Bringing Class Back In

Bringing Class Back In

Contemporary and Historical Perspectives

edited by
SCOTT G. MCNALL
RHONDA F. LEVINE
RICK FANTASIA

Westview Press
BOULDER • SAN FRANCISCO • OXFORD

Internal design by D. Gail Renlund. Cover design by Polly Christensen.

Published in 1991 in the United States of America by Westview Press, Inc., 5500 Central Avenue, Boulder, Colorado 80301, and in the United Kingdom by Westview Press, 36 Lonsdale Road, Summertown, Oxford OX2 7EW

Library of Congress Cataloging-in-Publication Data
Bringing class back in: contemporary and historical perspectives /
    edited by Scott G. McNall, Rhonda F. Levine, Rick Fantasia.
    p. cm.
    Includes index.
    ISBN 0-8133-1049-0—ISBN 0-8133-1050-4 (pbk.)
    1. Social classes. 2. Social conflict. 3. Ideology. I. McNall,
Scott G. II. Levine, Rhonda F. III. Fantasia, Rick.
HT609.B75 1991
305.5—dc20   90-44536
                                                             CIP

Printed and bound in the United States of America

The paper used in this publication meets the requirements
of the American National Standard for Permanence of Paper
for Printed Library Materials Z39.48-1984.

10   9   8   7   6   5   4   3   2   1

Contents

PART III
CLASS POWER, CONFLICT,
AND STRUGGLE 165

PART IV
CULTURE, IDEOLOGY,
AND CONSCIOUSNESS 239

Preface

The study of "class" has been curiously absent in recent "poststructuralist," "post-Marxist," and "state-centered" approaches emerging in historical and sociological scholarship. But it is our contention that far from ignoring recent developments in new approaches to sociological scholarship, the study of class has shaped and been shaped by them. It is also our contention that as class analysis changes and develops, it sustains itself as a powerful, refined working tool in helping scholars understand the complexities of social and historical processes.

This volume brings together scholars who are engaged in class analysis that addresses continuing debates over the relationship between class structure and human agency, the centrality of class relations, the dynamics of class formation, class culture, ideology, and consciousness. These essays are intended to provide a cross-section of the rich body of social theory and empirical research being produced by those employing a class analysis. We believe that this book demonstrates the variety, vibrancy, and continuing value of class analysis in historical and sociological scholarship.

We thank the University of Kansas, the American Sociological Association/National Science Foundation Small Grant Program, and the Colgate University Research Council for providing funds to make this book a reality. Special thanks go to Thelma Mayer and Mildred Tipton for secretarial assistance.

Scott G. McNall
Rhonda F. Levine
Rick Fantasia

1 | Introduction

SCOTT G. MCNALL
RHONDA F. LEVINE
RICK FANTASIA

Class is one of the most widely used and thoroughly contested concepts in the social sciences. There is little agreement among social scientists in general, and sociologists in particular, on the exact meaning of class or the explanatory power of the word itself. It resonates with political meaning for some, but for others it means no more than an individual's position on a scale that correlates years of education, income, and occupation.

Those who study class fall into two camps. On one side, we find class theorists who work in a tradition born in the 1960s and 1970s. Jerry Lembcke points this out in his chapter on the analysis of the U.S. working class in this volume. In the context of stalled campus and civil rights movements in the United States, many class theorists looked to the success of Marxist movements in other countries and pondered the role of the working class in transforming industrial societies. This led to questions about the changing composition of the working class and about whether that class, especially in advanced industrial countries, had retained its special role. That is, why wasn't the working class fulfilling the destiny identified for it by Marxist theory? This prompted these theorists to ask whether there were any real or meaningful differences between the working class and the middle class. Much effort has been expended in developing a Marxist map to help chart changed class structures and understand the nature of the middle or new classes.

The chapters that follow move beyond that concern. One of the primary goals of this volume is to recapture the central elements of a Marxist class analysis and show how and why it is more efficacious than other approaches for understanding class in comparative and historical perspective, as well as for understanding modern industrial societies. But before tracing the elements that such an analysis would involve, let us characterize the other theoretical camp, which uses the Weberian perspective, and consider why one perspective might be favored over another.

1

The hallmark of the Weberian perspective, as Löic J.D. Wacquant notes, is its multidimensionality. Class is understood as the summation or some weighted combination of a variety of position effects, e.g., property, income, occupation, authority, education, or prestige. Class is both objective and subjective and can be realized in the realm of consumption as well as the realm of production. In a Weberian schema, production and property relations are important but by no means sole determinants. Weberian conceptualizations, therefore, deny the antagonistic character of capitalist social relations of production and describe class in terms of exchange and market relations (see, for instance, Giddens [1973] and Parkin [1979]). In short, common life-chances define a basic class. In a Weberian system, classes can be divided and subdivided at will, as Erik Olin Wright notes. All that a theorist need do, for example, is show that people within certain categories, such as professional, technical, or managerial groups, have some sort of marketable skill that gives them an advantage over another category of people in the labor market. This method of conceptualizing classes has a number of limitations, as well as some advantages.

As we have already noted, Weberians take the market as given, ignoring the class struggles that led to the creation of a specific economic system. Neither the polity nor the economy are seen as actively created or as problematic. As a corollary, because class is seen as relational rather than oppositional, Weberians miss the dual nature of class formation and struggle. They neither assume nor look for underlying conflicts of material interest. Weberians are not interested in developing a schema to explain similarities and differences of classes across cultures and through time or in comparing and contrasting precapitalist and postcapitalist societies. The Weberian framework, then, imposes severe constraints on a theorist's ability to conceptualize and understand large-scale processes of social change.

Also, a Weberian perspective, because of its focus on skill level and individual attributes, does not examine class capacities, as Lembcke argues. Class capacity generally refers to the ability of the working class to liberate itself, as a class, from subordination to the capitalist class. If one believes class position and capacity are based on skill levels, then one would necessarily have to conclude that the potential for the working classes to effect political and economic change is presently limited. If, on the other hand, one believes class capacity is based on a collectivity that is more than the sum of its parts, then the situation is reversed. And, indeed, as Lembcke notes, scholars such as Rick Fantasia (1988) have found that cultures of solidarity are an important aspect of working-class culture—a finding that would not have been possible using a Weberian approach. What a Weberian perspective (Parkin 1979, p. 25) can do is draw a map of society that locates people in terms of differences in property, skills, or authority. It can compare, with relative ease, the class composition of different countries and quickly determine whether some category of people sharing the same life-chances is expanding or contracting, using such an additive model.

However, neither the Weberian nor the Marxian perspective is static. Moreover, the divide between the two approaches has been dissolving, as both Weberians and Marxists focus on problems of proletarianization, the role of credentials and culture in creating and maintaining class boundaries, and the independent role played by bureaucracies in structuring the middle classes. Both may also view status not as a passive attribute but as one means by which fractions of a class actively organize to protect their relative standing from challenges (Foster 1974, Wallerstein 1979).[1] Nevertheless, the Marxist model remains distinctive because of its focus on class conflict and its steadfast hold on the concept of exploitation.

Though classes are obviously of critical importance in Marx's view of history and the development of capitalism, he offers no systematic analysis of the concept of class. And generations of scholars since Marx have yet to arrive at a consensus over the various aspects of the concept of class (Wright 1980). The essential features for any Marxist analysis of class are that *classes are defined in relationship to other classes* within a given system of production, as Kathleen Stanley and Dean Braa, along with others, note in this work. The social relations of production form the material basis of class, rather than market relations or relations of exchange. Further, the nature of capitalism is such that social classes stand in contradictory and antagonistic relations with one another, and capitalist social relations are exploitative because one category of people must sell their labor power to survive, while another purchases labor power to make a profit. In other words, class struggle revolves around the relations of production; it is fundamentally a struggle over surplus value or the rate of exploitation (Godelier 1978; Prezworski 1980). The contradiction of capitalism, revealed in the age-old struggle between capitalists and workers, is expected to persist until a new system emerges, based on different social relations of production. In Marx's vision, the working class is the historical agent destined to change the system of exploitation.[1] *Class,* from a Marxist perspective, is therefore *"simultaneously an objective and subjective phenomenon,* both something independent of members' consciousness and something expressed in conscious thought and practice" (Therborn 1983, p. 39, emphases added).

One of the primary elements of class, as an objective phenomenon, is *class structure* (Hobsbawm 1984). This term simply refers to the diverse economic locations or positions (e.g., white-collar, blue-collar, managerial) that make up a society. Class structure is important because it sets objective limits to the historical development of class struggles (Zeitlin 1980). For example, at any given moment, one group might be numerically superior to another, which could heighten its chance for economic and political success (Katznelson 1986). Class struggle, on the other hand, can also affect class structure because it simultaneously "shapes and realigns the internal relations *within* classes and the relation *between* them. . . . In this sense, and to this extent, classes possess an inherently *contingent historicity.* They are determined by their place in a historically specific ensemble of production relations and by their self-activity, which constitutes and reconstitutes these relations and their place within them" (Zeitlin 1980, p. 3, emphases in original).

Here, we have an answer to those who challenge Marxist definitions of class on the grounds that the working class has not produced revolutionary movements throughout the world. First, as Aristide Zolberg (1986) has pointed out, though capitalism required a working class, it did not require it in a particular form. The working classes in some countries have been revolutionary, and in others they have not, depending on specific historical circumstances. This does not mean, however, that there is ever an absence of conflict. It means, as we will see from our contributors, that conflict can be channeled in ways that inhibit revolution. Second, there is no necessary correspondence between economics and politics in general, in spite of what Marx might have implied at points in his writing.

To summarize, we have noted that *class has an objective and subjective component, is a process, is defined in opposition to other class processes, and is historically contingent.* It is not, we hasten to add, that the economy does not count, simply that classes are made and unmade in history, not given. Let us consider the question of historical contingency by drawing on Zolberg (1986, pp. 431–50), who cited differences in British and U.S. class structures and explored the ways in which they were affected by differences in the mode of production and the polity.

British industrial development preceded that of the rest of the world by almost half a century. As a result, wage levels were higher there than in other countries, and an aristocracy of labor evolved. As Marc W. Steinberg demonstrates, the formation of British working-class ideology depended on how British workers crafted a vocabulary to deal with their circumstances out of available streams of discourse. Trade unionism was something of a folk invention. British workers were also an ethnically homogeneous group, huddled together into large industrial communities. These communities were welded together by common work experiences, leisure activities, and the local pub and music hall. And workers had no difficulty in seeing the differences between themselves and the owners. As E. P. Thompson (1963) and others (Hobsbawm 1984; Stedman Jones

1983) have demonstrated, a distinctive working class arose in the latter half of the 1800s *after* a strong state system had developed and *before* an elaborate mass party system was formed. When mass-based parties did develop, they tended to serve distinct class groupings, which meant that the working class had an organizational basis from which to mount an assault on the state and on other classes and with which to work for policies that served its distinct interests. The British working class was relatively effective in developing as a unique entity and defending its interests because it constituted the majority of the work force.

The situation in the United States was quite different. In the first place, the United States was actually more industrialized than Great Britain, if we measure industrialization by degree of capital intensity or calculate it in terms of horsepower per capita. This meant that fewer skilled and unskilled workers were needed to fuel the capitalist economy. One consequence was that a large white-collar class arose very early in the process of industrialization. Another important difference between Britain and the United States was that much of the U.S. labor supply came from immigration. By 1910, for instance, over one-fourth of the labor force was foreign born, with concentrations as high as one-third in manufacturing and one-half in mining (Zolberg 1986, p. 442). Many of these immigrants had no intention of staying, which contributed to the rise of business unionism for transient immigrant workers who were tied closely to the workplace and were interested, primarily, in higher wages. Again, because the work force was composed of immigrants, it was segregated by ethnicity, which contributed in the long run to the emergence of a segmented labor market that, of course, still exists. In addition, democracy preceded industrialization in the United States, which meant that transclass parties had developed *before* the end of the nineteenth century. These parties served to blur and mediate class tensions, as did other U.S. transclass organizations, such as churches and fraternal orders (see Orr and McNall, this volume). Paradoxically, then, and in contradistinction to what Marx thought, it was often in those countries where the impact of capitalism was most brutal that transclass political parties mitigated its effects by integrating people into the political sphere (Zolberg 1986, p. 452). This, of course, does not tell the whole story of class formation in Great Britain and the United States for we would also have to consider such factors as the world wars and how they suppressed class consciousness, the effect of ethnic divisions, and how the upper and middle classes mobilized (see, for example, Mintz and Roy in this volume). But this brief characterization does provide an illustration of what we mean when we say that class is contingent. However, this does not mean that we cannot talk meaningfully about the process of class formation or what the role of the polity or the economy will be. We must simply make reference to distinct historical and comparative examples to understand the process and the outcome.

Shelley Feldman suggests that if we are to understand contemporary class formation and class relations within Bangladesh (and thus, by extension, within any country), we must also (1) consider how a particular economy is inserted into the global marketplace, (2) consider those international class relationships that shape relations of accumulation, and (3) be aware of particular configurations of state-class relationships. Bangladesh has experimented over the last three decades with ways to expand the industrial sector and incorporate the rural proletariat. These experiments failed because the structural conditions necessary for success were lacking; the colonial experience and a devastating war of independence had eroded institutional infrastructures and provided no industrial elite. This left room for a rural elite to dominate in the countryside and control the flow of resources designed to transform production. The capitalization of Bangladeshi agriculture thus significantly increased the number of landless and marginal producers as well as the pressures on the rural labor market. At the same time, these landless laborers had few opportunities to move into the industrial sector, with the consequence that proletarianization was intensified. New programs have been designed to provide credit to simple commodity producers in rural areas, but these have caused family members to exploit themselves and one another (particularly men exploiting women in the family) as they strive to produce and pay back small loans. In short, another program for development is foundering on the shoals of previously existing class structures and relationships. The past continues to shape the future.

This is what Stephen Valocchi finds when he explains differences in the welfare systems of Britain, Sweden, and the United States. As he shows clearly, the state served to mediate the effects of class forces on policymaking in all cases; that is, no class was able to institute its entire agenda. However, some were more successful than others, which could be accounted for by seeing state structures as the products of previous class struggles and compromises and as embodying the interests of those who had won those struggles. Not surprisingly, as Valocchi points out, the winners of previous battles were the best organized members of the capitalist class. But the influence of this class on welfare policy was, in turn, determined by the extent to which precapitalist elites or other segments of capital had embedded themselves within the state. In short, historical class compromises and coalitions had become part of the state structure that influenced future policy decisions.

As Carl Strikwerda demonstrates, members of Belgian working-class communities in Ghent, Brussels, and Liège responded in very different ways to the process of industrialization. They did not form one united

Belgian working class because they were divided over the issue of religion and because, within the cities he studied, distinctive local politics and economic structures were key variables in determining class relationships and formation. Thus, multiple cultural identities and power relationships shaped the development of working-class formation. For instance, all three cities had Socialist movements, and all Socialists were vehemently anticlerical. For them, working-class consciousness was synonymous with opposition to Catholicism. This meant that Catholic workers' organizations and Socialist organizations could not always come together even over purely economic issues. It meant that Socialists sometimes joined with Liberal employers because of their mutual anticlericalism. It meant, too, that Liberals and middle-class Catholics sometimes found themselves allied against working-class Catholics. The Socialists struggled to mark off the workers as their "own," with the development of dense networks composed of cooperatives, mutual insurance societies, and unions, as well as funds for strikes, meeting places, and printing presses. The mix of Catholicism, local politics, and unique community histories produced, then, three very different socialisms in three Belgian cities. Class consciousness differed because workers' lived experiences and definitions of themselves differed in Liège, Ghent, and Brussels.

How do humans become class subjects, rather than subjects who emphasize their religion, ethnicity, or family? We must consider *class formation* to be a dual process (Therborn 1983, p. 39). It has, as we have noted, an objective aspect that accompanies a given mode of production and refers to the process by which people are distributed among different kinds of economic practices. In the late nineteenth century, England differed objectively from the United States because it had a greater concentration of industrial workers, which affected class formation. But class formation also has a subjective element because, as people develop an understanding of their relationship to the means of production and create ways to respond to their world, they also develop a variety of common ideological and political practices. In short, they develop various forms of *class consciousness*.

Eric Hobsbawm (1984, p. 18) has defined class consciousness as a group's awareness and understanding of itself that grows out of opposition to other groups. People may act to protect a way of life, a way of working and living. In organizing and confronting the world in which they live, people develop class consciousness; it grows out of action. However, this consciousness is not entirely created anew but refined (McNall 1987, p. 226). The importance of the lived experiences of people as the "material" from which classes are constituted has been clearly demonstrated by, among others, Herbert Gutman (1973). Gutman points out that language, stories, and ideas of harmony and brotherhood make a people and, hence, a class unique. Ideology enters significantly into the formation of classes (see Sewell [1985] for a discussion of the "independent" structuring role of ideology). Thus, class is *ideology* as well as structure.

Two chapters in this volume (Orr and McNall; Steinberg) deal explicitly with the role of ideology in class formation. James R. Orr and Scott G. McNall broaden the concept of class consciousness to include *language*, arguing that it is through both discourse and social practice that individuals are constructed as human subjects. Forms of discourse are grounded in the everyday experiences of people and are influenced by the mode of production, but they are also partially autonomous. For instance, in the United States, nineteenth-century workers had available to them a variety of languages with which to interpret their experiences. Some were embedded in emigrant communities with a socialist tradition, and, as a result, language was used to understand the emerging industrial order. Others were embedded in communities that used a religious rhetoric to analyze the human condition. In short, different languages produced different responses to material conditions. Orr and McNall argue that it is through discourse, then, that humans become conscious subjects before they become class subjects; different discourse streams flow together to produce different subjects and classes. To illustrate, nineteenth-century U.S. workers stood at the confluence of streams of religious rhetoric, republican ideology, German socialist ideology, and social Darwinism, to name but a few. These different streams produced, in varying locales and moments, different subjects.

Human subjects do not, however, passively accept just any language or symbolic system to interpret their material experiences. Social and political struggles are often waged over semantics, over the construction of new terms for old concepts (Hall 1985, p. 112). Pierre Bourdieu (1977, 1984, 1989) has argued persuasively that symbolic struggles are, at root, struggles over economic and political power. He has also noted (Bourdieu 1984, 1989) that elites maintain their positions of power through strategies of condescension, whereby they explain that they really are no different from those who occupy lower rungs on the economic ladder.

In his contribution to this volume, David Halle offers empirical support for the Bourdieu perspective, but he also departs from it in important ways. Arguing that a basic materialist approach to culture should not be abandoned, he finds class distinctions reflected in the expression of artistic taste in certain respects, although they are not as apparent in others. For Halle, the most salient material context for understanding the paintings displayed in the homes of the working and middle classes is not the mode of production but the house itself, the very material structure for which it has been purchased and in which it is displayed. Orr and

McNall, on the other hand, adopt a position closer to that of Bourdieu and argue that the rhetoric of brotherhood in the United States during the nineteenth century that was characteristic of fraternal organizations suppressed real and meaningful differences in economic and political power.

Steinberg examines the discourse of conflict used in a major industrial action by the cotton spinners of the Ashton-Stalybridge region of England in 1830. He makes an important point about discourse and active human agents: Actors struggle through discourse, rather than being impelled by its meanings. Discourse, especially that relating to conflict, is constructed from diverse streams as people seek to explain and develop a discourse that will allow them to challenge authority. By extension, then, a Marxist class framework stands in opposition to poststructuralist and postmodernist analyses of human behavior, which argue that first there was the word, and the word had meaning, and the word gave rise to the world. Language does not, by itself, give rise to or create human subjects.

Marx believed that worker consciousness would rise out of the basic contradictions of capitalist society. Workers would become class-conscious subjects because, as they labored, suffered, and were rewarded, they would come to see themselves as exploited and alienated—from themselves, from one another, and from their own labor. They would then act to overcome the situation in which they found themselves. Much has happened recently in the Soviet Union and Eastern Europe, in countries that had a socialist rhetoric, if not always a socialist economy. Hundreds of thousands of people have demanded new political and economic systems. Socialism and its rhetoric may have contained the seeds of their own destruction, as is evident from the material presented by Michael Burawoy in his chapter on "painting" socialism.

Burawoy (1985) has long argued that class is not simply a function of economic position. That is, regime production, which refers to how a person actually works, mediates between the development of a class-in-itself and a class-for-itself. And it is regime production that determines whether a class-in-itself is transformed into a class-for-itself. Burawoy worked as a furnaceman in a Hungarian steel mill on three separate occasions in the 1980s. What he found, in his discussions with his coworkers, was that the production regime of socialism was characterized by bureaucratic despotism. Each day, producers were called on to act out a version of socialism that was at odds with the reality around them. Workers were asked to perform, for show, jobs that did not relate to the needs of consumers or even to the needs of a Socialist state. They were, for example, asked to paint a dirty steel factory because a state dignitary was coming to visit; the assumption made by the bosses was that a painted plant would be more impressive than the real activity of the producers. Elsewhere, workers were confronted with the fact that people received different benefits, rights, and privileges depending upon their positions of power and authority. In short, the way in which they worked and lived their lives was at variance with the promise of socialism. One should understand the transformations racking Eastern Europe today in this context. Part of the demand for change flows from the fact that socialism, as defined by the producers, was a distant possibility, not the reality in which they lived.

Work experience is important in determining class consciousness, but it also contributes to and is mediated by *gender consciousness*. Michael Yarrow describes the hard and dangerous work of the coal miner whose manhood is forged daily in personal combat with the boss and with the work. The miner survives and benefits as an individual; it is his body and stamina that provide a living for himself and his family. Miners are tough, but in the long run this toughness undermines class solidarity in several ways. First, it omits women as class allies. Second, the strong value placed on individual autonomy makes it difficult for miners to cooperate with one another and to develop long-term strategies for collective survival, as is evident in the case of strikes. A tough man takes care of his own, which makes it difficult to turn to those outside the family for help during times of crisis. And finally, Yarrow argues, tough men look for tough leaders, who may be undemocratic and fail to build the kind of organizations that can sustain collective solidarity over extended periods of time.

Yarrow's work underscores the need to consider more than the job when constructing class. Class, as we have argued, is multidimensional. It formed not just at the point of production—if it were, people who do similar kinds of work would develop similar ideologies and politics—but in the community, among friends, and in the family, as Halle (1984) has shown.

Ideology, language, and consciousness are not created de novo. As Hobsbawm (1984, p. 28) has said, *consciousness is created through organization*. One of the ways that people learn about the nature of their oppression and how to articulate the values they wish to protect is through participation in class organizations. In mobilizing, in trying to change the economic and political system, people create themselves as a class (McNall 1988, p. 10). Class does not simply grow out of changed relations of production. It is created through organization and it is not just the working class that is actively created through time.

As William G. Roy demonstrates, the U.S. corporate class had its roots in the late nineteenth century. It was not fully determined by economic change but created itself as a class with distinct economic, political, and ideological aspects. On the economic level, this class established its hegemony through the fusion of financial and industrial capital, made possible, in large part, through the formation of corporations. Politically, the class was shaped by state actions, which it played a large role in determining and which gave the corporations great leeway and enormous power. For example, railroad corporations, which played a key role in the ascendancy of this class, received massive government subsidies and were protected from irate citizens and militant railroad workers. Finally, the class formed itself as a cohesive class segment in true Weberian fashion, by creating and controlling upper-class organizations. The debutante ball, the coming-out party, the exclusive country club, preparatory school, and private college—all became means by which the corporate class reproduced itself, linking families, building dynasties, and excluding outsiders.

The importance of organization in determining and shaping class is underscored by Sharon Reitman's examination of the contrasting political traditions of the Western Federation of Miners (WFM), which advocated socialism, and the coal miners' United Mine Workers of America (UMWA), which embraced the liberal reform movement of the progressive era. The WFM went on to found the revolutionary Industrial Workers of the World, whereas the UMWA became one of the more conservative affiliates of the American Federation of Labor. Why did similar work experiences produce such different outcomes? As Reitman suggests, the explanation hinges on the organizational structure that the miners confronted. In the case of Western metal miners, mining was highly capitalized and centralized, with a few owners dominating the scene. These owners were well organized, and they frequently and successfully called on the state to attempt to quell the miners. Coal mining, on the other hand, was not as well organized, and smaller entrepreneurial organizations mined a significant portion of the coal. Producers, then, were faced with two different structures: one that encouraged collective action and militance and another that encouraged localized actions and accommodationist strategies (also see Kimeldorf 1988 for an elaboration of a similar argument about the contrasting tradition of waterfront unions). Miners developed different organizations to respond to these structures and, in turn, developed as different classes.

Beth Mintz also deals with the process by which classes are actively structured. She demonstrates that an understanding of the structure of the capitalist class is a powerful tool for social research, specifically for understanding the emergence of the health care system in the United States. Instead of focusing on why the system is so poorly coordinated and so expensive, Mintz urges us to see the system as the outgrowth of the struggle between labor and capital. Any future changes or development in this system must be seen in light of this struggle. Battles by the poor and working class for health coverage have made it possible for one segment of the capitalist class to profit mightily, sometimes at the expense of other sectors. The conflict within capital over profitability and the conflict between labor and capital, Mintz suggests, will set the agenda for future struggles over the delivery of health care, although this does not mean that divergent interests among capitalists will provide a window for progressive social policies.

Health care policy has, of course, been heavily influenced by the state, but Mintz's main point is that state policy must be seen within the larger context of class formation. Class struggles gave rise to the state, providing it with a "logic," but class formation and struggle are a continuous process, shaped by past conflicts. State activity does not reduce to a simple reflection of the contours of class struggle. In fact, one cannot understand state policy without reference to the social forces that shaped its formation. Neither the editors of this volume nor the authors of individual chapters wish to usher the state to the analytic sidelines. But we contend that *the modern state cannot be understood outside the confines of class formation.*

The chapters that follow are organized into four sections, though it could be argued that any single chapter might be located elsewhere. The reason for this overlapping should by now be clear: Class is simultaneously structure, consciousness, and organization. Classes are forged in opposition to one another, over time. The majority of the chapters in this work exemplify, therefore, the trend toward comparative/historical sociology, a sociology that is not satisfied with mere classifications and formal model building. Rather, it seeks detailed historical and comparative analyses to understand how and in response to what classes come into being, to understand why some classes become revolutionary and others do not, and to understand the transformation of both capitalist and socialist societies. All of our authors, implicitly or explicitly, operate with a model that asks us to consider class as a dynamic, multidimensional process.

Notes

1. Current debates about the boundaries of classes are important for they relate to the project of locating the class most likely to carry out this historical charge.

References

Bourdieu, Pierre. 1977. *Outline of a Theory of Practice.* Translated by Richard Nice. Cambridge: Cambridge University Press.

———. 1984. *Distinction: A Social Critique of the Judgement of Taste.* Translated by Richard Nice. Cambridge: Cambridge University Press.

———. 1989. "Social Space and Symbolic Power." *Social Theory* 7:14–25.

Burawoy, Michael. 1985. *The Politics of Production.* London: Verso.

Fantasia, Rick. 1988. *Cultures of Solidarity: Consciousness, Action, and Contemporary American Workers.* Berkeley: University of California Press.

Foster, John. 1974. *Class Struggle in the Industrial Revolution.* London: Weidenfeld and Nicholson.

Giddens, Anthony. 1973. *The Class Structure of Advanced Societies.* New York: Harper and Row.

Godelier, Maurice. 1978. "System, Structure and Contradiction in *Capital.*" In *Marx: Sociology, Social Change, Capitalism,* ed. Donald McQuarie, pp. 77–102. New York: Quartet.

Gutman, Herbert. 1973. "Work, Culture, and Society in Industrializing America." *American Historical Review* 78:531–88.

Hall, Stuart. 1985. "Signification, Representation, Ideology: Althusser and the Post-Structuralist Debates." *Critical Studies in Mass Communications* 2:91–114.

Halle, David. 1984. *America's Working Man.* Chicago: University of Chicago Press.

Hobsbawm, Eric. 1984. *Workers: Worlds of Labor.* New York: Pantheon Books.

Katznelson, Ira. 1986. "Working-Class Formation: Constructing Cases and Comparisons." In *Working-Class Formation: Nineteenth-Century Patterns in Western Europe and the United States,* ed. Ira Katznelson and Aristide R. Zolberg, pp. 3–44. Princeton, N.J.: Princeton University Press.

Kimeldorf, Howard. 1988. *Reds or Rackets? The Making of Radical and Conservative Unions on the Waterfront.* Berkeley: University of California Press.

McNall, Scott G. 1987. "Thinking About Social Class: Structure, Organization, and Consciousness." In *Recapturing Marxism: An Appraisal of Recent Trends in Sociological Theory,* ed. Rhonda F. Levine and Jerry Lembcke, pp. 223–46. New York: Praeger.

———. 1988. *The Road to Rebellion: Class Formation and Kansas Populism, 1865–1900.* Chicago: University of Chicago Press.

Parkin, Frank. 1979. *Marxism and Class Theory: A Bourgeois Critique.* New York: Columbia University Press.

Przeworski, Adam. 1980. "Material Bases of Consent: Economics and Politics in a Hegemonic System." In *Political Power and Social Theory,* ed. Maurice Zeitlin, pp. 21–66. Greenwich, Conn.: JAI Press.

Sewell, William H., Jr. 1985. "Ideologies and Social Revolutions: Reflections on the French Case." *Journal of Modern History* 57:57–85.

Stedman Jones, Gareth. 1983. *Languages of Class: Studies in English Working Class History 1832–1982.* Cambridge: Cambridge University Press.

Therborn, Goran. 1983. "Why Some Classes Are More Successful than Others." *New Left Review* 138:37–55.

Thompson, E. P. 1963. *The Making of the English Working Class.* New York: Vintage.

Wallerstein, Immanuel. 1979. "Social Conflict in Post-Independence Black Africa: The Concepts of Race and Status Group Reconsidered." In *The Capitalist World Economy: Essays by Immanuel Wallerstein*. Cambridge: Cambridge University Press.

Wright, Erik Olin. 1980. "Varieties of Marxist Conceptions of Class Structure." *Politics and Society* 9:323–70.

––––––. 1985. *Classes*. London: Verso.

Zeitlin, Maurice. 1980. "On Classes, Class Conflict, and the State: An Introductory Note." In *Classes, Class Conflict, and the State*, ed. Maurice Zeitlin, pp. 1–37. Cambridge: Winthrop.

Zolberg, Aristide R. 1986. "How Many Exceptionalisms?" In *Working-Class Formation: Nineteenth-Century Patterns in Western Europe and the United States*, eds. Ira Katznelson and Aristide R. Zolberg, pp. 397–455. Princeton, N.J.: Princeton University Press.

PART I | Class Structure

The four chapters in this section are primarily concerned with issues of class structure and the ensuing debates on questions of class capacity and boundary. Erik Wright argues for a clarification of the concept of class structure that will provide the precondition for developing a powerful theory on the relationship between class structure, formation, and struggle. For Wright, the main task for class analysis is "to understand the ways in which macrostructural contexts constrain microlevel processes and the ways in which the microlevel subjectivities, choices, and strategies of individuals can affect macrostructural arrangements." Hence, debates over the concept of class structure have concrete theoretical importance for the study of class formation and the impact of class on the lives of individuals. Löic Wacquant is particularly interested in the structural location of the middle class(es) in advanced capitalist societies. After reviewing both Marxist and Weberian views of this class, he argues that the boundary question of the middle class cannot be addressed at an abstract theoretical level but must be confronted through historical analysis.

Beth Mintz explores the structure of the capitalist class in the United States and examines the ways in which an understanding of capitalist class structure and the importance of both inter- and intraclass relations can shed light on the creation and transformation of health care provision in the United States. Jerry Lembcke raises the question of the relationship between the process of capitalist development and the capacity of the working class to act as an agent of social change. Reviewing both theoretical and methodological issues concerning working-class capacity, Lembcke argues that the prospects for meaningful social change in the United States presuppose an adequate understanding of this working-class capacity.

2 | The Conceptual Status of Class Structure in Class Analysis

ERIK OLIN WRIGHT

At the core of Marxian class analysis is the claim that class is a fundamental determinant of social conflict and social change. In trying to defend and deepen this intuition, contemporary Marxist theorists have been torn between two theoretical impulses. The first is to keep the concept of class structure as uncomplicated as possible, perhaps even accepting a simple polarized vision of the class structure of capitalism, and then to remedy the explanatory deficiencies of such a simple concept by introducing into the analysis a range of other explanatory principles. These might include divisions within classes or between sectors, the relationship between work and community, or the role of the state and ideology in shaping the collective organization of classes. The second impulse is to increase the complexity of the class structure concept itself in the hope that such complexity will more powerfully capture the explanatory mechanisms embedded in class relations. Basically, these alternative impulses place different bets on how much explanatory work the concept of class structure itself should do. The first strategy takes a minimalist position, seeing class structure as, at most, shaping broad constraints on action and change; the second takes a maximalist position, seeing class structure as a potent and systematic determinant of individual action and social development.

My work on class has pursued this second strategy. In my theoretical discussions of class structure, I have been preoccupied with the problem of the "middle class," with elaborating a class structure concept that would give a coherent and systematic theoretical status to nonproletarian employees. My conviction was that conceptually clarifying the structural location of the middle class was essential for understanding the process of class formation in contemporary capitalism. Above all, I felt it was essential for understanding the problem of the formation of coalitions of classes and segments of classes around radical democratic and socialist political projects. This led to the introduction of the concept of "contradictory locations within class relations" and, subsequently, the reformulation of that concept in terms of a multidimensional view of exploitation. The theoretical aspiration was that these reconstructions of the concept of class structure would enhance its explanatory power by more adequately representing the complexities of class interests in capitalist societies. This, in turn, would make it possible to more systematically map the variations in class structures across capitalist societies and account for the impact of those variations on processes of class formation.

That aspiration has yet to be fulfilled. Although I do feel that progress has been made in the conceptualization of class in the past decade, the goal of producing a class structure concept that is both theoretically coherent and empirically comprehensive remains elusive. In this chapter, I will try to clarify some of the metatheoretical foundations of this conceptual project. More specifically, I will try to accomplish three main tasks. First, I will briefly situate the concept of class structure within the broader enterprise of class analysis. Second, I will discuss the problem of elaborating what I will call a repertoire of class structure concepts that vary along two dimensions: their degree of abstraction and the extent to which they specify class structure at a macro- or microlevel of analysis. Finally, I will examine the relationship between Weberian and neo-Marxist approaches to class in terms of the problem of generating adequate, concrete, microlevel concepts of class structure.

Class Structure in Class Analysis

The concept of "class structure" is only one element in a broader theoretical enterprise that can be called "class analysis." Other elements include class formation (the formation of classes into collectively organized actors), class struggle (the practices of actors for the realization of class interests), and class consciousness (the actors' understanding of their class interests). The task of class analysis is not simply to understand class structure as such but to understand the interconnections among all these elements, as well as their consequences for other aspects of social life.

The most basic, underlying theoretical claim of this kind of class analysis is that *class structures impose limits on class formations:*

$$\text{class structure} \longrightarrow \text{limits} \longrightarrow \text{class formation}$$

What precisely does this mean? It means that, given a particular configuration of class relations in a given society, certain patterns of class formation will be relatively easy to forge and, once forged, easy to maintain, whereas others will be difficult to form and precarious once created, and still others might be virtually impossible to form. Class structures, in short, do not determine *actual* class formations; what they determine are the *probabilities* of given class formations. Or, to put it in somewhat different terms, our general understanding of the relationship between class structure and class formations tells us when we should be surprised by the concrete patterns of class formation we observe in the world. Without such a causal theory, we should, in principle, never be surprised by the forms of collective solidarities and struggle that actually occur because anything would be viewed as having an equal probability of happening.[1]

Figure 2.1 illustrates the relationship between class structure and class formation using the multidimensional-exploitation class structure concept I elaborated in *Classes* (1985). In this concept, class structures in capitalist societies can be represented as a three-dimensional matrix, each dimension being defined by a specific mechanism of exploitation. One is based on ownership of the means of production, one on control of organizational assets, and one on the possession of skill assets. The cells in this matrix are *not* classes as such; they should be thought of as *locations* within class relations. The matrix of such locations defines a class structure.

On the terrain of such a class structure, a range of class formations can be forged through struggle. Class formations do not simply "happen"; they are created through the strategies of actors attempting to build collective organizations capable of realizing class interests. The claim that class structure limits class formation, then, is a claim that not all conceivable outcomes of these strategies are equally possible or stable. In Figure 2.1, for example, the first three patterns of class formation could be considered among those more likely to occur. Empirical research seems to indicate that the pattern in contemporary Sweden is quite close to pattern 1, whereas the pattern in the United States is more like pattern 3. Pattern 4, in contrast, is less likely. It embodies coalitions that combine locations with quite distinct and potentially conflicting interests, thus making such patterns of class formation prone to unravel. Finally, pattern 6 should be viewed as impossible. It constitutes a configuration that would be so unstable and internally divisive that it could not be created, let alone reproduced.

This way of understanding the relationship between class structure and class formation, it must be emphasized, does not prejudge on a priori grounds whether class structures should be the central focus of analysis for a specific explanatory task. The claim that class structures impose limits of possibility on class formations means that, within this terrain of probabilities, other causal factors—embedded in the state, culture, ideology, gender relations, etc.—shape the actual strategies of actors that result in the social production of specific, concrete patterns of class formation. For a specific empirical problem under investigation, it may

KEY TO CLASS STRUCTURE MATRICES:

C	EM	SM	UM
SE	ES	SS	US
PB	EW	SW	W

C = capitalist
SE = small employer
PB = petty bourgeoisie
EM = expert manager
ES = expert supervisor
EW = expert worker

SM = skilled manager
SS = skilled supervisor
SW = skilled worker
UM = uncredentialed manager
US = uncredentialed supervisor
W = worker

KEY TO CLASS COALITIONS:

Bourgeois
Coalition

Middle-Class
Coalition

Working-Class
Coalition

EXAMPLES OF PATTERNS OF CLASS FORMATIONS:

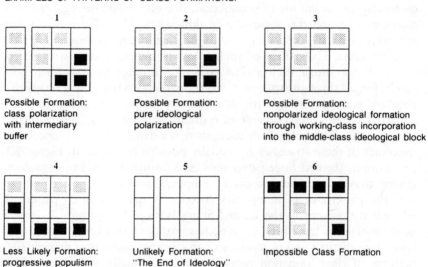

1
Possible Formation:
class polarization
with intermediary
buffer

2
Possible Formation:
pure ideological
polarization

3
Possible Formation:
nonpolarized ideological formation
through working-class incorporation
into the middle-class ideological block

4
Less Likely Formation:
progressive populism

5
Unlikely Formation:
"The End of Ideology"

6
Impossible Class Formation

Figure 2.1 Formable and Unformable Class Formations
in Contemporary Capitalism

well be that these causal processes should be at center stage for the analysis of class formation, with class structure treated simply as the context.

To develop an adequate theory of the relationship between class structure and class formation, it is essential, I believe, to have an adequate concept of class structure itself. To even speak of *class* formation or *class* struggle, as opposed to simply *group* formation or struggle, implies that we have a definition of "class" and know what it means to describe a collective actor as an instance of "class formation" or a conflict as a "class conflict."

Elaborating a coherent concept of class structure, therefore, is an important conceptual precondition for developing a satisfactory theory of the relationship between class structure, formation, and struggle.[2]

Underlying this preoccupation with clarifying the concept of class structure is a particular view of the relationship between the problem of *concept formation* and *theory construction*. My assumption is that the explanatory capacity of the theories we construct depends, to an important extent, on the coherence of the concepts we deploy within them. When concepts are loosely constructed and vaguely defined, it is much more difficult for the knowledge generated within a theory to have a cumulative character to it. Our capacity to learn from both our explanatory successes and our explanatory failures depends, in important ways, on the clarity and coherence of the basic categories used within those explanations. This does not imply that we cannot begin to study the world empirically and construct general theoretical explanations until we have a completely coherent inventory of concepts. But it does imply that a critical element in the advance of our capacity for theory construction is the elaboration of our basic concepts.

Building a Repertoire of Class Structure Concepts

The central thrust of my work on class structure has been the attempt to produce, within a broadly Marxist theoretical framework, a class structure concept capable of being used in analyses of microlevel processes at a relatively low level of abstraction. This preoccupation was driven by two overarching questions: How can we best explain the empirical variations in patterns of class formation across advanced capitalist societies? And under what conditions are class formations likely to embody projects of radical social change?

My assumption was that the elaboration of a concept of class structure that was both relatively concrete and specified at the microlevel of analysis was necessary to deepen our understanding of the causal relationships among class structure, formation, consciousness, and struggle. More specifically, I felt that viable democratic socialist politics in advanced capitalist societies had to contend with the problem of forming durable political coalitions between segments of the middle and working classes. Overly abstract and macrolevel concepts of class structure did not seem to provide the categories necessary for exploring the problem of forging such coalitions in the process of class formation. To study class formation in advanced capitalism in a politically relevant way, therefore, I felt it was necessary to produce a class structure concept that was much less abstract than existing ones and more suitable for microlevel analysis.

To situate this effort at concept formation, we must clarify what it means to produce a concept at a relatively "concrete" level of abstraction that is directed toward the relatively "microlevel" of analysis.

Levels of Abstraction

Although all concepts are abstract in the sense that they are mental constructions distinct from the "real objects" they attempt to represent, concepts differ in their "degree of abstraction" or concreteness.[3] The meaning of this expression can be clarified by introducing the distinction between "types" and "tokens" in the construction of concepts. The term "token" refers to the individual, concrete instances of some theoretical object—let us say, for example, my pet dog Micah. The term "type," on the other hand, refers to the more general theoretical categories under which this specific token could be classified: golden retrievers, dogs, mammals, animals, or living things. Within a given conceptual hierarchy, a more abstract concept is one that constitutes a classification of the variable forms of the less abstract concepts. Thus, the concept "dog" is more abstract than the concept "golden retriever" (because a golden retriever is one of many types of dogs) but less abstract than the concept "mammal." In these terms, in a given conceptual hierarchy, concrete concepts are nested within abstract concepts.

It is important to emphasize that a more "abstract" concept is not *less real* than a more concrete one, at least in the sense of attempting to identify real causal mechanisms. Thus, to describe Micah as a mammal is to identify causal mechanisms that are just as real as those captured by the description "golden retriever." Depending upon the specific theoretical question one is asking, the appropriate level of abstraction of the type-concepts used in the answer will vary, but, in each case, they will attempt to specify explanatory mechanisms.[4]

Within the Marxist tradition, at the most abstract level, the concept of class structure tries to differentiate distinct modes of production, such as capitalism and feudalism. Understood abstractly, for example, capitalism is defined by a perfectly polarized class structure consisting of capitalists and workers. They are bound together through a specific kind of production relation that is based on private ownership of the means of production, the sale of labor power on a labor market, and the appropriation of surplus by capitalists. More concrete concepts, accordingly, attempt to capture the ways in which the class structures vary over time and place within a given type of society.[5] One of the central objectives of my work on class structure has been to generate a concept capable of mapping, in a nuanced way, concrete variations in class structures across capitalist societies.

Micro/Macrolevels of Analysis

The distinction between micro- and macroconcepts involves the level of aggregation of social phenomena to which the concepts refer. As a macrolevel concept, class structures are meant to describe a crucial property of whole societies. When Marxists say, for example, that the private ownership of the means of production acts as a powerful constraint on potential policies of the state, they are generally making a macrostructural argument about the effects of the capitalist class structure on state institutions. As a microlevel concept, on the other hand, class structures define a set of "locations" filled by individuals. To be in a class location is to be subjected to a set of mechanisms that impinge directly on the lives of individuals as they think, choose, and act in the world. There is, of course, debate over what is most salient about these micromechanisms attached to the locations within class structures: Should they primarily be thought of as determining the material interests of individuals, as shaping their subjective understandings of the world, or as determining the basic resources they have available to pursue their interests? But, in any event, to develop a concept of class structure at the microlevel of analysis is to elaborate the concept in terms of mechanisms that directly affect individuals within class locations.

Such a microelaboration of the concept of class structure is essential, I believe, if we are to truly understand the causal relationship between class structures and class formations. By virtue of what characteristic does a given, objectively defined class structure make certain patterns of class formation easy and stable and others difficult and precarious? Part of the answer to this question involves explaining how individuals in different locations in a class structure come to subjectively identify with classes as collectively organized actors and participate—either through calculative choice (as modeled by rational-actor theory) or through some other form of subjective practice—in the collective activities of class formations. To explore such issues requires a coherent concept of "class location," i.e., of the microlevel concept of class structure.

The micro-macro distinction should not be confused with the abstract-concrete distinction. It often seems that microanalysis is more concrete than macroanalysis—for it deals with apparently concrete entities, "individuals"—but one can perfectly well develop very abstract concepts for dealing with microanalyses (as is often done in rational-actor models) or quite concrete concepts for dealing with macroanalyses (as occurs in many historical-comparative analyses of institutional development).

The Marxist concept of class structure has traditionally been developed most systematically as a highly abstract macrostructural concept. Class structures were defined in terms of models of pure modes of production (slavery, feudalism, capitalism, communism) and used to understand the broad, macrostructural dynamics of social development. This is not to say that Marxists have failed to engage in concrete or microlevel class analyses. Typically, however, the class structure concept deployed in such analyses has tended to be directly imported from the more abstract macrostructural arena, with relatively unsystematic amendments to make it suitable for concrete microanalysis.

The dominant objective of my work on the concept of class structure, then, has been to elaborate this concept in ways that would enhance its analytical power both in concrete analyses and in microanalyses. The goal was to generate a repertoire of class structure concepts that could be used both for comparative historical and institutional analyses of variations in the class structures of capitalist societies and for the analysis of the impact of class on the lives of individuals within those societies, while remaining consistent with the more abstract macroconcept of class characteristic of Marxist theory.

This concern with elaborating a class structure concept at the microlevel has led some critics to see my work as embracing principles of "methodological individualism."[6] This is, I think, an incorrect judgment. Much of my work has entailed developing the concept in a way that enables us to analyze, in a relatively fine-grained manner, the diverse ways in which individual lives intersect class structures. However, I have never argued that class structures are *reducible* to the properties of individuals, which is an essential claim of methodological individualism.[7] If Marxist class analysis is to advance, it must develop what is sometimes called "microfoundations," but this does not imply that all causal processes in class theory can be adequately represented at the level of individuals and their interactions. The task is to understand the ways in which macrostructural contexts constrain microlevel processes and the ways in which the microlevel subjectivities, choices, and strategies of individuals can affect macrostructural arrangements. To accomplish this, we must develop class structure concepts at both the macro- and microlevels of analysis.

In attempting this kind of task, we must decide how unified a conceptual field we should try to achieve. One aspiration is to establish a set of rules for producing new concepts such that the micro- and macroconcepts and the abstract and concrete concepts are theoretically integrated under a common logic. In this approach, the specific class structure concept we adopt will depend upon the kind of question we ask—we might, for example, use a simple polarized class structure concept for understanding the epochal dynamics of capitalism as a mode of production and a highly differentiated class structure concept with contradictory class locations for the analysis of coalition formation within class struggles in advanced capitalist societies. However, the different concepts are all integrated within a unitary conceptual logic. Alternatively, and more modestly, we can adopt a more eclectic and pragmatic strategy that is willing to acknowledge that different kinds of class concepts may be more or less appropriate for different explanatory tasks. It could be the case, for example, that Weberian class concepts work best for microanalyses or concrete analyses of institutional variations across capitalist societies, whereas Marxist concepts work best for the analysis of broad, epochal transformations.

My ambition has been to achieve as high a level of theoretical integration among these various class structure concepts as possible, on the assumption that, if such integration is achieved, the explanatory capacity of Marxist class analysis would be enhanced. This means that I have attempted, if not always completely consciously, to apply systematic rules to the derivation of new class structure concepts from the abstract concepts at the core of Marxist theory.

At the base of this project has been the problem of generating a satisfactory, microlevel concrete concept of the middle class within a Marxist concept of class structure. At the abstract, macrolevel of analysis, there is no middle class within Marxist theory: Class relations are viewed as perfectly polarized structures. In the abstractly conceived capitalist mode of production, there are capitalists and workers, bound together within a distinctive kind of social relation of production; no other class location is definable. My objective, then, was to maintain the integrity of this abstract, polarized, macrolevel class structure concept and introduce a set of strategies that would enable us to derive from this a more differentiated set of concrete and microlevel class structure concepts.

The basic strategy I adopted for moving from the abstract to the concrete was to see concrete class structures as consisting of different combinations of the class relations defined within abstract class structure concepts. Thus, for example, we can abstractly define the class relations of capitalism and feudalism and then describe a concrete class structure as a particular combination of these abstractly defined relations.

The basic strategy I have used for developing a more differentiated microconcept of class structure has been to elaborate the ways in which class relations are embodied in specific *jobs* because these are the essential "empty places" filled by individuals within the system of production. The traditional assumption of Marxian class analysis is that every job or location in the class structure was in one and only one class. In contrast, I have argued that individual jobs can, in different ways, have a multiple, and sometimes even a contradictory, class character. Thus, for example, in my initial class structure concept, I argued that managerial jobs were simultaneously in the capitalist class and in the working class.

Taking these two rules together, in principle, provides a way to link the abstract macroconcept of class structure rooted in the analysis of modes of production to the concrete and microconcept of class structure rooted in the analysis of individual lives. In the actual elaboration of my conceptual strategies, I have not been able to sustain such a neat and coherent conceptual space; nevertheless, I do think that these rules provide a general strategy that enhances the conceptual integration of the overall repertoire of class structure concepts.

The Weberian Temptation

The theoretical requirements we have just discussed for producing a coherent repertoire of class structure concepts have turned out to be quite arduous. In my own work, I have explored two different general approaches to the problem. These can be referred to as the *contradictory locations* approach and the *multidimensional exploitation* approach. Both strategies are attempts at providing a positive conceptualization particularly suited for a microlevel of analysis of the category "middle class." And each of these solutions, in my judgment, has attractive features. But, as many critics have pointed out, each also contains a range of problems and inconsistencies. The weaknesses of these conceptual strategies are discussed in considerable detail in the various critiques assembled in Wright et al. (1990). Though I do not feel that any of the existing alternative conceptualizations of class structure within the Marxist tradition provide a more satisfactory way of generating a microlevel, concrete concept of class structure, both of the strategies I have proposed fall short of the level of coherence to which they aspire.

Given these difficulties with the concepts of class structure built around contradictory class locations and multiple exploitations, there are several broad choices on how to proceed. First, we could retain the abstract, simple, polarized concept of class structure but abandon attempts to develop a repertoire of more concrete, microlevel Marxist class concepts derived from it. We could decide, for example, that, although the Marxist concept of class structure is analytically powerful for understanding the overall macrodynamics of capitalist societies in general, we cannot systematically derive from this abstract concept a concrete concept that is capable of explaining variations in such things as state policies or individual consciousness. Abandoning the goal of producing a microlevel, concrete concept of class structure, then, would open the door to a more eclectic choice of concepts for such microlevel problems. One could, for example, adopt Weberian class concepts for the analysis of variations in individual consciousness and retain the abstract polarized Marxist concept for understanding the structural dynamics of capitalism.

This response to the dilemmas of producing a satisfactory concrete, microconcept of class structure, might, in the end, be the best one can do, but it threatens to undermine the overall explanatory aspirations of Marxist theory. The explanatory force of the abstract, macrolevel Marxist concept of class would be greatly compromised if it were unconnected to corresponding microlevel concepts—concepts that are closely tied to the lives and conditions of individuals. And it is also true that the explanatory potential of Marxist theory would be undermined if its core concepts, in a particular class, are only useful for understanding the long-term, epochal dynamics of social change but not the variations across capitalist societies. If Marxist class analysis is to be theoretically powerful and politically useful, then, it seems necessary to continue the attempt at forging concepts at the concrete, microlevel of analysis that are consistent with the more abstract concepts.

A second possible response to the conceptual problems we have been discussing is to retain both the abstract class structure concept and the concrete derivations from that concept and simply decide to live with a certain level of conceptual incoherence. After all, all conceptual frameworks (in sociology at least), if pressed too hard, reveal inconsistencies and weaknesses, and Marxist theories of class are no exception. To do empirical work on class, one must, at some point, suspend the preoccupation with the reconstruction of foundational concepts and get on with the business of studying the world. And this generally requires a tolerance for a certain degree of conceptual ambiguity and inconsistency. This does not mean abandoning altogether the project of eliminating such inconsistencies; one can still try to forge new conceptual solutions, either by way of a synthesis of previous ideas or through the introduction of new conceptual elements. But it does mean adopting a certain pragmatic attitude toward research and not waiting until all conceptual problems are resolved. This is essentially the response I have adopted to these enduring conceptual problems in my empirical projects.

There is, however, a third possible response. One can decide that these conceptual issues have been so persistent and apparently intractable that they probably reflect deeper problems in the larger theoretical framework of which they are a part. Rather than continuing to struggle with the problem of constructing an adequate Marxist concept of the middle class in capitalist societies, therefore, analysts might call into question the general Marxist theory of class itself. I believe that there are compelling arguments against this alternative, but it is worth considering this more drastic remedy—namely, abandoning Marxist class analysis altogether.

Many of the conceptual difficulties bound up with the problem of the middle class within a Marxist framework appear to vanish within the Weberian tradition of class analysis. Of course, there are still plenty of

problems of operationalization within Weberian class structure analysis—
the concepts of "market situation" and "work situation" that are used
by Weberians such as John Goldthorpe both pose significant problems
of operationalization and measurement—but the middle-class category
does not pose the same kind of conceptual difficulties for Weberians that
it does for Marxists.[8]

Why is this so? Weberians have an easier time than Marxists in forming
a concept of the middle class because, in their tradition, the concept of
class structure is relieved of three theoretical burdens that must be dealt
with in one way or another within a Marxist framework:

1. *Class, Mode of Production, and the Theory of History.* For Weberians,
the concept of class structure does not have to be linked to an abstract
concept of "mode of production." Classes within the Weberian tradition
are viewed as categories of stratification specific to market societies; thus,
there is no need to develop a general schema of class analysis that applies
across different kinds of economic systems. And further, as a corollary
of this, the concept does not have to figure in any general theory of
history for Weberians as it generally does for Marxists. Even when, as
often occurs today, Marxists reject the general Marxist theory of history—
historical materialism—they nevertheless generally remain committed to
a class-based *structural typology* of historical variations. Thus, even without
the strong claims of historical materialism, the Marxist concept of class
is under the theoretical constraint functioning within a typology of
historical forms of class structure variation. The absence of this constraint
for Weberians means that the specific problem of conceptualizing classes
in capitalist society does not have to meet any criteria of coherence with
the analysis of class structures of pre- or postcapitalist societies.

2. *Exploitation and Antagonistic Classes.* Although the Weberian concept of class is relational (grounded in the problem of economic exchange
relations), it is not based on an abstract model of polarized, antagonistic
relations. In principle, then, Weberians can admit an indefinite number
of additional classes besides workers and capitalists without having to
postulate any underlying conflicts of material interest. All that is necessary
is that a given class be characterized by a distinctive work and market
situation or, more broadly, by distinctive economically conditioned "life-
chances" (to use a favorite Weberian expression). Marxists, on the other
hand, must produce concepts of specific class locations that are congruent
with the underlying antagonistic logic of class relations based in exploitation. This does not mean that every distinction among class locations
in a concrete, microlevel concept must, itself, be polarized to some other
distinction, but it must somehow be systematically embedded in an
analysis of such polarized, exploitative class relations.

3. *Ambitiousness of the Theoretical Ordering of Concepts.* The Weberian concept of class, at least as it has been elaborated by contemporary neo-Weberians, does not attempt to specify and defend a systematic hierarchy of conceptual elements. There is no effort, for example, to articulate a conceptual ordering of the problems of material interests, lived experiences, and capacities for collective action in the specification of class structures. This means that Weberians can deploy various kinds of criteria for defining aspects of class structures in a rather ad hoc manner without embarrassment. Weberians typically argue that class positions are defined by common work and market situations, but they do not attempt to construct a logical decomposition of these two concepts or to order them in a systematic way. Weberians are nearly always silent, for example, on the question of whether two jobs that share a common market situation but different work situations constitute divisions *within* a single class or *distinct* classes. Because they have lower aspirations for conceptual and theoretical integration than Marxists do, Weberians can adopt a rather pragmatic, empirical attitude toward the introduction of specific distinctions in a class structure analysis without worrying too much about the implications for a larger theoretical structure.[9]

The absence of these three theoretical constraints makes it much easier to locate categories like professionals, technical employees, and managers in the class structure. Thus, it is sufficient to demonstrate that the marketable skills of these categories give them distinctive economic advantages in the labor market. No conceptual difficulty is posed by the fact that ownership of skill assets does not correspond to any distinctive polarized social relation between skill-owners and nonowners. All that is necessary is that skills (or, in principle, any other attribute) constitute the basis for distinctively enhanced economic opportunities within exchange relations.

In a similar fashion, Goldthorpe (1982, pp. 167–70) argues that certain properties of work situations are the basis for the class structural differentiation of what he terms the "service class" from the working class. He argues that such characteristics as exercising managerial authority or having a great deal of discretion, autonomy, and responsibility on the job means that the employer-employee relation must involve high levels of *trust*. This trust element, in turn, means that, instead of a simple employment contract, the employment relation is constructed as a "service relation," the critical element of which is the centrality of *prospective rewards* rather than simply current remuneration. Primarily because these elements of the work situation systematically enhance economic opportunities (in the form of stable careers), they form the basis of a distinctive class—the "service class."[10]

The service class, defined in this way, is built around a distinctive kind of employment relation with superordinate employers (capitalists, corporate boards, the state). Within this definition, there is nothing inherently antagonistic about this relation, and certainly there is no implied *inherent* antagonism between the service and nonservice class employees.[11] Of course, conflicts, perhaps even explosive conflicts, may empirically occur among these classes, but the concept of class itself is based simply on a notion of distinctive *differences* in material interests and conditions among classes, not inherent cleavages.

Given the fact that the middle class is so much easier to contend with in a Weberian framework, one question clearly arises: Why not simply jump ship and adopt the Weberian approach? Frank Parkin, for one, has argued that an impulse in this direction is implicit in the neo-Marxists' efforts to grapple seriously with problems of class analysis: "The fact that these normally alien concepts of authority relations, life-chances, and market rewards have now been comfortably absorbed by contemporary Marxist theory is a handsome, if unacknowledged, tribute to the virtues of bourgeois sociology. Inside every neo-Marxist there seems to be a Weberian struggling to get out" (Parkin 1979, p. 25). Once we adopt a fairly differentiated Marxist class concept of the sort I have advocated, then, in practice, there is not much difference in the nature of the empirical class structure "variables" that are generated in neo-Marxist and neo-Weberian frameworks. After all, both acknowledge, in one way or another, that differences in property, skills/credentials/autonomy, and authority are bases for differentiating locations in the class structure. If you compare Goldthorpe's seven-category class structure schema (or the more elaborate eleven-category schema that contains a range of subclass divisions) with my analysis of class structure in terms of multiple-exploitation mechanisms, for example, you will find that, in practical empirical terms, the contrast is not great. Therefore, given that there is little empirical difference between many neo-Marxist and neo-Weberian class maps and given that the conceptual problems are greater within Marxist theory, why not just opt for the Weberian approach?

If the *only* reasons for adopting a Marxist approach to the concept of class structure was the practical usefulness of the categories derived from the conceptual framework for microlevel empirical analyses of class, there would be little reason to choose it over a range of neo-Weberian alternatives. The reason for adopting a Marxist strategy, then, must rest on a commitment to the theoretical constraints that Marxist theory imposes on class analysis. More specifically, unless one sees the value of embedding the concept of class structure in an abstract model of modes of production, in which classes are fundamentally polarized around processes of exploitation, there would be no reason to accept the difficulties this abstract framework generates for the concrete analysis of classes.

My personal commitment to these constraints is grounded on three broad considerations—one political or normative, one theoretical, and one methodological.

Politically, the Marxist tradition, broadly understood, continues to provide, in my judgment, the most comprehensive and compelling theoretical framework within which to understand the possibilities for and obstacles to emancipatory social change. A range of rival frameworks for radical social theory have emerged in recent years, but none has yet achieved the level of analytical power for understanding large-scale processes of social change that is offered by the Marxist tradition.[12]

Theoretically, if one wants the concept of class structure to simultaneously figure centrally in analyses of both epochal social change *and* systematically structured social conflict within given types of society, then something very much like these conceptual constraints is necessary. To borrow a metaphor from rational-choice theory, the goal of Marxist theory is to link systematically an account of conflict within a given type of game to an account of the fundamental shifts from one kind of game to another. *If* class structure is to figure in such a theory, then it must be subjected to the kinds of conceptual constraints indicated above.

Methodologically, I believe it is generally better to try to develop and reconstruct specific concepts within a clearly specified set of constraints than to do so in their absence. The Weberian tradition is, by and large, characterized by quite ad hoc and diffuse conceptual specifications. These may be grounded in certain abstract understandings of human action, but they are not systematically derived from a general theory of society and its development. The choice between Marxist and Weberian concepts of class, therefore, is not, strictly speaking, a choice between concepts with equal theoretical standing. Or, as Charles Camic has noted, the choice is not really between two theories of society but between a theory and a nontheory.[13]

The implication of this methodological point about the status of class concepts within the Marxist and Weberian traditions is that the choice of a concept cannot be reduced to a simple decision on their "explanatory power" in any given empirical setting. As a general metatheoretical proposition, we would expect that, in any particular empirical context, it is easier to construct empirical categories that are highly correlated with what we are trying to explain when the theoretical constraints on such constructions are relatively weak. This is precisely what gives "empiricism" as a strategy of concept formation such appeal: The researcher is relatively free to modify definitions and to juggle concepts (the categories of observation and analysis) in response to the specific exigencies of any given empirical analysis, without worrying about violating any theoretical constraints on concepts.

In these terms, the Weberian tradition of class analysis is relatively more "empiricist" than the Marxist tradition. The problem, of course, is that, at the end of the day, it may be much less clear what one has really *learned* cumulatively from such empiricist exercises, beyond the predictions and observations of the specific analysis, because the categories used are not orchestrated within an elaborated, more abstract framework. If we want to gain knowledge not simply *about* a particular empirical problem but *from* that problem, it is crucial that the concepts used in the analysis be as integrated into a general conceptual framework as possible.

These comments should not be interpreted as a devious way of getting a Marxist approach to class analysis "off the hook" of having to demonstrate its empirical power. *If*, indeed, it were true that Weberian categories were consistently better predictors of microlevel empirical phenomena— for example, individual class consciousness, variations in individual economic welfare, or propensities to participate in specific patterns of class formation—this would be a challenge for a Marxist approach.[14] It would then be incumbent upon a defender of class analysis in a Marxist framework to explain these Weberian-generated results within the theoretical constraints of Marxism. One hypothetical possibility, for example, might be something like the following:

> Let us introduce a distinction between the process of class formation under conditions of stable social reproduction in democratic capitalism and under conditions of systemic capitalist crisis. Under the first of these conditions, categories of economic actors become collectively organized on the basis of divisions of *immediate* material interests—divisions defined entirely within the "rules of the game" of capitalism. Under the second set of conditions, social categories have a much higher probability of becoming organized around "fundamental interests"—interests defined in terms of what game is to be played. Now, the kinds of distinctions in market situations embodied in Weberian class concepts do define divisions within immediate interests among sellers of labor power. Under conditions of stable reproduction, then, these are likely to become more salient as bases of social differentiation and collective organization. In short, Weberian class categories will have greater microlevel explanatory power under conditions of stable reproduction than under conditions of generalized economic crisis.

Other theoretical strategies for incorporating Weberian empirical results within a Marxist theoretical framework could also be entertained. These empirical findings could, perhaps, be treated as generated by the particular institutional organization of bargaining arrangements (as in the literature on corporatism) or as effects of the particular strategies of political parties (as in Adam Przeworski's analyses of social democracy). In each of these lines of theoretical argument, the empirical observations generated within Weberian class analysis would be taken seriously rather than simply dismissed out of hand. The task of Marxist class analysis, then, would be to explain the "conditions of possibility" of the Weberian patterns.

A critique of empiricism is thus not equivalent to a critique of empirical research or of empirically grounded knowledge. The point is simply that the task of adjudicating between alternative general approaches to class analysis—alternative "paradigms," as they are sometimes called—is an arduous one, and it cannot be reduced to the simple task of testing predictive power in a concrete empirical setting.

Weberian solutions, therefore, do represent a way of avoiding the conceptual knots generated by conceptualizing the middle classes within the Marxist tradition. But these solutions are purchased at the price of lowering the ambitiousness of one's theoretical aspirations and abandoning the attempt at consistency with the conceptual framework—Marxism broadly conceived—that remains the most coherent general approach to radical, emancipatory social theory. Sticking with that framework, however, creates headaches; because the conceptual knots will not disappear and cannot be indefinitely avoided by evasion, new efforts at untying them must be attempted.

Acknowledgments

This chapter is a slightly modified version of sections 1 and 4 of an essay, "Rethinking, Once Again, the Concept of Class Structure," which appeared as the concluding chapter of Erik Olin Wright, ed., *The Debate on Classes* (London: Verso, 1990) and is published here with permission. I thank Julia Adams, Ron Aminzade, Robin Blackburn, Sam Bowles, Johanna Brenner, Lisa Brush, Michael Burawoy, Val Burris, Ira Katznelson, Lane Kenworthy, Michael Mann, Scott McNall, John Roemer, Joel Rogers, Ivan Szelenyi, and Philippe Van Parijs for their extraordinarily helpful comments on the longer essay on which this chapter is based.

Notes

1. Note that this way of understanding the class structure/class formation relation is essentially equivalent to Bourdieu's (1987) formulation of the distinction between "classes-on-paper" and "real classes." However, I think that the expression

"classes-on-paper" is misleading for it implies that these are the arbitrary constructions of theorists and, thus, that the classes-on-paper do not have real effects in the world. If this were the case, they would also not have any determining effects on even the probabilities of "real classes" emerging. To say that X determines the probability of Y implies that X is a real mechanism, not just a description-on-paper.

2. The assumption here is that the concept of class structure imparts the essential content of the adjective "class" when it is appended to formation, consciousness, and struggle. Class formation is the formation of collective actors organized around class interests within class structures; class struggle is the struggle between such collectively organized actors over class interests; and class consciousness is the understanding by people within a class of their class interests. In each case, one must already have a definition of class structure before the other concepts can be fully specified.

3. In describing a concept as "representing" a real object, there is no implication that it is a simple *reflection* of that object, as in the metaphor of a mirror reflecting reality. Concepts are always active mental constructions, produced through a set of practices by people attempting to understand the world. To a greater or lesser extent, these constructions are constrained by the real objects they attempt to represent—i.e., if the world were different, the concepts that attempt to represent the world would be different—but they are never simple reflections of those objects. For a discussion of this kind of "realist" approach to the status of concepts, see Wright (1985, pp. 20–24).

4. Far from being "less real" than concrete concepts, there is a certain sense in which, for many explanatory problems, the causal mechanisms identified by more abstract concepts can be thought of as more "fundamental" than those identified by more concrete concepts. Thus, the mechanisms defined by the concept "dog" are more fundamental than those defined by the concept "golden retriever" in explaining a wide range of empirical properties of the specific token, Micah, where "more fundamental" means determining the limits within which the more concrete mechanisms operate.

5. In terms of the use of *words* in discussions of class structure and levels of abstraction, Marxists sometimes use the expression "social relations of production" to refer to the mode of production level of abstract, reserving the term "class structure" for more concrete levels of analysis. Thus, a (concrete) class structure consists of combinations of (abstract) relations of production, but the term "class structure" is not itself applied to the more abstract level. This is parallel to the distinction between elements and compounds in chemistry: Compounds are specific combinations of elements. In the present discussion, I will use the term "class structure" to refer to the theoretical object of the structural analysis of classes at whatever level of abstraction.

6. For examples of this kind of critique, see G. Carchedi (1990) and Paul Kamolnick (1988).

7. The core of methodological individuals is not simply the concern with microanalysis but the claim that macrophenomena are, in principle, fully explainable by micromechanisms (or, equivalently, that macrophenomena are reducible to

microphenomena). For a critique of this claim, see Sober, Levine, and Wright (1987).

8. John Goldthorpe (1980, pp. 39–42), for example, makes the following distinctions in developing his class structure concept: "high-grade" versus "low-grade" professionals; "higher-grade technicians" versus "lower-grade technicians"; managers in large versus small establishments; nonroutine versus routine non-manual employees in administration and commerce. In each case, there are difficult problems in defining nonarbitrary criteria for operationalizing these distinctions. Nevertheless, the conceptual status of these distinctions poses no difficulties within the overall class structure concept.

9. Val Burris, in a personal communication, suggests that the relatively low level of aspiration for theoretical integration of the distinct elements of class theory in the Weberian tradition is due to certain general properties of Weberian theory: "(1) As a theory of social *action,* the Weberian theory is absolved of having to specify structural forms of causation; (2) because Weberian theory is unabashedly *multicausal* and rejects the primacy of class relations, it is not forced to pack so much into its concept of class; (3) because Weberian theory focuses on *exchange* relations, it deals with phenomena that are closer to the empirical level of lived relations as compared with the production relations that Marxists must reconstruct theoretically." For a further discussion of these themes, see Val Burris (1987).

10. There are places where Goldthorpe seems to suggest that it is the possession of power and responsibility as such, rather than the way in which such powerholding constitutes the basis for a distinct kind of employment relation, that provides the rationale for treating the service class as a distinct class (e.g., Goldthorpe [1980, pp. 39–40]), but generally he seems to stress the ways in which work situations generate distinctive kinds of market situations (see especially Goldthorpe [1982, pp. 170–71]). Other writers, such as Lockwood (1980) and Giddens (1973), using a similar set of concepts, suggest in various places that the workplace *experiences* of actors under these different work situations also differ systematically and constitute part of the justification for treating these differences in work situations as the basis for class structural differences.

11. Indeed, there is no inherent social relation of any sort between the service class as a general category and nonservice class employees. Sometimes, an authority relation links these two but not invariably. The relationship between the service and working classes is basically understood via the distinctive differences in their respective relations to their employers rather than a relation that directly binds them to each other.

12. To avoid misunderstanding, two points of clarification are needed to this statement. First, the claim is about the Marxist *tradition,* defined in an ecumenical fashion, not about any particular theoretical position within that tradition. Second, the claim is not that this tradition provides the most fruitful framework for analyzing *every* question of relevance to radical projects of social change but simply that it provides the best overall framework for the general problem of understanding the obstacles to and opportunities for emancipatory transformation. Thus, for example, the Marxist tradition probably does not—and perhaps cannot—

provide adequate tools for understanding many of the important issues bound up with gender oppression. As a result, some kind of linkage between Marxism and feminism is essential for the study of gender. Nevertheless, in my judgment, Marxism remains the most comprehensive and productive general framework for developing a macrostructural theory of large-scale emancipatory possibilities.

13. Personal communication.

14. I do *not* think that the case for the empirical superiority of Weberian categories for microlevel analysis has been proven. In the one monograph-length, sustained, systematic empirical comparison that has been made of neo-Marxist and neo-Weberian class structure concepts (a comparison of my class structure concepts with those of John Goldthorpe, by Gordon Marshall, Howard Newby, David Rose, and Carolyn Vogler [1988]), the authors argue that the Weberian concepts are empirically more consistent and powerful, but, in general, the empirical differences they cite are small. The more striking general conclusion from their work is that these different concepts are empirically quite similar. (It should also be noted that there are significant methodological problems with the analyses in that book, in particular a lack of attention to the relationship between problems of operationalization and conceptual differences, which undermine their empirical conclusions.) Other less extensive cases of empirical comparisons between neo-Marxist and neo-Weberian class concepts have also failed to find dramatic differences in the brute "explanatory power."

References

Bourdieu, Pierre. 1987. "What Makes a Class?" *Berkeley Journal of Sociology* 32:1–17.

Burris, Val. 1987. "The Neo-Marxist Synthesis of Marx and Weber on Class." In *The Marx-Weber Debate,* ed. Norbert Wiley. Newbury Park, California: Sage Publications.

Carchedi, Guglielmo. 1990. "Classes and Class Analysis." In *The Debate on Classes* by Erik Olin Wright et al., pp. 105–25. London: Verso.

Giddens, Anthony. 1973. *The Class Structure of the Advanced Societies.* New York: Harper and Row.

Goldthorpe, John. 1980. *Social Mobility in Modern Britain.* Oxford: Clarendon Press.

———. 1982. "On the Service Class." In *Social Class and the Division of Labour,* eds. Anthony Giddens and Gavin McKenzie, pp. 162–85. Cambridge: Cambridge University Press.

Johnston, W., and M. Ornstein. "Social Class and Political Ideology in Canada." *Canadian Review of Sociology and Anthropology* 22:369–95.

Kamolnick, Paul. 1988. *Classes: A Marxist Critique.* Dix Hills, N.Y.: General Hall.

Lockwood, David. 1958. *The Blackcoated Worker.* London: Routledge and Kegan Paul.

Marshall, Gordon, Howard Newby, David Rose, and Carolyn Vogler. 1988. *Classes in Modern Britain.* London: Hutchinson.

Parkin, Frank. 1979. *Marxism and Class Theory: A Bourgeois Critique.* New York: Columbia University Press.

Sober, Elliott, Andrew Levine, and Erik Olin Wright. 1987. "Marxism and Methodological Individualism." *New Left Review* 162:67–84.

Wright, Erik Olin. 1985. *Classes.* London: Verso.

Wright, Erik Olin et al. 1990. *The Debate on Classes.* London: Verso.

3 | Making Class: The Middle Class(es) in Social Theory and Social Structure

Löic J.D. Wacquant

"Think of the tools in a tool-box: there is a hammer, pliers, a saw, a screw-driver, a ruler, a glue-pot, glue, nails and screws. The functions of words are as diverse as the functions of these objects. . . . The meaning of a word is in its use in language. . . . Of course, what confuses us is the uniform appearance of words when we hear them spoken or meet them in script and print. For their application is not presented to us so clearly."

Ludwig Wittgenstein

The question of the so-called "middle classes" in advanced societies— their theoretical status, social composition, and structural position—has been variously referred to as "one of the most intractable issues in contemporary sociology" (Abercrombie and Urry 1983, p. 1) and a major "embarrassment" for Marxist class analysis (Wright 1985, p. 13). Indeed, few problems in social science have proved more persistent and more strongly colored by both ideological commitments and political context.[1] The purpose of this chapter is to lay out the central features of this ongoing debate. After uncovering the historical origins of the puzzle, we survey the main contending views of the middle class, focusing on its structural location and on the factors determining its evolution, internal constitution, and political proclivities. For purposes of clarity and parsimony, these are regrouped in two broad categories, Marxist and Weberian. However, this distinction itself has become increasingly blurred of late, and its relevance will be questioned in the final section of this chapter, where a more dynamic and historical approach is outlined that takes seriously struggles over class (i.e., the political and symbolic dimensions of group formation) in the constitution of the middle classes.

Throughout, I point to the ways in which various theorists have confronted the question of the "boundary" of the middle class, arguing, in fine, that it cannot be adequately addressed at an abstract theoretical level and should thus be tackled, if at all, through historical analysis. I contend that intermediate regions of social space are, by their very nature, prone to being "cut up" in different and opposing ways and therefore that the question of the middle class(es) can only be resolved at the political and ideological level—that is, by the historical study of real class practices and not on paper.

The Puzzle of the Middle Classes: The Legacy of Marx and German Political History

Much of the current controversy surrounding the question of the "middle classes" can be traced back to Marx and to the rival interpretations that the ambiguities and/or deficiencies of his theory have generated in the political context of the German "revisionism" dispute of the 1890s. The common understanding of Marx attributes to him a theory of radical polarization and simplification of the class structure, where the maturation of capitalism eventually results in the mechanical subsumption of all intermediate groupings into a growing and increasingly homogeneous and militant working class (Bendix and Lipset 1966; Dahrendorf 1972; Aron 1964, p. 46). The locus classicus of this view is undoubtedly to be found in *The Communist Manifesto*, where Marx and Engels (Marx 1974a, p. 75) proclaim that

> the lower strata of the middle class—the small tradespeople, shop-
> keepers, and rentiers, the handicraftsmen and peasants—all these
> sink gradually into the proletariat, partly because their diminutive
> capital does not suffice for the scale on which modern industry is
> carried on, and is swamped in the competition with the large capi-
> talists, partly because their specialized skill is rendered worthless by
> new methods of production. Thus the proletariat is recruited from
> all classes of the population.

In opposition to this standard reading, a number of recent interpreters of the Marxian oeuvre have contended that, far from having ignored the expansion of salaried intermediaries, Marx was an early advocate, if not the originator, of the notion of a "new middle class" (e.g., Nicolaus 1967; Urry 1973; Rattansi 1985). They point to the numerous passages in his mature writings where the German political economist-cum-revolutionary discusses the growth of this social category. Thus, in *Theories of Surplus Value* (1863), Marx excoriates David Ricardo for forgetting "to emphasize . . . the continual increase in numbers of the middle classes, of those who are situated midway between the workers on one side and the capitalists and the landowners on the other" (in Bottomore 1985, p. 16). Later in the same volume, referring to Thomas Malthus, Marx writes: "His greatest hope . . . is that the middle class will increase in size and the working proletariat will make up a constantly diminishing proportion of the total population (even if it grows in absolute numbers). That is, in fact, the tendency of bourgeois society" (Bottomore 1985, p. 16).

Both of these interpretations are one-sided and inadequate. Sociology's conventional understanding of Marx is deficient because it grossly distorts his sociology in failing to acknowledge the degree to which he was aware of, and did speak to, the complexity of the class structures of his time and the functional and political importance of intermediate groups in them.[2] The presentist claims of the Marxologists who portray his work as the precursor of today's theories of the "new middle class" are equally flawed, inasmuch as Marx did not incorporate these insights regarding the changing composition of the class structure into his abstract model of the dynamics of capitalist society.

In point of fact, Marx's achievements and shortcomings set the basic parameters of the "middle class" debate that has preoccupied sociology and Marxism for nearly a century now. The questions he left unresolved have been at the core of the subsequent controversy on the status of these groups in contemporary capitalism. And the general, if divergent, theoretical directions he indicated have oriented much of the debate. They can be summarized as follows. Are the middle classes a transitional category or are they here to stay? Are they becoming proletarianized or not? Do they constitute a generic class or comprise several classes, or do they somehow stand outside the class structure? And how exactly do they differ from and relate to the working class?[3]

It fell upon the successors of Marx to elucidate the import of his pronouncements on these issues in light of the rapid expansion of middle strata at the turn of the century (Turner 1986). This gave rise to the "revisionism" controversy among theorists of the German Social Democratic party (SPD) and, in large part as a reaction to it, to a flurry of sociological studies aimed at pinning down for good the class nature of white-collar employees in the Weimar regime (the *Angestelltefrage*). It is at this time that the expression "new middle class" was invented—by Gustav Schmoller—and the basic contours of the modern "middle class" problematic were decisively shaped.

Faced with the "anomalous" growth of white-collar occupations, the German Social Democrats divided into two interpretive camps. In typically economistic fashion, the defenders of the Marxian orthodoxy, who represented the dominant tendency, clung to an inclusive definition of the proletariat as embracing almost all those who worked for a wage or a salary. Thus, Karl Kautsky based his analysis on a sharp distinction between class-in-itself and class-for-itself (Przeworski 1977) to argue that, although at the subjective level salaried employees fancied themselves part of the bourgeoisie, they were objectively part of the working class. He rejected the notion of a "new middle class" and predicted that, with the growing oversupply of educated labor and the continued rationalization of commercial and clerical activities, "the time is near when the bulk of these occupations will be distinguished from the others only by their pretensions" (Kautsky 1971, p. 40). Against this polarized conception of class as defined solely by the capital ownership versus wage-labor divide, advocates of the revisionist thesis, such as Eduard Bernstein, insisted that "the middle ranks between the apex and the bottom of the social pyramid" (Bernstein 1961) were not being absorbed into the proletariat; on the contrary, the number and variety of white-collar employees was increasing both relatively and absolutely. For Kautsky, this phenomenon was residual or transitory, but for Bernstein it was the wave of the future and expressed the increasing differentiation of the class structure, as revealed by income statistics and other indicators of economic improvement. Yet, Bernstein stopped short of treating those "in the middle" as a full-blown class, and, like his rival, he believed that they would eventually side with factory workers in the class struggle, once the SPD had shifted from a revolutionary to a gradualist strategy.

As the anticipated fusion of white- and blue-collar workers failed to materialize (I will show why below), other revisionists went well beyond Bernstein in emphasizing the distinctive social status and ideology of salaried employees; they also expressed strong reservations about their politics (see Burris 1986, pp. 324–34). That the white-collar work force did occupy a position roughly similar to that of industrial workers in the economic structure could not offset the massive effects of their distinctive lifestyle (Suhr 1928), their close contact with employers, and the prestige derived from their education and higher social recruitment (Speier 1939, as cited in Abercrombie and Urry 1983). This combined with the powerful hold of occupational ideologies emphasizing autonomy and independence in the organization of work (Croner 1928) and a status consciousness sustained by the complexification of bureaucratic hierarchies (Dreyfus 1933) to make the white-collar wage earners a specific class. Regarding their political proclivities, a consensus slowly emerged that, due precisely to their infatuation with status, salaried employees could not be expected to incline naturally toward the Left, a view that later evolved into an obdurate belief that their lower ranks were quintessentially reactionary.

Intermediate Strata, White-Collar Proletarians, or (New) Class Sui Generis? Recent Marxist Approaches to the Middle Class

Marxist views on the middle classes have since diversified along the lines defined by these earlier controversies. The recent positions can be arrayed in three categories, covering a broad spectrum from those that reduce intermediate groupings to a mere agglomeration of strata to those that acknowledge their reality only to make them "wither away" under the onslaught of proletarianization to those that fully recognize them as genuine class(es) endowed with specific (if contradictory) interests, possibly including that of imposing their own rule upon society.[4] The first remains strictly confined within the self-imposed limits of pure objectivism, propounding a steadfastly economistic conception of the middle class as determined exclusively by relations of production. The latter two recognize, timidly or wholeheartedly, that other dimensions of social life—ideology and politics, market relations and culture—have relevance for the theoretical understanding of the middle classes.

The first position consists in arguing that something like a middle class exists but that it is "structurally flawed" and subject to progressive erosion into the working class with the development of monopoly capitalism, i.e., becoming proletarianized.[5] The principal exponents of this theory, of which L. Corey (1935) and F. D. Klingender (1935) were evident forerunners, are Harry Braverman (1974), Guglielmo Carchedi (1975a, 1975b), and Rosemary Crompton and Jon Gubbay (1978). Braverman's main focus is on the impact that the transformations of the labor process under monopoly capitalism have had on the objective structure of the working class. But the two trends he identifies—the growing separation of conception and execution and the penetration of capital into the realm of clerical, trade, and service activities—have massive consequences for white-collar workers as well. The "Taylorization" of clerical labor, for instance, rationalizes office work by separating and concentrating its mental component in an ever-smaller group, while the brunt of the employees are confined to progressively deskilled, fragmented, and externally-controlled manual or quasi-manual tasks. Concludes Braverman (1974, pp. 355, 325–26):

> The apparent trend to a large nonproletarian "middle class" has resolved itself into the creation of a large proletariat in a new form. . . . The traditional distinction between manual and "white-collar" labor represents echoes of a past situation which have virtually ceased to have meaning in the modern world of work.

Guglielmo Carchedi's (1975a, 1975b) analysis represents a formal (and somewhat tortuous) elaboration of this basic thesis. Under monopoly capitalism, there develops, on the one hand, the "collective laborer" (that is, an advanced differentiation and coordination of workers to carry out an increasingly complex labor process) and, on the other, "global capital" (that is, equally complex bureaucratic apparatuses designed not only to unify but, more crucially, to exert control and surveillance over labor for purposes of accumulation. The middle class is defined by the fact that it performs both the functions of global capital and of the collective laborer: It promotes accumulation but does not own the means of production, and it supplies surplus value by participating in the detailed division of labor. To be more precise, the middle class is divided into three layers defined by the "mix" of these functions. According to Carchedi's model, technological changes spurred by accumulation result in both wage-goods devaluation and the technical dequalification of labor, which in turn lead to the proletarianization of middle-class labor power. In other words, the internal composition of the middle class, which, like its boundaries, is given by the particular "mix" of the two fundamental functions, is continually being lowered.

A third way of conceptualizing the middle class, especially popular in French Marxist sociology, portrays the new professional, technical, and bureaucratic workers as a segment of the petty bourgeoisie and underlines the structural factors that make them profoundly different from their industrial counterparts. For Nicos Poulantzas (1974, 1977), it is non-sensical to believe that "strata" that are not part of the class structure can exist; insofar as they do not belong to the bourgeoisie or the working class, white-collar employees, ex definitio, constitute (part of) a definite class, the "new petty bourgeoisie." It is determined concurrently by three criteria: at the economic level, by exclusion from both ownership of the means of production and productive labor; at the political level, by the exercise of authority and supervisory control over the activities of pro-ductive workers; and at the ideological level, by the tendency to monopolize knowledge and conception of the labor process at the expense of the latter. Put another way, the new petty bourgeoisie comprises all unpro-ductive, supervisory, mental wage earners. Poulantzas contends that, together with the traditional petty bourgeoisie of self-employed workers, it constitutes a genuine class. But he immediately qualifies this proposition by adding that it is not a "fundamental" class in the way the bourgeoisie and proletariat are: Its structural determination is chiefly at the political and ideological, rather than economic, levels. The sociological significance of the new petty bourgeoisie, then, lies primarily in its ability to mediate capitalist legitimacy in the ideological and political spheres. And because it does not have a "long-term autonomous interest," its politics and

ideology—or "ideological sous-ensemble" for it does not have an autonomous ideology either—are characterized by inconstancy and instability,
shifting in accord with the general balance of power between capital and
labor. Consequently, great caution should be exercised by the Left in
negotiating political alliances with it.[6]

Another way of treating the middle classes as a class is provided by
Erik Olin Wright's (1978, 1985) theory of contradictory class locations.[7]
Wright claims that class structures should be conceptualized strictly in
terms of exploitation and, drawing on the work of economist John Roemer
(1986), he proposes to define exploitation as any "economically oppressive
appropriation of the fruits of the labor of one class by another" flowing
from the unequal distribution of productive assets (Wright 1985, p. 77).
In pure capitalism, the material basis of exploitation is ownership of the
means of production, which defines the two polarized and fundamental
class locations of capitalist and worker. But any actual capitalist society
also contains secondary forms of exploitation that are decisive in accounting
for the structural position of the middle class. These noncapitalist mechanisms of exploitation are founded upon control over organizational assets
and upon ownership of monopolized skills. The various relations of
exploitation thus defined intersect in complex ways. Some propertyless
individuals, for instance, possess scarce credentials that allow them to
extract returns over and beyond what they would get without the operation
of institutionalized means of restricting the supply of such skills. Or
they may hold a position within an organization that enables them to
appropriate more than their share of the social product. The middle
classes can be defined, then, as locations in the class structure that have
discrepant coordinates along the three fundamental axes of exploitation—
they are the exploited in terms of property ownership, but the exploiters
with respect to (either or both) credentialed skills and organizational
authority. Their boundaries become somewhat fuzzy because they come
to depend on where the analyst decides to situate significant cutoff points
in the measurement of the various types of exploitation-generating assets.[8]
This reconceptualization allows Wright to give full theoretical status to
the concept of middle class and to construct a "historical trajectory" of
middle classes across modes of production, based on which specific
combination of exploitation relations structure the society. The middle
class appears, in this abstract typology, as the "bearer" of the principle
of class organization that always anticipates the next stage of societal
development (Wright 1986, p. 129). The political consequences of this
theory are clear enough: The working class can no longer be assumed
to be the chief or only rival to the bourgeoisie in the contention for
class power in capitalist society. Middle-class strategies—of individual
ascension, hegemonic collusion with capitalists, or rapprochement with

the proletariat—will decisively affect not only alliances but also the historical possibility and outcome of political transformation.

Finally, a number of Marxist or Marxoid writers have put forth the thesis that the middle classes contain the embryo of a new dominant class in statu nascendi. "New Class" theories are extremely diverse (Szelenyi and Martin 1988) and appear strongly rooted in particular national contexts. What they share is a concern for the role of science, culture, and bureaucratic authority in the creation of class. This is particularly obvious in the thesis of Barbara and John Ehrenreich (1977). The Ehrenreichs argue forcefully, contra theorists of proletarianization, that educated wage-labor cannot be viewed as proletarian. Technical workers and cultural producers not only have interests fundamentally at variance with those of both workers and capitalists but they must also be sharply distinguished from clerical and sales employees (who compose the new middle class) and from the older petty bourgeoisie. They form a distinct class in monopoly capitalist society, the "Professional-Managerial Class" (PMC), "whose major function in the division of labor may be described broadly as the reproduction of capitalist culture and capitalist class relations" (Ehrenreich and Ehrenreich 1977, p. 12). As a class, the PMC has evolved its own organizations (professional associations), its own ideology (technocratic liberalism), and its own centers of recruitment and indoctrination (elite universities). Much of the political protest of the 1960s in the United States can be interpreted as the result of the PMC's mounting opposition to late capitalism. But it also has the effect of deflecting working-class antagonism to capital and encouraging conservatism, sexism, and racism among workers. In other words, the crystallization of the PMC has irremediably transformed the landscape of class relations in advanced society.

This assessment finds a resonant cord in the neo-Hegelian sociology of class propounded by Alvin Gouldner (1979). For him, the New Class encompasses both technical intelligentsia and bureaucrats, whose base of power is essentially cultural: It consists of "cultural capital" and what he calls the "culture of critical discourse." The decisive relationship here is not that with the working class but that with the ruling class. The New Class enters in contention with whomever controls the machinery of production and administration—businessmen in the West, party leaders in the East—not because of structural contradictions at the economic level but because of heightened tensions between their objective and subjective situations and aspirations. Among these, Gouldner (1979, p. 58) singles out

the blockage of their opportunities for upward mobility, the disparity between their income and power, on the one side, and their cultural capital and self-regard, on the other; their commitment to the social totality; the contradictions of the technical, especially the blockage of their technical interests.

The New Class, which has grown in proportion to the centrality of science and rational discourse in the functioning of capitalism, does not yet rule, but it is quite possible that it will in the future. And its politics are ambivalent, at once progressive and potentially undemocratic: "The paradox of the New Class is that it is both emancipatory and elitist . . . a flawed universal class" (Gouldner 1979, p. 84).

Status, Authority, and the Market: The Middle Class in Stratification Research and Weberian Class Analysis

Weberian perspectives on the middle class(es) are, if anything, even more diverse than Marxist ones. This is because the hallmark of Max Weber's treatment of class, which forms their generative matrix, is its celebrated multidimensionality: Class is understood as the summation or weighed combination of a variety of positional effects on partly orthogonal scales or divides—of property, occupation, authority, education, and prestige. It entails both objective and subjective factors and arises in the sphere of consumption no less than in that of production (Weber 1947). Of paramount importance in almost all Weberian theories is the rift that allegedly separates blue- and white-collar workers. In what follows, I briefly summarize three influential approaches—those of David Lockwood, Ralf Dahrendorf, and Anthony Giddens—that typify, build on, or take off from these insights. Before I do, a few comments are in order on conceptions of the middle class in conventional stratification research.

The Weberian theme of status has been adopted and elevated to paramount importance in U.S. sociology where class has been effectively reduced to socioeconomic status, if not to subjective status tout court (Warner 1949; Goffman 1951; Lenski 1952; Gordon 1958; Coleman and Rainwater 1979). Even when the chief criterion of class position is occupation, occupations themselves are generally ranked in terms of income, education, and prestige, where these are assumed to reflect their "functional importance" for the social system (Davis and Moore 1945). In this perspective—whose Weberian credentials are admittedly dubious— the middle class is composed of those who stand in the middle in the statistical distribution of income and prestige, i.e., white-collar workers and professionals for the most part.[9] Thus, the manual-nonmanual line is considered to mark the boundary of the middle class[10] and is the main hurdle to mobility in a fundamentally open class structure (Blau and Duncan 1967).

Lockwood's (1958) theory of the middle class is spelled out in the course of an investigation of differences in consciousness between manual and clerical workers. Noting that both are propertyless yet have very divergent outlooks, he concludes that they must belong to different classes. He then proposes that class is determined by three sets of factors: market situation, "consisting of source and size of income, degree of job-security, and opportunity for upward occupational mobility"; work situation, that is, "the set of social relationships in which the individual is involved at work by virtue of his position in the division of labor"; and status situation, as defined by standing in the hierarchy of prestige (Lockwood 1958, p. 12). He proceeds to show how the "blackcoated worker" differs from manual wage earners in all three of these respects. He finds that, though it is true that the pay and income gaps between the two groups have tended to narrow, clerks still enjoy a better market position. Likewise, status differences have taken a more attenuated form over the years, but they continue to be significant. Of the three dimensions of class, however, the work situation dominates, and here Lockwood acknowledges the possibility that, even though the work situation of clerks has remained quite distinctive so far, it could become more similar to that of industrial workers. The class position of the blackcoated worker could, therefore, change in the future. For now, though, they are still part of the middle class and favor status politics over class politics. Lockwood's occupational scheme does not show how clerks fit in the overall class structure because his conventionalist epistemology does not require that he draw definite boundaries around his middle class: These would presumably vary with the purpose of the investigation. It is nonetheless clear that, as in C. W. Mills's (1956) earlier work, the manual/white-collar divide marks the lower frontier of the group.

The works of Mills, Lockwood, and U.S. stratification theorists share a strong empiricist focus on research, rather than on class theory per se, and typically remain close to the data. This is true of most Weberian views on the middle class (Mann 1986). Two notable exceptions are Dahrendorf (1972) and Giddens (1973) who have, each in their own way, developed more structural frameworks.[11] Dahrendorf's theory is also peculiar in that it generates not a gradational but a (multi)dichotomic picture of the class structure that, in effect, dissolves the middle class. Dahrendorf engages in a part-Machiavellian, part-Weberian reconstruction of Marx's theory in which authority is the more general category from which property, and thus class, is derived. Classes, for him, "have never been and are not economic groupings" but "groups of social conflict whose determining factor lies in participation in, or exclusion from, the exercise of authority within any imperatively-coordinated association" (Dahrendorf 1972, pp. 139–41). Because authority is always dichotomic, there can only be two classes. Those "in the middle" thus become split by falling on either side of the class divide, depending on whether they wield authority (bureaucrats) or are subjected to it (employees). There is no middle class, then, not because it has been proletarianized but because the very nature of authority "pulverizes" it into a multiplicity of dominated or dominant groupings across a range of organizations, inasmuch as Dahrendorf's conception logically implies the possibility of an indeterminate plurality of classes.

Where Dahrendorf stresses authority as the dividing line passing through "the middle," Anthony Giddens singles out the market as the foundation of a three-fold class structure generic to capitalist society. He explicitly rejects the German sociologist's authority-centered theory because of its inability to specify the boundaries of the middle class. Instead, he contends that "the structuration of classes is facilitated to the degree to which mobility closure exists in relation to" three fundamental sorts of market capacity (Giddens 1973, p. 107): ownership of the means of production, which defines the upper class; possession of manual labor power, which creates the working class; and possession of educational or technical qualifications, which yields the middle class. It is these different market capacities that produce the variety of economic and sociocultural differences observable between manual and white-collar workers through the distinct clusters of mobility, life-chances, and lifestyle they determine. "Proximate structuration," i.e., the division of labor and authority relations within the firm and distributive groupings such as neighborhoods and status communities, further reinforces the cleavage between the middle and working classes. This cleavage is not being eroded by changes in the organization of white-collar activities: Giddens maintains that the mechanization and automation of office work do not entail proletarianization of nonmanual employees. The middle class is a class sui generis in capitalism and is not about to fade away.

A number of common themes emerge in these Weberian treatments of the middle class, in addition to the ones directly or indirectly derived from Weber. First, with a few exceptions (e.g., Dahrendorf 1972, Barbalet 1986), there is clear agreement that some group or groups exist "in the middle," distinct and separate from both workers and the bourgeoisie. Second, the majority opinion seems also to hold that this grouping is heterogenous, multiple, diverse, and possibly even fragmented; many think it is becoming polarized.[12] Third, a plurality of criteria is necessary to identify the middle class; more precisely, several bases of middle class membership are given. In all versions, economic criteria (notably property and wage-labor) are insufficient to identify the middle class, and status or market variables have to be called in. At the same time, there is strong divergence on what the significance of this class might be for the understanding of advanced societies; on what its actual size is; on how it is evolving with contemporary changes in work, markets, and culture; and, last but not least, on whether it *is* a class in the strict sense of the term.

More importantly, though, all of the above points identify widening areas of overlap and convergence between Marxist and Weberian approaches as well. Writers on both sides of this divide have recently become centrally concerned with the question of proletarianization, the role of credentials and knowledge in social inequality, and the independent contribution of markets and bureaucratic organizations to the structuration of the middle class (Parkin 1979, pp. 23–25). New Class theorists, for instance, draw as much on Weber as they do on Marx (especially Ivan Szelenyi and Bill Martin [1988] and Gouldner [1979]). Marxist sociologists such as Erik Wright and John Urry have produced less deterministic and more differentiated pictures of the middle class, and Weberian theorists like Giddens (1973) and Parkin (1979) have developed more structural models emphasizing property and power. In any case, this emerging synthesis between "production-centered" and "market-centered" approaches seems far more convincing than any of these views taken alone (Abercrombie and Urry 1983; Bottomore 1983, p. 334). The ritual opposition of these two traditions of class theory is no longer meaningful and profitable. One must now build on both of them to try to transcend their common limitations.

The Marxist and Weberian analyses reviewed here suffer from several similar shortcomings. First, they have paid too little attention to their own political import and context of formation. Hindsight makes it quite obvious that theories of the middle classes are, to varying degrees, both responses to preexisting sociopolitical perceptions of these groups and attempts to influence these perceptions. Like much of social-scientific discourse on class, they have a performative dimension and fulfill functions that are inseparably descriptive and prescriptive, cognitive and political (Bourdieu 1984a; Boltanski 1979): Through them, social theorists try, more or less consciously, to shape social reality by "doing things with words," as John Austin (1962) says. Because they are insufficiently reflexive, class analysts have overlooked the fact that the changing geometry of the middle classes in sociological writings has as much to do with the desires of intellectuals to act upon the social world as with their desires to explain it.[13] Second, Marxists and Weberians alike have tended to treat the middle class as an entity already given and preconstituted in the social structure, whether on the basis of purely economic criteria or on grounds of authority, credentials, and market relations. Because of this essentialist conception of class, both of these strands of theory have privileged substances at the expense of relationships and concentrated too heavily on abstract typologizing and formal argumentation at the expense of historical analysis. They have sought to arrive at a unitary, universal model of the middle classes that is ill equipped to capture their diverse and variable character. Most theories of the middle class, be they Marxist or Weberian, suffer from the urge to solve "on paper" what is not resolved in reality. Thus, they tend to be rather static and ahistorical. In opposition to this view, we must recognize, with Przeworski (1985, p. 66), that "classes are not given uniquely by any objective positions because they constitute effects of struggles, and these struggles are not determined uniquely by the relations of production," exploitation, consumption, or authority. The juristic impulse behind many theories has prevented them from fully recognizing the essentially contested nature of classes in society and of the middle classes in particular. The result has been that the latter remain almost as inscrutable today as they were nearly 100 years ago.

To state that "classes are continually organized, disorganized, and reorganized" as an effect of struggles—economic, political, and ideo-logical—that are partly indeterminate from the standpoint of the structure (Przeworski 1977) implies that the structural position and formation of the middle classes are two sides of the same coin that cannot be analytically separated. One cannot understand class structure (i.e., the bases and forms of interclass systems of material and symbolic relations) without, at the same time, understanding class formation (intraclass relations). Therefore, we must forsake the essentialism implied in the will to decide in abstracto, by pure theoretical fiat, what group is what and where its "boundaries" lie. Groups and boundaries are made and unmade in history, not in theory. If the end goal of sociological theory is, in this case, to account for the definition, organization, and practices of historical actors situated somewhere in "the middle" of the social structure, the focus of inquiry must be shifted from abstract, formal typologizing and a priori pigeonholing to the historical and comparative analysis of concrete processes of class formation. The task is to elucidate the dialectic between class structure and class agency and the mechanisms that link one to the other and back, rather than endlessly elaborate the supposedly independent variable of structure, as does Wright (1990). Class lies neither in structures nor in agency alone but in their relationship as it is historically produced, reproduced, and transformed. That is, political and symbolic factors necessarily play a crucial role in the constitution of the middle class (and of any class, for that matter): Class identities, practices, and "lived experience" are not "afterthoughts" tacked on preexisting classes; they enter into the very making of these classes

(Thompson 1963, Wood 1982). The middle class does not exist prior to its symbolic and political organization—it results from it. The work of Pierre Bourdieu (1978, 1979, 1984a, 1988) exemplifies this shift from abstract theorizations of "objective" class boundaries flowing from economic structures to a focus on the structured formation or self-production of class collectivities through struggles that simultaneously involve relationships between and within classes and determine the actual demarcation of their frontiers. Bourdieu replaces the concept of class structure with that of social space, understood as the multidimensional distribution of socially effective forms of power (or capital, be it economic, cultural, or social) underlying social positions. To speak of social space, he says, means that "one cannot group anyone with anyone while ignoring fundamental differences, particularly economic and cultural ones. But this never entirely excludes the possibility of organizing agents in accordance with other principles of division" (Bourdieu 1984a, p. 9).

For social space is at once a field of objective forces and a field of struggles over the very criteria of group formation. This brings the symbolic moment of class to the heart of Bourdieu's sociology (Bourdieu 1988). In the latter, the core of class theory does not lie in "constructing the (w)right classes" (Rose and Marshall 1986) at a structural level but rather in exploring the "movement from theoretical to practical group, that is to say, the question of the politics and the political work required to impose a principle of vision and division of the social world, even when this principle is well-founded in reality" (Bourdieu 1987, p. 8). In this perspective, the nature, composition, and dispositions of the middle classes cannot be directly "deduced" from an objectivist map of the class structure; their boundaries cannot be "read off" objective (i.e., theoretical) criteria of classification. Rather, they must be discovered through analysis of the whole set of creative strategies of distinction, reproduction, and subversion pursued by all the agents—not just middle-class ones—situated at the various theoretically pertinent locations in social space. Sketching a historical comparison of the emergence of the German *Angestellten* and of the French *cadres* will highlight this independent efficacy of symbolic struggles and political class action and, most importantly, of the classification struggles (over criteria of identity, inclusion, and exclusion) that are "indeed a forgotten dimension of the class struggle" (Bourdieu 1979, p. 483).

Jurgen Kocka (1981, 1989) examines how, in early twentieth-century Germany, a uniquely marked divide developed between manual workers and salaried employees that transformed the latter from an analytic category into a real group. And he demonstrates conclusively that the sharpness and shape of the "collar line" were, at bottom, conditioned by historical processes in which the interplay between class structuration, interest-group formation, and government policy was of central importance. Kocka starts by observing that, in the 1880s, differentiations between German blue- and white-collar workers remained fragmented and vague, peripheral to public opinion, and politically irrelevant. By the second decade of the twentieth century, however, the concept of *Angestellte* was fully established, was beginning to refer to a real social collective (with its own associations and politics), and was the subject of considerable public debate in and out of the parliament. What had happened? Rapid technological advance and economic growth had effected important changes in the occupational structure of Germany. Kocka points out that this was also the case in the United States and England, yet no hardening of the collar line occurred in these countries. The solution to the riddle must be sought not in the economy or in the abstract configuration of class locations but in the way historic class relations and political struggles "processed" these economic transformations. Kocka singles out three factors. First, the resilience of eighteenth-century bureaucratic and corporate traditions and the peculiar route of modernization taken by Germany supplied a specific repertoire of cultural and organizational models for thinking and materializing this cleavage. Second, the formation of the *Angestellten* came primarily as a reaction to the political organization of the industrial working class. The growing militancy and pressure of the latter created a practical situation that reminded salaried workers of their self-image and promoted a feeling of communality based on not being a worker. The specific features of the German labor movement, itself a reaction to the repressiveness and archaisms of the German social and political structure,

> provoked or facilitated a very pointed and politicized antiproletarian and anti-Socialist rejection by most of the middle and upper classes . . . not belonging to the proletariat thus became a political issue, in addition to a status issue that it had been in the past (Kocka 1981, p. 71).

By contrast, the United States and England did not have a mass-based, class-conscious labor movement, and, therefore, no pressure toward such a symbolic blurring of the differences internal to the salaried categories was exerted. The third critical factor was Germany's mode of state intervention in society and the economy. More specifically, the public insurance system created by Otto von Bismarck was the key issue that caused white-collar workers to organize nationally and separately. As its coverage expanded, the threat of being handled by new government programs in the same way as "inferior" workers spurred the creation of a distinct white-collar pension system in 1911, patterned after the pension schemes of civil servants. Simultaneously, new ideologies and rhetorics were forged to justify the differences and superiority of white-collar employees; associations sprang forth, and loose federations were created to apply legislative pressure as legal debates raged over the official definition of the *Angestellte*.

But why did these legislative demands succeed? They prevailed because they garnered the support of bourgeois parties and of the government, which hoped to thereby keep this quickly growing mass of salaried employees outside the Socialist camp. Thus, "Politics partly determined who would be an *Angestellte* and who would not. . . . The exact location of the line of differentiation between *Arbeiter* and *Angestellte* resulted from a political compromise" (Kocka 1981, p. 74). Kocka makes it abundantly clear that this was not merely an academic question but a vitally practical one. And, indeed, it was solved in practice: The more laws differentiated in this way, the more relevant the blue-collar/white-collar line became for real life-chances, consciousness, and action. Social distinctions became transmuted into political, and thence legal, demarcations. Most importantly, under such conditions of juridical objectification, the distinction survived the erosion of its own origins. Thus, even when the material conditions of salaried employees worsened dramatically, as they did during World War I and the inflationary 1920s, the *Angestellte* still defined themselves—and consequently acted—very much in opposition to industrial workers.

No comparable category of employees emerged in France, other than as a statistical construct. Instead, a uniquely French social animal took shape in the period from 1934 to 1945: the *cadre*. Luc Boltanski's (1982) magisterial study of the "invention" of this group, of its symbolic and organizational constitution, and of the collective "amnesia of its genesis" provides a useful counterpoint to Kocka. It fully brings out the necessity of studying the middle class at the level of its historical formation, rather than simply elaborating abstract typologies that formally define the boundaries of a group that may have no existence other than in the minds and taxonomies of social theorists.

In the years prior to the mid-1930s, there was no trace of the *cadre* in cultural products such as novels, movies, or plays. Nor did this social persona appear in official censuses until after World War II. Of course, agents existed who occupied positions in firms and fulfilled functions similar to those now held by *cadres,* but they had not acquired the principle of their identity and unity. Boltanski (1979, 1982) sets out to analyze how this principle was produced as a result of class struggles and how, in turn, it served to preserve the structure of class relations by revolutionizing its social representation. The making of this new figure, through processes of regrouping and redefinition which progressively aggregated around a core constituted of Catholic engineers a whole gamut of occupations ranging from executive directors to accountants to foremen, was intimately linked with changes in the internal composition, and in the strategies, of France's bourgeoisie and petty bourgeoisie. Indeed, the use of the term *"cadre"* as a unifying concept and the constitution of the *cadres* into a real group, endowed with official representatives, bureaus, logos, etc., is the direct outcome of attempts to restore social order in the face of the massive sit-down strikes of 1936 and of the growing threat posed by the Popular Front. In this disrupted political conjuncture, precipitated by economic uncertainty and significant class realignments, it became imperative to restructure the "inert masses" of the "middle strata" into a class capable, by virtue of its volume and cohesion, of checking and defeating the mounting power of the working class. The effect of the appearance of the *cadre* as a group that was officially recognized and named, positioning the "executive" component of the middle classes as a tertium quid between the working class and the employers, was two-fold: It served symbolically to break up the bourgeoisie and allowed its dominant fraction to veil the widening gulf between itself and other "middle class" groups, and it mobilized the declining fractions of the petty bourgeoisie in defense of the established order. The stake of this symbolic struggle was nothing other than

> the imposition of a ternary representation of society centered upon the "middle class," as the "healthy" and "stable" component of the "nation," a representation which was itself patterned after the representation of political space which was being shaped by the vanguard of the new right with its "Third Way" [*troisieme voie*] mediating between the two extremes of "collectivism" and "capitalism" (Boltanski 1982, p. 63).

This ideology would not have been efficacious, however, had it not met with social contradictions and conflicts—between large and small employers, the public sector and private enterprise, the self-employed and salaried fractions of the bourgeoisie and petty bourgeoisie—that gave it an objective foundation. There was also a rich fount of symbolic resources to draw upon in projecting this new image of the social order: The large body of writings devoted to the middle classes and the executive that flourished in the 1930s, particularly after 1936, borrowed much of its materials from corporatist ideology, social Catholicism, and Italian fascism. But, as in the case of German employees, it was the legal consecration granted by the state that eventually caused the full crystallization of the group. By inserting it in the administrative taxonomies of its "Charter of Work," by recognizing that its representatives were entitled to speak in the name of the collective, by laying down in juridical terms its boundaries, the Vichy regime gave official recognition—and therefore existence—to the group. The postwar Parodi agreements established for good and all the tripartite representation of the social world it entailed. All these movements and symbolic maneuvers culminated in the creation of the Confédération Générale des Cadres (CGC), an official "union" representing the interests of the *cadres* (which, as in the German case, was first devoted to advocating and managing separate pension benefits). This officialization of the group through political representation went hand-in-hand with a transformation of the mode and content of its social representation: A new kind of literature quickly developed that codified the identity, mission, and values of the cadre. And despite—or rather thanks to—its objective diversity, the group has succeeded in maintaining its cohesion for some fifty years now. This is because its heterogeneity and the very wooliness of its boundaries benefit all those who can lay claim to membership in it. Bourgeois managers can dissimulate the permanence of their rule by confounding themselves into its "middle mass," and junior administrators, technicians, and foremen reap the symbolic profits attached to being identified with superior occupations. "In other words, the benefits each fraction gains from its inclusion in the category are essentially due to the presence of the other fractions in the same aggregate" (Boltanski 1982, p. 477).

There are several striking parallels between the formation of the German *Angestellte* and of the French *cadre*. In both cases, a heterogenous collection of agents who, on purely objective grounds, had dispersed interests and positions in social space were made into a unified social body, recognized by both its members and other groups. In both cases, these middle-class segments acceded to collective existence as a reaction to the political organization and active mobilization of the working class (under the Confédération Général de Travail in France, the SPD in Germany).[14] In both cases, their emergence was facilitated by, and for the most part served the interests of, the dominant class. And in both instances, the actions of the state, especially the legal recognition and nomination of the group and the setting of its boundaries, were decisive in the success of these symbolic struggles of class making. Many factors explain the different outcomes, but chief among them are the cultural and ideological heritage of each country, preexisting rifts in the class structure, and the objective social conditions of the crisis under which these came to be activated. Finally, both Kocka (1981, 1989) and Boltanski (1979, 1982) illustrate the extent to which struggles over class react upon and help shape the objective structure of classes.

The greatest merit of these two studies is that they do not set up a conceptual opposition—indeed, a false antinomy—between structure and agency but endeavor to construct a series of analytic bridges between the underlying distribution of objective resources that define a theoretical middle class, on the one hand, and the strategies, identities, and specific organizations actually developed as vehicles for group formation by middle-class actors, on the other. They fully recognize that, as Bourdieu (1979, pp. 559–64) has insisted, one cannot create any group randomly: Symbolic struggles have an objective base, and their efficacy depends on whether they can activate real, material differences. At the same time, they prove incontrovertibly that class is largely underdetermined at the structural level and that symbolic, or ideological and political, relations of power enter decisively in the very constitution of class. And this is particularly true of the middle classes.

Conclusion

In this discussion of the state of the sociology of the middle class, my aim has been to suggest that much of the debate has been pegged at the wrong level and in pursuit of a fictitious goal. The epistemic ambition of defining, once and for all, the correct classification, of discovering the "real" boundaries of the middle class, is doomed to failure because it rests on a fundamentally mistaken conception of the ontological status of classes: The middle class, like any other social group, does not exist ready-made in reality. It must be constituted through material and symbolic struggles waged simultaneously over class and between classes; it is a historically variable and reversible effect of these struggles. As much as these struggles are limited by the underlying structure of social space, they still determine, in large part, the shape and nature of the groups that will emerge in its intermediate regions. Consequently, one can say only that the middle class has no frontiers other than the historically shifting and disputed ones that are continually produced and transformed through these conflicts, and these cannot be defined abstractly.

Because "it is in these intermediate zones of social space that the indeterminacy and the fuzziness of the relationship between practices and positions are the greatest, and that the room left open for symbolic strategies designed to jam this relationship is the largest" (Bourdieu 1987, p. 12), the middle class is necessarily an ill-defined entity. This does not reflect a lack of theoretical penetration but rather the character of reality. Theories of the middle class should consciously strive to capture this essential ambiguity of their object rather than dispose of it: The indeterminacy, wooliness, and contention that exist and partly define it should not be destroyed but preserved in sociological models of this reality. In short, the question of what group or groups occupy the intermediate regions of the class structure cannot be settled ex cathedra on paper because it is never fully resolved in society in the first place.

The emerging agenda for the sociology of the middle class, then, is not to produce better theoretical "maps" in which to fit the middle class, to refine formal criteria of inclusion or exclusion,[15] but to engage in historical and comparative investigations of how agents situated at various points of the "middle" zones of social space can or cannot be assembled, through a political work of delegation and nomination (Bourdieu 1984b; Maresca 1983), into a collective resembling something like one or several "middle classes." For this, it is necessary to study dynamically the whole set of relationships that links them to those groups situated above and below them, paying special attention to the types of organizations and strategies other classes develop, as well as the role of the state in classification struggles. Although there is no need to adopt a "state-centered" approach to class, it would seem to be an improvement to move beyond stateless theories of the middle class.[16] None of this, of course, makes the business of class analysis any easier. But, then, the beauty of the sociology of class also lies in its difficulty.

Acknowledgments

I thank George Phillip Steinmetz, Adam Przeworski, Raymond T. Smith, Michael Burawoy, and Pierre Bourdieu for their critical comments and suggestions on an earlier version of this chapter. The final product remains my sole responsibility. Support of a Lavoisier Fellowship from the French government is gratefully acknowledged.

Notes

1. The inherent difficulties and contestation involved in the use of the concept of class itself (Martin 1987; Calvert 1982) are, of course, other critical issues in social science. However, this chapter concentrates on disputes on the middle class, not on the middle class itself.

2. Indeed, without this, Marx's (1974b) historical analyses of class struggles would have been strictly impossible. Mainstream exegeses of Marx have failed to recognize this because they do not understand how his theories work in different "analytical zones"—his views on class are pegged at various levels of abstraction (from the general mode of production to specific conjunctures) and have different foci (structure versus relations) and varying time frames (cf. Wacquant 1985, pp. 33–37; also Giddens 1973, pp. 28–31).

3. Note that nearly all theories of the middle class(es) take the notion of working class (and bourgeoisie) itself as rather unproblematical. This Archimedean point could well be one of the most serious, if little discussed, weaknesses of middle-class theory.

4. This classification does not preclude overlap between categories, as will be seen. A fourth position, which need not concern us here because no serious analyst advocates it any longer, is to deny the very existence of intermediate groupings in advanced society. This stance was defended most prominently by theoreticians of the French Communist party in the mid-seventies (cf. Ross 1978, pp. 165–70). According to them, there are only two real classes in monopoly capitalism: the "monopoly caste" of employers/top managers and the industrial working class. There are no old or new "middle classes" to speak of, only a heterogenous collection of intermediaries that stand outside the class structure and are bounded, at one end, by participation in exploitation and, at the other, by inclusion in production labor.

5. The term "proletarianization" is generally used in a loose way, as a short-hand formula of analogical reasoning establishing a parallel between white-collar employees and industrial workers. As Sarfatti-Larson (1980, p. 133) points out, it is often more appropriate to speak of "rationalization" or "industrialization" of nonmanual labor processes.

6. An interesting mix of the petty-bourgeoisie and proletarianization arguments is offered by Baudelot, Establet, and Malemort (1973), for whom the new petty bourgeoisie is not a survival from a previous mode of production but a class actively created by capitalism to perform nonproductive but necessary services in capital circulation, commercializatio and administration. They further divide the petty bourgeoisie into three fractions with divergent political tendencies: the traditional, right-wing-oriented fraction of small commercial propertyholders (artisans and shopkeepers); the individualistic and procapital new petty bourgeoisie of encadrement (supervisors, technicians, and executives in the private sector); and the left-leaning, public-sector fraction of the petty bourgeoisie in charge of managing the "state compromise." Thus, like Poulantzas, Baudelot and his associates insist that there is a petty bourgeois class in France, but they demarcate it sharply from the new white-collar proletarians. They also part with the former in their belief that the political orientations of the petty bourgeoisie are quite predictable and decidedly nonleftist.

7. Wright's (1978, 1985) theory has shifted significantly over time, moving from structuralist to analytical Marxism, from a domination-centered to an exploitation-centered concept of class, and from a one-dimensional to a three-dimensional map of the class structure. Here, I only consider his later conceptualization of the middle class.

8. Indeed, a case could be made that, for all its talk of exploitation, Wright's scheme is neither fully rooted in production nor consistently relational but gradational because it operationally defines (9 of 12) classes in terms of what are, in real life (and in stratification research), two continuous hierarchies, bureaucratic authority and education.

9. For a pungent critique of the "de-Marxified" interpretation of Weber's view of stratification prevalent in U.S. social science, see Parkin (1978).

10. The upper boundary of the middle class is typically left unspecified. In many class schemes used in mobility research particularly, the (upper) middle class represents the apex of the class structure, making its label of "middle" paradoxical, to say the least, and its ideological function of sociodicy quite plain.

11. A third exception is Frank Parkin (1974, 1979), whose "closure theory" is not discussed here for lack of space and because it is essentially concerned with class as "collective action" rather than as structure; it also has "dissolved" the middle class in a fashion similar to Dahrendorf's (for a useful review and critique, see Murphy [1986]).

12. Goldthorpe (1982) suggests that it contains the embryo of a "service class" of professionals and credentialed managers and administrators who enjoy privileged economic and market positions protected by way of institutionalized monopolies, in sharp contrast to the degraded condition of lower clerical and sales worker.

13. See Ross (1987) for an illuminating discussion of this dialectic in the case of French theories of the "new middle strata" from the 1960s to the present.

14. Note that in neither case was there a mobilization of all categories belonging to a "theoretical" middle class.

15. However, this is a necessary moment in any sociology of the middle class. Lest I be misunderstood as advocating the kind of "free-for-all" relativist nominalism that is behind empiricist and subjectivist conceptions of class, let me reassert once more that there is an objective structure to class; however, this objective structure does not uniquely determine what social collectives emerge out of it and in what form and thus does not suffice to define class. See Wacquant (1989, 1990) for elaborations.

16. It would also be an improvement to move beyond gender-blind theories, as well. Because of severe limitations of space, I have chosen not to address this central dimension of the process of class making. For very insightful leads on this thorny topic, see Scott (1988).

References

Abercrombie, Nicholas, and John Urry. 1983. *Capital, Labour and the Middle Classes.* London: George Allen and Unwin.

Aron, Raymond. 1964. *La lutte des classes.* Paris: Gallimard.

Austin, John L. 1962. *How to Do Things with Words.* Oxford: Oxford University Press.

Barbalet, J. M. 1986. "Limitations of Class Theory and the Disappearance of Status: The Problem of the New Middle Class." *Sociology* 20:557–75.

Baudelot, Christian, Roger Establet, and Jacques Malemort. 1973. *La petite bourgeoisie en France.* Paris: Maspero.

Bendix, Reinhard, and Seymour Martin Lipset. 1966. "Karl Marx's Theory of Social Classes." In *Class, Status and Power,* eds. Reinhard Bendix and Seymour Martin Lipset, pp. 6–11. New York: Free Press.

Bernstein, Eduard. 1961. *Evolutionary Socialism: A Criticism and Affirmation.* New York: Schocken Books.

Blau, Peter M., and Otis Dudley Duncan. 1967. *The American Occupational Structure.* New York: John Wiley and Sons.

Boltanski, Luc. 1979. "Taxonomies sociales et lutte de classes. La mobilisation de la 'classe moyenne' et l'invention des 'cadres'." *Actes de la recherche en sciences sociales* 29:75–105.

————. 1982. *Les cadres: La formation d'un groupe social.* Paris: Editions de Minuit. (Trans. *The Making of a New Class.* Cambridge: Cambridge University Press, 1987.)

Bottomore, Tom. 1983. "Middle Class." In *A Dictionary of Marxist Thought,* eds. T. B. Bottomore et al., pp. 333–34. Cambridge: Harvard University Press.

————. 1985. *Theories of Modern Capitalism.* London: George Allen and Unwin.

Bourdieu, Pierre. 1978. "Capital symbolique et classes sociales." *L'arc* 72:13–19.

————. 1979. *La distinction: Critique sociale du jugement.* Paris: Editions de Minuit. (Trans. *Distinction.* Cambridge: Harvard University Press, 1984.)

————. 1984a. "Espace social et genèse des 'classes'." *Actes de la recherche en sciences sociales* 52–53:3–15. (Trans. "Social Space and the Genesis of Groups." *Theory and Society* 14:723–44).

————. 1984b. "Delegation and Political Fetishism." *Thesis Eleven* 10:56–70.

————. 1987. "What Makes a Class? On the Theoretical and Practical Existence of Groups." *Berkeley Journal of Sociology* 32:1–18.

————. 1988. "Social Space and Symbolic Power." *Sociological Theory* 7:14–25.

Braverman, Harry. 1974. *Labor and Monopoly Capital: The Degradation of Work in the Twentieth Century.* New York: Monthly Press.

Burris, Val. 1986. "The Discovery of the New Middle Class." *Theory and Society* 15:317–50.

Calvert, Peter. 1982. *The Concept of Class: A History.* New York: Saint Martin's Press.

Carchedi, Guglielmo. 1975a. "On the Economic Identification of the New Middle Class." *Economy and Society* 4:1–86.

————. 1975b. "Reproduction of Social Classes at the Level of Production Relations." *Economy and Society* 4:361–417.

Coleman, Richard P., and Lee Rainwater. 1979. *Social Standing in America: New Dimensions of Class.* London and Boston: Routledge and Kegan Paul.

Corey, L. 1935. *The Crisis of the Middle Class.* New York: C. Friede.

Crompton, Rosemary, and Jon Gubbay. 1978. *Economy and Class Structure.* New York: Saint Martin's Press.

Croner, Fritz. 1938 [1928]. *The White-Collar Movement in Germany Since the Monetary Stabilization.* New York: Department of Social Science, Columbia University.

Dahrendorf, Ralf. 1972 [1957]. *Classes et conflits de classes dans la société industrielle.* Paris and The Hague: Mouton.

Davis, Kingsley, and Wilbert E. Moore. 1945. "Some Principles of Stratification." *American Journal of Sociology* 10:242–49.

Dreyfus, Carl. 1938 [1933]. *Occupation and Ideology of the Salaried Employee.* New York: Department of Social Science, Columbia University.

Ehrenreich, Barbara, and John Ehrenreich. 1977. "The Professional-Managerial Class." *Radical America* 11-2 & 3.

Giddens, Anthony. 1973. *The Class Structure of the Advanced Societies.* New York: Harper and Row.

Goffman, Erving. 1951. "Symbols of Class Status." *British Journal of Sociology* 2:294–304.

Goldthorpe, John. 1982. "On the Service Class." In *Social Class and the Division of Labour*, eds. A. Giddens and G. McKenzie, pp. 162–85. Cambridge: Cambridge University Press.

Gordon, Milton M. 1958. *Social Class in American Sociology*. Durham, North Carolina: Duke University Press.

Gouldner, Alvin W. 1979. *The Future of Intellectuals and the Rise of the New Class*. New York: Oxford University Press.

Kautsky, Karl. 1971 [1910]. *The Class Struggle*. New York: W. W. Norton and Co.

Klingender, F. D. 1935. *The Condition of Clerical Labour in Britain*. London: Martin Lawrence.

Knottnerus, J. David. 1987. "Status Attainment Research and Its Image of Society." *American Sociological Review* 52:113–21.

Kocka, Jurgen. 1981. "Class Formation, Interest Articulation, and Public Policy: The Origins of the German White-Collar Class in the Late Nineteenth and Early Twentieth Century." In *Organizing Interests in Western Europe*, ed. Suzanne Berger, pp. 63–82. Cambridge: Cambridge University Press.

———. 1989. *Les employes en Allemagne, 1850–1980: L'histoire d'un groupe social*. Paris: Editions de la Maison des Sciences de l'Homme.

Lenski, Gerhard E. 1952. "American Social Classes: Statistical Strata or Social Groups?" *American Journal of Sociology* 68:139–44.

Lockwood, David. 1958. *The Blackcoated Worker: A Study in Class Consciousness*. London: George Allen and Unwin.

Mann, Michael. 1986. "Classes, Swedes and Yanks." *Contemporary Sociology* 15:837–39.

Maresca, Sylvain. 1983. *Les dirigeants paysans*. Paris: Editions de Minuit.

Martin, Pete. 1987. "The Concept of Class." In *Classic Disputes in Sociology*, eds. R. J. Anderson, J. A. Hughes, and W. W. Sharrock, pp. 67–96. London: George Allen and Unwin.

Marx, Karl. 1974a. *The Revolutions of 1848*. New York: Vintage Books.

———. 1974b [1852]. "The Eighteenth Brumaire of Louis Bonaparte." In *Surveys from Exile*. New York: Vintage Books.

Mills, C. Wright. 1956. *White Collar*. New York: Oxford University Press.

Murphy, Raymond. 1986. "The Concept of Class in Closure Theory: Learning from Rather than Falling into the Problems Encountered by Neo-Marxism." *Sociology* 20:247–64.

Nicolaus, Martin. 1967. "Proletariat and Middle Class in Marx: Hegelian Choreography and the Capitalist Dialectic." *Studies on the Left* 7:22–49.

Parkin, Frank. 1974. "Strategies of Closure in Class Formation." In *The Social Analysis of Class Structure*, ed. Frank Parkin, pp. 1–18. London: Tavistock Publications.

———. 1978. "Stratification." In *A History of Sociological Analysis*, eds. T. B. Bottomore and R. A. Nisbet, pp. 599–632. New York: Basic Books.

———. 1979. *Marxism and Class Theory: A Bourgeois Critique*. New York: Columbia University Press.

Poulantzas, Nicos. 1974. *Les classes sociales dans le capitalisme aujourd'hui*. Paris: Le Seuil.

_____. 1977. "The New Petty Bourgeoisie." In *Class and Class Structure,* ed. Alan Hunt, pp. 113–24. London: Lawrence and Wishart.

Przeworski, Adam. 1977. "The Process of Class Formation from Kautsky's 'The Class Struggle' to Recent Controversies." *Politics and Society* 7:343–401.

_____. 1985. *Capitalism and Social Democracy.* Paris and Cambridge: Editions de la Maison des Sciences de l'Homme and Cambridge University Press.

Rattansi, Ali. 1985. "End of an Orthodoxy? The Critique of Sociology's View of Marx on Class." *The Sociological Review* 33:641–69.

Roemer, John. 1982. "New Directions in the Marxian Theory of Exploitation and Class." *Politics and Society* 11:253–88.

Rose, David, and Gordon Marshall. 1986. "Constructing the (W)right Classes." *Sociology* 20:440–55.

Ross, George. 1978. "Marxism and the New Middle Classes: French Critiques." *Theory and Society* 5:163–90.

_____. 1987. "Destroyed by the Dialectic: Politics, the Decline of Marxism and the New Middle Strata in France." *Theory and Society* 16:7–38.

Sarfatti-Larson, Magali. 1980. "Proletarianization and Educated Labor." *Theory and Society* 9:131–75.

Scott, Joan Wallach. 1988. *Gender and the Politics of History.* New York: Columbia University Press.

Suhr, Otto. 1928. *Allgemeiner Frier Angestelltenbunde: Angestellte und Arbiter, Wan . . . in Wirtschaft or Gesellschaft.* Berlin: Frier Folks.

Szelenyi, Ivan, and Bill Martin. 1988. "Three Waves of New Class Theories." *Theory and Society* 17:645–68.

Thompson, E. P. 1963. *The Making of the English Working Class.* Harmondsworth, England: Penguin.

Turner, Bryan S. 1986. *Citizenship and Capitalism: The Debate over Reformism.* London: George Allen and Unwin.

Urry, John. 1973. "Towards a Structural Theory of the Middle Class." *Acta Sociologica* 16:175–87.

Wacquant, Löic J.D. 1985. "Heuristic Models in Marxian Theory." *Social Forces* 64:17–45.

_____. 1989. "Social Ontology, Epistemology, and Class." *Berkeley Journal of Sociology* 34:165–86.

_____. 1990. "Action collective et conscience ouvrière en Amerique." *Sociologie du travail* 2 (April), in press.

Warner, W. Lloyd. 1960 [1949]. *Social Class in America.* New York: Harper and Row.

Weber, Max. 1947 [1921–1922]. "Class, Status, Power." In *From Max Weber: Essays in Sociology,* eds. H. H. Gerth and C. Wright Mills, pp. 180–95. New York: Oxford University Press.

Wood, Ellen Meiksins. 1982. "The Politics of Theory and the Concept of Class: E. P. Thompson and His Critics." *Studies in Political Economy* 9:45–75.

Wright, Erik Olin. 1978. *Class, Crisis and the State.* London: New Left Books.

_____. 1985. *Classes.* London: Verso.

———. 1986. "What Is Middle About the Middle Class." In *Analytical Marxism,* ed. John Roemer, pp. 114–40. Cambridge and Paris: Cambridge University Press and Editions de la Maison des Sciences de l'Homme.

———. 1990. "Rethinking, Once Again, the Concept of Class." In *The Debate on Classes,* eds. Erik Olin Wright et al. London: Verso.

4 | The Role of Capitalist Class Relations in the Restructuring of Medicine

BETH MINTZ

Over the last decade, research on the structure of the capitalist class has identified a series of important actors and locations crucial to the process of class rule. At issue in this literature is the question of unified class action: What are the mechanisms that transform a group of individual capitalists into a cohesive class? Typically, the answer offered is either financial institutions, capitalists themselves, or the state, and the contribution of each to the process of class formation has been explored in detail.[1]

As we sharpen our understanding of the ways in which capitalist unity is achieved, however, we have not applied our findings to other areas of study, either in terms of the implications of class rule or as part of a theoretical discussion of class structure. For example, although the labor process has been an extremely active field of inquiry, the extent to which elite unity contributed to the ability of capitalists to reorganize the labor process has not been addressed. Similarly, studies of segmented labor markets have not explored the role of unified class action in the process of market segmentation; we have little understanding of the impact of unified class rule on U.S.-Third World relations, on the growth of militarism, or on relations with the larger international community.

Thus, although research on the structure of the capitalist class has been successful in identifying the mechanisms that transform a series of important actors into a unified class, it has not addressed the implications of these results. We have not explored what these findings can tell us about the consequences of class rule, both for social policy and for broader questions of class relations. This chapter investigates this issue by exploring the ways in which our understanding of capitalist class structure may be applied to substantive questions and, thus, used to analyze the implications of class rule. It focuses on one particular problem, the restructuring of the health care sector, to investigate the role of the capitalist class in the creation and transformation of health care provision, emphasizing the importance of both interclass and intraclass relations in such an analysis.

The Role of Interclass Relations

Although the organization of capital offers a framework for exploring a variety of questions ranging from health care restructuring to changes in the nature of the labor process, applications of this sort have been scarce for two important reasons: the emphasis, in the larger literature of recent years, on the role of the state rather than on the role of capital and our inattention to the details of a class analysis.

To the extent that the role of the state has been framed in terms of its relative autonomy, the question of the organizational capacity of the capitalist class has been of secondary concern because it is the state— not the class—that is assumed to develop policies that serve the larger interests of capital. As investigations of the state turn to arguments about potential autonomy and agency, however, and the dynamics of class struggle at particular historical junctures are again considered, the role of the capitalist class takes on renewed importance. Thus, as the emphasis on the general attributes of the capitalist state is replaced by investigations of specific circumstances, the role of capital becomes an integral part of these analyses.

To be of value in understanding state function, however, clarity in our conceptualization of capital as a class becomes increasingly important. One point, in particular, must be considered carefully in this regard: the impact of class conflict on the organization of the capitalist class.

Much of the debate about the role of the capitalist state turns on the extent to which and the process whereby the state mediates among the interests of different fractions of capital, on one hand, and the needs of the working class, on the other. This concern stems from the traditional Marxist analysis of capitalist relations that takes as its starting point class conflict based on the exploitation of one class by another. This framework is based on a relational concept of class that not only views the working class as a revolutionary force in the long run but as a group that continuously transforms current conditions.

These assumptions suggest that the organization of the capitalist class is directly affected by its relationship to the working class. Moreover, because capital is itself divided in the ways in which it pursues maximum profits, different fractions of capital confront the working class in different ways and on different issues. Thus, the interests of individual fractions of capital are conditioned by the details of distinct conflicts with capital.

The literature on the structure of the capitalist class has assumed that the divisions within capital must be examined in this context. Noting that the internal differentiation of the capitalist class is organized around varying locations in the production and appropriation of surplus value (Zeitlin 1980), the importance of class conflict has been suitably noted.

All too often, however, the traditional analytic category of conflict between classes is lost in more immediate investigations of lines of division and sources of unity within capital itself. My work (Mintz and Schwartz 1985) on the hegemonic role of financial institutions within the corporate system illustrates this tendency. Although it is demonstrated that control of capital flows effectively constrains the behavior of non-financial corporations, undeveloped in this analysis is the process by which capital needs themselves are conditioned by interclass relations. The Eastern Airlines strike of 1989, for example, redefined Eastern's relationship with its capital suppliers; on a systemwide level, capital-labor struggles condition the environment in which financial and nonfinancial institutions interact.

Inattention to this fact masks the underlying dynamic of class structure, encouraging an analysis in which capitalist class organization is examined independent of its relations with other classes. The portrait that emerges is one in which the major enemy of the capitalist is other capitalists; the role of exploitation as the fundamental relation in capitalist society is not addressed. For the capitalist class to be a useful category in sociological analysis, then, the impact of interclass relations on the internal organization of capital must be a starting point of inquiry. Only with an understanding that such relations modify and condition class structure can we examine the impact of capitalist class formation on social policy. Moreover, it is only then that we can explore the extent to which and the conditions under which classes and class struggles shape state activity.

In sum, then, use of the capitalist class as an analytic category in an investigation of social relations can be an extremely valuable tool for general sociological inquiry. However, a more carefully constructed conceptualization of class relations is necessary. In the following investigation of the U.S. health care system, I will explore the role of interclass relations in changing health care patterns, demonstrating that a class analysis remains relevant to modern intellectual inquiry.[2]

The Health Care Crisis

Health care in the United States is drawing increased attention as costs continue to spiral and more fundamental questions are raised about the distribution and quality of available care. These problems are not new, but the situation is becoming more alarming as predictions suggest that within the next few years health care will account for over 14 percent of the GNP (gross national product) (*Wall Street Journal,* September 29,

1987). Although this crisis is extremely complicated, with many contributing factors, two particularly important elements include efforts at cost containment and the privatization of health provision. And the major actors in both processes include many of the same groups typically studied in research on the capitalist class. The business community, in particular, has been actively engaged in developing strategies for cost control (Leyerle 1984), which is understandable because the corporate world is the major consumer of health care services. As an employer, it purchases health insurance for about 40 million workers (Leyerle 1984), which, in 1988, translated into an average per employee cost of $2,354, up 18.6 percent from the former year (*HealthWeek*, March 6, 1989).

Interests within the business world are divided, however, and a small proportion of large corporations are profiting greatly from expanded health care usage. Commercial health insurance carriers, for example, are accounting for a larger and larger share of health insurance dollars. In addition, pharmaceuticals and medical supply houses have been enjoying record profits; giant corporations, including Greyhound, Union Carbide, Firestone, and 3M, have entered the lucrative health care market (McKinlay 1978), demonstrating the extent to which medical care has become a source of profit for an increasingly diverse collection of large companies.

Perhaps the most interesting development in recent years in terms of profit seeking, though, is the increasing privatization of medical delivery itself. Until very recently, health care provision was not highly concentrated but dominated by large, urban teaching hospitals, organized on a not-for-profit basis. In comparison, the quickly expanding "new medical industrial complex" is composed of investor-owned multiunit hospitals, nursing home corporations, diagnostic labs, mental health centers, and hemodialysis providers, as well as freestanding ambulatory and emergicare centers (Relman 1980; Starr 1982; Salmon 1984).

The extremely lucrative health care market is attracting new participants continually, as additional opportunities for profit making present themselves. Most spectacular of all is the growth of investor-owned multihospital systems. By 1983, one out of seven U.S. hospitals and nearly 10 percent of all U.S. hospital beds belonged to investor-owned systems. The four largest—Hospital Corporations of America, Humana, National Medical Enterprise, and American Medical International—owned or managed 75 percent of those beds (Ermann and Gabel 1986). By 1986, about a third of all acute-care hospitals in the United States belonged to a multiunit system, but expansion had begun to slow as profitability declined in the face of cost-cutting strategies implemented by Medicare, Medicaid, and private insurers (Light 1986).

These figures suggest that, though the corporate community as a whole is struggling to remain profitable in the face of skyrocketing health care benefits for its workers, some segments of the business world have realized very nice returns on invested capital. This should not be surprising for we know that capital accumulation is a contradictory process: It provides enormous potential for growth and profitability for some but not for all. Also as expected, this, in turn, has resulted in conflict in the corporate community, both within the health care sector (as firms compete for health care dollars) and among different sectors (as health provision becomes a more and more expensive commodity).

Moreover, the health care issue affects a variety of groups in addition to the larger business community. Unions, for example, have been strong advocates of medical cost containment, initially because they feared that increased health care costs paid by employers would limit potential pay raises. These concerns, however, have been replaced by more immediate fears that health care benefits themselves will be cut, and trends in this direction are becoming clearer and clearer. Between 1985 and 1988, 79 percent of all participating employers have turned to higher employee deductibles in their health coverage (*HealthWeek,* February 6, 1989).

The interests of the state in this process are contradictory. Assuming for a moment an independent role for the state, we note that increasing health care costs are a continuing threat to the stabilized inflation rates of the 1980s and that public revenues are being diverted to the health care sector disproportionately in the form of Medicare and Medicaid (Light 1988). At the same time, the employment opportunities accompanying the growth of health delivery services are crucial to economic stability. Since 1975, more than 900,000 jobs have been created in direct health services (Appelbaum and Granrose 1986).

As this brief overview suggests, the health care crisis of the 1980s illustrates some of the contradictions inherent in the capital accumulation process: In certain periods, some sectors are extremely profitable, and this may occur at the expense of other segments of capital. The conflict within the corporate world generated by these differences—differences based on one's relation to the production and appropriation of surplus value—is exactly the type of issue that has attracted the attention of those interested in the internal differentiation of the capitalist class.

Thus, the divergent interests within and between classes makes health care a particularly good field with which to explore the ways that our understanding of the structure of the capitalist class may be applied to broader questions about social relations. Moreover, it provides an excellent arena for studying the dynamics of class conflict and demonstrating the impact of interclass relations on the development of social policy.

Interclass Conflict and the
Internal Differentiation of Capital

Demands by poor and working-class people for greater accessibility to health care services in the 1960s led directly to the establishment of Medicare and Medicaid, the most inclusive health provision legislation in the history of the United States. Despite vigorous oppositional lobbying by the American Medical Association, Medicare and Medicaid were signed into law in 1965 as the hallmarks of the Great Society programs.

Although Medicaid and Medicare resulted directly from demands for increased health care coverage, implementation was based on an over-medicalized, technologically based system in which profit seeking, rather than public health, drove development (Salmon 1984). Despite the fact that they were implemented to increase accessibility and were successful in this regard, these programs are responsible for many of the problems in health care today—most particularly, the high cost and ineffectiveness of medical provision.[3]

Medical technology is a crucial factor in the health care crisis, and its role was exacerbated by the entitlement programs of the 1960s that provided what seemed to be a limitless source of funds for use of new technologies. However, it is important to note that technological medicine, which has so successfully become the normative model of health delivery worldwide, is not the "natural" direction for health care development, and many argue that it is far from the best (Salmon 1984). According to Brown (1979), it is rooted in a fifty-year struggle between the medical profession and the ascendant segment of capital over the rationalization of medical delivery.[4] This long-term conflict has created its own contradictions, forming the environment in which Medicare and Medicaid were introduced. Neither side understood the implications of the legislation; nor did the recipients who fought for extended coverage.

In the short term, Medicaid and Medicare resulted in economic boom for providers and vast profit potential for capital. The huge infusion of funds with which the federal government subsidized the purchase of medical services attracted a wide assortment of new entrants into medical delivery, resulting in the formation of the "new medical industrial complex" mentioned earlier.[5] As important as the availability of federal funding to expand coverage, however, was the reimbursement system. Continuing the popular fee-for-service method in force at the time, Medicare and Medicaid automatically paid for any procedure ordered by an appropriate health care provider; the more procedures, the higher the provider's salary and the faster the implementation of new and more sophisticated—and expensive—equipment. For all intents and purposes, this produced a blank check for health expansion.

Almost twenty-five years later, we find that the compromise on health care provision that was negotiated between the poor, the elderly, and the uncovered working class, on one hand, and capital, on the other, leaves us with important divisions within the corporate community over profitability, as well as crucial consequences for the poor, the working class, and, increasingly, the salaried intermediaries. Today, over 31 million people in the United States are without health insurance of any sort, a group disproportionately composed of black and Hispanic people (*Statistical Abstracts of the United States,* 1989). And though the general trend has been toward a health care system that is geared for the productive and excludes the unemployed, the underemployed, and, increasingly, the elderly, even this is changing. The highly nonunionized service sector continues to be the major employment site of inadequately covered workers, but health insurance coverage is becoming more precarious for all. As employers continue their attempts at reducing their share of health insurance payments, a majority of U.S. citizens will be faced with lower coverage and higher out-of-pocket costs.

The current crisis in health care, then, can be analyzed in terms of both interclass conflict and the fragmentation of capital. Large profits resulting from demands by poor and working people for increased health care coverage offered extremely attractive investment opportunities for some fractions of capital. In turn, cost containment became a more and more important reaction of that segment of capital paying for, but not profiting from, health care delivery. At the same time, rising expectations and an aging population further increased pressures for reasonable health care coverage.

On the side of capital, two separate postures toward medical delivery—attempts to control the costs of health care provision by those paying for employee health insurance versus the appropriation of surplus value from that provision by those involved in health care—merge to produce strikingly similar effects for clients and workers within the health care industry.

The Working Class and the Poor

As health care costs escalate and profit margins become more important in medical delivery, the gap between the well-insured and the under- or uninsured continues to widen. This is rooted in the absence of a national health plan and exacerbated by long-term attempts by capital to minimize the cost of health coverage for its workers.

Over the years, as such coverage was won as part of labor's compensation package, U.S. capital looked for ways of cutting costs, and its success laid the foundation for the two-tiered system of provision found today.

A particularly important piece in this development can be traced to the establishment of Blue Cross/Blue Shield and its replacement by commercial insurance carriers as the largest source of health care reimbursement.[6]

Legislation that benefited Blue Cross and, a decade later, Blue Shield included favorable tax provisions as a method of underwriting their mission, which was to provide health coverage to all at a similar rate. The plan was designed so that differential usage by the poor and/or elderly was averaged over an entire community, with the cost of provision distributed over the larger group (Leyerle 1984, p. 29). Commercial insurance carriers were not subject to the same constraints and, thus, were able to offer lower rates to groups that were likely to use fewer services. As union contracts increasingly included employer-financed health care plans, corporations turned to commercial carriers who were not required to subsidize the poor or elderly. In 1945, Blue Cross accounted for 61 percent of hospital insurance, as compared to 33 percent for commercial carriers. By 1969, Blue Cross was down to 37 percent, with private insurance accounting for 57 percent (Leyerle 1984), and, at present, the future of "the Blues" is highly uncertain.

Thus, "cream skimming," a term used in health care circles to describe the practice of serving only the most cost-effective portion of the client community, finds its roots in the early reaction of corporations to financing care for their workers. And this trend is intensified by the development of for-profit medicine, as proprietary hospitals are making it abundantly clear that their responsibility to the poor is minimal. They do not serve the uninsured, and their share of Medicaid patients is disproportionately small (Kennedy 1984).[7] Health maintenance organizations, relatively recent entrants into the health care market, combine the incentives of cost containment with, in their increasingly privatized form, the need for profitability. This has made them famous for skimming, as well.

This example suggests that the victories of labor in the long-term struggle to win health care coverage for workers, coupled with capital's search for ways of minimizing the cost of those victories, laid the foundation for cream skimming, an all too common practice in contemporary medicine. In the same way that the success of the social movements of the 1960s produced Medicare and Medicaid that, in turn, became major contributors to the health care crisis of the 1980s, cream skimming illustrates the dialectical nature of interclass relations. Reactions of capital to health care costs influenced the future development of the system, and increased demands for coverage by broader segments of the population influenced that development in still other ways.

The two examples together illustrate that victories for labor can translate into investment opportunities for capital—or at least some fractions of capital—that, in turn, undermine those victories. Moreover, even the differences of interest within capital, produced by labor's success, do not necessarily generate different conditions for subject classes, even when the various fractions pursue their own profitability. With cream skimming, though employers seek health coverage for their workers in more and more restricted groups, a comparable process is occurring within health provision: Care is offered to increasingly narrow segments of the population.

This process leads, among other things, to patient dumping, which explains the condition of public hospitals that are quickly becoming the only source of care for the nonproductive segment of the economy. In New York City, patients are experiencing longer and longer waits; understaffing, overcrowding, and poor quality care are commonplace. In nonprofit and municipal hospitals in the New York metropolitan area as a whole, occupancy rates are averaging around 90 percent, compared with a national rate of 64.3 percent, and more than one-third of these hospitals have rates of 100 percent or higher (*HealthWeek*, November 14, 1988).

The poor, the elderly, and the underinsured are not the only members of society affected by these developments. The internal differentiation of capital, in this case via splits produced by the successes of the poor and working class in obtaining increased health care benefits, has translated into the dual dynamic of cost containment versus the appropriation of surplus value. This makes employers more reluctant to cover total health care charges even for workers who have traditionally been well provided for in terms of health care benefits. This suggests that the long-term outcome of class conflict has important consequences for social policy in general and that the particular actors in a struggle are far from the only ones affected by it.

Health Care Workers

The interests of the capitalist class in the organization of health care also have important consequences for those working within the health delivery system. The differences generated by the need for cost containment, on the part of one fraction, versus health care as a location for the appropriation of surplus value, for another fraction, suggest that these groups have very different motivations for developing strategies for profit maximization. But both forces impact on health care workers in markedly similar ways. The broader struggle between labor and capital over health care benefits, therefore, has important implications for the structure of work within the health care sector itself.

Both forces—cost containment and the appropriation of surplus value—have contributed to employers' attempts to increase control over health care workers. Their need to do so becomes quite clear when we note that health care is an extremely labor-intensive activity: Employment costs account for 60 to 70 percent of a typical hospital budget (McKinlay 1984). Cost containment, then, translates into tighter demands on employees because this is the most obvious—and historically familiar—place to cut costs. The need for profitability works in a similar manner: Increased returns are needed to attract and maintain invested capital. Thus, in both cases, we see attempts to increase the rate of exploitation of workers. To study this process, we must consider the impact of technological growth on modern medical employment requirements.

As an employment sector, health care is among the fastest growing segments of the economy, and a major characteristic that distinguishes medicine from other industries is the impact of technology. Within the productive sector of capitalist enterprise, technological innovation has consistently been found to displace workers; within the field of medicine, however, technological advances have created new positions and spurred employment increases. The number of totally new occupations and job categories has far outpaced job losses, and the overall growth in health care employment has been spectacular. Combining the higher demand for health services with the labor needs of increasingly sophisticated technology, health care employment accounted for 14 percent of all new wage and salary jobs in the private sector between 1960 and 1984. In numerical terms, this translates into nearly 4.6 million new positions; by 1984, health care sector employment accounted for 7.4 percent of all nongovernmental U.S. jobs (Kahl and Clark 1986).

This employment expansion has contributed to the "transformation of American medicine" (Starr 1982), and it has accompanied the change from small-scale, office-based medical practice to an increasingly centralized, hospital-based, high-tech industry (Himmelstein and Woolhandler 1984; Aries and Kennedy 1986). This move toward centralized delivery systems was demanded by the high capital investment costs of technological medicine; as technology progressed, physicians became increasingly dependent upon it for diagnosis and treatment, and, thus, the centralized form became normative.

This institutionalization of technological medicine has produced striking changes in health care employment patterns, as new occupations emerged to handle equipment and provide other developing services. In 1900, for example, one out of three health care workers was a physician; by 1980, it was one in sixteen, with the most dramatic growth in the field found among technologists and technicians (Aries and Kennedy 1986). Accompanying these changes has been the development of a large administrative apparatus, a change typically corresponding to centralization. Between 1950 and 1980 the number of health care administrators grew by 1,189 percent (Aries and Kennedy 1986).

The development of technological solutions to medical problems, then, has changed the nature of health delivery, both in terms of medical practice and in the organization of work within the sector. The expansion of health care as an employment site can be traced to numerous factors, with a special importance given to new technologies. This peculiarity—that technological innovation creates, rather than displaces, work—is the result of cost-based reimbursement policies that have offered little incentive to limit employment growth because increased costs have been transferred directly to health care purchasers. This has distinguished medicine from other industries and has spared it from the imperatives of capital accumulation.

Current changes in health financing are altering this situation in a fundamental way. Attempts at cost containment via new fixed-cost reimbursement practices, coupled with the privatization process, are transforming medicine into a typical capitalist industry in terms of accumulation needs and labor relations. Concepts familiar in analyses of capitalist enterprise are becoming applicable to the health care sector.

This does not suggest that health care has, to this point, escaped the standard types of labor relations practices that characterize the larger service sector. Health care occupations have been organized in a manner familiar to U.S. workers. Jobs have been hierarchically arranged, with the bottom layers occupied overwhelmingly by black, Hispanic, and female workers. Most positions lack career ladders linking various occupations and, thus, offer very little occupational mobility. Moreover, the health care sector (hospital-based health care most particularly) has been exceptionally active in union busting.

The reorganization of medical delivery is exacerbating these trends. The interests of capital, both the fraction that is appropriating surplus value and those committed to containing costs, are accelerating levels of managerial control over the labor process. The result is decreased staffing, coupled with increased levels of exploitation, encouraging further labor unrest.

This suggests that, although the internal differentiation of capital does not always produce divergent interests vis-à-vis labor, relations within capital and relations between capital and other classes can provide a framework for analyzing the changing structure of the work within the health care industry. Although the development of the health delivery system has been guided by many different forces and is sensitive to a wide range of inputs, class relations offer a powerful analytic focus for understanding changes within the system. At the present time, it is expected that labor relations will become more and more problematic and an analysis of the interests of capital in this arena provides a framework for exploring these developments.

A Note on the Role of Physicians

The role of the physician as pivotal in modern medical delivery systems is changing as capital continues both its attempts at cost containment and its trend toward privatization. These changes are not occurring smoothly for capital and the physician now compete for control over a well-developed division of medical labor.

As in the case of both patient care and health workers as a whole, the two contradictory tendencies within capital impact on physician practice in similar ways. The most obvious point of conversion is in physician salaries, which are often viewed as an important factor in health care inflation rates and which alone account for about 20 percent of medical costs (Starr 1982). Given that the modern physician is no longer self-employed, salary levels have become a conspicuous target for cost control, on the one hand, and for increasing exploitation, on the other.

More important than salaries in overall costs, however, is the fact that physicians generate about 70 percent of all health care expenses through their diagnostic and treatment procedures (Starr 1982). This suggests that the richest arena for both cost control and profit extraction is not necessarily in salary adjustment but in the control of physician practice itself. And because physicians define and legitimize appropriate medical services, this has implications for the overall structure of health delivery.

Conflict between the physician and capital, therefore, may be seen most clearly as a struggle for control over medical practice, with competing fractions of capital fighting for greater control over the process. Because salaried intermediaries are being explored in the class structure literature as class actors, the struggle between physicians and capital can be framed in terms of interclass relations. Of particular interest in this regard are the implications of this conflict for the structure of medical care—the relationship between physicians and other health care workers, the quality and availability of medical services, and the details of health care organization.

Conclusion

Central to this analysis of class relations within health care is the assumption that the structure of the capitalist class provides a powerful analytic focus for social research. When the health care example is explored within a framework that examines the impact of capitalist class formation on the development of health care provision, we turn from a portrait of a system driven by increased demands for services in the face of a poorly coordinated and decentralized group of small producers to an analysis that bases the development of health care delivery in the long-term struggle between labor and capital. Moreover, the types of changes that we are likely to see in the future will be conditioned by this dynamic.

Three specific conclusions flow from this analysis. First, interclass relations have particularly important implications for both the internal differentiation of the capitalist class and for the formation of social policy. In the health care example, profits generated from victories by the poor and working class for health coverage produced highly profitable investment opportunities for some, but not all, fractions of capital, resulting in important splits within the capitalist class. They also contributed to the current crisis in health care, characterized most importantly by high cost and decreasing availability. The next stage of the U.S. health care system will develop from these conditions. Conflict within capital over profitability and conflict between labor and capital over levels of coverage will define the agenda for the battle over the future organization of health care delivery. Such conflicts produce the environment in which current changes are proceeding, and their outcomes will determine health care policy in the years ahead.

Second, when the profitability of different fractions of capital is in contradiction, alternative conditions for the working class are not necessarily generated. Attempts to control the cost of health care provision by that fraction of capital that pays for, but does not profit from, health delivery impacts on workers and clients in ways similar to those stemming from strategies designed by the fraction that appropriates surplus value from the delivery of care. This suggests that, although the internal differentiation of capital reflects important splits and divergent interests within the capitalist class, other classes do not necessarily profit from these divisions; alliances between labor and capital fractions will not necessarily develop. Divergent interests, therefore, cannot be expected to produce opportunities for progressive social policy formation even when, on the surface, interests seem to coincide.

Third, investigations of class relations, in general, and the internal structure of the capitalist class, more specifically, provide the materials needed to explore the role of the modern state. The recent debate between class-centered and state-centered theories of capitalist organization turn on the extent to which state policies are formulated to serve the larger interests of capital. In the health care example, state involvement has taken many forms over the years, ranging from regulation and oversight to tax incentives and entitlement programs.

In each of these instances, state activity has developed in the context of a system with an ongoing logic—a system that itself is in the process of formation. The specific circumstances of modern health care underscore the notion that when the state becomes active in a particular issue it is often at a point at which other forces have already been at play. The historical development of health care provision defined the environment in which specific health care legislation was introduced. If E. Richard Brown (1979) is correct in stating that the direction of modern medicine was a result of a long-term struggle between capital and providers over the very definition of health care, then this, too, is the context that state policy addressed.

This suggests that, although state activity may not necessarily reduce to a reflection of the contours of class struggle, an investigation of the role of the state in the health care case cannot be undertaken without a careful consideration of the social forces that framed its formation. This chapter has argued that an analysis of the structure of the capitalist class, in terms of both intraclass and interclass relations, offers a powerful framework for investigating the health care system. An analysis of the role of the state in this particular issue, therefore, would profit from the same framework.

This does not imply that class relations are the only relevant dynamic in the study of the medical field. Looking only at economic dimensions omits, as J. Craig Jenkins and Barbara Brent (1989) suggest, an analysis of political processes. And, as Rhonda Levine (1987) points out, Theda Skocpol's (1985) emphasis on the role of state structures is an important corrective to an overdetermined view of economic primacy. Nevertheless, to investigate state activity in the context of the current health care crisis as an autonomous structure is to deny the impact of larger social forces. Thus, the health care example demonstrates the value of exploring class relations as they impact specific social issues. Moreover, this case illustrates some of the ways in which our understanding of capitalist class structure may be applied to specific areas and thereby be used to explore the implications of class rule. Thus, this chapter is a call for bringing class— the capitalist class, in particular—back into our research agenda, both in terms of general social relations and in the formation of social policy.

Acknowledgments

I thank Peter Freitag, Rhonda Levine, Patrick McGuire, and Reeve Vanneman for their helpful comments on this manuscript.

Notes

1. For a sampling of this literature, see Bearden and Mintz (1988); Clawson et al. (1986); Domhoff (1983); Glasberg (1989); Kotz (1978); Mizruchi (1982); Mizruchi and Koenig (1986); Quadagno (1984); Schwartz (1987); Useem (1984); Whitt (1979); and Zeitlin and Ratcliff (1988).

2. This, of course, is not the first time a class analysis has been applied to the field of health care. For examples of analyses of this kind, see Navarro (1975, 1976, 1986), McKinlay (1978, 1984), and Salmon (1977).

3. Although studies over the past twenty-five years have consistently found the average accuracy of medical diagnoses to be only about 50 percent (Spitz 1987), a more devastating critique addresses the overall effectiveness of modern medicine itself. A former editor of the *New England Journal of Medicine* suggests that, assuming that 80 percent of medical problems are either self-curing or untreatable, 20 percent would benefit from medical intervention. However, about half of the time "give or take a point or two, the doctor may diagnose or treat inadequately, or [s]he may just have bad luck. Whatever the reason . . . the balance of accounts ends up marginally on the positive side of zero" (Ingelfinger 1977, pp. 448–49).

4. Brown (1979) argues that capital's interest in medicine had several dimensions. First, scientific medicine was viewed as a vehicle for improving the health of workers and thus contributing to increased worker productivity. Second, the ideological function of health care was seen as an effective way of winning loyalty to the idea of industrial capitalism. Finally, emphasis on disease rather than inequality as the cause of ill health diverted attention from the health consequences of capitalist development.

5. The legislation establishing Medicaid and Medicare encouraged the development of proprietary hospitals by allowing depreciation, interest on debt, and allowances for generous returns on investment to be calculated into reimbursement charges. In this way, public funds have subsidized the attractive profit rates found in health care and encouraged the formation of direct for-profit medicine.

6. The establishment and implications of Blue Cross/Blue Shield have many interesting parallels to the Medicare/Medicaid example, including opposition from the medical community and the availability of a stable payment pool that allowed for the rapid and substantial growth of the delivery system.

7. Medicare, which provides coverage for the elderly, is also becoming less adequate in its provision, and the supplement provided by private insurers to fill the gap between actual costs and Medicare reimbursement levels is becoming more expensive. In 1989, premium increases were as high as 75 percent (*HealthWeek,* March 6, 1989).

References

Aries, Nancy, and Louanne Kennedy. 1986. "The Health Labor Force." In *The Sociology of Health and Illness,* eds. Peter Conrad and Rochelle Kearns, pp. 196–207. New York: St. Martin's Press.

Appelbaum, Eileen, and Cherly Skromme Granrose. 1986. "Hospital Employment Under Revised Medicare Payment Schedule." *Monthly Labor Review* August:37–45.

Bearden, James, and Beth Mintz. 1988. "The Structure of Class Cohesion: The Corporate Network and Its Dual." In *Intercorporate Relations,* eds. Mark Mizruchi and Michael Schwartz, pp. 24–43. New York: Cambridge University Press.

Brown, E. Richard. 1979. *Rockefeller Medicine Men.* Berkeley: University of California Press.

Clawson, Dan, Allen Kaufman, and Alan Neustadtl. 1986. "The Logic of Business Unity." *American Sociological Review* 51:797–811.

Domhoff, G. W. 1983. *Who Rules America Now?* Englewood Cliffs, N.J.: Prentice-Hall.

Ermann, Dan, and Jon Gabel. 1986. "Investor-owned Multihospital Systems: A Synthesis of Research Findings." *For-Profit Enterprise in Health Care,* pp. 474–91. Washington, D.C.: National Academy Press.

Glasberg, Davita Silfen. 1989. *The Power of Collective Purse Strings.* Berkeley: University of California Press.

HealthWeek. Biweekly. *HealthWeek* Publications. Oakland, Calif.

Himmelstein, David, and Steffie Woolhandler. 1984. "Medicine as Industry: The Health Care Sector in the United States." *Monthly Review* 35:13–25.

Ingelfinger, Joseph. 1977. "Health: A Matter of Statistics or Feeling?" *The New England Journal of Medicine* 296:448–49.

Jenkins, J. Craig, and Barbara Brents. 1989. "Social Protest, Hegemonic Competition, and Social Reform." *American Sociological Review* 54:891–909.

Kahl, Anne, and Donald E. Clark. 1986. "Employment in Health Services: Long-term Trends and Projections." *Monthly Labor Review* August:17–36.

Kennedy, Louanne. 1984. "The Losses in Profits: How Proprietaries Affect Public and Voluntary Hospitals." *Health/PAC Bulletin* November-December:5–13.

Kotz, David. 1978. *Bank Control of Large Corporations in the United States.* Berkeley: University of California Press.

Levine, Rhonda. 1987. "Bringing Classes Back In: State Theories and Theories of the State." In *Recapturing Marxism: An Appraisal of Recent Trends in Sociological Theory,* eds. Rhonda Levine and Jerry Lembcke, pp. 96–116. New York: Praeger.

Leyerle, Betty. 1984. *Moving and Shaking American Medicine: The Structure of a Socioeconomic Transformation.* Westport, Conn.: Greenwood Press.

Light, Donald. 1986. "Corporate Medicine for Profit." *Scientific American* 255:38–45.

———. 1988. "Social Control and the American Health Care System." In *Handbook of Medical Sociology,* eds. Freeman and Levine. Englewood Cliffs, N.J.: Prentice-Hall.

McKinlay, John. 1978. "On the Medical-Industrial Complex." *Monthly Review* 30:38–42.

———. 1984. *Issues in the Political Economy Health Care.* New York: Tavistock Publications.

Mintz, Beth, and Michael Schwartz. 1985. *The Power Structure of American Business.* Chicago: University of Chicago Press.

Mizruchi, Mark. 1982. *The American Corporate Network: 1904–1974.* Beverly Hills, Calif.: Sage Press.

Mizruchi, Mark, and Thomas Koenig. 1986. "Corporate Political Consensus." *American Sociological Review* 51:482–91.

Navarro, Vincente. 1975. "The Political Economy of Medical Care." *International Journal of Health Services* 5:65–94.

———. 1976. *Medicine Under Capitalism.* New York: Prodist Press.

———. 1986. *Crisis, Health and Medicine: A Social Critique.* New York: Tavistock Publications.

Quadagno, Jill. 1984. "Welfare Capitalism and the Social Security Act of 1935." *American Sociological Review* 49:632–47.

Relman, A. S. 1980. "The New Medical-Industrial Complex." *The New England Journal of Medicine* 303:963–70.

Salmon, J. Warren. 1977. "Monopoly Capital and the Reorganization of Health Care." *Review of Radical Political Economics* 9:125–33.

———. 1984. "Organizing Medical Care for Profit." In *Issues in the Political Economy of Health Care,* ed. John McKinlay, pp. 143–86. New York: Tavistock Publications.

Schwartz, Michael. 1987. *The Structure of Power of American Business.* New York: Holmes and Meier.

Skocpol, Theda. 1985. "Bringing the State Back In: Strategies in Analysis in Current Research." In *Bringing the State Back In,* eds. Peter Evans, Dietrich Rueschemeyer, and Theda Skocpol, pp. 3–43. New York: Cambridge University Press.

Spitz, S. A. 1987. "Diagnostic Dilemmas." *Science for the People* July/August:19–21.

Starr, Paul. 1982. *The Social Transformation of American Medicine.* New York: Basic Books.

Statistical Abstracts of the United States. 1989. Washington, D.C.: U.S. Government Printing Office.

Useem, Michael. 1984. *The Inner Circle.* New York: Oxford University Press.

Wall Street Journal. September 29, 1987.

Whitt, J. Allen. 1979. "Toward a Class-Dialectical Model of Power: An Empirical Assessment of Three Competing Models of Political Power." *American Sociological Review* 44:81–99.

Zeitlin, Maurice. 1980. *Classes, Class Conflict and the State.* Cambridge, Mass.: Winthrop Press.

Zeitlin, Maurice, and Richard E. Ratcliff. 1988. *Landlords and Capitalists: The Dominant Class of Chile.* Princeton, N.J.: Princeton University Press.

5 | Class Analysis and Studies of the U.S. Working Class: Theoretical, Conceptual, and Methodological Issues

JERRY LEMBCKE

The development of class analysis since the early 1970s has greatly enhanced our understanding of how capitalist class interests are advanced (Domhoff 1980; O'Connor 1973) and clarified the definitional problems involved in studies of the middle class (Poulanzas 1978; Wright 1978). Great strides have also been made toward an identification of the historical origins and role played by the professional managerial stratum in the capitalist societies (Walker 1979). Unfortunately, however, we know scarcely more about the working class—particularly the U.S. working class—today than we did fifteen years ago.

Why is this? The answer surely does not lie in the quantity of work done for the production of historians, working in the social history tradition of the British Marxist historians and the social scientists exploring the terrain of workplace conflict brought into focus by Harry Braverman (1974), has been abundant. But if the volume of scholarship on the working class compares favorably to that produced on other classes, its analytical quality does not. Studies adorned with the terminological rubric of class analysis are plentiful, but real confrontations with the theoretical, conceptual, and methodological issues have generally been avoided by their authors.

This chapter sets in relief three issues that are embedded in recent studies of the U.S. working class but that, for lack of visibility, have not been addressed on their own terms. The first is a theoretical question involving the relationship between the long-term capitalist development process and the capacity of the working class to act as an agent of social change. The second is a conceptual question concerning the definition of working-class capacity. This is important because the way in which it is answered determines, to a great extent, how the first question is addressed. The third set of issues are methodological: What do we study, and how do we study it? I will address these issues, show how they are linked, and conclude with some comments bearing on the political significance of the issues.

The Theoretical Issue: Capitalist Development and Class Capacities

Is the capitalist development process contradictory? Does capitalism bring into existence its own means of destruction, the working class? Does the progressive development of capitalism empower the working class or render the working class impotent as a historical agent capable of playing a transformative role in the capitalist epoch?

Since C. Wright Mills (Horowitz 1972), most of the work done in the United States by radical scholars has concluded that capitalism has sidelined the working class as an agent of historical change. One of the most influential contributions to this trend was Harry Braverman's *Labor and Monopoly Capital*.[1] In the wake of Braverman's work there flowed volumes, each of which argued that the process by which the working class had progressively become deskilled under capitalism had the added consequence of neutralizing that class as a historical actor (Marglin 1974; Ehrenreich and Ehrenreich 1976; Aronowitz 1983). Despite its apparent departure from the liberal, pluralist paradigm of labor studies that had preceded Braverman's volume (Lipset et al. 1956), the work process school retained the most important premises of its predecessor.[2]

The unit of analysis continued to be the individual or, as it was for Braverman, the properties of individual job positions. Working-class power, in these studies, was equated with aggregated individual sovereignty, albeit sovereignty in the workplace rather than in a political process. All these studies were characterized by a strongly normative bias holding proletarianization or deskilling to be "bad" and attempts at resisting proletarianization to be virtuous. Finally, these studies located the cutting edge of history at the interface between monopoly and competitive forms of production, and they elevated the central importance of the labor aristocracy and petty bourgeoisie in the process of history. In sociology, the result has been a virtual preoccupation with the middle class.

The task of retheorizing the U.S. working-class experience lies ahead. Retheorizing means, in the first instance, getting the problem out of the atomizing "work process" discourse. It means focusing on *class* rather than individual workers as the unit of analysis, and it means we must try to understand the contradictory, rather than the normative, implications of the proletarianization process. Retheorizing also means clearly defining what the object of analysis actually is. It seems clear to me that this object is class capacities, not skill level per se.

For Marx, the problem was not whether technology deskilled but rather how the capitalist development process empowered the working class (Marx and Engels 1972, p. 186; Marx 1967, p. 43). The "independent variable," capitalist development, was a sociological, not a technical, variable. Marx treated the level of technology as but a single aspect of development, with a dialectical relationship to other aspects of the development process. His "dependent variable" was empowerment, an aspect of working-class formation. Most importantly, the relationship between these "variables" was a contradictory one: As capitalist development occurred, working-class empowerment increased. With the loss of individual control over production and the workplace, social individualism would be broken down and the groundwork laid for the collective struggle of workers for the social ownership and control of capital (Engels 1975, pp. 418, 529).

The Conceptual Issue: How Do We Understand Working-Class Capacity?

Capacity, in this instance, means the capability of the working class to act in its own interests (that is, against the interests of the capitalist class) in a way that transforms the basic social relations of capitalism. It refers, in other words, to the means available to the working class to liberate itself from its subordination to the capitalist class. The significance of how we conceptualize working-class capacity is enormous because the way we do it answers, in effect, the question about the relationship between capitalist development and working-class capacity. If class capacity is based on an aggregation of sovereign individuals, that relationship is probably inverse; if it is based on collectivity, the relationship can probably be shown to be contradictory.

One of the most important developments in class analysis in the last decade is the specification of class capacities by Claus Offe and Helmut Wiesenthal (1980) and Goran Therborn (1983). Offe and Wiesenthal make it clear that capitalist class power is based on its accumulated capital, and working-class power is based on the "association" of workers. The capitalist class mobilizes capital in pursuit of its objectives, and the working class mobilizes human resources—people.

Therborn agrees with Offe and Wiesenthal that different classes have different sources of power, but he adds two important refinements. First, he provides further specification for the notion of class capacities by distinguishing between *petty bourgeois* sources of power and *working-class* sources of power. For the petty bourgeoisie, the source of power is autonomy in the labor process; for the working class, the source of power is its collectivity. Offe and Wiesenthal's "working class" thus is decomposed by Therborn into two classes, each with its own, distinct source of power. In effect, Therborn shows us not two but three "logics of collective action." This is an important point because it is a conceptual crossroad that offers two alternatives upon which to build an analysis and strategy of anticapitalist social forces. Autonomy—be it in the production of surplus value or in knowledge—is not the only noncapitalist source of power, and the petty bourgeoisie/middle class is not the only class from which opposition to capitalism might come. It is at this juncture that we can locate a path leading away from rational-choice theory.[3]

Second, he distinguishes between the *intrinsic capacity* that classes have—the power resources available to them (as described in the previous paragraph)—and the *hegemonic capacity* of classes—their ability to deploy their intrinsic capacity against opposing classes. The essence of hegemonic capacity rests on the ability of one class to intervene in the process by which the opposite class generates its own intrinsic capacity. Moreover, Therborn points out, class power is not a zero-sum game, and the power of one class is not necessarily the weakness of its opposite. Thus, working-class deskilling and economic immiseration resulting from the capitalist class's accumulation of wealth does not necessarily mean that the working *class* is left weaker by the process. Rather, the process that increases capitalist class power through capital accumulation simultaneously and contradictorily collectivizes the working class and thus empowers it, not in material ways but in social ways.

The key insight here is that the capitalist class's success depends on its ability to maintain the accumulation process (and thus continue to generate *its* intrinsic capacity) while blocking the contradictory effects of accumulation by mitigating the collectivization of the working class—that is, to exercise hegemonic capacity. One way of doing that is for the capitalist class to *displace* collectivizing forms of organization that are intrinsic or indigenous to the working class with organizational forms that are intrinsic to the capitalist class. For example, if the capitalist class can convince workers that the notion of labor unions' reliance on larger treasuries and high-paid legal experts is more effective than rank-and-file mobilization, the capitalist class will essentially be able to place the class struggle on its own court, played by its own rules.

The spatial dimension of this process provides the key to an understanding of U.S. working-class capacity. Therborn (1983, p. 41) argues that "the extent to which the public practices of the working class are coextensive with the territorial range of the supreme political power which the class must confront" is a key determinant of which class will hold sway at any historical moment. In other words, there is a sense in which the history of class relations under capitalism can be understood as a series of flanking actions, with the capitalist class first attempting to expand its geographical options and then attempting to block working-class efforts to keep pace. In the United States, successful working-class mobilizations on local levels during the late nineteenth century (Brody 1960; Greer 1979) were countered by capital with corporate forms of organization that opened up new geographic regions. Following the success of the industrial workers' movement in basic industry during the 1930s, capital began to shift from the Great Lakes states in the post–World War II years (Gordon et al. 1982). During the 1970s, capital moved in wholesale quantities to Third World locations.

The implication of the Braverman tradition is that the casting of the working class in a central role for contemporary socialist strategies is mistaken precisely because the degradation of work under capitalism has rendered that class incapable of independent action. Consistent with these conclusions (and those of liberal pluralism), many socialist organizations have targeted middle-class and "new working-class" segments of the population for their organizing activities.

The failure to identify the dialectical properties of the capitalist development process has produced a kind of static and unimaginative quality in the U.S. socialist movement that looks *outside* the labor capital relation for historical agency. That approach has, at times, frustrated monopoly capitalism with tactics that are reactive, defensive, and protectionist, but it has not been able to advance socialism in the United States.

Therborn's formulation is consistent with the premises of classical Marxist theory, and its challenge to neo-Marxist work on the U.S. working class carries important strategic implications. Understanding that working-class capacity lies in its collectivity and that working-class collectivity exists in a dialectical rather than zero-sum relationship with capitalist class capacity, he is able to interpret capitalist development in a way that keeps the working class central to the socialist strategies. Although a focus on collectivity suggests a new research direction for working-class studies, it also brings new methodological issues to the fore. Some of these are addressed in the next section.

The Methodological Issue: What Do We Study and How?

I have argued that we need to reconceptualize how we think about working-class capacity. Specifically, I have pointed to a reductionist fallacy in the liberal pluralist and work degradation traditions and argued in favor of an approach that asks questions about the properties of the working class, qua class. This is a significant break with dominant approaches to U.S. working-class studies because it asks us to consider the subject in a manner that understands class as sui generis—that is, having properties that are its own and that are distinguishable from the properties of its parts (individuals, institutions, etc.)—and that understands the dialectical relationship between class as a whole and the component parts of the class.

This approach presents problems that confound conventional methods. How does one study the properties of a whole class? If working-class capacity is based, as I have suggested, on collectivity, how does one study that? Where and how does one "see" collectivity? How does collectivity manifest itself? What are the empirical referents for collectivity?

The trend among scholars interested in these questions is to pursue them through the conventional methods of survey research. Implicitly, survey research equates class capacity with class consciousness, and, finding little evidence of a working-class consciousness, sociologists have generally concluded that working-class agency is minimal. As a result, the efficacy of independent working-class action has been questioned by union leaders and the public, and strategies for social change have become increasingly premised on political and legal tactics that marginalize the working class.

But Rick Fantasia (1988, p. 8) contends that survey research has asked the wrong questions and, as a result, arrived at answers that, if not wrong, are "so narrow that the most important and interesting dimensions of class relations and experience are often missed." The problem, Fantasia says, is based in "an overemphasis on class imagery at the expense of class action," which, in turn, is rooted in the "widely held belief among academic observers that it is somehow necessary for men and women to encompass society intellectually before they can attempt to change it" (Gordon Marshall quoted in Fantasia [1988, p. 8]).

Fantasia uses the concept "cultures of solidarity" in place of class consciousness and argues that such culture is "formed out of friction and opposition" (Fantasia 1988, p. 233) and must, therefore, be studied in the context in which it is formed. "Ideas," he argues (Fantasia 1988, p. 236), "should be considered in the context of class behavior." Collective *action*, in other words, might be a better indicator of working-class consciousness than the attitudes and values indicated by survey research.

By taking the purely superstructural and ideational notion of "consciousness" and redefining it as "cultures of solidarity," Fantasia grounds the object of his analysis in social relations and thereby restores its *material* dimension. The shift from consciousness to culture as our primary object of analysis is a breakthrough because it restores an element of *holism* to the project of understanding class properties. Fantasia employs the methods of participant observation to study three cases of worker mobilization, and the contrast between his findings—that solidary behavior is an important aspect of working-class culture—and the findings of survey researchers are dramatic.

But the expressions of solidarity observed by Fantasia only indicate the existence of a solidary culture—what of the culture itself? Can we get closer to what it is that actually enables solidary behavior? In the cases studied by Fantasia, why was the balance between capitalist-class hegemonic capacity to disrupt working-class collectivity and intrinsic working-class capacity to act collectively tipped as favorably toward working-class collectivity as it was? And what were the mechanisms by which the balance ultimately tipped the other way in each case? Asked in this way, these become questions about working-class *capacity*.

How can the study of working-class collective culture be translated into a study of that class's capacity? What is the social chemistry that enables individual workers to overcome the atomization of capitalist social relations and act collectively? That social chemistry, I argue, is the stuff of working-class capacity, and it manifests itself as an organizational phenomenon. Collectivity materializes, in other words, through forms of organizations, which are the best empirical referents we have for the notion of collectivity.

Recent studies (Grenier 1988; Sacks 1988; Fantasia 1988) have significantly improved our understanding of the circumstances in which collective culture manifests itself. But the cultural capacities that workers draw upon for particular struggles have spatial and temporal dimensions, as well. It is the time-space matrix that is the essence of class capacity, and we need to know more about that.

The capacity of workers to defeat capital in one location, for example, is a function of how united they are with workers in another location where capital might strategically relocate. That kind of cross-space unity is an extremely important factor of working-class capacity in an era of rapid capital mobility like the late twentieth century, and it can only be adequately studied as an organizational phenomenon.

I elaborated the organizational basis of spatial capacity in my study of twenty-seven unions affiliated with the Congress of Industrial Organizations (CIO) in the late 1930s. I showed that craft and skill-based unions formed in an earlier period of capitalist development premised the allocation of resources for organizing on a pecuniary or per capita logic—those who pay the most have the most say in how, where, and when organizing resources are deployed. Industrial unions, on the other hand, tended to base the allocation of resources on unit logic—one group of workers with an identifiable interest has the same power, the same *amount* of claim, on resources as another, regardless of its size and its level of *paid* participation.

These two forms of organization, I argued, were expressions of different levels of collective culture, with identifiable bases in specific fractions of the working class. It was clear, moreover, that ongoing organizing activities that were in the best interest of the *class* were facilitated by the "unit form" of organization and impeded by the "pecuniary form"; further, the more proletarianized industrial workers developed the most efficacious form of organization. In those unions with the purest form of per capita decisionmaking structure, organizing was the most sluggish.

The methodological point to be made here is that, although a site-specific method like participant observation could presumably have recorded individual *expressions* of collectivity,[4] collectivity at the level of *class,* including its essential spatial dimension, is only observable in manifest forms of social organization. The methodological difference, in other words, lies between an analysis of capacity that is limited to a particular space and one that, holistically, captures the totality of the relationship between parts of the class that are located in geographically distinct locations. By examining forms of organization, the study of culture moves, in this case, from the level of community to the level of class.

This point can be further illustrated by considering the temporal dimension of class capacities. The tenacity of a working-class culture of collectivity has been noted in several recent studies (Montgomery 1979; Nelson 1984; Rosenzweig 1983), but only occasionally (Bensman and Lynch 1987) is it suggested that this culture is reproduced intergenerationally. The mechanisms by which collective culture is reproduced and transmitted from one generation to another are even less studied.

What can be gained through an analysis that captures the temporal dimension of class capacity is demonstrated in Harold Benenson's (1985) reexamination of the Braverman skill-degradation thesis. Benenson (1985, p. 112) notes that "the fundamental strategic issue for labor [at the turn of the century] was the reorientation of the organized skilled sector toward a concept of inclusive, industrialism unionism" that could accommodate the swelling mass of semiskilled and unskilled workers in manufacturing. The barriers to inclusive unionism often took the form of hierarchical social relations (between, for example, skilled and unskilled workers), and, for the most part, the radical scholars of the 1970s and 1980s attempted to understand the dynamics of early twentieth-century class formation on this vertical plane. Typically, the analyses of failed working-class formation done during this period cite the protectionist attitudes and behavior of white, male, native-born, skilled workers as a factor in the exclusion of people of color, women, foreign-born individuals, and unskilled workers from participation in unions and other would-be class-based organizations.

What is missed in these analyses, according to Benenson, is the gender-specificity of the industrial changes taking place during this period and the centrality of the working-class family to the way the changes were

matrix can best be achieved through study of organizational forms that reflect class properties.[6]

Summary and Conclusions

What is widely recognized today as "class analysis" was born twenty years ago in the context of stalled campus and civil rights movements. The success of Marxist-led revolutionary movements abroad led to a renewal of interest in classical Marxist analysis and especially to the proposition that the working class would play a central role in the transformation of capitalism. Examinations of the working-class movements in advanced capitalist countries raised questions about the changed composition of the working class since Marx wrote. They also raised important questions about the political potential of new elements within the class. As radical movements waned during the late 1970s and early 1980s, however, the lines between Marxist and non-Marxist notions of class began to blur, and the questioning led away from the "new" working class to concerns about the middle class. Today, "class analysis" is almost synonymous with studies of the middle class, and its agenda differs little from that of general stratification studies.

Meanwhile, the United States is witnessing political economic devastation seldom seen in its history. Unemployment and underemployment, homelessness, hunger, the declining quality of health and educational systems, and the rise of racism and national chauvinism combine to portend a crisis-ridden future. The suffering of large numbers of working people and others who have been economically cast off is increasing. And it has been increasing for at least a decade.

Yet, the prospects of a meaningful, effective response to those conditions by a left-wing, socialist movement appear distant. Thus, for example, political economist Leo Panitch observed at a recent conference that the failure of the Bronx, New York, is the failure not of capitalism but of the socialist movement's ability to respond effectively. By comparison, ten years into the Great Depression of the 1930s, the U.S. Left was mobilized and playing a central role in the resolution of the crisis. It should be noted that *class* was central to the analysis and strategic vision of the movement, and the working class was the social base on which that movement was built.

Theoretically, it is true that the working class should not be granted a priori primacy. But the proof of the pudding is in the eating. The strategies and tactics based on analyses that have sidelined the working class have produced nothing. It is time to rethink. A movement that bases its strategies on an incorrect assessment of its intrinsic capacities is likely to fail.

By analogy, envision a basketball team, the home team, whose players are short by the standards of the game. They are also very fast and exceptional shooters from the three-point range. However, common wisdom, fostered by coaches of teams stacked with seven-foot players, is that basketball is "an inside game." Their discourse is one of "getting the ball inside" and "getting the ball down low." They counsel the hometown coach to install a "low-post offense" like they have. So he follows the trend and plays the best "inside game" he can with his small players—and he has a losing season.

Not a smart coach, you say? The political Left in the United States has made the same mistake—it has played the political economic game for too many years on the other team's court, using the other team's strategy. Clearly, this is not a smart tactic. What is needed is a reassessment of the *intrinsic* capacities of the working class and a new game plan established on the basis of that work. It is time to rethink and reformulate the agenda of class analysis.

Notes

1. My thinking on the issues in this chapter has been enormously stimulated by the work of Braverman and his followers. Without them, the ideas expressed here would never have taken shape.

There are others, however, who have contributed to the marginalization of the working class during the last period. Mike Davis's "Why the U.S. Working Class Is Different" argues that it is the cumulative effects of successive failures suffered by the U.S. working class that explain its incapacitation. See Tabb and Sawers (1978), Piven and Cloward (1977), and Gordon, Edwards, and Reich (1982) in regard to urban development, social movements, and industrial organization, respectively.

2. This point is expanded in my book *Capitalist Development and Class Capacities* (1988).

3. Rational-choice Marxism is also known as analytical Marxism, neoclassical Marxism, and game-theoretic Marxism. The best critique of this literature is Michael Lebowitz's "Is 'Analytical Marxism' Marxism?" in *Science and Society* 52:191–214.

4. I do not mean to minimize the importance of local expressions of solidarity. They are part of the time-space matrix, and they can be very important guides to properties of the class as a whole. In my study, for example, union convention proceedings recorded the rhetoric of individual members as they spoke for one or another form of organization. The workers from more craft-oriented fractions typically invoked the rhetoric of "taxation without representation" to argue for per capita forms of representation, and workers from more proletarianized fractions spoke in a more egalitarian rhetoric consistent with a culture of solidarity and collectivity. (For examples drawn from convention proceedings of CIO unions, see Lembcke [1988, pp. 65–132]).

5. Intergenerational links are also broken through the upward or downward *social* mobility of workers. The upward mobility, or embourgeoisment, of workers has been studied (e.g., Goldthorpe 1968) but primarily as a study of the attitudes of individual workers, not as a problem of class capacity. Except in periods of industrial restructuring when whole new class strata are created (e.g., the creation of the professional-managerial stratum at the turn of the century), working-class capacity is probably not greatly affected by social mobility, however. And in those cases, social mobility occurs in conjunction with the geographic mobility of capital, as I argue in this section.

6. For studies of the U.S. working class in a framework of uneven class formation, see Howard Kimeldorf (1988), Lembcke (1988), and Sharon Reitman's chapter in this volume.

References

Aronowitz, Stanley. 1983. *Working Class Hero.* New York: Pilgrim Press.

Benenson, Harold. 1985. "The Community and Family Bases of U.S. Working Class Protest, 1880–1920: A Critique of the 'Skill Degradation' and 'Ecological' Perspectives." In *Research in Social Movement, Conflicts and Change,* ed. Louis Kriesberg, pp. 109–32. Greenwich, Conn.: JAI Press.

Bensman, David, and R. Lynch. 1987. *Rusted Dreams: Hard Times in a Steel Community.* New York: McGraw-Hill.

Blee, Kathlene. 1982. "The Impact of Family Settlement Patterns on the Politics of Lake Superior Communities, 1890–1920." Ph.D. dissertation, University of Wisconsin, Madison.

Bluestone, Barry, and B. Harrison. 1982. *The Deindustrialization of America: Plant Closings, Community Abandonment and the Dismantling of Basic Industry.* New York: Basic Books.

Braverman, Harry. 1974. *Labor and Monopoly Capital.* New York: Monthly Review Press.

Brody, David. 1960. *Steelworkers in America: The Non-union Era.* New York: Harper and Row.

Davis, Mike. 1980. "Why the U.S. Working Class Is Different." *New Left Review* 123 (September-October):3–44.

Domhoff, G. William. 1980. *Power Structure Research II.* Published as a special issue of *The Insurgent Sociologist* 9:2–3.

Dunn, Marvin. 1980. "The Family Office as a Coordinating Mechanism Within the Ruling Class." *The Insurgent Sociologist* 9:8–23.

Edwards, Richard. 1978. *Contested Terrain.* New York: Basic Books.

Ehrenreich, John, and Barbara Ehrenreich. 1976. "Work and Consciousness." *Monthly Review* Summer:10–18.

Engels, Frederick. 1975. The Condition of the Working Class in England. *Collected Works of Marx and Engels IV.* New York: International Publishers.

Fantasia, Rick. 1988. *Cultures of Solidarity.* Berkeley: University of California Press.

Gillis, John R. 1984. "Peasant, Plebeian, and Proletarian Marriage in Britain, 1600–1900." In *Proletarianization and Family History,* ed. D. Levine, pp. 129–62. Orlando, Fla.: Academic Press.

Goldthorpe, John. 1968. *The Affluent Worker.* Cambridge: Cambridge University Press.

Gordon, David. 1978. "Capitalist Development and the History of American Cities." In *Marxism and the Metropolis: New Perspectives in Urban Political Economy,* eds. William Tabb and L. Sawers, pp. 25–63. New York: Oxford University Press.

Gordon, David, R. Edwards, and M. Reich. 1982. *Segmented Work, Divided Workers.* Cambridge: Cambridge University Press.

Greer, Edward. 1979. *Big Steel.* New York: Monthly Review Press.

Grenier, Guillermo. 1988. *Inhuman Relations: Quality Circles and Antiunionism in American Industry.* Philadelphia: Temple University Press.

Horoweitz, Irving L. 1972. *Power, Politics and People: The Collected Essays of C. Wright Mills.* New York: Oxford University Press.

Howe, Carolyn. n.d. "Beyond the Four Walls: Finnish Immigrant Women and Family Ideology." Manuscript.

Lebowitz, Michael A. 1988. "Is 'Analytical Marxism' Marxism?" *Science and Society* 52:191–214.

Lembcke, Jerry. 1988. *Capitalist Development and Class Capacities: Marxist Theory and Union Organization.* New York: Greenwood Press.

Lipset, S. M., M. A. Trow, J. S. Coleman. 1956. *Union Democracy.* New York: Anchor Press.

Kimeldorf, Howard. 1988. *Reds or Rackets? The Making of Radicals and Conservatives on the Waterfront.* Berkeley: University of California Press.

Marglin, Stephen. 1974. "What Do Bosses Do?" *Review of Radical Political Economy* 6:60–112.

Marx, Karl. 1967. *Capital.* New York: International Publishers.

Marx, Karl, and F. Engels. 1972. *Selected Works In One Volume.* New York: International Publishers.

Montgomery, David. 1979. *Workers' Control in America: Studies in the History of Work, Technology, and Labor Struggles.* New York: Cambridge University Press.

Nelson, Bruce. 1984. " 'Pentecost' on the Pacific: Maritime Workers and Working-Class Consciousness in the 1930s." In *Political Power and Social Theory,* eds. M. Zeitlin and H. Kimeldorf, vol. 4, pp. 141–82. Greenwich, Conn.: JAI Press.

O'Connor, James. 1973. *The Fiscal Crisis of the State.* New York: St. Martin's Press.

Offe, Claus, and Helmut Wiesenthal. 1980. "Two Logics of Collective Action: Theoretical Notes on Social Class and Organizational Form." In *Political Power and Social Theory,* ed. M. Zeitlin, vol. 1, pp. 67–115. Greenwich, Conn.: JAI Press.

Piven, Frances Fox, and R. Cloward. 1977. *Poor People's Movements.* New York: Pantheon.

Poulanzas, Nicos. 1978. *Classes in Contemporary Capitalism.* London: Verso.

Rosenzweig, Roy. 1983. *Eight Hours for What We Will: Workers and Leisure in an Industrial City, 1870–1920.* Cambridge: Cambridge University Press.

Sacks, Karen. 1988. *Caring by the Hour: Women, Work, and Organizing at Duke Medical Center.* Urbana: University of Illinois Press.

Stone, Katherine. 1975. "The Origins of Job Structures in the Steel Industry." In *Labor Market Segmentation,* eds. Richard Edwards, M. Reich, and D. Gordon, pp. 113–73. Lexington, Mass.: Lexington Books.

Tabb, William, and Larry Sawers. 1978. *Marxism and the Metropolis.* New York: Oxford University Press.

Therborn, Goran. 1983. "Why Some Classes Are More Successful than Others." *New Left Review* 138 (March-April):37–55.

Walker, Pat. 1979. *Between Labor and Capital.* Boston: South End Press.

Wright, Eric Olin. 1978. *Class, Crisis and the State.* London: Verso.

PART II | Class Formation

The three chapters in this section are concerned primarily with the formation of classes into collectively organized actors. James R. Orr and Scott G. McNall examine the manner in which fraternal orders acted to limit working-class organizational capacity in nineteenth-century Kansas. They argue that the myth of brotherhood actually served to prevent working-class members from both seeing class conflict and developing a language of class conflict. By examining class formation as a process involving an analysis of structural position, ideology or consciousness, and organization, Orr and McNall are able to explain why working-class men might have joined fraternal organizations and how this promoted and diffused the emerging capitalist order. Shelley Feldman focuses on the process of class formation in rural Bangladesh. Instead of concentrating on issues of class consciousness, Feldman studies the structural development and expansion of the small and cottage industries sector that was essential in establishing the conditions for rural industrialization and the consequent transformation of relations among rural nonagricultural producers. She examines the ways in which institutional credit contributed to efforts to transform petty commodity producers into an entrepreneurial class and the contradictory effects this process had on rural producers. Finally, William G. Roy argues that the formation of the corporate class segment of the U.S. capitalist class in the decades around 1900 was not merely a result of structural consequences in the relations of production. He examines the rise of financial institutions and the role of the railroad as important factors in explaining the growth of this segment of the capitalist class. Yet, he suggests, this economic factor must be understood in conjunction with the role the state played on the political level in forming the corporate segment, as well as the role of elite social organizations that cemented cohesion within the segment and, secondarily, the creation of organizations that symbolized upper-class solidarity.

6 | Fraternal Orders and Working-Class Formation in Nineteenth-Century Kansas

James R. Orr
Scott G. McNall

Werner Sombart once said that "socialism in America came to grief on roast beef and apple pie." Though there is some truth in this familiar joke, we will argue here that socialism never emerged as a dominant political force in the United States because members of the working class failed to develop strong, autonomous organizations. We will also contend that they failed to do so because they were embedded in organizations that crosscut and defused class interests.

Many reasons have been advanced to explain the failure of U.S. workers to advance a proletarian revolution,[1] but only recently have researchers (Clawson 1985, 1989; Montgomery 1976; Rosenzweig 1977) begun to explore the role fraternal orders played in limiting the growth and development of strong working-class organizations. Fraternal orders (such as the International Order of Odd Fellows, the Knights of Pythias, or the Masons) were enormously popular in the United States during the late nineteenth century and early twentieth century (Dumenil 1984, p. XI). B. H. Meyer (1901, p. 650) estimated that in 1901 5 million U.S. citizens belonged to more than 600 separate orders, and by 1927—the point at which membership began to decline—30 million were members of some fraternal group (Schmidt 1980, p. 3). If this figure is accurate, it would mean that almost one-half of the population (60 million in 1920) belonged to some fraternal organization. To put these figures in perspective, union membership stood at only about 1 million in 1900 and 5 million in 1920 (Nash et al. 1986, p. 702). In short, fraternal affiliations far outnumbered union affiliations.

But did members of the working class belong to fraternal orders? And, if so, were they likely to come into contact with members of the middle and upper classes? Although some early writers, such as David Montgomery (1976) and Roy Rosenzweig (1977), argued that fraternal orders were class homogenous, recent studies of membership lists from late nineteenth-century organizations by Lynn Dumenil (1984), Mary Ann Clawson (1985, 1989) and McNall and Orr (1988) have found that, for such groups as the International Order of the Odd Fellows, the Knights of Pythias, and the Masons, membership typically consisted of both the middle *and* working classes.

Dumenil (1984) found that about 25 percent of the members in an 1880 Oakland, California, Masonic lodge were skilled, semiskilled, or unskilled workers. Thirty-one percent of the Masons owned businesses, and 35 percent were white-collar workers. Clawson (1985, 1989) found an even higher proportion of working-class members in the Knights of Pythias in late nineteenth-century Belleville, Illinois, and Buffalo, New York. On a citywide basis, 52.2 percent of the Knights in Belleville could be classified as blue-collar; the rest were white-collar. McNall and Orr (1988) found a similarly diverse social composition in a study of Masons and Odd Fellows in four late nineteenth-century Kansas industrial towns. About 22 percent of the Masons and 47 percent of the Odd Fellows were classified as skilled or unskilled workers.[2] In two of the towns they studied, membership in fraternal orders exceeded male membership in churches and included almost 50 percent of the adult (over age 19) male population.

The fraternal lodge, then, was a place where workers rubbed shoulders with merchants, bankers, politicians, and white-collar employees. Lodge brothers were bound to one another by an elaborate hierarchical system that utilized rituals, oaths of secrecy, and pledges of fraternity and mutual assistance. Did the pledge of brotherhood mute class conflict and limit the workers' ability to articulate their grievances and form autonomous organizations? We think it did and will offer evidence to substantiate this claim. Clawson (1985, 1989), whose work urges us, usefully, to see class as actively constructed and contested, makes a different claim. Although admitting that fraternal orders acted to limit working-class organizational capacity, she argues that a large block of workers within a given lodge could serve to enhance the potential for working-class organization and mobilization within a specific locale (Clawson 1989, pp. 94–107). We are skeptical of this claim for three reasons. First, we can find no evidence in Kansas that lodges served to bring members of the working class together in a way that empowered them. Second, as we will show, the myth of brotherhood undercut the potential for both *seeing* class conflict and developing a *language* of class conflict. And finally, membership in both a fraternal order and a union does not mean that the ideology of the union was privileged as Clawson (1989, p. 100) seems to claim. Even if it were, we must remember that the ideology of many unions was neither radical nor even pro–working class.

Class Formation

Under what conditions do humans become class subjects, rather than subjects who emphasize their ethnicity, their religion, or even their family? How are cohesive classes made? To answer such questions let us first consider what is meant by class.

Eric Hobsbawm (1984) has identified two meanings of class. The first conception refers to those broad aggregates of people who share some common attribute, such as their relationship to the means of production. The *structure* of capitalist society at any particular moment affects the potential for a group of people to become a class by determining, among other things, whether one group is numerically superior to another (Katznelson 1986). Thus, in considering the potential for Kansas workers who were also Masons and Odd Fellows to become a class, we must consider the nature of capitalist development in nineteenth-century Kansas.

However, to understand more about actual class formation, we must look to Hobsbawm's second meaning of class, which deals with *class consciousness*—whether a gap exists between a group's interests, as defined by its structural position, and that group's awareness and understanding of its position. As Hobsbawm (1984, p. 16) has said, "Class in the full sense comes into existence at the historical moment when classes begin to acquire consciousness of themselves as such." For Hobsbawm, this consciousness develops in opposition to other groups. This struggle can and often does occur at the level of ideology.

Therefore, class is problematic, not given. Nothing can be assumed from class position or structure alone; classes on paper are not necessarily classes in society. Even if we can separate people into distinct categories, all we have learned is that some group has the *potential* for becoming a class. We do not know, from structural position alone, whether members of a group actually are conscious of, or act on the basis of, their economic or structural position. Groups who share a common location in the social structure may act in very different ways; some may act collectively, others will not, and still others may act in ways seemingly contrary to their interests as a class (Katznelson 1986).

We must broaden Hobsbawm's conception of class consciousness to include *language* for it is through both discourse and social practice that individuals are constructed as human subjects (MacDonell 1986, p. 19). Forms of discourse are grounded in the everyday experiences of people and are influenced by the mode of production; they are also partially autonomous (Hall 1985, p. 110). For instance, nineteenth-century workers had available to them a variety of different languages to interpret their experiences. Some were embedded in emigrant communities with a socialist tradition, and, as a result, this language was used to understand the emerging industrial order. Others were embedded in communities that used a religious rhetoric to analyze the human condition. In short, different languages produced different responses to material conditions. It is through discourse, then, that humans become conscious subjects before they become class subjects; different discourse streams flow together to produce subjects and classes. As we will see, the nineteenth-century U.S. worker stood at the confluence of streams of religious rhetoric, republican ideology, German socialist ideology, and social Darwinism, to name but a few. These different streams produced, in varying locales and moments, different subjects.

Human subjects do not, however, passively accept just any language or symbolic system to interpret their material experiences. Social and political struggles are often waged over semantics, over the construction of new terms for old concepts (Hall 1985, p. 112). Pierre Bourdieu (1977, 1984, 1989) has argued persuasively that symbolic struggles are, at root, struggles over economic and political power. He has also noted (Bourdieu 1984, 1989) that elites maintain their positions of power through strategies of condescension, whereby they explain that there really is no difference between them and those who occupy lower rungs on the economic ladder. As will be seen below, the rhetoric of fraternal brotherhood acts to suppress real and meaningful differences in economic and political power.

Thus, ideologies and languages are not created de novo. They grow out of real experiences and are refined and sharpened through organization. Organizational capacity is critical to class formation and is closely tied to language. As McNall (1988, p. 10) has emphasized, "One of the ways people have learned about the nature of their oppression and about how to articulate the values they wish to protect, is through their participation in class organizations. In mobilizing, in trying to actually change the economic and political system, people create themselves as a class."

Therefore, to answer the question of why U.S. workers tended not to be revolutionary, one must examine three separate components of class formation: structure, class consciousness (which is determined by language and ideology), and organizational capacities. This means that we must look at the class structure of late nineteenth-century Kansas, study the ideology of the organizations workingmen joined, and speculate on how membership in fraternal orders may have inhibited the development of autonomous working-class organizations.

Socioeconomic Conditions in
Late Nineteenth-Century Kansas

Between 1860 and 1900, the population of Kansas grew from 107,000 to 1,470,000, a nearly fourteen-fold increase (Clark and Roberts 1936). Throughout this period, the majority of Kansans were farmers. In 1860, the state was primarily a preindustrial agricultural society, though this situation would quickly change. Agriculture became highly capitalized, and Kansas farmers were tightly linked to international and national capital and commodity markets. As agricultural production expanded, so did manufacturing. By 1890, there was major growth in the capital goods sector, and after 1880, a large percentage of new investment was devoted to manufacturing and transportation.

There was a concomitant change in the labor force between 1880 and 1900. The population was becoming less rural as growth in the non-agricultural sector of the labor force outpaced that in agricultural labor. The urban population of the state jumped from 10.5 percent in 1880 to 22.5 percent in 1900 (Clark and Roberts 1936). The nonagricultural labor force increased 87 percent between 1880 and 1890 and went up another 16 percent by 1900. In terms of actual numbers, this meant that jobs in manufacturing increased from 11,800 in 1880 to 30,100 by 1900. This still placed Kansas well below the national average for it had only 0.7 percent of the nation's manufacturing labor force in 1900. Food and food production, particularly milling and slaughter, dominated the manufacturing sector, and a substantial number of men worked for the railroads. In short, Kansas did not have what we would think of as real factory towns, which meant there were few concentrations of workers and few opportunities to develop a working-class culture (McNall 1988, pp. 111–13). In the absence of worker communities and organizations, fraternal orders would hold an important appeal.

Though Kansas did not have large factory towns, its people experienced the effects of proletarianization, which is both an objective and a subjective process (Tilly 1979). During the late nineteenth century, both national and state economic conditions were turbulent. The rapid economic expansion of the state, due primarily to increases in the population, was accompanied by a series of economic crises. The nation as a whole experienced a major depression in 1873, which limited growth in Kansas. The eastern sector of the state was particularly hard hit because it depended on Eastern capital, which dried up with the depression (Wright

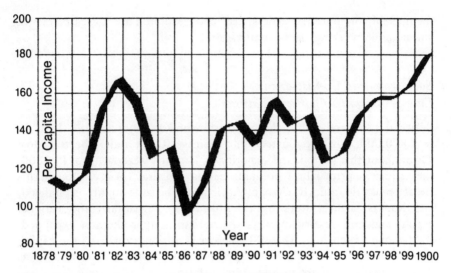

Figure 6.1 Per capita income in Kansas from 1878 to 1900
Source: Derived from Madden 1968.

1941). The following year, Kansas endured a severe and prolonged drought, after which a plague of grasshoppers arrived to destroy both the farmers' crops and the businesses of those who depended on the farmers' prosperity. These natural calamities wiped out agricultural production in some areas, led to foreclosures, and bankrupted local merchants. The state recovered from this blow, only to suffer another series of setbacks with the depression that lasted from 1887 until 1896, when a measure of prosperity again returned.

Figure 6.1 illustrates the tumultuous nature of these years by charting the changes in per capita income between 1878 and 1900. Per capita income fell 75 percent between 1882 and 1886 and did not return to 1882 levels until 1889. These crises fell on the shoulders of farmers, merchants, and workers alike. In fact, local businessmen were more likely to fail than were farmers. According to McNall (1988, p. 108), between 1865 and 1900, 84 percent of the businesses in Fort Scott, Kansas, failed within five years. McNall (1988, p. 107) attributes this to three factors: "First, the merchant's prosperity was linked to the farmers'. . . . Second, their prosperity was false insofar as it was based on protection from the national markets. This protection would end with mass production and lower railroad rates. Third, competition among merchants themselves was intense."

These crises led to massive social dislocations. Raymond Miller (1925) calculated the population loss in towns of over 4,000 to be 36 percent between 1887 and 1892, and James Malin (1935) estimated that between

1885 and 1895 there was a 50 percent turnover among farm owners. Seeing one's neighbors fail and leave the county or state threatened old forms of association and solidarity. As Ronald Aminzade (1979) found in his study of nineteenth-century workers in Toulouse, France, when old solidarities are threatened, people turn to the cultural and social resources at hand to construct new solidarities. In sum, as we deal with the structural component of class formation in Kansas, we find workers and others experiencing a process of proletarianization, changing conditions of work, and an uncertain economic future. But workers were a minority of the laboring population throughout the state, which meant that they seldom possessed their own organizations or resources for mobilization. This would mean that fraternal orders would offer them a haven from the harsh changes that swept the state.

The Nature and Appeal of Fraternal Orders

What were these organizations like, and why might they have appealed to workers? We can identify five related reasons: They offered financial security, business advantages, prestige, and a sense of community, and their ideology was compatible with the dominant Republican ideology of the age.

Financial Security

During the economic crisis spurred by the collapse of financial markets in 1873, many Kansans were hard pressed to meet basic needs. Yet, when the poor appealed to those who had money, particularly town merchants, they were spurned. The level of hostility and indifference can be gleaned from comments such as those in a letter written by one angry man to the Wichita, Kansas, *Eagle* (July 17, 1874). The writer was responding to previous comments by a "lady of the town" and said, "What is to be done for the poor and destitute of this country? Let them . . . suck their thumbs as the generous lady said, or 'let them starve and be damned' as a high toned gentleman in Wichita said last week? . . . A majority of those needing help have families of small children to support. One lady in Wichita said last week that they had no business to have a lot of young-uns to support. . . . But it is a fact, and it can't be got over." In short, public assistance was virtually nonexistent in Kansas and other states in the nineteenth-century. The Masons, Odd Fellows, and other orders helped fill this important economic breach in several ways.

When Max Weber (1958, pp. 307–8) visited the United States at the turn of the century, he related that "it was striking to observe many

men among the American middle classes . . . wearing a little badge (of
varying color) in the buttonhole. . . . When asked what it meant, people
regularly mentioned an association with a sometimes adventurous and
fantastic name. And it became obvious that its significance and purpose
consisted in the following: Almost always the association functioned as
a burial insurance, besides offering greatly varied services."

In addition to providing burial insurance, the pledge of brotherhood
meant that members of groups such as the Masons and Odd Fellows would
help one another in difficult times. In fact, we find frequent references in
Masonic and Odd Fellow literature to how generous their financial benefits
were, an obvious selling point. A writer for the Odd Fellows (Beharrell
1881, p. 15) said that the "Maxim of Odd Fellowship" was: "We visit the
sick, relieve the distressed, bury the dead, and educate the orphan." The
Odd Fellows were supposed to, and usually did, have an orphan fund in
every lodge to provide clothing and education for surviving children.
Widows of deceased members were also provided for, and if a member
became sick, a lodge brother was available to help the wife take care of
the invalid. These were not just token benefits. The Odd Fellows Constitution described the financial help available to members:

Any brother who's attained the third degree, and has been a
member of the same lodge for 6 months . . . who shall be disabled
by sickness or injury . . . (providing such sickness or injury shall
not have been occasioned by his own improper conduct), shall be
entitled to benefits . . .

If dues are $4–5/year	$2/week benefits
$5–6/year	$3/week
$6–7/year	$4/week
$7–8/year	$5/week
$8–10/year	$6/week

To put this in perspective, a skilled worker in nineteenth-century Kansas
made an average of about $10 a week.

Another important financial benefit was life insurance. Many fraternal
orders began during the late nineteenth century as insurance companies
for the working classes. These organizations met an important need:
providing insurance to workers at lower rates than could be obtained
from commercial insurance companies. These "fraternal beneficiary societies" combined the qualities of nonprofit insurance companies with
the structure and ideology of the lodge system (Smith 1979, p. 4).[3]

The Odd Fellows 1894 proceedings of the Grand Lodge of Kansas
indicate that 83 percent ($15,743) of the state lodge's expenses were

paid as death benefits to the relatives of forty-six lodge members who died (the average payment was $342.24, almost a year's wages). The state lodge employed some Odd Fellows as insurance agents, who specialized in writing life insurance policies for members.[4] As described in the January 1888 issue of *The Ezel* (the Kansas Odd Fellows magazine), the Odd Fellows actively recruited members to sign up for insurance: "There are many names of Odd Fellows on the books of outside Insurance Companies. When there is an Odd Fellows Accident Insurance Company it is your positive duty to enlist with such a one. Small sums invested this way always insure profitable returns."

The Masons also had a life insurance division within their organization, although it was only available to Master Masons. The Masonic Mutual Benefit Society brochure of 1890 states that its purpose was to give financial aid and benefit to the widows, orphans, and dependents of deceased members. The benefits were limited to either $1,000 or $2,000, depending on the plan one opted for. There was an initial $5 fee to join, and yearly payments ranged from 90¢ to $1.80, depending on age. The 1886 *Light*[5] indicated that $32,000 in benefits were paid in 1885, at a total cost to the insured (2,241) of $1,561.[6]

It would seem, from an examination of their records and publications, that the Odd Fellows were involved in a greater range of projects than the Masons to help needy members, perhaps simply because the Odd Fellows were poorer. The 1875 proceedings of the Grand Lodge contain the details of a program in which 800 Odd Fellows from Kansas and surrounding states donated $5,400 worth of corn, potatoes, buckwheat, and fall wheat seed to 443 lodge members who could not afford to buy seed to plant the next spring.[7]

There were other—indirect—benefits that smoothed the financial path for lodge members, especially during an era of high population turnover and mobility. The Odd Fellows described some of these benefits in the July 1888 issue of *The Ezel*:

> Its attentive benefits, its mutual and reciprocal aid and the many privileges and advantages accompanying membership, should be taken into consideration. By its laws, an Odd Fellow in a strange land, or while traveling, receives the same attention, care and assistance, that he would in his own home. If he is unfortunate he is assisted, if sick, is visited, watched over and nursed, and if he dies is decently buried, or his remains are sent to his home lodge in the place where he died.

A corollary benefit, then, was that lodges could serve as *labor exchanges* for a mobile population. A man could go into a town, claim affiliation with a lodge, and seek the legitimation and assistance of his brothers in securing employment.

It is not surprising, considering the orders' emphasis on the financial benefits of brotherhood, that brothers would sometimes cynically manipulate others or join for the wrong reasons. The orders were careful to warn that such people violated the true spirit of brotherhood, and they cautioned their members to be on guard against those who claimed to be members but were not. The Masons' *Light* (April 1, 1886) issued this notice: "One S. Hamlin, claiming to be a member of Pineville Lodge, No. 534, of Kentucky, is endeavoring to visit lodges in the southern part of the state. The Secretary of the Pineville Lodge writes that there is no member of that lodge of the name. A man giving the name of Franklin Jones, claiming to be a member of Ancient Landmark Lodge, No. 5, at St. Paul, Minn., has been 'doing' Lawrence. No such name appears on the rolls of that lodge."

But for legitimate members, the lodges provided an important source of financial support during the latter part of the nineteenth and early twentieth centuries. They would also give their members the legitimation they needed to succeed in business.[8]

Business Advantages

We have already noted that Weber was fascinated by the preponderance of fraternal orders when he visited the United States in 1904. One of the things that impressed him was how similar lodge membership was to affiliation with a religious denomination (Weber 1958, p. 307): "Today the kind of denomination [to which one belongs] is rather irrelevant. It does not matter whether one be Freemason, Christian Scientist, Adventist, Quaker, or what not. What is decisive is that one be admitted to membership by 'ballot,' after an examination and an ethical probation in the sense of the virtues which are at a premium for the inner-worldly asceticism of protestantism and hence, for the ancient puritan tradition." Weber's specific reference was to the fact that a man could claim to be ethical and engage in fair business dealings by virtue of the fact that he was a member of some denomination or fraternal organization. Weber recounted how an assistant professor of Semitic languages in an eastern university told him he regretted not having become "master of the chair" in the Masons for then he could go back into business and present himself in a role famous for respectability. "He could beat any competition and would be worth his weight in gold" (Weber 1958, p. 307). Little wonder that we find a preponderance of merchants and professionals in nineteenth-century fraternal organizations.

In Kansas, over 68 percent of the Masons and 51 percent of the Odd Fellows were merchants, professionals, agents, or salesmen who could expect to profit from business contacts made through the orders or from the status associated with lodge membership. Though they were not supposed to, businessmen, doctors, and lawyers who were Masons sometimes advertised this fact in their windows, on their business cards, or on the lapels of their suits.

As we have already noted, lodge membership could benefit working-class members by increasing their opportunities for securing employment and by providing the means to forge links with powerful members of the community. The status of lodge membership, combined with the opportunity to develop contacts with important men, helped many obtain the credit needed to start a business and move out of the ranks of skilled workers.[9] This motive for joining a lodge was acknowledged in the literature of both orders. The Masons noted: "A few join the Freemasons from curiosity, others to enhance their business interests, others join thinking the society will be of great benefit to them in times of adversity, while still others imagine that by joining it will give them social standing" (*Light*, December 1884). Most were not disappointed.

Prestige

Lodges were centers of middle-class respectability (Dumenil 1984, p. 72), where class divisions of the external world were ignored and the internal rankings and hierarchy of the lodge were substituted (Clawson 1985). The secrecy of the lodge functioned, as Georg Simmel (1906, p. 442) noted, to establish another, private world alongside the outer world. One was admitted to this secret world by invitation only and by a vote of the membership. One "blackball" was sufficient to deny a prospective member entry. In a small community (and nineteenth-century Kansas towns were small), an individual could experience social prestige and feel important because he was a member of an exclusive group, with private rituals and ranks.

The groups themselves and, by extension, their members were socially approved. Dumenil (1984, p. 30) has linked the prestige of nineteenth-century Masons to their ideology: "Masonic leaders, sensitive to popular attitudes, molded Masonry to reflect the religious and moralistic viewpoints of the Protestant middle class. In offering [its members] identification with a religious and moralistic organization that upheld societal norms, Masonry provided men with a vehicle for expressing their commitment to the respectable virtues of industry, sobriety, self-restraint, honesty, and faith in God."

Sense of Community

The lodges became separate moral communities, made possible through secrecy and ritual. Rituals were the means by which the principle of brotherhood was affirmed and members drawn together. Even if this were not a deliberate strategy of condescension, as Bourdieu (1989, p. 16) would label it, it did mean that members were more attuned to a rhetoric that emphasized something other than the possibility of class war. As Simmel (1906, p. 481) said, "Since the symbolism of the ritual stimulates a wide range of vaguely bounded feelings, touching interests far in excess of those that are definitely apprehended, the secret society weaves these latter interests into an aggregate demand upon the individual." The ritual is the means by which the secret society is expanded into a comprehensive totality and unity. Initiates of fraternal orders did not just go to "meetings," they went to a "court, nest, tent, homestead, circle, encampment, pond, forest, conclave, hive, or clan" (Schmidt 1980, p. 9). As an Elk, Mason, Odd Fellow, or Red Man, one was a member of a brotherhood. Fraternal orders served, as Clawson (1985, p. 41) has argued, as *fictive kinship organizations.*

Masons and Odd Fellows made much of the fact that their members lived in troubled and uncertain times. In our analysis of Odd Fellow literature, it was clear that the world was seen as harsh and merciless, full of deception, conflict, and moral depravity. The lodge was portrayed as a sanctuary from this and a force for good in the world. It was a fraternity of brothers in which one could find mutual encouragement, support, and solace. Class divisions did not exist in the moral view of the lodge.

Republican Ideology

People must first be able to think about themselves in conflict with and in opposition to other groups before they can constitute themselves as class subjects. The language of brotherhood, a language that stressed that both capitalist and worker were God's children, limited the potential of workers who were embedded in these centers of respectability to develop as an autonomous class; it even limited their ability to "see" how capitalism operated. Republican ideology, which stressed the equality of all, opportunity, and the wonders of entrepreneurial behavior, dominated nineteenth-century U.S. life, and this language was reinforced within fraternal orders.

That is why we are doubtful that fraternal orders were vehicles for working-class mobilization, even when workers might have been in the numerical majority. Clawson (1989, pp. 100–103) notes that some lodges harbored labor leaders among their members and concludes that the lodge might have provided support for working-class mobilization. This may have characterized Eastern lodges or those in heavily industrialized cities, but it was not the case in Kansas. Furthermore, one must consider that the rhetoric of nineteenth-century labor leaders was more often than not accommodationist and procapitalist—in part, of course, because, to get any kind of hearing in a social climate that stressed a social Darwinist philosophy and condemned anybody who did not subscribe to the myth of capitalist growth and prosperity, one had to speak softly. Consider the comments from some of the representatives of organized labor. The leader of the Order of Railway Conductors of America said that socialism was completely impractical and that the real problem was people's "selfishness." He suggested, as a solution to U.S. labor problems, that convict labor be abolished and foreign immigration stopped, a common suggestion at the time. The national president of the Boilermakers and Iron Ship-Builders of America said that U.S. citizens need not worry about labor organizations because "the true principles of organization are opposed to strikes, and favor the settlement of all grievances by arbitration, using all efforts to create and maintain harmonious relations between labor and legitimate capital," by which he meant nonmonopolies, something most inveighed against (Kansas Bureau of Labor 1895, pp. 185–211).[10]

Individual independence was another linchpin of republican ideology (Ross 1985, p. 3). Of course, it was over the issue of economic independence that much working-class conflict was based, and, in a capitalist economy, there was an inevitable conflict between independence and cooperation. In their publications, both the Masons and Odd Fellows indicate they were aware of the contradictions, but their position in relation to the state and outside world ranged from accommodationist and retreatist (Odd Fellows) to explicit and enthusiastic support for the emerging capitalist order (Masons). This, of course, reflected their different class compositions. In their state magazines, both Odd Fellows and Masons carried articles that portrayed fraternal orders as helping members to adjust to the emerging capitalist order:

The fraternal orders are a national blessing. They promote thrift, economy and sobriety, without freeing the soul to enter into selfishness, as is apt to be the cause in the usual struggle for wealth or high social position. They bring men into closer social relations and cherish those feelings that drive and put forth blossoms in each other's welfare. They make men thoughtful and hopeful, expanding the sentiments of love, charity and good-will (*The Ezel,* June 1888).

Thus, membership in fraternal orders undermined the potential for workers to develop their own organizational capacities because it meant that they were likely to accept and believe in the republican ideals of cooperation and harmony preached by the fraternal order.

In short, where Clawson sees fraternal orders as complex, multiclass organizations, communicating diverse messages, we argue, on the basis of our findings (which may be influenced by locale) that, though their class membership was diverse, their language was not.

Conclusion

Class formation is a process involving three distinct, though related, elements: structural position, ideology or consciousness, and organization. The analysis of these elements was central to our project and our attempt to explain both why working-class men might have joined fraternal organizations and what the results of their joining implied about class formation. We have argued that Kansas laborers, like those elsewhere in the United States, were subject to a process of proletarianization but that, unlike workers elsewhere, there were few, if any, working-class organizations or networks that could provide the solidarity necessary to deal as a class with the changing conditions of work, economic problems, and the lack of political power. Instead, the most common and ubiquitous resource available for forging new bonds of solidarity was the fraternal order. Membership in such orders muted class conflict by embedding workers in personal ties with members of the bourgeoisie, inhibiting class conflict, and directing energy away from the formation of autonomous working-class organizations. Fraternal orders played an important role in promoting and diffusing the emerging capitalist order.

But why would workers join such organizations, rather than trying to create ones that might better serve their interests? The appeal was multifaceted. These organizations, functioning as Simmelian total organizations, created a bond of brotherhood, shielding people from an economically chaotic and harsh society. Fraternal orders offered their members increased financial security, served as labor exchanges, enhanced business opportunities, served as an important source of social prestige, helped provide workers with a sense of community, and promoted in them a vision of society that meshed with the republican ideals of cooperation and a harmony of interest.

Notes

1. Some of these include: the separation of the workplace from home and community (Katznelson 1981), widespread suffrage, high immigration levels, high numbers of immigrant workers, the urban locale of industrialization, large numbers of white-collar workers, the availability of cheap land and widespread property

ownership (Zolberg 1986), the influence of a republican ideology (Ross 1985), the incorporation of workers and worker movements into the political and social mainstream by trade unions and political machines (Shefter 1986), and the hegemony of the U.S. capitalist class (Friedman 1988).

2. Skilled laborers included, among others, craftsmen, bakers, blacksmiths, bookbinders, butchers, carpenters, gas fitters, tailors, and wheelwrights. Unskilled laborers included gardeners, day workers, and common laborers. It is important to mention that class boundaries were "fuzzy" in frontier communities and may have been elsewhere. That is, carpenters and other skilled workers sometimes may have been independent contractors and entrepreneurs, differing little from the owner of a store in structural position or ideology.

3. Dean Smith, in his book *A Nickel a Month,* describes the history of the Security Benefit Life Insurance of Topeka, a large, private insurance company that began in Topeka in 1892 as a fraternal insurance organization called the "Knights and Ladies of Security."

4. Most fraternal orders offered some form of life insurance, but not all could pay the claims. To attract new members, some offered unreasonably generous benefits with disastrous consequences for the lodge. Insurance rates were not based on actuarial tables until much later, though the orders would pioneer in this area (Clawson 1989).

5. This was the magazine of the Kansas Masons, published in Topeka, Kansas.

6. In both orders, the local lodge was responsible for collecting and distributing sick benefits. Life insurance was administered at the state level.

7. This does not mean that most Odd Fellows were farmers, though a substantial number were. Frequently, local merchants or skilled craftsmen also farmed as a way to provide for themselves and their families.

8. It is interesting to speculate as to why the lodges began to lose members in the 1930s. One reason was suggested by the grand secretary of the Odd Fellows in Topeka, Kansas, when he said that "the programs of the New Deal" contributed to the decline.

9. It would be useful, though we have not yet been able to do so, to trace the social mobility of skilled workers and determine to what extent upwardly mobile workers were more likely to be lodge members than those who were not as mobile.

10. The Kansas Bureau of Labor sent questionnaires to leaders of labor, as well as university presidents and other leading citizens, and published the results under a heading entitled "Sociology."

References

Aminzade, Ronald. 1979. "The Transformation of Social Solidarities in Nineteenth-Century Toulouse." In *Consciousness and Class Experience in Nineteenth-Century Europe,* ed. John M. Merriman, pp. 85–105. New York: Holmes and Meier.

Beharrell, T. G. 1881. *Odd Fellows Monitor and Guide.* Indianapolis: Robert Douglass.

Bourdieu, Pierre. 1977. *Outline of a Theory of Practice.* Trans. Richard Nice. Cambridge: Cambridge University Press.

_____. 1984. *Distinction: A Social Critique of the Judgement of Taste.* Trans. Richard Nice. Cambridge: Cambridge University Press.

_____. 1989. "Social Space and Symbolic Power." *Social Theory* 7:14–25.

Clark, Carroll D., and Roy L. Roberts. 1936. *People of Kansas.* Topeka, Kans.: The Kansas State Planning Board.

Clawson, Mary Ann. 1985. "Fraternal Orders and Class Formation in the Nineteenth-Century United States." *Comparative Studies in Society and History* 27:672–95.

_____. 1989. *Constructing Brotherhood: Class, Gender, and Fraternalism.* Princeton, N.J.: Princeton University Press.

Dumenil, Lynn. 1984. *Freemasonry and American Culture: 1880–1930.* Princeton, N.J.: Princeton University Press.

Friedman, Gerald. 1988. "The State and the Making of the Working Class." *Theory and Society* 17:403–30.

Hall, Stuart. 1985. "Signification, Representation, Ideology: Althusser and the Post-Structuralist Debates." *Critical Studies in Mass Communications* 2:91–114.

Hobsbawm, Eric. 1984. *Workers: Worlds of Labor.* New York: Pantheon Books.

Kansas Bureau of Labor. 1895. *Annual Report of the State Board of Agriculture,* vol. 11. Topeka, Kans.: State Printer.

Katznelson, Ira. 1981. *City Trenches.* New York: Pantheon Books.

_____. 1986. "Working-Class Formation: Constructing Cases and Comparisons." In *Working Class Formation,* eds. Ira Katznelson and Aristide R. Zolberg, pp. 3–44. Princeton, N.J.: Princeton University Press.

MacDonell, Diane. 1986. *Theories of Discourse.* New York: Basil Blackwell.

Madden, John Langston. 1968. *The Kansas Economy in Historical Perspective.* Ann Arbor, Mich.: University Microfilms International.

Malin, James C. 1935. "Turnover of Farm Population." *Kansas Historical Quarterly* 4:339–72.

McNall, Scott G. 1988. *The Road to Rebellion: Class Formation and Kansas Populism, 1865–1900.* Chicago: University of Chicago Press.

McNall, Scott G., and James Orr. 1988. "Nineteenth Century Fraternal Organizations: Blocks to Class Formation." Paper presented at the Midwest Sociology meetings in Minneapolis, Minnesota.

Meyer, B. H. 1901. "Fraternal Beneficiary Societies in the United States." *American Journal of Sociology* 6:646–61.

Miller, Raymond Curtis. 1925. "The Background of Populism in Kansas." *Mississippi Valley Historical Review* 11:469–89.

Montgomery, David. 1976. "Labor in the Industrial Era." In *The United States Department of Labor History of the American Worker,* ed. Richard B. Morris, p. 124. Washington, D.C.: United States Government Printing Office.

Nash, Gary B., and Julie Roy Jeffrey. 1986. *The American People: Creating a Nation and a Society.* New York: Harper and Row.

Rosenzweig, Roy. 1977. "Boston Masons, 1900–1935: The Lower Middle Class in a Divided Society." *Journal of Voluntary Action Research* 6:123–24.

Ross, Steven J. 1985. *Workers on the Edge.* New York: Columbia University Press.

Schmidt, Alvin J. 1980. *Fraternal Organizations.* Westport, Conn.: Greenwood Press.

Shaver, William M. 1898. *A Pocket Monitor of Ancient Craft Masonry.* Newton, Kans.: Henry F. Toevs.

Shefter, Martin. 1986. "Trade Unions and Political Machines: The Organization and Disorganization of the American Working Class in the Late Nineteenth Century." In *Working Class Formation,* eds. Ira Katznelson and Aristide R. Zolberg, pp. 197–276. Princeton, N.J.: Princeton University Press.

Sheridan, Richard. 1956. *Economic Development in South Central Kansas: An Economic History: 1500–1900.* Lawrence: University of Kansas.

Simmel, Georg. 1906. "The Sociology of Secrecy and of Secret Societies." *The American Journal of Sociology* 2:441–98.

Smith, Dean L. 1979. *A Nickel a Month.* St. Louis: Mid-America Publishing Co.

Tilly, Charles. 1979. "Did the Cake of Custom Break?" In *Consciousness and Class Experience in Nineteenth-Century Europe,* ed. John M. Merriman, pp. 17–44. New York: Holmes and Meier.

Weber, Max. 1958 [1904]. "The Protestant Sects and the Spirit of Capitalism." In *From Max Weber,* trans. and eds. H. H. Gerth and C. Wright Mills. New York: Oxford University Press.

Wright, Chester. 1941. *Economic History of the United States.* New York: McGraw Hill.

Zolberg, Aristide R. 1986. "How Many Exceptionalisms?" In *Working-Class Formation,* eds. Ira Katznelson and Aristide R. Zolberg, pp. 397–455. Princeton, N.J.: Princeton University Press.

7 | Rural Industrialization: The Shaping of "Class" Relations in Rural Bangladesh

SHELLEY FELDMAN

Central to analyses of agrarian change and processes of rural differentiation in the contemporary Third World are the issues of class formation and class relations. The debate within which these issues are addressed is often grounded in a historical materialism that assumes the transitional nature of the peasantry. This debate also generally assumes that as capital encroaches upon precapitalist forms it subsumes them and transforms extant relations into capitalist relations, thus completing the transformation toward a fully capitalist mode of production (Vergopoulous 1978; Patnaik 1987; Rudra 1988). Alternatively, there is the thesis that the uneven development of capitalism is not captured by the logic of capitalist class relations but is better understood, at least in the contemporary period, by what has come to be called a peasant mode of production (Alavi 1978, 1979; Shanin 1973, 1974). This peasant mode is distinct from the capitalist mode and has been shaped within the particular set of colonial and postcolonial relations characteristic of newly independent, agriculturally dominant social formations. Each of these arguments locates its empirical focus in **agrarian social relations** as distinct from **rural class relations,** although both draw attention to processes of rural differentiation (Mencher 1974; Omvedt 1981).

These analyses of rural differentiation processes are embedded within a nondialectical logic of social change. They assume, for example, that the penetration of capital is direct and from above, an approach that is reminiscent of a view of the peasantry as a set of passive actors having no significant or autonomous engagement in the making of history. In this view, peasants are among those subsumed, without struggle, by processes of capitalist penetration. Such structural interpretations of class formation are undoubtedly correct to note the relative power of capital as a progressive force in history, capable of incorporating forms of production that may have reached their limits of productive capacity. It does not necessarily follow, however, that the peasantry does not struggle for its own interests and generate new forms of accommodation within an increasingly dominant capitalist mode.[1]

This structuralist approach also tends to measure the degree of the capitalization of agriculture in terms of the existence of wage labor or the extent of indebtedness among agricultural producers. The concern with measurement results in a mechanistic interpretation of development outcomes, whereby landholding patterns or the proportion of hired labor on a farm enterprise gauges capitalist penetration within particular economies. Within this approach, class formation is examined as a **consequence** of capitalist penetration rather than as a **dialectical process** of the **social relations** between various forms of production in the creation of a historically specific expression of capitalist articulation.

This chapter explores one aspect of the process of rural class formation in Bangladesh:[2] the development and expansion of the small and cottage industries sector essential in establishing the conditions for rural industrialization and the consequent transformation of relations among rural nonagricultural producers. I will examine the ways in which institutional credit contributes to efforts to transform petty commodity producers into an entrepreneurial class and the contradictory effects of this process on rural producers. The salient role of development assistance in shaping this process, the ideology of entrepreneurship, and the new relations of indebtedness, exploitation, and inequality that are shaping rural life are central themes here.

The chapter is divided into three parts. The first suggests that a number of conceptual issues make a generalized definition of class formation difficult to operationalize. This section of the chapter argues for a historically specific understanding of the term class formation. Section two provides an overview of the political economy of Bangladesh and alerts the reader to the importance of foreign assistance in shaping the processes by which the rural economy is increasingly characterized by patterns of capitalist penetration. Here, attention is focused on the failure to expand agricultural production and generate a climate for industrial growth. This failure to realize economic "take-off" has forced a rethinking of the role of rural industrialization in the process of employment generation where the recent deployment of a rural entrepreneurship strategy has generated new opportunities for rural class formation. The final section of the chapter examines how particular policy reforms shape and are shaped by extant relations in the countryside. What emerges are the contradictory effects of the processes by which the state attempts to distance itself from the responsibility of providing for social reproduction.

What Does Class Formation Mean?

In analysis of the industrialized countries, class formation generally refers to processes of organizing class segments, with varying degrees of revolutionary class consciousness, into a class-for-itself. In these discussions, the class structure is assumed, and explanation is focused on the reasons why class-conscious actions have yet to generate a revolutionary class movement (Wright 1989). Throughout this chapter, the term "class formation" is operationalized in a simpler and what arguably is a dynamically richer sense to mean the generation of conditions that pattern relations of accumulation. Here, class structure is not assumed but is analyzed as it is shaped by noncapitalist forms of production that articulate with patterns of capitalist accumulation and come, in turn, to depend on their insertion within the capitalist mode for their reproduction.

Employing this approach in the analysis of the social construction of a working class in contemporary Bangladesh means that the process of class formation must be problematized and analyzed rather than assumed.[3] The analysis of class formation, in other words, must include an explanation of the pattern of global insertion and dependency that shapes relations of accumulation and the particular configuration of state-class relations as these shape the changing "class" relations.[4] In this context, problematizing class formation includes, but cannot be limited to, the analysis of class consciousness because attention must also focus on forms of class alliances and coalitions, as well as the relations of accumulation and legitimacy that generate conditions for the reproduction of relations of production.

What follows is an elaboration of the structural changes that have molded the political economy of Bangladesh since its independence was declared in 1971. This includes: (1) a summary of the significant changes within the agricultural sector that expand the demand for work in the rural nonfarm labor market, (2) the failure of early rural industrialization strategies to generate employment sufficient to meet the growing labor demand, and (3) the changing demands of debt servicing that have reduced state support for welfare reform and thus generated conditions for a myriad of self-reliance schemes, including the implementation of entrepreneurship programs.

The Political Economy of Bangladesh

Bangladesh traditionally has depended on agricultural exports to meet its financial and trade requirements. In 1973–1974, for example, income earned from agricultural exports, including jute, fisheries, and processed food originating from agriculture, represented approximately 95 percent of total exports. Agriculture also accounted for about 80 percent of total employment. At the same time, agriculture was undercapitalized: The sector received only 10 to 15 percent of total public development expenditure (excluding water and flood control spending), 10 percent of institutionalized bank credit, and 7 to 9 percent of total private investment (de Vylder 1982, p. 29). By 1972–1973, in other words, nonagricultural private investment was already an arena for productive capital. After 1974, jute and leather exports stagnated, and there were only modest increases in tea exports. This decline of traditional exports encouraged efforts to expand nontraditional ones and set the domestic stage for a focus on industrial production (Chr. Michelsen Institute 1988).

These shifts in the structure of agricultural production contributed to pressure on the industrial sector to meet the growing demand for off-farm employment. The growth in rural agricultural underemployment and unemployment corresponded to the declining proportion of agriculturalists engaged as small-scale owner-cultivators: By 1978, the total number of landless households was estimated at approximately 29 percent of the rural population. Including those households that are functionally landless or that own less than one acre increases to almost 80 percent the proportion of the rural population likely to require off-farm employment. This figure excludes members of households owning between 1 and 2.5 acres, who are also likely to seek off-farm work to subsidize reproduction costs, and the small proportion of households with more than 2.5 acres, who supplement agricultural incomes with agricultural wage labor (United Nations Development Program 1988, pp. II–3). Thus, there is a growing demand for off-farm employment among households needing to subsidize subsistence and family reproduction and to diversify investments and earnings.

Unfortunately, the demand for agricultural labor is not anticipated to increase by more than between 200,000 and 300,000 person-years per year, and the number of households likely to secure work as agricultural laborers is expected to decline (United Nations Development Program 1988, p. II). This growing demand on the agricultural labor market has effectively brought the nonfarm rural sector into sharper focus and provoked an increased and more explicit programmatic and policy commitment to the development of nonfarm employment alternatives. Much of this concern is indicated by the initiatives of the donor community that are centered on rural entrepreneurship programs and support for an expanded informal sector (World Bank 1986).

It should be emphasized, however, that agricultural wage labor has never been the sole arena of off-farm employment, nor has the agricultural labor market ever been expected to provide sufficient opportunities for the growing demand placed on it by changing agrarian relations. Even during the early years of the Green Revolution (1961–1971), it was recognized that increased opportunities for off-farm work would be generated by the demand for new inputs, such as irrigation facilities and machinery, as well as by the trade and marketing networks necessary to support an increasingly capitalized agricultural sector. This includes employment in small factories, agro-based industries, machine repair shops, and market and input distribution services.

It is not surprising to find, therefore, that efforts to expand rural employment opportunities began in the 1960s with the establishment of industrial estates. These estates were intended to provide a social and technical infrastructure to support medium-size enterprises, to expand investment opportunities for local entrepreneurs, and to generate employment for the growing numbers of rural unemployed. Despite these intentions, however, the situation twenty years later was not much improved. Most of the estates had only partially been supplied with water, power lines, and roads, and these facilities were insufficient to stimulate capital investment. Moreover, credit facilities and a fully developed domestic market were still lacking. This limited both investment and demand; thus, employment generated by the estates was relatively insignificant (Feldman 1984).

During the 1970s, national policy initiatives to stimulate industrial growth also were only partially successful. Major donor agencies supported credit extension and infrastructural development of both the Ministry of Industries and institutionalized credit institutions to promote increased domestic resource mobilization among small-scale rural entrepreneurs. The Bangladesh Small and Cottage Industries Corporation (BSCIC), for example, began to work with women to increase the type of handicrafts and improve the quality of the goods they produced.

More recently still, the 1980s witnessed a proliferation of semiautonomous and nongovernmental organizations providing credit and training opportunities for nonfarm production activities to village and provincial town entrepreneurs to increase employment and generate a demand for hired labor (Feldman and McCarthy 1984). Although most of these efforts have produced a cadre of self-employed, they have been less successful at substantially increasing the demand for hired labor because a significant portion of the labor used in these enterprises is household labor. That is, given the scale of production and the amount of credit available, entrepreneurship programs have tended to reduce the demand for agricultural and off-farm work by providing credit to those traditionally engaged in cottage industries, rather than generating a significant demand for daily or contract labor. Thus, traditional craftspeople and artisans may now put fewer demands on the agricultural and unskilled rural labor market to subsidize their small production units.

Despite the increasing importance of the nonfarm sector in providing employment to a growing, disenfranchised rural population, the salience of this sector continues to be underestimated in analyses of the rural economy. Such analyses still focus on the agricultural sector, landholding patterns, agricultural labor, and agrarian relations, almost to the exclusion of the contribution of nonfarm activities to rural production relations.[5]

One arena of rural nonfarm production for which some data is available to help illuminate the complexity of the rural economy—and the importance of nonfarm employment in shaping rural class relations—is the small and cottage industries sector (SCI). The range of activities among petty commodity producers in this segment of the labor force is one indication of the diversity within the rural economy. The increasing importance of this sector in generating rural commodities is based on the assumption that the lack of income depresses domestic demand for consumer goods and thus creates a vicious cycle of poverty and economic stagnation.

Support for the development of the small and cottage industries sector is premised on the following SCI attributes: (1) the creation of employment opportunities due to the labor-intensive nature of SCI production, (2) the promotion of entrepreneurship, (3) the expansion of indigenous enterprises through the effective mobilization of local resources, (4) the limited capital investment required to expand productive capacity, (5) the dependence on indigenous technology that can build on and expand local expertise, (6) the contribution of the sector to regional growth, enhancing more equitable regional resource distribution, and (7) the promotion of people's participation in industrial development.

Theoretically, these attributes contribute to lower capital-labor ratios and thus take advantage of the high demand for employment. In addition, commodity production, manufacture, or processing within SCI is premised on the utilization of local resources and is therefore assumed to be a foreign exchange saver to the extent that the production of local goods replaces the need for imports. The SCI sector is also seen as a production arena that can contribute to the generation of foreign exchange through the export of traditional handicrafts and other locally produced items.

Begun in 1957, the Bangladesh Small and Cottage Industries Corporation is the oldest public-sector organization responsible for the development of rural enterprises. Support for sector development in the form of infrastructural facilities (including market, extension, and advisory services, technical assistance, and credit) has been provided by a number of multi- and bilateral development agencies (e.g., World Bank/International Development Agency, U.S. Agency for International Development,

Norway, and Saudi Arabia). The interests of the aid community in sector expansion include its potential to expand domestic production, to generate a domestic market in goods and services, and to contribute to social stability by providing employment to the increasing number of unemployed, assetless people.

The technical infrastructure provided by BSCIC to enhance loan accessibility and the reorganization of the corporation to include extension officers are attempts to diversify its program and increase the participation of even very small producers in the credit scheme. BSCIC officers are also charged with project review and the provision of technical assistance to new and continuing enterprises, as well as outreach and extension to identify new entrepreneurs and product markets for local development. These officers examine the viability of each project, study the appropriateness and need of the requested loan, and recommend projects to bank representatives in efforts to expand the productive capacity of selected goods.[6]

Loans for cottage industries are granted for a maximum of five years, with a one-year grace period followed by monthly installments. Interest is 13 percent, and equity financing has been set at a minimum of 10 percent. Loans average Tk 10,000 (US$333), with a ceiling of Tk 25,000 (US$833). Among the traditional artisans and the newly landless willing to initiate production, the 10 percent equity financing makes program participation difficult. Thus, the very poor are unlikely to benefit from this scheme, although they are part of a growing number who may try to sell their artisan skills or operate small shops with noninstitutionalized credit. Alternatively, they may be a source of cheap labor for small entrepreneurs.

In this context, it is quite clear how differential access to credit helps to shape processes of rural differentiation. Some small producers are able to capitalize their enterprises, hire minimal amounts of wage labor, and expand production. For others, the lack of credit may reduce their competitiveness in the local economy and thus lead to increasing impoverishment. With the growing capitalization of the local economy, those without access to credit may be forced to seek work in a context that has been relatively unsuccessful in generating employment sufficient to meet the growth in demand. Moreover, because labor relations in this sector generally fall outside government and legal protection as far as minimum wage levels, health and safety standards, and overall labor conditions, those able to secure employment are among the least protected workers: They typically find work only as daily laborers, and they are the least likely to organize on their own behalf.

Small-scale entrepreneurs, as distinct from those in the cottage sector, are able to secure better credit terms: an interest rate of 7.6 percent and a maximum investment for machinery set at Tk 2.5 million (US$83,333). Loan security is provided in the form of land and building mortgages with the lending institution, or, if rented land and buildings are used, it is based on an agreement with the landlord to maintain the tenant for at least the term of the loan. Equity participation of at least 20 percent is required, although it has been recently suggested that it be reduced (NORAD 1984). Loans are extended for a maximum of fifteen years, with a grace period of five years. Given the size of equity financing, even if only loosely adhered to, these loans tend to meet the needs and interests of a financially secure segment of the rural and urban petty bourgeoisie. It has been anticipated that support for small-scale industries development will help stimulate rural industrialization, expand employment opportunities, strengthen the domestic producer and consumer market, and better deploy local resources. Unfortunately, the total employment generated by this sector, compared to the demand, has been relatively insignificant.

A survey of the sector reveals that, as of 1978, there were 24,005 small enterprises, compared to 16,331 in 1963. This represents a 47 percent increase or an annual growth rate of 2.8 percent for all industries, excluding the handloom subsector. In 1963, the cottage industries sector had 233,534 units, which increased to 321,743 units (excluding handloom and sericulture) at the end of 1981, for an approximate annual growth rate of 2 percent (BSCIC 1984). Specific information on 305,410 cottage enterprises reveals an average investment ranging from Tk 7,500 (US$250) to Tk 99,500 (US$3,317).

Not surprisingly, significant interregional differences emerge regarding the distribution of enterprises. Dhaka, as the country's capital, has more resources, a technical and social infrastructure to support enterprise development, and a greater number of people with experience in securing institutionalized credit than the national average. Loans to Dhaka-based enterprises are twice as numerous as those for any other district. Chittagong, the country's major port city, and Rangpur, a medium-sized northern town, tie for second and third place and indicate the competitive advantage of urban entrepreneurs in securing credit and capitalizing larger-scale enterprises.[7] These enterprises get additional support from the institutional capacities, including marketing and transport facilities, that are more likely to be found in urban areas. In short, financial subsidies to SCI provide the structural context for the emergence of a highly differentiated industrial sector.

Also of interest in the data available on 305,410 enterprises is their fixed capital investment. The average investment per enterprise was only Tk 15,093 for Dhaka, compared with Tk 15,878 for Chittagong, Tk 68,328 for Patuakhali, and Tk 99,542 for Kushtia. Although the proportion of enterprises funded could be explained by regional differences in population density, the larger investments in less urbanized districts (Patuakhali and Kushtia) are more likely to be explained by the differential control of BSCIC funds by petty bourgeois interests in these areas. That is, local elites who control the political machinery tend to use their personal alliances with BSCIC and bank staff to gain access to additional resources (Jahangir 1979; Rahman 1986). The implementation of this rural entrepreneurship policy, in other words, supports both rural and urban petty bourgeois interests. This segment of the population is often in conflict over the urban resource bias (Lipton 1977; Byres 1981; de Vylder 1982).

Most small industries (we have data for at least 72 percent of them) produce, manufacture, or process food and allied products. Of these, the majority are rice mills, followed by bakeries, flour mills, light engineering works, hosiery mills, and oil mills. The cottage industries sector, on the other hand, is largely represented by textiles, apparel, and leather products, followed by food, beverage, and tobacco products. Overall, 27 percent of the production units are engaged in textile, apparel, and leather products, and 26 percent in food products. These cottage industries also include a significant proportion—22 percent—of units engaged in wood finishing and furniture making.

What is most illuminating in this distribution of industries is the extent to which such enterprises exploit local resources and contribute to and shape the domestic market in goods and services. Most units operate in the "traditional" or agro-based sectors of the economy, have low capital investments, are labor intensive, generally engage family labor, and integrate production and marketing within a single enterprise.

The policy environment that supports the increased availability of credit to cottage and small-scale producers has been an explicit effort to transform these production units into increasingly capitalistic ones, dependent on the development of new labor relations and new relations of indebtedness. The acceptance of new inputs, however, is neither uniform nor evenly disbursed throughout the sector. Rather, the sector is becoming increasingly differentiated between a small capitalized segment of the rural economy and an increasingly indebted segment that is forced to depend on the exploitation of family labor for reproduction.

Both of these enterprise types—those engaged in the slow capitalization of the "firm" in order to expand production and maximize profits and those that operate as small, home-based producing units engaged primarily in providing family subsistence—are integrated within the formal credit matrix in new ways. These ways require that loans be repaid so that, despite differences in productive capacity and management strategy, each enterprise must realize sufficient returns to meet its loan repayment schedule. Such credit relations indicate the ways in which even subsistence producers are integrated within state and international efforts to foster opportunities for capitalist accumulation. And the differentiation within the sector suggests the differential costs diverse segments of the rural community bear in their efforts to provide subsistence or create employment.

This differentiation of the SCI sector and of the rural economy is likely to be underestimated in discussions of rural entrepreneurship. This is because this sector is treated as relatively homogeneous, as are the entrepreneurs that seek and secure credit for enterprise expansion. For example, credit extended to small-scale industries is likely to generate different opportunity structures and demands for labor than credit extended to those engaged in cottage industries. Among small-scale industrialists, the status of entrepreneur reflects the emergence of a class of petty bourgeois rural producers that is increasingly likely to hire labor. For those in cottage industries, small loans to stabilize or initiate production tend to generate indebtedness and increased dependence on purchased machinery, which tie them into a capitalist commodity market and transform the household division of labor. The penetration of capital through increased credit opportunities, in other words, molds the uneven processes of class formation within Bangladesh.

As of the mid-1980s, the small and cottage industries sector was assumed to employ 75 percent of the country's total industrial labor force and contribute 37 percent of the value added in the national economy (BSCIC 1984, p. 8). Employment in the sector was estimated at 322,126 people, 86 percent of whom were production workers engaged in 4,005 small units (BSCIC 1984, p. 4). It was estimated that 916,806 people were employed in the cottage industries sector. Of those employed in the 321,743 units, 715,732 or 78 percent were family laborers and 201,074 were hired workers (BSCIC 1984).[8]

Data available from a NORAD credit scheme to BSCIC provides more specific information on employment creation among 305,410 enterprises (NORAD 1984, p. 14). On average, only 16 percent of those engaged in cottage industry production are hired laborers, although this average masks differences that may emerge by both industry type or size of operation. Available information also masks the kind of hired labor deployed: Is it full-time or part-time? Is it casual or daily labor? A sample of 250 entrepreneurs who received NORAD credit showed that female labor tends to be unpaid family labor, and male labor is more likely to be of a casual kind. Of the small proportion employed on a regular, full-time basis, the majority are males employed by male entrepreneurs.

Different proportions of hired and family labor by district indicate the diverse skills and occupations that characterize regional economies. Rajshahi, for example, is a region known for its silk spinning, reeling, and weaving, and it is the location of numerous small enterprises. Loans to entrepreneurs engaged in these enterprises typically represent production units that depend on female labor for spinning and reeling operations and male labor for silk weaving. Women are considered low-skill production workers who labor in units that employ more than 20 laborers and use imported as well as locally produced machinery, including mechanized weaving machines. In this area, it is not surprising that wage labor provides a larger proportion of the total labor than in other districts. Differences in labor deployment, in other words, is a consequence of the prevalence of particular industry types rather than of specific regional differences in hiring practices.

In the Chittagong Hill Tracts, the high proportion of hired labor likely indicates that BSCIC loans were received by Chittagonian businessmen, who organized small wood and furniture businesses and hardboard, box, newsprint, and other paper-related enterprises. Laborers in the Hill Tracts tend to be male, semiskilled workers hired on yearly contracts. In Tangail and Pabna districts, on the other hand, cotton weaving and knitting of saris and undergarments are the traditional occupations of local dwellers. These operations tend to be organized around family labor, although hired laborers may be employed to supplement efforts.

Cottage enterprises embrace a myriad of labor relations: Family members may be engaged as direct producers, as unpaid family laborers, or as disguised wage laborers. The hiring of labor in these enterprises is similarly complex: Laborers may secure permanent, long-term employment, serve as contract laborers, or be hired as daily workers. Most cottage enterprises rely on the flexibility of hiring labor on a daily or contract basis to perform very specific tasks or in response to short-term demand. Thus, efforts to generate employment through the cottage industries sector is likely to offer workers very limited security.

To the extent that cottage industries operate as home-based production and consumption units dependent on family labor for reproduction, access to credit is likely to place increased demands on family labor to expand production to meet loan repayment schedules. Changes in intrahousehold labor relations and in the household division of labor put particular burdens on women and children to provide unpaid family labor. These burdens arise because women and children do not generally control production decisions or the income earned from the sale of the commodities produced. Moreover, women are subordinated by patriarchal relations embodied in the cultural construction of *purdah*, which limits women's access to other forms of remunerated work. These relations include the household gender division of labor that is premised upon husband and paternal authority, which tends to mask the emergence of relations of exploitation within the cottage industries sector.

Although patriarchal relations did not emerge in response to new forms of dependence on credit and markets, the incorporation of household production within more capital-dependent relations forms intrahousehold and interhousehold relations to local resources. For example, an examination of loan recipients reveals the importance of the relationship between entrepreneurs and those who control community-based resources, including institutional forms of credit. Access to small rather than cottage industry credit means higher interest charges, shorter grace periods, and a lower credit ceiling. And obtaining such credit may depend on access to village elites who control decentralized government offices and serve as gatekeepers to local resources. This differential resource access structures the household division of labor and the differentiation of the industrial sector. It is reflected in the fact that fully 64 percent of all loans fall below Tk 5,000 (US$167) and are distributed among those most likely to depend almost completely on family labor. When hired labor among these producers is sought, it is usually of a casual or temporary kind sufficient to carry out a specific task and, as such, epitomizes the development of the most insecure segment of the labor force. The small industries sector, on the other hand, usually depends on semi-skilled production workers engaged in more permanent employment, although without protective labor rights.

Emerging Class Relations

The tying of different rural commodity producers to institutionalized credit suggests the ways in which national policy reforms financed by international assistance structure processes of class formation. And the structure and implementation of such reforms are contingent upon extant relations of production and exchange. For example, the capitalization of Bangladeshi agriculture significantly increased the number of landless and marginal producers and placed new demands on the rural labor market. Early efforts to expand rural employment, however, were relatively unsuccessful for they depended upon an incipient industrial class and a skilled labor force, both lacking during the Green Revolution. Credit and input subsidies and the expansion of infrastructural support to establish rural industrial estates were, not surprisingly, unable to mobilize existing resources. That is, subsidies carried through a program to foster medium- and large-scale industrial activity and to generate a demand for a full-time wage labor force were unattractive to surplus agricultural producers who could more profitably invest in moneylending and trade. Nor, surprisingly, has this constrained the development of a strong, competitive rural industrialization program, especially one able to create employment for the growing numbers of unemployed and underemployed agricultural laborers. Of investments made in the sector, the majority represent the interests of the rural power brokers who do very little to transform nonagricultural rural production but who derive personal benefit from their ability to appropriate existing local resources for self-aggrandizement.

By the early 1980s, it was apparent that the strategy to mobilize development assistance for capital investment in large-scale enterprises able to incorporate—and create—the rural proletariat had failed. The lesson to be learned was that the conditions necessary to realize an expanding industrial sector were contingent upon structural conditions, which included an incipient bourgeoisie and an available labor force. The colonial experience under the British and then the Pakistanis, followed by a devastating independence war, had left the country without a strong institutional infrastructure and without an entrenched industrial class. This provided an arena for the rural elite to continue to dominate the countryside and the resources allocated to capitalize the agricultural sector. But it did not establish conditions for their transformation, and it limited the extent to which those pushed out of agriculture could be trained and incorporated into the industrial work force. Moreover, the postindependence state of Mujibur Rahman, characterized by the nationalization of the major industrial sectors previously owned by West Pakistani industrialists, was also unable to effectively expand industrial production. A more adequate implementation of this strategy may have produced opportunities that did not emerge with the subsequent regimes of Zia Rahman and General Ershad. This represents an increasingly liberalized economy and a push to remove government subsidies and expand private investment. As a result of these policy swings and their failure to establish an entrenched and coordinated industrial sector and a cadre of skilled laborers, those pushed out of agriculture have sought employment in the informal sector as petty commodity producers or daily laborers in agriculture or industry. And for those traditionally engaged in off-farm production, limited access to credit has constrained their capacity to expand and significantly increase their demand for hired labor.

To the extent that the development discourse has cast the rural economy in terms of agricultural relations, it has masked the needs and demands of nonfarm producers and limited policy initiatives that strengthen their productive interests. For example, only since the early 1980s has it been recognized that the agricultural sector is unlikely to provide employment for the vast majority. It also has been conceded that the 1982 New Industrial Policy, focused on the larger industrial sector and the promotion of exports, will be unable to generate sufficient employment for the creation of an organized working class.[9] These understandings have shifted national development policy toward an exploration of the needs and demands of the SCI sector and the artisan community.

It is not surprising, therefore, that, since the mid-1980s, larger investments have been made for private sector development, including increased credit opportunities and technical assistance to cottage and small-scale producers. Although support for this sector may be said to have begun with investments in the industrial estates, it is only recently that a decentralized approach to credit extension has supported efforts to capitalize the sector. In the 1970s and increasingly in the 1980s, in other words, more explicit attempts were made to mobilize the capital and skills of nonfarm petty commodity producers with subsidized financing. This policy reform, strengthened by the encouragement of international assistance and the reformulation of development policy to privatize all productive sectors, has helped to sustain and diversify a process of capitalist penetration and class formation within the rural economy.

The increased interest in this segment of the rural economy has been developed within an ideology embraced by the concept of entrepreneurship and self-reliance and premised upon the creation of new forms of indebtedness among petty commodity producers and traditional artisans. This entails a reorganization of household production relations and support for family-based enterprises, suggesting the petty-bourgeoisification of petty commodity producers. For a segment of those engaged in the SCI sector, this is, indeed, what is occurring: Small-scale entrepreneurs with access to credit are able to expand production and increase capital investments and the demand for hired labor. This is made possible through the creation of a production environment that is increasingly tied into and dependent upon the market for inputs, sales, and labor.

Very small producers, paralleling those generally considered part of the informal sector and engaged in cottage industries, are also increasingly involved in market and credit exchanges to meet production goals. However, unlike small-scale producers who are likely to expand the demand for hired labor, those engaged in cottage industries are increasingly linked with processes of production that require them to reduce labor costs in order to meet loan repayment schedules. As the majority of these petty commodity producers rely on family labor, reducing the value of one's labor (what is sometimes called processes of self/family exploitation) increasingly characterizes these cottage enterprises. In this context, all household members take on heavier burdens in production, but male members continue to dominate market relations and thus tend to control incomes. The household remains both the production and consumption unit but loses the security once enjoyed by subsistence producers because generational and social reproduction is now dependent on the market (de Janvry and Deere 1979). Moreover, male control of market relations establishes new forms of patriarchal dominance as women continue to be only marginally represented in market exchanges.[10]

Given the conditions of cottage-based production and the processes of indebtedness and reproduction that characterize loan recipients in the BSCIC entrepreneurship program, it may be more apt to argue that such producers operate more like disguised wage laborers than entrepreneurs. The banks, those who control the market, the middlemen who control inputs, and the unpaid family laborers who do not earn enough for either self- or family reproduction increasingly live as a class of rural workers for they control neither the means of production nor, often, the sale of what they produce.

Under these conditions, production is individuated, with some household members forced to secure additional income as daily laborers to maintain family subsistence. Furthermore, labor relations within the household do not provide the contextual basis for worker organization. They do, however, remove the responsibility from the state for developing protective legislation to guarantee rights to debtors and small-scale entrepreneurs and artisans. These relations of individualized family production also tend to hinder the development of worker consciousness, playing as they do on the cultural tradition of the independent agricultural producer transformed into a private, self-reliant entrepreneur. However, as cottage industry entrepreneurs maintain or expand production, they do so as increasingly dependent consumers of credit and technical assistance. In short, they enter the market as debtors.

The concept of the entrepreneur thus embraces the notions of capitalist market and capitalist relations of production, independent manager, organizer, and risk-taker. Such a concept differs markedly from that of the petty commodity producer, who engages in forms of production requiring little or no investment cost and utilizes family labor. A gender division of labor may characterize forms of petty commodity production, including control of the labor process and the general integration of productive and reproductive tasks. But the capitalization of the sector means that forms of individuated, market-dependent production are a significant alteration in the ways in which families and household members ensure their own survival. Unfortunately, to the extent that producers engaged in the sector gain access to credit and become involved in new forms of indebtedness, they do not seem to benefit from the opportunities that capitalist relations provide to an entrepreneurial class. This is because they are unlikely to be able to expand production and therefore come to depend on exploitative wage relations to realize profits. Furthermore, they are typically limited to an expanded use of family labor to meet their credit and investment responsibilities.

Conclusion

Through an explanation of the complex rural economy in Bangladesh and the identification of petty commodity producers, this chapter has examined the way in which national policy reform, with financial support from the international lending community, has helped to structure the transformation of rural production relations. State policies, in concert with the expanded availability of technical resources to rural off-farm producers, have differentiated petty commodity producers into a class of petty bourgeois entrepreneurs and a cadre of indebted artisans and cottage industry producers forced to increasingly rely on forms of self- and family exploitation to maintain reproduction. Though small-scale entrepreneurs will probably increase their use of hired labor, growth in the sector is unlikely to play a significant role in meeting the needs of the rural unemployed. On the other hand, those in this sector are likely to reduce their demand on the agricultural labor market but bear the burden of both increased indebtedness and forms of reproduction that are dependent on nationally based patterns of economic restructuring, fueled by a changing global capitalism.

What do these findings suggest theoretically? First, they underscore the importance of the social construction of the labor force: The development of a class of industrialists and a class of workers is neither a "natural process" nor one that is simply imposed. Rather, it is a contingent process shaped by existing relations of production and dependent upon the establishment of new conditions of existence and policies that structure new forms of resource access and dependence. Class formation in this context is not the identification of the emergence of or constraints upon class consciousness, the transformation of a class-in-itself to a class-for-itself. It is the very process by which class relations emerge.

Theorizing on the rural economy has been constrained by a focus on the agricultural sector. This has inhibited analyses of rural class formation and the historical significance of petty commodity producers in this process. These producers and the forms of commodity production in which they are engaged provide the context for individualized, home-based cottage enterprises. Lastly, as I suggest in this chapter, family labor is important in disguising the process of rural proletarianization, and women are critical actors for the development of cottage-based, capital-dependent production enterprises. Despite the ideology characterizing independent entrepreneurship and self-reliance, credit dependence helps to transform subsistence relations of production to increasingly wage-like labor relations. Thus, it establishes the structural bases for the formation of a working class.

Acknowledgments

Special thanks are due to the editors of this volume and to the participants of the conference on "Bringing Class Back In" for their thoughtful comments. Research for this project was funded by NORAD, and data came from a review of small and cottage industries carried out by the Bangladesh Small and Cottage Industries Corporation (BSCIC 1984), a field study of the Norwegian lending program to the BSCIC (NORAD 1984), and an analysis of loan recipients to explore credit use and loan realization (Feldman and Banu 1985). Additional information came from an analysis of the New Industrial Policy and an examination of female employment generation (Feldman and Banu 1985; Feldman 1984, 1988).

Notes

1. See James Scott 1985, 1986.

2. Here, the distinction between class formation and proletarianization is significant for the latter tends to refer to the transformation of agricultural producers into wage laborers and the term "class formation" captures both agricultural and nonagricultural rural producers.

3. This is distinct from an analysis of processes of class consciousness and the development of a class-for-itself.

4. Quotation marks are used here to indicate that it may be premature to assert the existence of class relations in what might continue to be preclass forms. I am reserving the term "class" to refer particularly to capitalist relations and using "class" to refer to segments of the population that have yet to be defined by a predominantly capitalist character.

5. Underestimating the importance of the nonfarm rural sector in theorizing on rural change and an inadequate data base on this segment of the rural work force are problems that limit a full assessment of this population.

6. There are charges that special interest groups are more likely to receive access to credit and technical assistance than would be expected under competitive grant and loan conditions. Evidence exists to support this contention, but the point of this chapter is not to indicate who gets access to credit but how access reinforces and transforms class relations and spawns new class interests in the countryside.

7. It is noteworthy that this data is premised on participation or registration with the BSCIC rather than on an analysis of the SCI sector as such. By definition, this ignores the myriad of informal or nonregistered operations that are scattered throughout the towns and countryside and along roads and footpaths that link rural villages, providing the market for local production.

8. These figures are extremely sketchy and "guesstimated" at best because the infrastructure to support and maintain adequate monitoring is simply not available.

Moreover, to the extent that a major proportion of these enterprises (particularly those in the cottage sector) are "informal" operations and do not secure institutionalized credit, they are unlikely to be included in such figures.

9. The New Industrial Policy was characterized by trade and tariff reform, the denationalization of public enterprises, and the liberalization of the economy to enhance foreign investment.

10. A rigid gender division of labor is eroding among these lower middle-class rural households, but this division continues to inhibit women's control over income. The point to emphasize here is that, despite changes in these relations, patterns of female seclusion still shape intrahousehold and market relations.

References

Alavi, Hamza. 1978. "Capitalism and Colonial Transformation." Paper presented at the seminar on "Underdevelopment and Subsistence Reproduction in Southeast Asia," University of Bielefeld, Germany, April 21–23.

———. 1979. "The Structure of Colonial Social Formations." Paper prepared for the "Conference on Underdevelopment—An International Comparison," University of Bielefeld, Germany, July 1–7.

Bangladesh Small and Cottage Industries Corporation. 1984. "State of the Art Review on Small and Cottage Industries in Bangladesh" (draft). Dhaka, Bangladesh: BSCIC.

Byres, T. J. 1981. "The New Technology, Class Formation and Class Action in the Indian Countryside." *Journal of Peasant Studies* 8:405–54.

The Christian Michelsen Institute. 1988. *Bangladesh: Country Study and Norwegian Aid Review.* Bergen, Norway: DERAP.

de Janvry, Alain, and Carmen Diana Deere. 1979. "A Conceptual Framework for the Empirical Analysis of Peasants." *American Journal of Agricultural Economics* 61:601–11.

de Vylder, Stefan. 1982. *Agriculture in Chains—Bangladesh: A Case Study in Contradictions and Constraints.* London: Zed Press, Ltd.

Feldman, Shelley. 1984. Field notes from Fulbright Islamic Civilization Research Program, Grant No. 83–006–IC.

———. 1988. "Crises, Islam and Gender in Bangladesh." Paper prepared for "Workshop on Economic Crises, Household Survival Strategies and Women's Work," Cornell University, Ithaca, N.Y., September 2–5.

Feldman, Shelley, and Fazila Banu. 1985. Field notes from "An Evaluation of the NORAD Loan Scheme."

Feldman, Shelley, and Florence E. McCarthy. 1984. *Rural Women and Development in Bangladesh.* Oslo, Norway: Ministry of Development Cooperation.

Jahangir, B. K. 1979. *Differentiation, Polarisation and Confrontation in Rural Bangladesh.* Dacca, Bangladesh: Centre for Social Studies, Dacca University.

Lipton, M. 1977. *Why Poor People Stay Poor: A Study of Urban Bias in World Development.* London: Temple Smith.

Mencher, Joan P. 1974. "Problems in Analysing Rural Class Structure." *Economic and Political Weekly* 9:1495–1503.

NORAD. 1984. *Field Study Concerning Norwegian Financial Assistance to Small and Cottage Industries in Bangladesh.* Dhaka, Bangladesh: NORAD.

Omvedt, Gail. 1981. "Capitalist Agriculture and Rural Classes in India." *Economic and Political Weekly* 16:A-140–A-159.

Patnaik, Utsa. 1987. *Peasant Class Differentiation.* Delhi, India: Oxford University Press.

Rahman, Atiur. 1986. *Peasants and Classes.* London: Zed Press Ltd.

Rudra, Ashok. 1988. "Emerging Class Structure in Indian Agriculture." In *Rural Poverty in South Asia,* eds. T. N. Srinivasan and P. K. Bardhan, pp. 483–500. New York: Columbia University Press.

Scott, James C. 1985. *Weapons of the Weak: Everyday Forms of Peasant Resistance.* New Haven, Conn.: Yale University Press.

———. 1986. "Everyday Forms of Peasant Resistance." *Journal of Peasant Studies* 13:5–35.

Shanin, Teodor. 1973. "The Nature and Logic of the Peasant Economy, I: A Generalization." *Journal of Peasant Studies* 1:63–80.

———. 1974. "The Nature and Logic of the Peasant Economy, II: Policy and Intervention." *Journal of Peasant Studies* 1:186–206.

United Nations Development Program. 1988. *Bangladesh Agriculture: Performance, Resources, Policies and Institutions.* Dhaka, Bangladesh: Bangladesh Agriculture Sector Review.

Vergopoulos, Kostas. 1978. "Capitalism and Peasantry Productivity." *Journal of Peasant Studies* 5:446–65.

World Bank. 1983. *Bangladesh: Selected Issues in Rural Development.* World Bank Report No. 4292-BD.

———. 1986. *Bangladesh: Recent Economic Developments and Medium Term Prospects, Vol. 1: Executive Summary and Main Report.* World Bank Report No. 6049.

Wright, Erik Olin. 1989. "The Conceptual Status of Class Structure in Class Analysis." Paper presented at the conference on "Bringing Class Back In," University of Kansas, Lawrence, Kansas, April 14–15.

8 | The Organization of the Corporate Class Segment of the U.S. Capitalist Class at the Turn of This Century

WILLIAM G. ROY

The United States in the late nineteenth and early twentieth centuries witnessed the creation of a new segment of the capitalist class based on the fusion of financial and industrial capital in large corporations—the corporate class segment. The new segment was not fully determined by economic change, but it acted to create itself as a class with economic, political, social, and ideological aspects. The creation of a new class segment cannot be explained by any inevitable process by which economic consolidation creates social cohesion. Instead, the process of class formation is a historically contingent process, delicately balanced within the dialectic between people making their own history and the circumstances within which they find themselves.

This chapter describes how the fusion of financial and industrial capital structured the new segment's relation to the means of production and how the segment organized itself in pursuit of institutional class hegemony in the context of class conflict. Economically, the corporate form socialized capital throughout the class segment and provided the organizational form for it to dominate the capitalist class. Politically, the segment owed its origins to state actions, especially the ways in which the state shaped the corporation itself and the institutional environment in which corporations operated. Socially, the class segment formed itself as a cohesive class by creating and controlling upper-class organizations.

Theoretically, three strands of Marxist analysis of the internal organization of the capitalist class come into play here: (1) the analysis of segmentation within the capitalist class; (2) the interrelationship of productive and extraproductive aspects of class organization in a reciprocal rather than a deterministic fashion; and (3) an institutional focus, extending the concept of hegemony into the analysis of specific social institutions as sites of class relations. These three cornerstones provide the foundation for an analysis of the organization of the capitalist class at the turn of the century.

After briefly addressing recent literature on social class, I will explain how the corporation altered the relationship of capitalists to the means of production and how the new class segment organized itself politically and socially. In economic, political, and social aspects, the new class segment acted to form itself into a formidable class organization.

Recent Trends in Historical Class Analysis

Segmentation Within the Capitalist Class

Rather than treating the capitalist class as a monolith, both Marxist and non-Marxist writers have increasingly examined its internal segmentation by focusing on a bifurcation of the class after the late nineteenth century. They have generally agreed that the rise of large corporations was the decisive economic development in this nation's history, paralleled only by industry's victory over agriculture in the aftermath of the Civil War. But they have disagreed about the effect of the bifurcation on capitalist power. Non-Marxists argue that the corporation separated ownership and control, essentially dissolving the capitalist class. And as ownership separated from control (Berle and Means 1932), the economic function of the capitalists eroded (Schumpeter 1951), the decline of heredity dissolved the ruling class (Bell 1961), the basis of power shifted from relations of production to relations of authority (Dahrendorf 1959), and a new managerial stratum arose to administer the economy (Chandler 1977). All these authors treat corporations as the dominant economic force, with any persisting entrepreneurial or family capitalism seen as economically and socially marginal. But corporate strength stems from organizational power, not class power. That is, this group of theorists sees no theoretical or empirical differences between large corporations and other large organizations, such as governments, universities, or hospitals.

In contrast, Marxists—at least some of them—have argued that the corporation segmented the capitalist class but did not dissolve it, changing capitalists' relationship to the means of production without severing it. Theorists of finance capital depict the rise of a distinctively new segment, clearly differentiated and visible in the Eastern establishment and Wall Street, sharply contending with other capitalist interests, and parasitically extracting rentier interest from industrial profits (Fitch and Oppenheimer 1970). Others, like Paul Sweezy (1953, 1956) and David Kotz (1978), have adopted Lenin's formulation of a merger between financial and industrial capital. Maurice Zeitlin (1974) has marshalled convincing data as well as logic to demonstrate that there has been no separation of ownership and control—that the owners still control.

Marxists more accurately portray the enduring saliency of class in the twentieth-century United States, but they have too often neglected to specify exactly how different segments are related to the means of production or describe how the organization of the segments differs in specific historical contexts. James O'Connor's (1973) distinction between monopoly, competitive, and state sectors has made substantial gains in this direction. Although vulnerable to the charge that he has abandoned class analysis for "sector" analysis, he does successfully specify regularities of a class nature within his sectors. For example, the competitive sector grows by extracting absolute, rather than relative, surplus value. Michael Soref (1980) argues that the managerialist argument is incorrect because, although corporations are formally separate, they are unified by a network of financial, social, and kinship ties. He shows that finance capitalists— individuals with ties to both financial and industrial concerns—are (1) a "special social type," with more links to exclusive social clubs and the largest companies, and (2) located strategically in economic terms, that is, more likely to hold positions allowing them to coordinate intercorporate activities.

My perspective on intraclass relations is that, at the turn of this century, financial and industrial capital fused two theretofore separate segments. However, the fusion was only partial, bifurcating industrial capital into a new corporate class segment and a continuing entrepreneurial segment that was changed by virtue of a new economic context, by conflict with the new segment, and by the altered nature of class conflict wrought by the new segment's effect on the working class.

Productive and Extraproductive Class Organization

Dissatisfaction with a purely materialist orientation has stimulated renewed interest in the relationship between productive and extraproductive aspects of class structure and class conflict (Roy 1984). Much recent Marxist scholarship has rejected the economic determinist interpretation that treats social classes purely in terms of the abstract relations of production. Instead, a more historically contingent approach draws on the political works of Marx, with attention to extraproductive social and political factors. Classes are treated as historically situated—real people in real situations, not abstract categories. As E. P. Thompson is often quoted, "Class is defined by men as they live their own history, and, in the end, this is its only definition" (Thompson 1963, p. 11). The emphasis is on class struggle as a theory of social change, rather than class structure as social anatomy. The relationship of productive and extraproductive levels is seen as interactive, by which the forces of production not only structure class relations but are transformed by class struggle.

Erik Olin Wright (1978) argues that classes are actively formed in historically constructed social relations within and between classes. Class formation concerns the social links generated directly by the structural development of capitalist society and those constituted by the conscious organization of that class. Class formation consequently affects class capacity, which is the potential basis for the realization of class interests within the class struggle. The relationship between class formation and class structure is reciprocal: Classes cannot be defined outside of class struggle, and part of the struggle is over the process of class formation.

In a similar vein, Adam Przeworski (1977) has argued that the economic determinism of "orthodox" Marxism is attributable more to Karl Kautsky and, in rebuttal, Lenin than to Marx himself. Like Wright, he holds that class struggle concerns conflict over class as well as struggle between classes. Viewed in this light, the lack of a class-conscious working-class movement in the United States is a result of class struggle, not an indication of its absence. His agenda for class conflict is less an effort to explain its presence or absence than an attempt to specify its dynamics and consequences. Rather than conceptualizing class struggle as the conflict over objectively structured class interests, Przeworski maintains that the positions in production are themselves the consequence of class struggles, which are shaped by both productive and extraproductive forces.

My analysis of the corporate class in the United States shows that the emergence of the segment cannot be explained without reference to class conflict at the political level. I reject both the conventional view (Van Hise 1912; Nelson 1959; Porter 1973; Chandler 1977), which identifies the rise of corporate capitalism purely in terms of technological and economic processes of capital concentration, and the views of revisionist historians (Kolko 1963; Weinstein 1968), who see economic concentration as causally prior to corporate political power.

Nonproductive factors, especially state actions, were critical in shaping the new class segment. In the first place, the corporation—the institutional keystone of the new segment—was initially created by the state to serve a public purpose, such as transportation, communication, or education. As such, corporations were held publicly accountable and only gradually treated as private entities (Seavoy 1982; Handlin and Handlin 1945; Horwitz 1985; Hurst 1970). And the holding company that served as the initial vehicle for uniting financial and industrial capital would not have been possible without the Fourteenth Amendment and subsequent court interpretations that extended individual rights to corporations, as well as the New Jersey laws legalizing the holding company. Even the Sherman Anti-Trust Act of 1890 facilitated the penetration of finance into industry. These legal changes were not just the superstructural manifestations of inexorable economic forces pounding a path through time; they were nondeterministic outcomes of a class-based political and ideological struggle set in the context of economic bounds. Secondly, there would have been no national railroad network without national and state government capital assistance, and there would have been no corporate capitalism without the railroads; the private capital market could never have mobilized the necessary capital. The U.S. government provided legal assistance, financial support, and land, not only as right-of-way for tracks but as financial incentive. The relationship was further strengthened by administering railroad finance within institutions created for government finance—the institutions of New York-based investment banking and stock exchange.

Institutions and Class

A third trend in recent Marxian social analysis has been an institutional focus, examining how institutions reproduce class relations and how classes struggle over and within institutions. The state has not been the only area of inquiry; others include: education (Bowles and Gintis 1976; Katz 1971; Spring 1972; Wrigley 1982; Katznelson and Weir 1985; Rubinson 1986), medicine (Navarro 1976), the media (Schiller 1973; Erlich 1974; Ginsberg 1986), social clubs (Domhoff 1967, 1979), religion (Thompson 1963; Wallace 1978), policy formation organizations (Eakins 1966; Domhoff 1979; Weinstein 1968; Ratcliff et al. 1979; Alpert and Markusen 1980), and the family (Laslett 1975; Zaretsky 1976; Sennett 1974; Dunn 1979–1980). Although these various studies adopt different theoretical orientations with different conceptions of class, they share the assumption that social institutions are part of a social-class system. Implicitly or explicitly, they deal with the notion of hegemony (Gramsci 1971). As Carl Boggs (1976) reminds us, hegemony is a variable or historically specific concept, not a statis constant or a relationship of omnipotence. A ruling class is hegemonic to the extent to which social institutions serve to reproduce the social relations defining and benefiting that class.

This brief review of the three dimensions of class analysis forms the context for the following discussion of the emergence of the corporate class segment in the late nineteenth-century United States. The segment is treated in terms of the organization of the capitalist class, and the focus is on social relationships within that class, rather than on interclass relationships. Much of the struggle surrounding the developing segment concerned its emergence: Had its opponents succeeded, the segment would not have developed in the form that it did—and possibly not at all. Ultimately, the creation and reproduction of the segment depended on its ability to successfully shape or penetrate social institutions, especially on the national level. And the reorientation of those institutions from the local to the national level was not only a goal of the segment but critical to its formation. At first, the institutional relationships of the segment contributed cohesiveness to the class (class formation, in Wright's terms). But over time, members of the class increasingly penetrated into institutions that spanned across classes, thereby broadening their hegemony.

The Corporate Class Segment and Production

A class segment is a grouping within a mode of production that has a particular relationship to the means of production and a particular set of interests (Zeitlin et al. 1976). It shares class interests with the rest of its class, especially in conflict with other classes, but holds interests at odds with other segments of its own class. Interclass conflict revolves around the creation of surplus value at the point of production; intraclass conflict stems from different modes of appropriating surplus value and from different forms of capital. The deepest division within the bourgeoisie has historically been between landed property and industrial capital (Marx 1974, p. 174), but capital can take various forms in different historical circumstances.

In the United States, industrialization was initially capitalized from mercantile capital and institutionalized through family holdings and commercial banks. As industrialization proceeded, many family fortunes were diverted from mercantile to industrial pursuits as merchants and their sons capitalized industrial enterprise. Other industrialists capitalized enterprise through commercial banking, much of which was based on mercantile profits. After the Civil War, mercantile capital receded, and industrialization was increasingly capitalized from industrial profits, including both internally generated capital and industrial capital administered by commercial banks. The capitalist class segment based on this form of production can be called the entrepreneurial class segment.

Later, another segment arose based on the institutions of investment financing. Early canals and railroads sparked the creation of investment institutions, including stock exchanges, investment banking houses, and trust companies. Full development of these institutions was stimulated by financing the Union debt during the Civil War. Further railroad development, especially the intercontinentals financed by federal and state government, enabled these institutions to mature. By the 1870s, these basic institutions existed in much the same form as they do today (Chandler 1977). The capital they administered was vast but narrowly circumscribed within a few industries, deepening the unevenness of U.S. development. Despite unprecedented amounts of capital flowing through the system, financiers did not invest in manufacturing but only in transportation and communication. Thus, Wall Street's role in the creation of surplus value did not operate through ownership of the means of production but through its indirect appropriation, primarily via the railroad. During this period, finance capital was not productive capital. This separation was not inherent in finance capital or in the structure of U.S. productive relations; it was due to the specific institutional structure of the political economy and the specific historical origins of U.S. finance capital. Finance capital was institutionalized in the railroad and government.

The railroad was the "first big business" in the United States (Chandler 1965) and is generally credited with setting the mold that shaped the twentieth-century economy. By 1890, it accounted for half of the total capital in the entire nation. But in terms of ownership, financing, and style of operation, it remained apart from the vast majority of industrial enterprises. Although the railroad's contribution to aggregate economic growth, especially through wider and cheaper marketing, has been widely treated (Jenks 1944; Chandler 1965; Cochran and Brewer 1966), the relationship of the railroads to production has been relatively neglected.

The railroad industry formed a segment of the capitalist class that, like the financial community with which it was associated, was dependent on the creation of surplus value in other enterprises. Railroad revenues came from the value appropriated by industrial entrepreneurs and farmers. For manufactured goods and agricultural products, middlemen bridged the market and the point of production. It was these men—jobbers, factors, wholesalers, and the like—who realized the profits for manufacturers. These middlemen, in turn, depended on the purchasing power of U.S. consumers. It was also the middlemen who directly supplied the railroads with revenues. Surplus value—or, in the case of most farmers, direct value—was thus funneled from the realization process to the investment community. This was the source of railroad profits.

The connection between the ultimate and the proximate sources of profit was a long and tortuous route, often revealed only in times of economic collapse. One of the distinctive features of finance capital was the dynamic of the capital market, making possible short-term profits divorced from the creation of surplus value. The "pure" accumulation process, in which value appropriated from workers is realized in the market and then transformed into capital for further accumulation, was altered for the railroad. Capital generated in other pursuits, often existing as speculative paper but also coming from government sources and international investors, was invested into railroad securities, underwriting large-scale construction and providing the opportunity for speculation on a similarly large scale. Once the capital was invested, it became necessary to mobilize revenues to continue operation and secure dividends on stock. If this could not be done by receipts on traffic, the railroad companies could return to the capital market, usually by issuing mortgage bonds with a fixed interest rate and due date. Revenues in the long run were necessary if the investments were to continue to return a profit, but specific railroads could remain solvent without meeting their costs through receipts from traffic, at least in the short run.

The link between revenue and capital was thus severed by socializing capital within the class (Roy and Bonacich 1988). Because ownership was not held by any specific individual but distributed throughout the class (and beyond), any failure to realize a profit through the market could be compensated for by further investment from the class. Just as an individual entrepreneur can use personal funds (surplus value appropriated elsewhere) to sustain an ailing firm, the socialization of investment capital made it possible for railroads to exist without short-term viability. Moreover, the relationship between revenues and solvency came to be mediated by the institutions of finance. A weak railroad could continue operation by issuing bonds or other securities. When these became due, new bonds could be issued to cover the older ones, as long as the dominant financiers gave their blessing (a distinct social relationship in economic garb). By the 1890s, many railroads were carrying first, second, and third mortgage bonds, common and preferred stock, and miscellaneous forms of indebtedness (*Poor's Manual of Railroads,* passim). If investment bankers were willing to market the securities (and recommend them to customers who could buy them with money borrowed on other securities), the railroads could remain solvent. Consequently, railroad companies were often extraordinarily overburdened with debt. Thus, revenues had to be split between operations and interest payments. In the early 1890s, U.S. railroads as important as the Union Pacific allocated almost half their gross revenues to interest payments (Campbell 1938)—half of every dollar a farmer or merchant paid to ship a bushel of wheat or a barrel of nails was forwarded directly to Wall Street. Typically, the wealth so mobilized went right back into the railroads to buy more securities (along with mansions and yachts). And very little of that wealth (only the minute proportion of securities owned by individual manufacturers) was invested in industrial production. The relationship of industrial production to the railroads was almost entirely conducted through market transactions, the shipping of goods. The New York Stock Exchange, *The Wall Street Journal,* investment banks, trust companies, stockbrokers, and the "wire" constituted a world apart from the manufacturer.

During the 1880s, the structure of industry began to change, along with its relationship to the railroad and to the financial community. Centralization and finance capital began to penetrate into the industrial realm. The fusion of finance and industry began in a core of new industries and then spread outward. The new corporate class segment developed cumulatively, each new addition being built on the central core (Roy 1983). This fusion did not occur independently from industry to industry; rather, each industry's transformation was critically affected by the structure of the growing core. By the second decade of the twentieth century, the corporate mode of organization was the institutionalized mode of organizing large-scale industry, the only means by which new enterprise could be created on any significant scale.

The change was less a transformation of the forces of production than of the social relations within the capitalist class, set within changing institutional structures. First came the trust, by which several companies surrendered control of their assets to a group of trustees who managed it for the presumed benefit of all owners while preventing any single owner from destructive competition. Although individual owners lost autonomy, industrialists as a group maintained control, and the capital was socialized under the industrialists' aegis. Thus, the trust did not change the basic structure of capitalist class segments.

Standard Oil, the first trust, was formed in the context of a basically competitive economy. John D. Rockefeller used the industrial supremacy he had achieved with his special relationship to railroad companies to mobilize the other oil entrepreneurs. Stiff competition within the mushrooming industry eroded profits that were vulnerable to any significant fluctuation in production and distribution costs. The disproportionately high transportation costs for the refined oil loomed large in the competitive market. But Standard's railroad rebates enabled the company to lower total costs enough to force smaller companies into Rockefeller's trust (U.S. Bureau of Corporations 1906, 1907). Other early consolidations followed a similar path. (For sugar, see Eichner 1969; for whiskey, Jenks 1944 and U.S. Industrial Commission 1900–1902; for meat packing, Clemen 1923, Yeager 1980, and Corey 1950). In a trust, industrialists maintained control over enterprise. A few were even able to wield influence beyond the industrial sector by gaining seats on the boards of directors of railroads (for example, Philip Armour, the Chicago meatpacker, John Searle, a sugar lawyer, and William Rockefeller, brother of John D.).

The major institutional change precipitating new relations among class segments was the rise of the holding companies, which provided a mechanism for financiers to wrest control from industrialists. By the beginning of the depression in 1893, there were a few industrial securities, but they were not popular. Industrialists did not think in terms of the

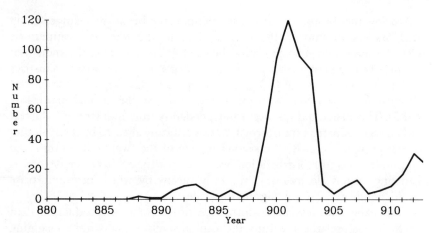

Figure 8.1 Number of Companies Listed on Stock
Exchanges for First Time, 1880–1913
Source: Manual of Statistics

stock market as a ready source of capital, and investors did not trust
industrial securities as a safe investment (Navin and Sears 1955). But
the stage was set for a change, a change that the depression brought to
fruition. The paper empire of the railroads collapsed. Within a year, by
June 1894, a quarter of all railroad capital was in receivership (Campbell
1938), and it soon became obvious that railroads were not necessarily
more secure than manufacturing. In the process, the investing community
gained a new appreciation for industrial securities. So the corporation
became the vehicle for the fusion of industrial and financial capital. After
the depression, industry experienced the largest consolidation movement
in its history. The major corporations that still dominate many critical
industries were formed in the 1890s and the first decade of the new
century.

The transformation of manufacturing capital was explosive, as displayed
in Figure 8.1. Starting from virtually nothing before 1890, the aggregate
amount of capital in publicly traded manufacturing companies rose until
1893, when the depression stalled economic expansion. The value of
common stocks in publicly held industrial firms jumped from $33 million
in 1890 to $210 million the following year. But these figures were small
compared to multi-billion-dollar totals after the turn of the century. By
itself, the food industry common stocks totaled $210 million in 1901.
The most volcanic eruption, at least in absolute terms, began after 1897.
The total common stock of publicly held industrial corporations in 1898
was a little over a half billion dollars. It doubled in 1899 to $1.2 billion,
nearly doubled again the following year, and topped $4 billion in 1903.
It then fluctuated around the $4 billion mark until the outbreak of World

War I (*Manual of Statistics*, passim). These figures confirm the conventional wisdom that the years 1898 to 1903 witnessed a major transformation from one economic system to another. Before that watershed, the stock exchanges served government, transportation, and communication. The large publicly traded corporation, although clearly in private hands, was used primarily to serve functions with a public character. Railroads and telegraph companies not only were functionally part of the infrastructure, they were legally mandated and regulated as common carriers to serve the public interest. Industries, including large firms, were privately held by a few individuals or partners; even Carnegie Steel, the world's largest steel firm, was a limited partnership. The years around the turn of the century marked a new corporate order in manufacturing. The total par value of manufacturing stocks and bonds listed on the major exchanges in 1904 was $6.8 billion, more than half the $11.6 billion book value of all manufacturing capital enumerated in the 1904 census (U.S. Bureau of the Census 1975, p. 684).

The enormous growth of corporations tells only half the story. The large corporation dominated but did not constitute the U.S. economy; rather, the capitalist class had split into two segments, the entrepreneurial class segment and the corporate class segment. The difference between the two lay first and foremost in the nature of the ownership of the means of production, which had ramifications for interclass relations at the point of production, relations with the market, and political and ideological orientations.

In the entrepreneurial class segment, owners directly controlled the means of production on an individual, partnership, or family basis. Capital took the form of personal property; assets were fixed and tangible. The predominant relationship to production was through absolute surplus value. Like the competitive sector of the late twentieth century discussed by James O'Connor (1973), economic growth was achieved by increased labor power, usually through an expanded labor force but sometimes through intensified extraction of value. As the capitalist class split into two groups, the labor force became increasingly segmented, with the entrepreneurial segment drawing primarily from the secondary labor market (Gordon et al. 1982). Wages were lower, turnover was higher, and unionization was less frequent. All of these characteristics, especially the personal nature of ownership, meant that firms in this segment were more vulnerable to swings in the economic cycle. They were more sensitive to changes in the product market than changes in the capital market. When markets collapsed, there were few sources of security. Unless owners had personal fortunes to draw on or unless commercial banks could extend further credit, failure was a very real possibility. Beyond this, personal fortunes were irregularly distributed, and commercial banks were themselves dependent on the same enterprises that needed more credit.

On the other hand, the corporate class segment was characterized by socialization of ownership throughout the segment and use of capital from beyond the segment itself in exchange for atomized bits of legal ownership without control. The segment was the main site of the "Second Industrial Revolution," shifting the mode of expropriation from absolute to relative surplus value. Growth depended more on technological development and enhanced productivity than on expansion of the work force. Meanwhile, this work force was increasingly confined to a specialized labor market—the primary labor market—especially through internal recruitment, and jobs were increasingly stratified in a bureaucratically dictated hierarchy (Jacoby 1985; Edwards 1979). The segment resisted unionization but less fiercely than the entrepreneurial segment had, not because they were any less opposed but because they could more easily assimilate unions due to their higher organic composition of capital. Unionization, in turn, stimulated further technological development. Thus, the corporate segment had higher wages, lower turnover, and more unionization. Because capital was socialized through the segment, there was less vulnerability to the swings of the economic cycle. Short-term profitability could be maintained in the face of market decline. And despite higher fixed costs requiring regular revenue, these firms were less affected by market fluctuations; a collapse in the market could be mitigated by issuing more securities. Taken together, the foregoing differences combined to form a very different set of economic relationships for the two segments and a very different set of objective interests, as well.

Political Origins and Organization

The emerging corporate class segment stimulated and benefited from new political forms. The entrepreneurial segment tended to work through the mode of electoral politics, and the corporate segment, through both electoral and bureaucratic politics (Roy 1981b). The entrepreneurial segment continued the nineteenth-century tradition of the businessman-politician, the responsible leading citizen active in party affairs, electoral campaigns, and, occasionally, public office. The rise of special interest groups was initiated by the corporate class segment (Chandler 1965; Key 1958; Brady 1943), but, after the turn of the century, such groups increasingly characterized the entrepreneurial segment. By the time the two segments were distinctively articulated, the entrepreneurial segment conducted its political activity through lobbying, campaign contributions, and special interest groups. Mobilization took the form of trade associations, trade journals, individual participation in political parties, and general associations (Roy 1981a; Brady 1943). The National Association of Manufacturers (NAM) was typical. Formed in 1896 to stimulate U.S. exports, it soon became an active antiunion organization. Clearly a special interest group, it lobbied, supported candidates, and coordinated the actions of individual businessmen. It functioned as a stereotypical "business politics" organization, as it does today.

In contrast, the corporate class segment operated not only through conventional electoral politics but also through bureaucratic politics. Pioneers in the rise of modern U.S. pluralism through interest groups, the members of the segment found that conventional electoral politics were too expensive and too undependable to assure their interests. The election of 1896, in which the Populist candidate William Jennings Bryan came perilously close to winning, was a sobering experience for big capital, exposing the vulnerability of electoral politics. Learning from the lessons of the Interstate Commerce Commission and the Bureau of Corporations, this group increasingly sought to vest their interests in government bureaucracies, in which the payoff was embedded in administrative procedures and internally reproduced through bureaucratic operation (Roy 1982). Consequently, they more frequently used conventional political means to remove jurisdiction over critical processes from the electoral and parliamentary arena. They continued to mobilize through such devices as trade associations and, more and more, through "public interest" organizations like the National Civil Service Reform League, the National Civic Federation, or the American Association for Labor Legislation (Eakins 1966; Weinstein 1968). Unlike the NAM, these organizations were not special interest organizations but identified their realm as the public interest. Businessmen were joined by labor leaders and representatives of the "public," such as university presidents. They did not lobby but offered consultation, including model legislation. They did not always articulate a "business perspective," but they could be liberal, reflecting a basic ideological contrast between the two segments (Lustig 1982).

Corporate liberalism, a distinctly new political ideology that has dominated most of the twentieth century, emerged as an interpretation of (and at times was directly influenced by) the rise of the corporate class segment (Weinstein 1968; Lustig 1982; Sklar 1988). The meaning of liberalism and conservatism was radically altered. What had been liberal— Smithian laissez-faire economics, the central place of liberty, and the Jeffersonian ideals of individual freedom and democracy—became conservative to the political world and "classical liberalism" to the academic world (Wolfe 1977). The word "liberal" became associated with rationality instead of liberty, government regulation rather than an untamed market, and management rather than leadership. Both ideologies were offered as solutions to problems based in class conflict, and both, if put into operation as desired by their proponents, would achieve solutions beneficial not only to the capitalist class as a whole but to their particular segment, as well.

Class Organization

Class structure necessarily includes cultural orientation and organization, not only as a consequence of economic relations but also as a force affecting these relations. The members of the entrepreneurial segment were organized on a local level and were typically members of organizations like the Masons, Elks, and other fraternal clubs. They were likely to attend middle- or upper-middle-class churches (Congregational or Presbyterian, for example), although many toward the lower end were Methodists and others at the upper end, Episcopalians. Few were Catholics or Jews. The local political party—usually Republican—served both as a means of furthering their interests at the state house and to draw the segment into a more cohesive group. In sum, many were the cream of the local elites in towns across the United States.

The corporate class segment, on the other hand, was organized locally *and* nationally. Members were more likely to reside in large cities, where they belonged to such high-status clubs as the Union League or the Century Club, which arose with the segment after the Civil War. By the end of the century, these clubs were joined into a national network through interlocking memberships between cities (Baltzell 1964). Starting in the 1880s, the members were sending their children to nationally recognized schools like Groton (founded in 1884), St. Paul's, and others, then on to the traditional Ivy League colleges. A formal system of prestige recognition also developed with the advent of social registers and blue books (started in the 1880s) and debutante balls, which solidified the network of intermarriage. All of these socially elite organizations not only developed cohesion within the class but separated the social elite from the rest of society. It is significant that this national elite, with the corporate class segment at its core, did not develop until the final decades of the nineteenth century. It was not an elite that the segment penetrated, but an elite that was created concomitantly with the segment and that actually helped to develop that segment. A brief look at the lives of two businessmen, one a small manufacturer, the other associated with both finance capital and major corporations, will illustrate the contrast.

Joseph E. French was a leading shoe manufacturer and member of the firm of French, Shriner and Urner, a medium-sized Massachusetts business. Born in the Bay State in 1838, he attended public schools but not college, going straight to work at an early age. He learned the shoe trade and quickly worked his way up to foreman and general manager. His first business venture was a partnership, French and Hall, that lasted until the elder partner retired. Then French joined in the founding of French, Shriner and Urner, first as a partner and then, when it incorporated in 1893, as vice president and director. He later founded J. F. French Company of Rockland, Massachusetts. Like most businessmen of the period, he was active in local civic and religious affairs, joining the Rockland Commercial Club and serving as a trustee of the Rockland Savings Bank. He was also a deacon of the First Baptist Church (McDermott 1918).

Robert L. Belknap was not one of the more renowned business figures of the day, but he was typical of the breed of rising corporate officials. Born in 1848 in an old U.S. family, he held positions of responsibility in nine firms in six industries over his lifetime. He attended preparatory schools before entering Columbia University, where he graduated in 1869. From his first job in a mercantile firm, he rose quickly to prominence. At the age of thirty-one, he was elected treasurer of the Northern Pacific Railroad, later serving as officer or director in public utilities, banking, real estate trust companies, and others. Socially, he was active as a trustee in hospitals, the American Bible Society, and the Presbyterian church. He was a member of "preservation" societies like the Sons of the Revolution, honorary societies, and elite social clubs, including the Union League and several yachting and riding clubs. He was also a Republican (*National Cyclopedia of American Biography* 1893). Unlike French, Belknap's world was not confined to one region. Although a lifelong resident of New York City, he was president of companies in Minnesota (where he also belonged to elite social clubs), Indianapolis, and Washington, D.C.

Both these men experienced intragenerational mobility but in very different forms. French's mobility was from one small business to another, but Belknap moved not only up the ladder within organizations but from small to larger organizations. Both were affiliated with banking, but French's ties were with local commercial banking and Belknap's with financial institutions serving a national clientele. French belonged to social clubs that included other local notables; Belknap belonged to clubs in several cities, each of which included both local and nonlocal members, tying together a burgeoning national network. Thus, their class situations far transcended their relations to the means of production.

Class Formation and Social Affiliations

Throughout the last quarter of the nineteenth century and into the twentieth, corporate capitalists increasingly formed organizations, created linkages among colleagues, and acted collectively on behalf of their common interests. Their organization as a class segment not only resulted from their domination of industry but also facilitated their movement *into* industry. By the turn of the century, when finance capital entered the industrial arena, the capitalists were already organized nationally and utilized their national economic, political, and ideological organizational bases to overcome the resistance from populist, working-class, and anti-monopoly movements. The social and cultural apparatus of the new segment was being constructed before the proliferation of industrial corporations. A brief look at social clubs, religious organizations, educational affiliations, philanthropic activity, high-culture involvement, and preservationist commitments illustrates how the corporate segment organized itself socially. At least in the period before 1905, corporate capitalists selected organizational affiliations that facilitated class formation rather than activities that exercised class rule.

The most important organizations of the manifestly social aspects of class formation were the men's clubs (including country clubs, athletic clubs, or riding clubs) and the elite clubs (including such exclusive urban men's clubs as the Union League and Century Club in New York, the Pacific Union in San Francisco, and the Duquesne Club in Pittsburgh). Most major cities had at least one such club. Also important was identification of upper-class status via listings in the *Social Register,* the *Blue Book,* etc.

E. Digby Baltzell (1964) notes that country clubs started in the early 1880s and quickly spread from city to city. A few of the elite clubs started earlier (the Union Leagues, for example, were founded during the Civil War), but most were organized in the 1870s and 1880s, when they became a common feature of large U.S. cities. Baltzell further notes that "British and American gentlemen, especially after the urban bourgeoisie replaced the provincial aristocracy, soon realized that the club was an ideal instrument for the gentlemanly control of social, political, and economic power" (Baltzell 1964, p. 136). It was here that successful men could gather in a congenial atmosphere, free from the pressure of daily tasks and the fetters of public gaze. The first *Social Register* was published in 1887, and, by the turn of the century, it was published in most major cities. It was important primarily as an instrument of national integration. Local high society did not need formal and published designation of social acceptability, but as upper-class individuals traveled across the nation, reliable certification of status was valuable.

F. L. Allen, in writing about leading businessmen at the turn of the century, noted, "One of the most striking things about this group of men—and one of the things in which they were representative of their financial generation—was their piety" (Allen 1966, p. 87). For the United

States as a whole, the 1890s witnessed a religious revitalization, paralleled only by the 1830s and perhaps the 1970s. Evangelism swept the cities and the campuses, accompanied by an upsurge of missionary spirit, symbolized by John R. Mott's "Evangelization of the World in Our Generation" movement for the young and Walter Rauschenbusch's "Social Gospel" for the progressives. But despite the general growth of religion, corporate capitalists as a whole were joining fewer religious organizations (Roy 1984). At the same time, religion seemed to be shifting from a period of intraclass cohesion to one in which interclass relations dominated. U.S. mainstream Christian churches, with generous upper-class support, focused their attention on the lower classes. Both the evangelical movement and the social gospel were means by which the privileged sought to alleviate the spiritual and material poverty of the less fortunate. For example, the elite Episcopal church was one of the first to support what would become known as the "social gospel," by founding the Association for the Advancement of the Interests of Labor in 1887.

The capitalist class did not reach out to others through religion merely because they were pious or because religion was indelibly embodied in the U.S. mind. As Herbert Gutman points out, labor leaders before the turn of the century often adopted religious imagery and appealed to workers' religious sentiments. With the exception of Daniel DeLeon and Samuel Gompers, unionists, including many radicals, "shared a common faith in a just God, effused perfectionist doctrine, and warned of divine retribution against continuing injustice" (Gutman 1977, p. 97). Christianity condemned greed and justified resistance against an individualistic and capitalist social order. Thus, religion became a site of class conflict. The social gospel and evangelism could fight fire with fire. The social gospel provided justification for the rising industrial order and shared a strong affinity with the developing corporate liberal ideology. As Ernest May puts it, "The Christian social movement . . . owed its existence more to the impact of labor conflict than any other single cause" (May 1949, p. 111). After the turn of the century, the religious imagery dropped out of union symbolism. The evangelical movement receded, but the social gospel continued through much of the progressive era.

Education was an institution that facilitated both intraclass cohesion and interclass domination. During the years surrounding the turn of the century, the structure of education changed substantially as it became more stratified by class. Schools were being founded for upper-class youth, nationally consolidating class socialization at a small number of Eastern boarding schools; J. P. Morgan, for example, helped found Groton and served on its board for many years. Such schools socialized new members into the class, facilitated intermarriage within the class, and thus enhanced class formation and reproduction.

While religion and education had both inter- and intraclass aspects, charity and hospital institutions were solely interclass. The conventional view highlights business's growing concern with such philanthropic activities, but some evidence challenges this view. The conventional wisdom is that, after a period of unbridled business abuses, a new breed of responsible business statesmen arose: The wealthy found a conscience. John D. Rockefeller gave dimes to people on the street and millions to medical and charitable concerns. Andrew Carnegie donated libraries and concert halls while preaching his gospel of wealth that any man who died rich died disgraced. Pragmatism coincided with generosity for his class was having a knotty problem with the working class at the time. As Carnegie put it, "The problem of our age is the proper administration of wealth, so that the ties of brotherhood may still bind together the rich and poor in harmonious relationship" (cited in Kirkland 1964, p. 147). Or, as Edward Kirkland (1964) labeled the motive for the new enthusiasm for charity, "Don't shoot the millionaire." Although debate has centered on whether philanthropy was genuinely altruistic or strategic, some have questioned whether corporate capitalists were any more charitable than earlier generations of the wealthy. Ferdinand Lundberg (1937) argues that the percentage of wealth given to the needy declined with the rise of plutocracy, that the concentration of wealth outstripped giving. Certainly, some major businessmen *did* become actively involved in charitable and philanthropic endeavors, but classic bourgeoisie culture had always encouraged generosity. My collective biography revealed that the personal involvement of corporate officials in charitable and hospital organizations was no greater in 1905 than in 1886 (Roy 1984).[1]

Institutions of symbolic representation both facilitated intraclass cohesion and interclass superiority. High culture, such as art, music, literature, drama, and fine architecture, represented the superiority of the capitalist class in contrast to working-class culture or low art. It also effectively dispelled the popular image of the crass, cigar-chomping robber baron and projected the capitalist as a better social type. High culture was "high" because of its association with "better" people; at the same time, it made those associated with it seem "better" as well (Cochran 1972; DiMaggio 1982).

Preservation organizations, which conserved family and cultural heritage, included historical and genealogical societies, public libraries, and scientific institutes. Beginning in the 1880s, they quickly proliferated, especially genealogical and historical associations like the Sons of the Revolution (1883), Colonial Dames (1890), the Daughters of the American Revolution (1890), and the Holy Roman Empire in the Colonies of America (1892) (Baltzell 1964). In the late 1880s, only religion and education groups surpassed these in terms of business' memberships (Roy

1984). Preservation organizations enhanced class cohesion by creating a common, white Anglo-Saxon identity, sharpening the distinction between their members and lower-class (especially immigrant) groups. The associations were still popular after the turn of the century, but the fad was passing.

Looking at the total pattern of organizational affiliations of corporate officials in that era, it appears that the emerging corporate class segment embraced the strategy of class cohesion over class domination. Elite clubs were founded and attracted members from all parts of the country, as their rates of membership climbed rapidly. Meanwhile, institutions that both achieved intraclass cohesion and spanned classes generally declined. Institutions bridging the classes showed stable rates of membership; in those symbolic of class eliteness, rates fell. Socially, this was a period of class formation rather than class co-optation or control (Roy 1984).

Class formation took precedence over class rule not only because cohesion "logically" precedes dominance but also because class conflict, especially intrasegment conflict, made the very existence of the segment a contentious issue. The entrepreneurial class segment, especially the businessmen who were being driven out of business, wanted to do more than regulate the corporations; they wanted to break them up. A major component of the antitrust movement threatened to "bust" all the trusts. It would be incorrect to say that class conflict "caused" such class formation, but the process cannot be explained without considering the dynamics of conflict. Class formation and the concomitant institution building was thus a critical part of conflict over class formation; class formation was a critical part of conflict between class segments and ultimately, of course, of conflict between classes.

Conclusion

In addressing the issue of the organization of the U.S. capitalist class in the late nineteenth and early twentieth centuries, the point of departure here has been three-fold: a historical treatment of capitalist class segmentation, a reciprocal orientation toward the productive and extra-productive aspects of social class, and an institutional focus, concentrating on the formal affiliations held by corporate officials in social organizations.

The bifurcation of the capitalist class into the corporate and the entrepreneurial class segments has been one of the critical episodes of U.S. history, perhaps paralleled only by the consolidation of landed power following the American Revolution and the entrepreneurial segment's ascendance after the Civil War. Industrial capital split into two segments, one wedded to financial capital and institutionalized through the large corporation, the other more closely tied to commercial and local banking capital, maintaining the predominance of personal ownership. Contrary to the managerial perspective, the rise of the corporation did not change the fundamental relations of capitalist production. But it did have profound effects on the internal organization of the capitalist class, which was split into two interdependent but often hostile segments. The essence of capital was not obviated, but its structure was transformed. A new structure of ownership was erected, starting with the railroad companies, in which financial institutions provided an organizational framework for socializing ownership (unevenly distributed) through the new segment of the capitalist class while using the formal apparatus of ownership (corporate stock) to mobilize capital from outside the segment and redistribute it within. The institutions of finance capital, administering the capital affairs of the railroad companies, coexisted uneasily with U.S. industry until the 1890s' depression provided a motivation and an opportunity for such capital to penetrate industry and for strategically situated industrialists to tap the immense capital wealth expropriated by the railroads. The ensuing process was one of fortunes and failures, robber barons and impoverished industrialists, consolidation and conflict. These events cannot be explained, however, in purely economic terms.

The emerging class segment organized itself, enhancing its ability to act politically and preserve its gains while warding off attempts to dismantle the new structures. The segment developed the capability to contend on the economic, political, and social front against labor, agrarian, and entrepreneurial attempts to recreate the old order or at least prevent further encroachment.

The changing capacities for politicization parallel the changing structure of the state. The centralization of power during the Civil War and the ensuing elimination of Southern planters from the polity created a more fertile political field for subsequent events. The federal government planted the seeds for the growth of finance capital by marketing its own bonds and by financing and providing land grants to the transcontinental railroads. After the turn of the century, federal executives gradually gained the decisive edge within the state as a bureaucratic mode of politics undermined the electoral mode, centralizing the state even further and thereby benefiting concentrated economic organizations.

Socially, the new corporate class segment formed itself as a class by creating upper-class organizations. They were building an internally cohesive structure, bounded from the rest of society. The new organizations not only sustained the honor and legitimation of upper-class prestige but provided a framework for class reproduction that was consonant with the changing structure of ownership in the corporation. The new corporate capitalist departed from the traditional bourgeois model of businessman as civic and community leader, at least for the first generation. At the same time, this group created new organizations (like the urban men's clubs that underlay the emergence of the national upper class), institutions of formal class recognition (like the *Social Register*), and institutions that contributed to class reproduction and socialization (like elite prep schools). They thus formed themselves into a national social elite, whose economic base was the corporate class segment.

Three lessons can be drawn: (1) The transformation of the late nineteenth century often described in such economic terms as "the great merger movement," "the rise of big business," "the corporate revolution," or "the rise of modern business enterprise" cannot be explained in purely economic terms; although technological change, economic cycles, and economies of scale were necessary factors, the political, social, cultural, and, especially, institutional factors must be taken into account; (2) although the structure of the capitalist class was transformed, the fundamental dynamics of capital accumulation remained intact; the capitalist class was bifurcated but not liquidated; and (3) the capitalist class, as well as the working class, undertakes the activities of class formation; its members pursue their interests as they interpret them to construct institutions that embody class structure, and they, too, act under circumstances not entirely of their own choosing to make their own history.

Acknowledgments

The research for this chapter was supported by the National Science Foundation and the Academic Senate of the University of California. It has benefited from the helpful comments of Scott McNall, Charles Perrow, and Rachel Parker.

Notes

1. This does not necessarily indicate any conclusions about the actual degree of commitment or even the amount of giving because two factors must be considered. In the first place, there was much individual charity, and most charity was personal rather than organizational. Even John D. Rockefeller was not affiliated with many charitable organizations throughout most of this period and did not establish his foundation until 1911. Secondly, these data do not include charitable work by the women of the class, which was and continues to be an important activity. Nonetheless, the collective biography adds no support to any notion of increased charitability.

References

Allen, Frederick L. 1966. *The Lords of Creation.* Chicago: Quadrangle.
Alpert, Irvine, and Ann Markusen. 1980. "The Professional Production of Policy, Ideology, and Plans: Brookings and Resources for the Future." *Insurgent Sociologist* 9:94–106.

Baltzell, E. Digby. 1964. *The Protestant Establishment: Aristocracy and Caste in America*. New York: Random House.

Bell, Daniel. 1961. *The End of Ideology*. New York: Collier-Macmillan.

Berle, Adolf A., and Gardiner C. Means. 1932. *The Modern Corporation and Private Property*. New York: Macmillan.

Boggs, Carl. 1976. *Gramsci's Marxism*. London: Pluto Press.

Bowles, Samuel, and Herbert Gintis. 1976. *Schooling in Capitalist America*. New York: Basic Books.

Brady, Robert A. 1943. *Business as a System of Power*. New York: Columbia University Press.

Campbell, E. G. 1938. *The Reorganization of the American Railroad System, 1893–1900*. New York: Columbia University Press.

Chandler, Alfred D., Jr. 1977. *The Visible Hand: The Managerial Revolution in American Business*. Cambridge: Belknap.

Chandler, Alfred D., Jr., ed. 1965. *The Railroads: The Nation's First Big Business*. New York: Harcourt, Brace and World.

Clemen, Rudolf. 1923. *The American Livestock and Meat Industry*. New York: Ronald Press.

Cochran, Thomas C. 1972. *Business in American History*. New York: McGraw-Hill.

Cochran, Thomas C., and Thomas B. Brewer, eds. 1966. *Views of American Economic Growth: Volume 2: The Industrial Era*. New York: McGraw-Hill.

Corey, Lewis. 1950. *Meat and Men: A Study of Monopoly, Unionism, and Food Policy*. New York: Viking Press.

Dahrendorf, Ralf. 1959. *Class and Class Conflict in Industrial Society*. Palo Alto, Calif.: Stanford University Press.

DiMaggio, Paul. 1982. "Cultural Entrepreneurship in Nineteenth-Century Boston: The Creation of an Organizational Base for High Culture in America." *Media, Culture, and Society* 4:33–50.

Domhoff, G. William. 1967. *Who Rules America?* Englewood Cliffs, N.J.: Prentice-Hall.

———. 1979. *The Powers That Be: Processes of Ruling Class Domination in America*. New York: Vintage.

Dunn, Marvin. 1979–1980. "The Family Office as a Coordinating Mechanism with the Ruling Class." *Insurgent Sociologist* 9:3–23.

Eakins, David. 1966. "The Development of Corporate Liberal Policy Research in the United States, 1885–1965." Ph.D. dissertation, University of Wisconsin, Madison.

Edwards, Richard. 1979. *Contested Terrain: The Transformation of the Workplace in the Twentieth Century*. New York: Basic Books.

Eichner, Alfred S. 1969. *The Emergence of Oligopoly: Sugar Refining as a Case Study*. Baltimore: Johns Hopkins University Press.

Erlich, Howard. 1974. "The Politics of News Media Control." *Insurgent Sociologist* 4:31–44.

Fitch, Robert, and Mary Oppenheimer. 1970. "Who Rules the Corporations?" *Socialist Revolution*, vol. 1, no. 1, pp. 73–107; no. 5, pp. 16–114; no. 6, pp. 33–94.

Ginsberg, Benjamin. 1986. *The Captive Public: How Mass Opinion Promotes State Power.* New York: Basic Books.

Gordon, David, Richard Edwards, and Michael Reich. 1982. *Segmented Work, Divided Workers: The Historical Transformation of Labor in the United States.* Cambridge: Cambridge University Press.

Gramsci, Antonio. 1971. *Selections from the Prison Notebooks.* New York: International Publishers.

Gutman, Herbert G. 1977. *The Black Family in Slavery and Freedom, 1750–1925.* New York: Vintage.

Handlin, Oscar, and Mary F. Handlin. 1945. "The Origins of the American Business Corporation." *Journal of Economic History* 5:1–23.

Horwitz, Morton J. 1985. "Santa Clara Revisited: The Development of Corporate Theory." *West Virginia Law Review* 88:173–224.

Hurst, J. E. 1970. *The Legitimacy of the Business Corporation in the Law of the United States, 1780–1970.* Charlottesville, Va.: University of Virginia Press.

Jacoby, Sanford M. 1985. *Employing Bureaucracy: Managers, Unions, and the Transformation of Work in American Industry, 1900–1945.* New York: Columbia University Press.

Jenks, Jeremiah W. 1889. "The Development of Whiskey Trust." *Political Science Quarterly* 4:296–319.

Jenks, Leland H. 1944. "Railroads as an Economic Force in American Development." *The Journal of Economic History* 4:1–20.

———. 1968. *The Irony of Early School Reform.* Boston: Beacon Press.

Katz, Michael B. 1971. *Class, Bureaucracy and Schools: The Illusion of Educational Change in America.* New York: Praeger.

Katznelson, Ira, and Margaret Weir. 1985. *Schooling for All: Class, Race and the Decline of the Democratic Ideal.* New York: Basic Books.

Key, V. O. 1958. *Politics, Parties and Pressure Groups.* New York: Cromwell.

Kirkland, Edward C. 1964. *Dream and Thought in the Business Community, 1860–1890.* Chicago: Quadrangle.

Kolko, Gabriel. 1963. *The Triumph of Conservatism: A Reinterpretation of American History, 1900–1916.* Chicago: Quadrangle.

Kotz, David M. 1978. *Bank Control of Large Corporations in the United States.* Berkeley: University of California Press.

Laslett, Barbara. 1975. "Household Structure on an American Frontier: Los Angeles, California, 1850." *American Journal of Sociology* 81:109–28.

Lundberg, Ferdinand. 1937. *America's Sixty Families.* New York: The Vanguard Press.

Lustig, R. Jeffrey. 1982. *Corporate Liberalism: The Origins of Modern American Political Theory, 1890–1920.* Berkeley: University of California Press.

Manual of Statistics. passim. Various publishers.

Marx, Karl. 1974. "The Eighteenth Brumaire of Louis Bonaparte." In *Political Writings Vol. 2: Surveys From Exile,* ed. David Fernbach, pp. 143–249. New York: Vintage.

May, Ernest. 1949. *Protestant Churches and Industrial America.* New York: Harper and Bros.

McDermott, Charles H. 1918. *A History of the Shoe and Leather Industries of the United States*. Boston: John W. Denehy and Co.

Navarro, Vicente. 1976. *Medicine Under Capitalism*. New York: Prodist.

Navin, Thomas R., and Marian V. Sears. 1955. "The Rise of a Market for Industrial Securities, 1887–1902." *Business History Review* 29:105–38.

Nelson, Ralph L. 1959. *Merger Movements in American Industry, 1895–1956*. Princeton, N.J.: Princeton University Press.

O'Connor, James. 1973. *The Fiscal Crisis of the State*. New York: St. Martin's Press.

Poor's Manual of Railroads. passim. New York: H. V. and H. W. Poor.

Porter, Glenn. 1973. *The Rise of Big Business, 1860–1910*. Arlington Heights, Ill.: AHM.

Przeworski, Adam. 1977. "From Proletariat into Class: The Process of Class Formation from Karl Kautsky's 'The Class Struggle' to Recent Controversies." *Politics and Society* 7:343–402.

Ratcliff, Richard, Mary E. Gallagher, and Kathryn S. Ratcliff. 1979. "The Civic Involvement of Bankers: An Analysis of the Influence of Economic Power and Social Prominence in the Command of Civic Policy Positions." *Social Problems* 26:208–23.

Roy, William G. 1981a. "The Vesting of Interests and the Determinants of Political Power: Size, Network Structure, and Mobilization of American Industries, 1886–1905." *American Journal of Sociology* 86:1287–1310.

——— . 1981b. "From Electoral to Bureaucratic Politics: Class Conflict and the Financial-Industrial Class Segment in the United States, 1886–1905." In *Political Power and Social Theory*, vol. 2, ed. Maurice Zeitlin, pp. 173–202. Greenwich, Conn.: JAI Press.

——— . 1982. "The Politics of Bureaucratization and the U.S. Bureau of Corporations." *Journal of Political and Military Sociology* 10:183–99.

——— . 1983. "The Unfolding of the Interlocking Directorate Structure of the United States." *American Sociological Review* 48:248–56.

——— . 1984. "Institutional Governance and Social Cohesion: The Internal Organization of the American Capitalist Class, 1886–1905." In *Research in Social Stratification and Social Mobility*, eds. Robert V. Robinson and Donald Treiman, pp. 147–71. Greenwich, Conn.: JAI Press.

Roy, William G., and Philip Bonacich. 1988. "Interlocking Directorates and Communities of Interest Among American Railroad Companies." *American Sociological Review* 53:368–79.

Rubinson, Richard. 1986. "Class Formation, Politics, and Institutions: Schooling in the United States." *American Journal of Sociology* 92:519–48.

Schiller, Herbert. 1973. *The Mind Managers*. Boston: Beacon Press.

Schumpeter, Joseph. 1951. *Imperialism and Social Classes*. New York: Augustus M. Kelley.

Seavoy, Ronald E. 1982. *The Origins of the American Business Corporation, 1784–1855: Broadening the Concept of Public Service During Industrialization*. Westport, Conn.: Greenwood Press.

Sennett, Richard. 1974. *The Fall of Public Man*. New York: Vintage.

Sklar, Martin. 1988. *The Corporate Reconstruction of American Capitalism, 1890–1916: The Market, the Law, and Politics.* Cambridge: Cambridge University Press.

Soref, Michael. 1980. "The Finance Capitalists." In *Classes, Class Conflict and the State,* ed. Maurice Zeitlin, pp. 62–82. Cambridge: Winthrop.

Spring, Joel. 1972. *Education and the Rise of the Corporate State.* Boston: Beacon Press.

Sweezy, Paul. 1953. *The Present as History.* New York: Monthly Review Press.

———. 1956. *The Theory of Capitalist Development.* New York: Monthly Review Press.

Thompson, E. P. 1963. *The Making of the English Working Class.* New York: Vintage.

U.S. Bureau of Corporations. 1906. *Report of the Commissioner of Corporations on the Transportation of Petroleum, Vol. 1.* Washington, D.C.: U.S. Government Printing Office.

———. 1907. *Report of the Commissioner of Corporations on the Transportation of Petroleum, Vol. 2.* Washington, D.C.: U.S. Government Printing Office.

U.S. Bureau of the Census. 1975. *Historical Statistics of the United States: Colonial Times to 1970.* Washington, D.C.: U.S. Government Printing Office.

U.S. Industrial Commission. 1900–1902. *Reports,* 19 vols. Washington, D.C.: U.S. Government Printing Office.

Van Hise, Charles. 1912. *Concentration and Control: A Solution of the Trust Problem in the United States.* New York: Macmillan.

Wallace, Anthony. 1978. *Rockdale: The Growth of the American Village in the Early Industrial Revolution.* New York: Knopf.

Weinstein, James. 1968. *The Corporate Ideal and the Liberal State, 1900–1918.* Boston: Beacon Press.

Wolfe, Alan. 1977. *The Limits of Legitimacy: Political Contradiction of Contemporary Capitalism.* New York: Free Press.

Wright, Erik Olin. 1978. *Class, Crisis, and the State.* London: New Left Books.

Wrigley, Julia. 1982. *Class Politics and Public Schools.* New Brunswick, N.J.: Rutgers University Press.

Yeager, Mary. 1980. *The Development of Oligopoly in the Meat Packing Industry.* Greenwich, Conn.: JAI Press.

Zaretsky, Eli. 1976. *Capitalism, the Family and Personal Life.* New York: Harper and Row.

Zeitlin, Maurice. 1974. "Corporate Ownership and Control: The Large Corporation and the Capitalist Class." *American Journal of Sociology* 79:1073–119.

Zeitlin, Maurice, W. Laurence Neuman, and Richard Earl Ratcliff. 1976. "Class Segments: Agrarian Property and Political Leadership in the Capitalist Class of Chile." *American Sociological Review* 41:1006–30.

Class Power, Conflict, and Struggle

The four chapters in this section focus on the practices of actors in the realization of class interests. Stephen Valocchi examines the origins of welfare policy in Britain, Sweden, and Germany. He argues that the variations in these policies can be attributed to the different trajectories of class relations and class struggles. In all instances, state structures mediated the effects of class forces on policymaking, and Valocchi contends that differences in state structures and the policy outcomes are best seen as products of previous class struggles and class compromises. Carl Strikwerda examines the divergent responses of members in working class communities in three Belgian cities to industrialization between 1870 and 1914. Strikwerda suggests that divisions over religion, distinctive local politics, and economic structures were important variables in preventing the formation of a united Belgian working class. Sharon Reitman asks why similar work conditions produced different political traditions for metal miners associated with the Western Federation of Miners (WFM) and coal miners associated with the United Mine Workers of America (UMWA). She suggests that, with contrasting organizational and political capabilities, industrial conflicts in the Western mining industry involved substantially more political struggle than those in the Eastern coal mining industry; as a result, the WFM advocated socialism and the UMWA embraced liberal reforms. Finally, Kathleen Stanley and Dean Braa examine how the Irish peasantry became a class-for-itself during the Land War of the late nineteenth century. They demonstrate the interconnections between material, political, and ideological dimensions of class, moving beyond a simple "structure versus agency" dichotomy.

9 | The Class Basis of the State and the Origins of Welfare Policy in Britain, Sweden, and Germany

STEPHEN VALOCCHI

Despite massive increases in social spending, extensions of benefits to previously ineligible groups, and the introduction of new programs and services in the post–World War II period, the origins of the welfare systems of Great Britain, Sweden, and Germany in the late nineteenth and early twentieth centuries established principles of intervention into the capitalist market that remain essentially unaltered today (Flora 1986, p. XIV). The British reforms of 1908–1911 established centralized systems of relief for old age,[1] accident, health, and unemployment based not on a means test but universal criteria and flat-rate insurance contributions. The framers of the reforms wanted to establish a national minimum under which certain groups of industrial workers who shared the same condition (e.g., old age, unemployment) would not be permitted to fall (Furniss and Tilton 1977, p. 102). The programs were self-financing, and the benefits from these programs were only marginally tied to income. The former characteristic ensured that these programs would not threaten the British state's credit position with the financial community; the latter guarded against any possible work disincentives (Gilbert 1966).

The foundation of West Germany's welfare system is its earnings-related, status-differentiated insurance system, which compensates individuals according to their earnings records and insurance programs (Alber 1988, p. 6).[2] These organizing principles were established soon after the unification of Germany in 1871, with the introduction of health insurance (1883), accident insurance (1884), and disability and old-age insurance (1889). Unlike the early British reforms, benefits in the early German schemes were directly tied to income: policymakers transferred distinctions in income and status at work into the public provision of benefits. In this sense, welfare had the same distributional consequences as the market (Valocchi 1986, pp. 290–91).

Although many of the interventionist features of the Swedish welfare system are attributed to the influence of Social Democratic governments beginning in 1932, the universalistic thrust of its insurance system emerged in 1913 with the provision of flat-rate pension benefits to all citizens at age 67 (Heclo 1974, p. 191; Rosenthal 1967). The Swedish state, however, did not extend the insurance principle to provisions for other social contingencies, as was the case in Britain and Germany. The state provided substantial supplements, but provisions for accident, sickness, and unemployment in Sweden remained the responsibility of local governments and voluntary programs (Hovde 1943, p. 632). Neither work disincentives, status inequalities, nor private borrowing requirements was the chief organizing principle of these early reforms.

Explaining Welfare System Differences

How can we account for these differences? The three approaches to the study of the welfare state that recognize important cross-national differences in welfare policy and view them in interventionist terms are the Social Democratic, the state-centered, and the neo-Marxist approaches. The Social Democratic literature distinguishes welfare systems according to the degree to which benefits are related to wage labor, which class bears the brunt of the cost of these benefits, and the degree to which benefits usurp business prerogatives in the labor and capital markets.

The Social Democratic literature (see Shalev 1983 for a review of this literature) explains these differences with a model of policymaking that emphasizes the strength and nature of working-class interests outside the state and the ability of labor parties to both mold and represent such interests. John Stephens (1979) emphasizes the differential strength of organized working-class interests in explaining the differences in the post–World War II welfare systems of seventeen Western nations. Gosta Esping-Andersen (1978) does not simply emphasize the direct effects of the class strength on state policy in his comparison of Scandinavian social policy. Rather, he sees this strength as being molded and redefined by past policy and present party strategy; policy and party, however, affect class strength unmediated by state structure. He does not consider that state structures may vary in their receptivity to working-class parties in shaping policy, nor that this receptivity may be the product of past balances of class forces presently institutionalized within the state.

A second theoretical approach, the state-centered approach, also views welfare systems in interventionist terms (see Skocpol and Amenta 1986 for a review of this literature). A concern with such a definition of welfare differences emerges in Margaret Weir and Theda Skocpol's (1985) analysis of national responses to the Great Depression. They ask why

Sweden moved in the direction of full employment policy and universalistic social programs after 1936 while Great Britain, with a more firmly entrenched system of unemployment provision, did not integrate these programs with a full employment policy. Extending the analysis to the United States, they ask why national policymakers made overtures in the direction of full employment and universalism in the late 1930s but could not extend or institutionalize these policy initiatives. Their research questions are guided by interventionist concerns: the relationship between labor market status and qualification for benefits and the relationship between social and economic policies.

Although the state-centered literature defines differences in interventionist terms, as does the Social Democratic approach, it does not explain these differences vis-à-vis the nature and strength of organized class interests. State-centered analyses contend that for states to impose their policy objectives on a population they must possess fiscal, administrative, and political resources and establish structures that organize and implement these resources. Specifically, these structures must have the ability to raise revenue (i.e., fiscal resources), make collective decisions that are viewed as legitimate by relevant political actors (i.e., political resources), and implement these decisions in a prescribed manner (i.e., administrative resources). Differences in the nature of these state structures account for differences in the nature of welfare policy across democratic capitalist nations.

This approach recognizes the ability of the state to act independently of organized interests and to shape policy outcomes according to such organizational variables as bureaucratic characteristics (Fainstein and Fainstein 1978), electoral characteristics (Katznelson 1985; Skocpol 1980), and policy legacies (Ashford 1986). However, it sees this ability as derived mainly from the internal characteristics of states. It does not consider the possibility that bureaucratic and electoral characteristics or the construction of a policy legacy may incorporate class interests into state structures and that these interests interact with the formal and informal characteristics of states to shape welfare policy.

Neo-Marxist approaches do recognize class biases within the state and thus insist that analyses of policymaking must involve an investigation not simply of the strength and nature of class interests nor of the organizational capacities of states but of the interaction of class power and state structures both outside and within various state structures. The theoretical work of Nicos Poulantzas (1973; 1978) has informed a growing number of empirical analyses of policymaking that have taken seriously this interaction of economic power with state structures (Levine 1988; Quadagno 1988; Quadagno and Meyer 1989).

Poulantzas asserts that states in capitalist societies have the institutional capacity to act independently of the interests of individual capitalists and, indeed, must act independently if state managers are to serve as "the factor of cohesion" and the "factor of reproduction" of the conditions of production of a system (Poulantzas 1973, p. 245). This function requires that state managers pursue policies that may "select in" some fraction of capital and, if necessary, some segment of the working class in order to guarantee the general conditions of profitable capitalist production and ensure the stability of a class-based social structure. The process of policymaking, therefore, is a process of embedding the balance of class power within the structure of the state (Poulantzas 1978, pp. 123–63).

This neo-Marxist approach would not deny the importance of the fiscal, political, and administrative structures of the state in understanding differences in the nature of welfare policy. Poulantzas would contend, however, that the manner in which states generated the resources necessary to build these structures was due, in part, to the class-based conflicts over what role the state would play in a capitalist economic system. In addition, the continued generation of these resources requires that the interests of the class or class fractions that supply these resources be given preference within the policymaking process. What is suggested, then, is a model of policymaking that posits an interaction of class interests with state structures within the state.

This model assumes a direct relationship between class relations in society and the fiscal, administrative, and political characteristics of the British, German, and Swedish states. The balance of class power outside the state is institutionalized in the form of biases in those structures of the state, and it is this institutionalized bias that has a direct impact on the shape of welfare reform. The following section specifies the ways that class interests became incorporated into the fiscal, administrative, and political characteristics of the British, Swedish, and German states prior to the extensions of their early welfare systems. Identifying both the nature of the dominant economic classes as well as the preexisting state structures influenced by them is a necessary prelude to understanding the politics of the early welfare reforms.

Class Interests and State Structures
Prior to Welfare Reform

Before welfare reform, the dominant economic classes in Britain, Sweden, and Germany were relatively successful in transforming economic power into political powers. The points where this transformation occurred, however, differed across these nations. In Britain, a legacy of activist politics prevented the aristocracy from building an insulated centralized state without compromising with the emerging capitalist class. In Sweden, industrial capitalists did not have to confront a powerful aristocracy but a monarchy that created a centralized bureaucracy with openness to the peasantry and small farmers. Only in Germany did the preexisting structure of the state facilitate a powerful political alliance of the aristocracy and industrial capitalists without the simultaneous creation of structures to represent the working class.

Britain

Prior to the British reforms of 1908–1911, Parliament very rarely proposed national taxes to finance welfare reform. This hesitancy derived from the economic power of the commercialized landed property (Ashford 1986, p. 68). This group saw their local tax rates increase throughout the early nineteenth century, as land consolidation and enclosures made the peasantry increasingly dependent on the Poor Law. Landed magnates whose interests turned more and more on profits derived from rents and exports became increasingly unable to control the costs of local relief; the last thing they wanted was national taxation for welfare reform (Brundage 1978, pp. 1–14).

In addition to these local pressures against national taxation, the centrality of British capital in underwriting domestic and foreign industrialization made growing numbers of politicians wary of doing anything to jeopardize the value of the pound. These politicians simply mimicked the concerns of the lawyers and bankers that made up the finance-trading complex of the City of London (Gamble 1981, pp. 56, 71–75), who were managing and investing the profits made from agricultural exports and textiles by both landed and industrial capitalists.

The interests of this small group of capitalists also determined the ways in which the British state credentialized the civil service and routinized many of the state's administrative and policymaking functions. The 1870 Civil Service Reform Act, together with a number of public orders in the 1860s and 1870s, opened up the senior civil service to members of the professional middle class brought into existence by the accounting and legal requirements of an expanding market economy. This access was contingent, however, on obtaining a classical education at either Oxford or Cambridge University (Shefter 1977, p. 436). These reforms also established a pattern of closed consultation between department heads and senior civil servants apart from the systematic input of party MPs, and they placed the treasury department at the apex of the civil service. Taken together, the reforms gave the finance-trading complex of the city easy access to policy circles (Gowan 1987, p. 19; Roseveare 1969, p. 227).

The rise of mass party organization represented the major inroad made by the working classes in what had been a closed political system staffed and controlled by the aristocracy. Although spearheaded by the middle class, the extensions of the franchise and the subsequent reform of the patronage-based party system were accompanied by working-class movements for broader political representation in Parliament (Cowling 1967, pp. 242–66). This accessibility to Parliament made political issues that were previously debated and resolved by a small circle of large landowners the object of party competition. Working-class access to parliamentary politics, however, was initially contingent on participation in either of the two mass-based parties, the Conservatives or the Liberals.

By the early twentieth century, the period prior to welfare reform, the British state had a newfound capacity to act. However, this enhanced capacity was the result of an implicit alliance between the landed and industrial segments of capital, designed to extend the market basis of society and to protect that basis from a restive working class. Although shielded from the process of policymaking, the working class did manage to gain a limited voice in party politics. As we will see below, this would prove crucial in prodding the Liberal government to overcome some of the fiscal constraints on national welfare reform.

Sweden

In contrast to both Britain and Germany, the aristocracy played only a peripheral role in the development of a capitalist state in Sweden (Roberts 1967, p. 42). In the late seventeenth century, the monarch, in a successful struggle for power with the aristocracy, dramatically reduced landholdings and distributed these among small farmers and the Swedish state (Roberts 1967, p. 212). As an additional bulwark to the demands of the aristocracy throughout the nineteenth century, the monarch encouraged commercial and industrial activity by removing restrictions on trade and promoting investment by foreign capital (Tilton 1974, p. 564). In turn, the Swedish state became increasingly reliant on taxes from this commercial and industrial activity.

The state's encouragement of the capitalist market was part of a larger agenda that included not only economic development but also a heightened political defense of the constitutional monarchy against demands by both the aristocracy and urban liberals for greater political freedoms (Alestalo and Kuhnle 1987, p. 10). Toward this end, the Swedish state pursued a number of administrative reforms in the early nineteenth century that emphasized a close association between civil servants, party leaders, state ministers, and local administrators (Koblik 1975, p. 37). Foremost among these was a committee structure that jointly involved all parties in identifying problems, drafting consensus-based solutions, and implementing these solutions throughout the countryside (Meijer 1969).

Although these administrative changes did give small farmers and agricultural workers indirect access to policymaking circles, the structure of the Riksdag did not give industrial workers any political voice until the second franchise reform in 1909. A 1866 electoral reform gave those with urban property the vote, thus allowing the typically urban concerns of poor relief and unemployment to receive a hearing in the Riksdag during the latter half of the nineteenth century (Rustow 1955, pp. 23–25). The reform, however, did not alter the bias in the more powerful first chamber of the parliament in favor of a few large landowners and capitalists in the timber, mining, and shipbuilding industries.

In the latter part of the nineteenth century, an already centralized state with ties to the countryside became dependent on industrial capitalists for fiscal and political resources. As we will see, the rural bias of the Swedish state, expressed in its committee structure, gave peasants and small farmers some influence over the shape of the early welfare reforms. The capitalist-class bias in the political and fiscal structures of the state, however, prevented the replacement of the locally based welfare system with a more uniform national system.

Germany

The fiscal characteristics of the German state owed much to the influence of both large landowners centered in Prussia (Anderson 1974, pp. 236–78) and industrial capitalists involved in heavy industry (Blackbourn 1984, pp. 238–60). The early state proposed taxes in administrations without ministerial responsibility and relied not on the more representative lower house of parliament (Reichstag) to authorize these taxes but on the upper house (Bundesrat) where the bulk of the members were appointed by the Prussian king and prime minister (Dragnich and Rasmussen 1982, p. 329). With unification, landed capitalists managed to deflect taxes from themselves to the peasantry, and in 1879, industrial capitalists engineered a system of tariffs that protected both grain producers and iron and steel manufacturers from international competition (Lambi 1961).

The coalition between landed and industrial capitalists was also responsible for many of the administrative characteristics of the prereform German state. Like the Swedish state, it had a long tradition of administrative autonomy prior to national welfare reform. Rulers of the German territories had historically relied on members of the aristocracy as paid royal servants who enjoyed a great deal of power as policy advisers and as liasons in the implementation of policy in the sometimes remote areas of the realm (Badie and Birnbaum 1983, p. 116). These royal servants were drawn from the Prussian nobility and exercised complete control over the peasantry.

Although the credentialization of the civil service in 1807 expanded its ranks to include members of the professional middle class, these educated sons of merchants, lawyers, and teachers could not penetrate the upper civil service levels. Access there was determined by the Prussian rulers who, after the German Revolution of 1848, were wary of "liberalist" influence in the state (Blackbourn 1984, p. 255). Unlike the body of administrative law that developed around the Swedish civil service in the nineteenth century, however, the German law still gave preference to the interests of large landowners (Sheehan 1976, p. 73). With unification and the recognition by the kaiser and state ministers of the importance of industrial activity for domestic growth and international standing, this bias was extended to a variety of activities and associations involved in heavy industry.

The illusion of political representation existed in the Reichstag under the guise of universal male franchise for election to that body.[3] The Reichstag by itself, however, had very little power over policymaking. First, there was no ministerial responsibility; second, the little legislative power that existed rested with the nonrepresentative Bundesrat. Together, these parliamentary bodies (the Reichstag and the Bundesrat) exercised veto power over national budgets and thus had some minimal influence over the shape of policy formulated by the chancellor and his ministers (Rosenberg 1976, p. 51).

In the period prior to the early welfare reforms, a politically powerful landed class extended its influence by recruiting industrialists into the politics and administration of the new German state. But rather than working toward the elimination of certain landed biases within the state, this small segment of industrial capital traded, as Barrington Moore (1967, p. 437) said, "the right to rule for the right to make money." Implicit in this bargain, however, was the understanding that the state would address "the labor problem."

The Politics of Welfare Reform

In all three countries, working-class political pressure pushed the state toward welfare reform. Whether it was the parliamentary politics of the British Liberal-Labour coalition, the extraparliamentary protests of workers and peasants in Sweden, or the working-class politics of opposition by the German Social Democratic party and trade unions, political elites responded directly to this pressure with ameliorative social reforms. The precise shape of these reforms, however, owed less to this pressure itself and more to the ways in which it was registered in the class-biased state structures of these nations. The following section describes the ways in which the class biases of the British, Swedish, and German states interacted with working-class political pressure to shape welfare reform.

Great Britain

The onset of a prolonged trade depression in the 1880s increased trade union organization and militancy and created a variety of challenges to the British state's passive position toward labor and social issues (Fox 1985, p. 177). These challenges received a hearing in Parliament by way of the urban-based Liberal party and the small number of working-class MPs sponsored by the Labour Representation Committee. The will to act came in 1908 when party competition forced the Liberal party to introduce national systems of old age, health, and unemployment benefits to counter proposals from both the Conservative party and the growing number of Labour MPs (Harris 1972, p. 270).

Behind this party competition, however, stood class politics. Particularly influential for Liberal party proposals, for example, was the changing balance of power between the fledgling Labour party and the Liberals. Labour's growing presence in Parliament threatened to upset the delicate balance that existed between both parties' candidates in the two decades surrounding the turn of the century. During this period, the Liberal party agreed not to run candidates in certain districts where independent Labour candidates were also running. In return, the Labour candidates that were elected agreed to maintain the party discipline of the Liberals (Moore 1978, p. 18). As the nature of working-class organizations shifted from an emphasis on skilled and craft workers to unskilled and semiskilled workers, more Labour MPs rejected the Liberals' program for one of their own making (Eley 1984, p. 103). In an attempt to stave off further Labour defections from the Liberal-Labour coalition, then, the Liberals introduced welfare legislation that would primarily benefit the better organized members of the working class (Valocchi 1989, p. 358).

Working-class politics, however, had little impact on the policymaking process. Most aspects of Labour's social agenda were ignored in the behind-the-scenes discussions between state ministers and civil servants (see Marwick 1967 for a discussion of what was ignored). The specifics of the reforms were crafted in the relatively closed administrative and financial structures of the British state. Particularly influential in this process were the links established in the mid-nineteenth century between civil service recruitment processes and the elite universities of Oxford and Cambridge (Richter 1966). The civil servants produced by these universities saw their role as developing policy that would incorporate diverse groups and perspectives into the formation of state policies in a way that would preserve individual liberties yet mitigate class conflicts (Harris 1972, p. 285). These individuals were largely successful in inscribing principles of pragmatism and political liberalism into welfare policy because the administrative insulation of the cabinet allowed senior civil servants to set the terms of the debate in their negotiations with both British labor and business.

The most notable feature of these reforms was the break with the locally directed Poor Law and the introduction of nationally administered support for the various contingencies associated with industrial society. Running throughout the Liberal reforms was an emphasis on their supplementary nature. Winston Churchill expressed the nature of the reforms in a public speech on unemployment insurance: "We have not pretended to carry the toiler to dry land. . . . What we have done is to strap a lifebelt around him" (quoted in Bruce 1961, p. 154).

The causes of the minimal and market-oriented nature of the early British welfare reforms can be viewed from a state-centered perspective only if we recognize that the state structures most closely responsible for these reforms have class origins. These capitalist-class biases were institutionalized at the administrative level, and the partial openness to working-class interests at the parliamentary level enabled policymakers to construct a system that simultaneously addressed demands, incorporated the working class, and shielded the market from the possible work and investment disincentives of welfare policy.

Sweden

Many of the early Swedish reforms were simply extensions of previous programs: They were extended because the close links between local administrators, politicians, and the national bureaucracy enabled civil servants to detect local problems and respond on a national, albeit ad hoc, basis (Hammerstrom 1979, p. 184). The state's attention was drawn to these problems by a small group of Liberals and Social Democrats in the second chamber of the Riksdag who demanded national responsibility for old age, unemployment, and sickness programs and who commanded the support of a number of popular movements whose momentum threatened the uneasy legitimacy of the monarch in the Swedish countryside (Lundkvist 1975). Although this route allowed increased funding for a variety of local sickness, accident, and unemployment schemes, it could not control other aspects of the extensions— most importantly, the increase in taxes necessary to finance these extensions and the opposition to a more uniform, nationally coordinated welfare system.[4]

It was only in the case of pensions that the early welfare reforms did not utilize existing voluntary and local programs; in this one instance, Sweden moved toward a national insurance model similar to that of the British and Germans. This was because the committee system of the Swedish state allowed agrarian interests privileged access to policy approval. These interests, represented mainly in the Rural party, refused to sanction welfare reforms unless they were extended to small farmers and agricultural workers. The popularity of pensions among liberals and Social Democrats in the second chamber pushed the Rural party into giving their support to a national system of old age pensions, provided, of course, that it would not be limited to industrial workers (Heclo 1974, pp. 185–86).

The evolution of the state-provided universal pension, as well as the supplementary welfare assistance given by the state to already organized local, voluntary, and private programs, can be understood in state-centered terms only if we see the administrative relationship between civil servants and the monarch and the political relationship between the Riksdag and state ministers as the outcome of class-based processes. The power struggle between the crown and the aristocracy gave the Swedish state autonomous administrative power, the alliance between the crown and the small farmers gave agrarian interests disproportionate access to policymaking, and the alliance between state administrators and industrial capitalists impeded the growth of a centralized system of welfare provision.

Germany

Although Germany had a long tradition of social protection dating back to the mid-eighteenth century, rapid industrialization in the second half of the nineteenth century created increasing numbers of urban workers outside the guild and handicraft systems (Ullmann 1981, p. 134). Their employment in the new unprotected and unregulated industries made them dependent on the locally based Poor Law. The institutional links between the Poor Law administrators in the towns and rural provinces and state civil servants ensured that the increased financial burden placed on the law would find its way into political debate in the Bismarck government.

At the national level, these local concerns dovetailed with social concerns—the industrialists' concerns with the political and economic power of the working class. The depression that began in 1873 provided the opportunity for state ministers to introduce a variety of measures designed to control this working-class movement. Some took the form of sticks—for example, banning the meeting of all Socialist organizations and the publication of all Socialist literature in 1878. Others took the form of carrots. Chancellor Otto von Bismarck saw welfare reform as one of those carrots, a way to divert working-class loyalties away from working-class organizations and toward the state (Rothfels 1938, pp. 296–300). The administrative insulation of the German state gave Bismarck the opportunity to take the initiative, and the procapital biases within the state helped shape the specific proposals.[5] Although the mimimal influence accorded the legislative assemblies allowed a coalition of parties representing small business and Catholics to thwart some of the centralization tendencies within Bismarck's original proposals, the alliance with big business gave the government the political support needed to maintain the principle of status differences in the insurance reforms (Rimlinger 1971, pp. 119–120). From this alliance emerged several features of the early German welfare system: workers' contributions designed to wed working-class well-being to the interests of the state; the preservation of status distinctions in qualification for and benefit from insurance schemes in order to fragment the working class; and earnings-related benefit schemes intended to gain the support of the better paid unionized workers (Rimlinger 1971, pp. 112–16).

The lack of direct influence by the German Social Democrats on the shape of these reforms stands in contrast to the moderate influence of the Labour party on the British welfare reforms. This difference can largely be explained by differences in the ways in which class interests were institutionalized in the British and German state structures. British parliamentary processes were becoming more open, but the German Reichstag and Bundesrat accorded no real influence to working-class citizens. Furthermore, the Social Democrats were doubly scourged by the anti-Socialist laws. These state structures, however, were premised on class biases and, as in the British and Swedish examples, one cannot understand the shape of the early German reforms without considering the balance of class forces institutionalized in the policymaking process. Such forces in Germany included a bureaucratized landed class and a deputized segment of big business that was attempting to construct a welfare system that instilled national loyalty and status consciousness into the working class.

Conclusions

The extensions and partial centralization of protection for individuals in the event of unemployment, accident, sickness, and old age represent an important change in the political economies of the British, Swedish, and German societies. For the first time, these states recognized their responsibility to address problems that had hitherto been seen as the province of either the individual or the local community. To a large degree, this change was due to the political pressure exerted by the working class in these countries. This pressure, however, occurred outside state structures that had already been organized in ways that could deflect or channel this pressure. The process of capitalist statebuilding in each of these countries, therefore, delivered welfare policy that not only guaranteed political resources to compensate for the inadequacies of the market but also ensured that these resources would not challenge the structural inequalities of an emerging capitalist society. In a double sense, then, welfare reform is a contradictory process. It is contradictory in its *causes* in that pressures for reform came from both the working and the capitalist classes. It is contradictory in its *consequences* in that it compensates for the negative effects of the market even as it reaffirms the integrity of this market and reconstitutes the fault lines of a class society.

The foregoing analysis also speaks to the theoretical debates among the Social Democratic, state-centered, and neo-Marxist perspectives regarding the causes of welfare state development. It demonstrates that Social Democratic accounts of policymaking are only partly correct in pointing to balances of class power organized outside states as determinants of social policy. Although working-class pressure prodded the state to move from the locally based Poor Law to a national insurance system, it did not affect the nature of the resulting reforms. This had more to do with balances of class power within, rather than outside, the state, a conclusion consistent with the neo-Marxist perspective of the capitalist state offered by Nicos Poulantzas.

In every case, state structures mediated the effects of class forces on policymaking. These structures, however, were the products of past struggles and compromises, and they embodied the interests of the winners of those conflicts. Not surprisingly, these were the best organized segments of the capitalist class in each country; the precise influence of this class on welfare policy, however, was dependent on how firmly precapitalist elites or other segments of capital had embedded themselves within the state. The resulting class compromises and coalitions established policymaking structures that refracted working-class political pressures and yielded different patterns of welfare intervention into the market.

Future research must pay closer attention to the class nature of the state, specifying more precisely what type of class influence within the state is responsible for what dimension of welfare reform. This will allow comparative analyses of policymaking that can assess not only how different classes and class fractions "embed" themselves within state structures but also the effect this embeddedness has on specific dimensions of welfare policy.

Finally, this analysis adds a necessary corrective to the state-centered perspective on policymaking. Many of the features of states that this perspective sees as crucial to policymaking cannot be divorced from the class relations within which these features emerged and developed. The nature of the electoral system, the division of responsibility across administrative units, and the relationship of policymakers to legislative assemblies emerged from power struggles among social classes; the outcomes of such struggles were incorporated into the structure of the state, and these structures communicated these class biases in the policymaking process. "Bringing the state back in," therefore, should not entail keeping class analysis out.

Notes

1. The original pension program did not entail employee contributions: It was a flat-rate, noninterventionist scheme. It became insurance-based in 1926.

2. An individual contributes and benefits according to his or her earning record. Note here the difference between the British and German social insurance schemes: The British scheme is intended to provide a minimum to live; the German scheme is intended to provide a minimum to live in the style to which one is accustomed. In addition, one does not belong to a centrally administered fund, as in Britain, but to one of several hundred privately administered funds licensed by the state. Some distinctions and qualifications for benefits based on occupation and ability to pay exist. For example, those who do not want to join the public sickness scheme may join substitute schemes (Ersatzkassen) that have more generous benefits (Simanis 1971, pp. 20–21).

3. Blackbourn (1984) argues that the extension of the franchise in an essentially powerless parliament was Bismarck's attempt to conciliate small-business people who were becoming increasingly anxious over the concentration of wealth in the hands of a few powerful industrial concerns, as well as over the state's encouragement of this process.

4. Many Conservative members of the Riksdag believed social reform was draining resources necessary for a sound military. Only after the massive demonstrations for franchise reform in 1907 increased the access of the urban middle class and some better-off industrial workers to the Riksdag did the shift from defense to social policy occur. This shift was financed not through an increase in the taxes of commercial and industrial elites but through the diversion of tobacco monopoly revenues from defense to social expenditures (Verney 1972, p. 45).

5. Particularly influential was an iron and steel magnate, Fieherr von Stumm— a member of the Reichstag and founder of a lobbying organization that represented the interests of large corporations. Stumm's ideas, as well as those of his organization, informed many of Bismarck's social insurance proposals (Levine 1988).

References

Alber, Jens. 1988. "Germany." In *Growth to Limits: Volume 2,* ed. Peter Flora, pp. 1–154. Berlin: Walter de Gruyter Press.

Alestalo, Matti, and S. Kuhnle. 1987. "The Scandinavian Route: Economic, Social, and Political Developments in Denmark, Finland, Norway, and Sweden." In *The Scandinavian Model,* eds. Robert Erikson, E. J. Hansen, S. Ringen, H. Uusitalo, pp. 3–38. Armonk, N.Y.: M. E. Sharpe.

Anderson, Perry. 1974. *Lineages of the Absolutist State.* London: New Left Books.

Ashford, Douglas. 1986. *The Emergence of the Welfare States.* Oxford: Basil Blackwell Ltd.

Badie, Bertrand, and Pierre Birnbaum. 1983. *The Sociology of the State.* Chicago: University of Chicago Press.

Blackbourn, David. 1984. "The Discreet Charm of the Bourgeoisie." In *The Peculiarities of German History,* eds. D. Blackbourn and G. Eley, pp. 159–294. Oxford: Oxford University Press.

Bruce, Maurice. 1961. *The Coming of the Welfare State.* London: B. T. Batsford Ltd.

Brundage, Anthony. 1978. *The Making of the New Poor Law.* New Brunswick, N.J.: Rutgers University Press.

Cowling, Maurice. 1967. *1867: Disraeli, Gladstone and Revolution.* Cambridge: Cambridge University Press.

Dragnich, Alex, and J. Rasmussen. 1982. *Major European Governments.* Homewood, Ill.: The Dorsey Press.

Eley, Geoff. 1984. "The British Model and the German Road: Rethinking the Course of German History Before 1914." In *The Peculiarities of German History,* eds. D. Blackbourn and G. Eley, pp. 39–258. Oxford: Oxford University Press.

Esping-Andersen, Gosta. 1978. *Social Class, Social Democracy and State Policy.* Ann Arbor, Mich.: University Microfilms International.

Fainstein, Susan S., and Norman I. Fainstein. 1978. "National Policy and Urban Development." *Social Problems* 26:125–46.

Flora, Peter, ed. 1986. *Growth to Limits: Volume 1.* Berlin: Walter de Gruyter Press.

Fox, Alan. 1985. *History and Heritage: The Social Origins of the British Industrial Relations System.* London: Allen and Unwin.

Furniss, Norman, and Timothy Tilton. 1977. *The Case for the Welfare State.* Bloomington: Indiana University Press.

Gamble, Andrew. 1981. *Britain in Decline.* Boston: Boston Press.

Gilbert, Bentley B. 1966. *The Evolution of National Insurance in Great Britain: The Origins of the Welfare State.* London: Michael Joseph Ltd.

Gowan, Peter. 1987. "The Origins of the Administrative Elite." *New Left Review* 148:4–34.

Hammerstrom, Ingrid. 1979. "Ideology and Social Policy in the Mid-Nineteenth Century." *Scandinavian Journal of History* 4:163–85.

Harris, Jose. 1972. *Unemployment and Politics: A Study in English Social Policy 1886–1914.* Oxford: Clarendon Press.

Heclo, Hugh. 1974. *Modern Social Politics in Britain and Sweden.* New Haven, Conn.: Yale University Press.

Hovde, J. 1943. *The Scandinavian Countries, 1790–1865.* Boston: Chapman and Grimes.

Katznelson, Ira. 1985. "Working-Class Formation and the State: Nineteenth-Century England in American Perspective." In *Bringing the State Back In,* eds. Peter Evans, D. Rueschemeyer, and T. Skocpol, pp. 257–84. London: Cambridge University Press.

Koblik, Steven. 1975. *Sweden's Development from Poverty to Affluence, 1750–1970.* Minneapolis: University of Minnesota Press.

Lambi, Ivo N. 1961. "The Agrarian Industrial Front in Bismarckian Politics, 1873–1879." *Journal of Central European Affairs* 20:378–96.

Levine, Daniel. 1988. *Poverty and Society: The Growth of the American Welfare State in International Comparison.* New Brunswick, N.J.: Rutgers University Press.

Levine, Rhonda. 1988. *Class Struggle and the New Deal.* Lawrence: University of Kansas Press.

Lundkvist, Sven. 1975. "Popular Movements and Reform." In *Sweden's Development from Poverty to Affluence, 1750–1970,* ed. Steven Koblik. Minneapolis: University of Minnesota Press.

Marwick, Arthur. 1967. "The Labour Party and the Welfare State in Britain, 1900–1948." *American Historical Review* 73:380–403.

Meijer, Hans. 1969. "Bureaucracy and Policy Formulation in Sweden." *Scandinavian Political Studies* 4:103–16.

Moore, Barrington. 1967. *The Social Origins of Dictatorship and Democracy.* Boston: Beacon Press.

Moore, Roger. 1978. *The Emergence of the Labour Party, 1880–1924.* London: Hodder Stoughton.

Poulantzas, Nicos. 1973. "The Problems of the Capitalist State." In *Ideology in Social Science,* ed. R. Blackburn, pp. 238–53. New York: Random House.

———. 1978. *State, Power, and Socialism.* London: New Left Books.

Quadagno, Jill. 1988. *The Transformation of Old Age Security.* Chicago: University of Chicago Press.

Quadagno, Jill, and Madonna Harrington Meyer. 1989. "Organized Labor, State Structures, and Social Policy Development: A Case Study of Old Age Assistance in Ohio, 1916–1940." *Social Problems* 36:181–96.

Richter, M. 1966. "Intellectuals and Class Alienation: Oxford Idealist Diagnoses and Prescriptions." *European Journal of Sociology* 7:1–26.

Rimlinger, Gaston. 1971. *Welfare Policy and Industrialization in Europe, America and Russia.* New York: John Wiley and Sons.

Roberts, Michael. 1967. *Essays in Swedish History.* London: Wiedenfeld and Nicolson.

Rosenberg, Hans. 1976. "Political and Social Consequences of the Great Depression of 1873–1876 in Central Europe." In *Imperial Germany,* ed. J. Sheehan, pp. 39–60. New York: Franklin Watts.

Rosenthal, Albert H. 1966. *The Social Programs of Sweden.* Minneapolis: University of Minnesota Press.

Roseveare, Henry. 1969. *The Treasury: The Evolution of a British Institution.* London: Penguin Press.

Rothfels, Hans. 1938. "Bismarck's Social Policy and the Problem of State Socialism in Germany, Part 2." *Sociological Review* 30:288–302.

Rustow, Dankart. 1955. *The Politics of Compromise.* Princeton, N.J.: Princeton University Press.

Shalev, Michael. 1983. "The Social Democratic Model and Beyond: Two Generations of Comparative Research on the Welfare State." *Comparative Social Research* 6:315–51.

Sheehan, James J., ed. 1976. *Imperial Germany.* New York: Franklin Watts.

Shefter, Martin. 1977. "Party and Patronage: Germany, England and Italy." *Politics and Society* 7:403–51.

Simanis, Joseph G. 1971. "Health Insurance Legislation in West Germany." *Social Security Bulletin* June:20–21.

Skocpol, Theda. 1980. "Political Response to Capitalist Crisis: Neo-Marxist Theories of the State and the Case of the New Deal." *Politics and Society* 10:155–201.

Skocpol, Theda, and Amenta, Edwin. 1986. "States and Social Policies." *Annual Review of Sociology* 12:131–57.

Stephens, John D. 1979. *The Transition from Capitalism to Socialism.* New York: Macmillan Press.

Tilton, Timothy. 1974. "The Social Origin of Liberal Democracy." *American Political Science Review* 68:561–71.

Ullmann, Hans-Peter. 1981. "Germany Industry and Bismarck's Social Security System." In *The Emergence of the Welfare State in Britain and Germany,* ed. W. J. Mommsen. London: Croom Held Ltd.

Valocchi, Stephen. 1986. "Welfare Policy and Stratification Outcomes in Great Britain, West Germany and Sweden." *Research in Social Stratification and Mobility* 5:285–319.

––––––. 1989. "The Relative Autonomy of the State and the Origins of British Welfare Policy." *Sociological Forum* 4:349–66.

Verney, Douglas. 1972. "The Foundations of Modern Sweden: The Swift Rise and Fall of Swedish Liberalism." *Political Studies* 20:42–59.

Weir, Margaret, and Skocpol, Theda. 1985. "State Structures and the Possibilities for Keynesian Responses to the Great Depression in Sweden, Britain and the United States." In *Bringing the State Back In,* eds. Peter Evans, D. Rueschemeyer, and T. Skocpol, pp. 107–68. London: Cambridge University Press.

10 Three Cities, Three Socialisms: Class Relationships in Belgian Working-Class Communities, 1870–1914

CARL STRIKWERDA

A long tradition of historical and social scientific literature has seen the development of a militant, cohesive working class as the natural outcome of European workers' experience during industrialization. The position of these workers as disadvantaged wage earners, it is argued, produced a natural bonding that united them in opposition to other economic groups. Other influences on workers acted primarily as countervailing tendencies to the dominant influence of class solidarity. One proof that a self-conscious, united working class has, in fact, developed is some kind of movement or political party that claims to represent workers as a class. "Socialist consciousness *through organization*," writes Eric Hobsbawm, is "an essential complement of working class consciousness" (Hobsbawm 1984, p. 28, emphasis in original). Another body of historical and social scientific literature has recently argued that class relationships are only one of many power relationships in society. Workers could mobilize on the basis of a number of loyalties or identities—gender, religion, ethnicity, political ideology—as well as their identity as an economic class (Savage 1987; Smith 1982). As workers participated in multiple struggles, they sometimes united on the basis of class solidarity and divided over other loyalties.

The debate between these two positions is especially important when scholars try to understand one of the fundamental shifts in European working-class history. During the late nineteenth century, workers in almost every industrial country created mass movements that appeared destined to dominate the political system. By the 1940s, however, working-class movements became enmeshed in what has variously been called interest group or corporatist politics (Berger 1981; Cox and O'Sullivan 1988). Important groups of workers remained outside these movements, and, at times, their own membership became divided. Rather than seeing a confrontation between a united working class and its opponents, the period witnessed a variety of ideological and economic interest groups contending for power.

This "failure" of working-class movements to continue to grow or to take power on their own terms has been attributed to changes within capitalism, the adoption of reformist as opposed to revolutionary goals, the manipulation of the elites, or the tactics of labor leaders (Nolan 1981; Perrot 1974). Yet, it may also be seen as the result of a set of power relationships and social identities shaping workers' lives. Workers in Belgium, for example, formed two labor movements, Catholic and Socialist, and sometimes also created separate organizations of Dutch- and French-speakers. Solidarity in working-class organizations did not easily cross ideological or linguistic lines. I will look at how these divided loyalties in the pre–World War I era attracted workers into organizations and, at the same time, prevented the formation of one movement representing workers' interests. The language of class intersected with other discourses of ethnic rights, religions, and political ideology in ways that sometimes unified and at other times weakened working-class solidarity.

As the second country in the world to industrialize, Belgium presents a classic case of an industrial society with deep social divisions. The large working class created by the nineteenth-century Industrial Revolution helped the Socialists to become the second largest party in the Belgian Parliament by 1894. In three nationwide general strikes during the pre–World War I era, the Belgian workers caught the imagination of Socialists all over the world. At first glance, then, Belgium conforms closely to a classic pattern: A new working class, created by industrialization and urbanization, brought about a new kind of mass politics based on class conflict.

On the other hand, twentieth-century Belgium presents a quite different portrait in which a welter of compartmentalized communities contend for influence: Dutch-speaking Flemings in the north against French-speaking Walloons in the south; Catholics versus anticlerical Liberals and Socialists; and organizations of the lower middle class, big business, farmers, and labor unions jockeying with each other. For some scholars, the coexistence of these groups provides an intriguing example of "consociational democracy" or "segmented pluralism" (McRae 1974). One observer describes Belgian politics more critically as an "armed peace" (Huyse 1980). How did the Socialists, with their early lead in organizing the working class, become one in a set of competing interest groups? And what does this transformation say about class identity in an industrial society?

Because the crosscutting conflicts in twentieth-century Belgium are so complex, neither a national-level nor a community-level study can capture the set of factors at work. Instead, I will analyze the development of Belgian socialism and interest-group politics by comparing three cities, each with its own distinctive local politics, economic structure, and class relationships. The Socialist workers' movement is the center of concern because it claimed to express workers' solidarity as a class and because scholars use it as a prime example in international comparisons (Zolberg 1986). The three cities together capture much of Belgium's diversity in language, urban geography, and economic specialization. Ghent, a Dutch-speaking city whose economy rested on textiles, was a densely populated factory and harbor town. Liège, in the French-speaking region of the country, depended on sprawling coal and metallurgical industries that covered the city's hinterland. Brussels, meanwhile, was the bilingual capital of Belgium and possessed a diverse and rapidly growing mix of commercial, artisanal, and industrial occupations. The crucial issues in each case here are the confrontation between Socialists and Catholics, the divisions between linguistic groups, and the effect of urban geography that could oppose urban and commuting workers. Because almost all analyses of interest-group politics in the twentieth century focus on the battles over the welfare state (Quadragno 1987), the creation of unemployment insurance is also interesting for what it reveals about the distinctive class relationships in the local areas (Kiehel 1932).

Ghent: Socialists Versus Catholics

The most striking feature of Ghent was the organizational density and richness of its native working-class life and the success of the Socialists in utilizing this organizational life as a path to power. By the late nineteenth century, Ghent had been the "Belgian Manchester" for decades. Cotton and linen factories, where almost half of the employees were women, crowded into a town whose medieval walls had once made it the largest city in northern Europe outside of Paris. The result was that, despite the fact that Ghent was the third largest industrial city in Belgium, the metropolitan area still roughly approximated the core city's boundaries. (See Table 10.1.) In Brussels and Liège, workers lived in a dozen or more townships (*gemeenten* or *communes*), but almost 90 percent of Ghent's workers lived in the town of Ghent itself, which encouraged their identification with the city and their creation of a local culture. Ghent's native working class, furthermore, was fed by few immigrants or commuting workers from the countryside in the late nineteenth century because the city's textile industry experienced several recessions, beginning with the "cotton famine" of the American Civil War. Thus, by the time a small group of Socialists began organizing in Ghent in the 1870s and

TABLE 10.1   Socialist Union Membership and Socialist Party Strength in Ghent, Brussels, and Liège in 1900

	Socialist Union Members in Agglomeration	Industrial Workforce in Agglomeration	Percent of Workforce in Socialist Unions	Percent of Socialist Seats in Core Communal Council	Percent of Socialist Vote in Electoral Arrondissement
Ghent	10,625	46,997	22.6	36	16.1
Brussels	6,531	105,271	6.2	31	25.7
Liège	1,395 (est.)	54,456	2.3	31	46.4

Sources: Union Membership: *Vooruit,* 21 October, 1900; Parti Ouvrier Belge, Fédération Bruxelloise, *Rapport, Exercise, 1912–13;* Commission syndicale, *Congrès, 1901;* Workforce: calculated from Volumes I, II, and III of *Recensement des industries et des métiers, 1896;* Communal Council Representation: Jules Destrée and Emile VanderVelde, *Le Socialisme en Belgique* (Paris, 1898); Socialist Vote in Electoral Arrondissement: W. Moyne, *Résultats des élections belges entre 1847 et 1914* (Brussels, 1970).

1880s, the city possessed a dense, well-established network of mutual insurance societies, singing clubs, and small craft unions.

Although a number of Socialist leaders came from artisanal backgrounds, the key support for socialism came from industrial workers—cotton spinners, weavers, and metallurgists, many of whom were unskilled. With a loan from the weavers' union, the Socialists started an amazingly successful consumer cooperative, *Vooruit* ("Forward") in 1881, whose modern ovens soon drove down the city's bread prices to nearly the lowest level in the county. As a commercial enterprise, *Vooruit* did everything from selling dry goods to operating its own textile factories. At the same time, it loaned money to the unions, published a daily newspaper (also called *Vooruit*), and helped sponsor everything from women's leagues and a band and choir to a "freethinkers' first communion" for children and Marxist study clubs (Avanti 1908).

In all their activities, the Ghent Socialists systematically tried to pull workers away from traditional, local, or middle-class-dominated organizations into exclusively Socialist ones. When the Socialist party and *Vooruit* began a Socialist federation of mutual insurance societies, they did so in the face of the vociferous opposition of the cafe owners who depended on the old informal groups' clientele. Nor did either the small group of Socialist leaders or the rank and file tolerate much dissent: Those who criticized the party leader and former clerk Edouard Anseele too stridently for being a political boss were expelled and vilified. Nonetheless, with their wide range of organizations that brought working-class families, women, children, and male workers into the movement in a variety of ways, the Ghent Socialists created a new kind of working-class community.

As one observer described it, it was "a city within a city, a Socialist country within the national country" (Varlez 1899, p. 1).

Against this picture of Socialist success must be put the complex class relationships and political alliances with other workers and the lower middle class into which the Socialists became drawn. Here, the issues were religion, linguistic nationalism, and the countryside. It is ironic that the Socialists in Ghent were able to transcend all barriers to working-class solidarity—except religion. In a country where almost everyone was at least nominally Catholic and where the church had governmental support, this was a fateful choice. Socialists sponsored a Freethinkers' League, attacked religious burials, and allied themselves on anticlerical issues with the Liberal party that included some of the same factory owners whom the unions fought. As a result, a small but stubborn Catholic workers' movement arose in Ghent, the first in Belgium. By 1900, the Anti-Socialist League, as it was called, had organized about a third as many workers as its opponents and had done so in similar fashion: A Catholic consumer cooperative, *Het Volk* ("The People"), also with a daily newspaper of the same name, had grouped around it mutual insurance societies, clubs, women's groups, and labor unions (Strikwerda 1988).

The creation of this Catholic working-class community alongside the Socialist one demonstrates how workers fashioned different kinds of class consciousness. This division was not traceable to underlying economic divisions between Socialists and Catholics, and the distribution of occupations among Socialist and Catholic unionists was remarkably similar. The Catholic workers, however, also had the support of the Catholic lower middle class and the rural population. Beginning in the 1890s, farmers and lower-middle-class groups also began forming organizations under Catholic leadership. The introduction of universal male suffrage encouraged the Catholic elite to tolerate these organizations in hopes that some lower-class voters would still support the Catholic party. The creation of the Catholic workers' movement was part of the larger process in which the lower classes entered modern politics (Scholl 1965).

The workers and middle-class individuals who organized the Catholic unions used a vocabulary within working-class life that could support an alternative class consciousness to the Socialist one. Rather than contrasting those who labored against the possessing class, Catholics spoke of groups who labored alongside each other, as it were, each in its own unequal but distinctive place. The Catholic union and lower-middle-class press often described its audience as "Workers" (*Werklieden*) and "*Burgers*"—the latter term an almost untranslatable combination of citizen, petty bourgeois, commoner, and middle class. In particular, the opposition to the Socialist call for nationalization of private property united Catholic workers and the lower middle class: Leaders of both groups argued that property preserved their defined place in society. Catholic leaders sometimes used "estate" (*stand*), rather than class, to describe workers or the lower middle class. The strength of this "petty bourgeois" or less than completely capitalist mentality may have reflected the nature of the Ghent textile industry—split into small, undercapitalized firms with few ties to the big Brussels investment banks and unwilling to form effective cartels or trade associations. But it also drew on the tradition of distributive justice, in which the lower classes would cooperate with each other to demand that the upper class respect certain rights. Catholics tried to draw a distinction between the economic or "material" interests of social groups, which could be legitimately defended, and the "political" demands of the Socialists, i.e., the abolition of private property and exclusive control of the government by the working class. Although the distinction between "economic" and "political" may sound odd, in a way this pointed to the special claims of the Socialists. As reformist or pragmatic as the Flemish Socialists may appear by contrast with revolutionary left-wing movements, they consistently stressed their "political" goals. As the Socialist weavers in Ghent urged their fellow workers in a pamphlet: "Organize yourselves! Not in unions which strive for nothing else than higher wages and fewer hours, but in unions which also have as their goal to change the political power, the State" (*De Vier Getouwen* 1893, pp. 12–13).

Persistent opposition by Catholics meant that the Socialist workers, as well organized as they were, could be deprived of allies among other lower-class groups. The small group of Catholic workers had links to the government, which was under Catholic party control from 1884 to 1914, and to the rural population, which was heavily Catholic. One of the key political battlegrounds between Socialists and Catholics was control of the Labor Courts (*Werkrechtersraden/Conseils des Prud'hommes*) that judged minor employment disputes. After the Socialists won the elections to the Labor Courts, the Catholic-controlled government redrew the boundaries for the courts' jurisdiction so that it included a large area outside the city itself. As a result, many workers in small towns now voted in the elections. Although the Socialists won inside Ghent, by a 5,343 to 2,916 vote, outside the city they lost to the Catholics, 1,467 to 5,673, and thereby lost control of the courts.

The alliances between Catholics of different classes also meant that the Catholic workers, rather than the Socialists, could more easily align their movement with the cause of Flemish nationalism. Although Ghent, and Flanders as a whole, were Dutch-speaking, French remained the language of the upper levels of business, government, and education. The Catholic unions seized on the issue to recruit Flemish workers, especially commuting and small-town workers, and to smear the Socialists as internationalist and pro-French. With their justifiable pride in internationalism and their argument that linguistic oppression would disappear with class oppression, Socialists often found themselves on the defensive over the issue of Flemish nationalism. In Ghent especially, the use of French was closely tied to higher economic status: The Socialist newspaper *De Vlasbewerker* (1898, p. 2) once called a workers' delegation a *"comité de defense"* and complained, "In front of the bosses, one always has to use French."

Stymied by Catholic opposition, the Socialists chose to compromise, albeit reluctantly. In almost every industry where Catholic unionists could not be ignored, the Socialist unions formed joint committees with Catholics for strikes and bargaining. Some of the Socialist leaders obviously hoped that common occupational interest would pull the Catholics into a permanent alliance. The executive secretary of the Catholic unions, in fact, warned that the joint committees had to be dissolved as soon as strikes or negotiations were over or the committees, dominated by the Socialists, would replace the unions. But the pull of economic interest could work against the Socialists, as well. Their party and union federation leadership had an ongoing battle with the cotton workers' union to stop its continual collaboration with the Catholics. This union was reputedly the most "English" (that is, nonideological) of all the Socialist unions (Varlez 1899, pp. 8–9, 34).

The crowning edifice of cooperation, furthermore, came from the leadership itself: Socialist and Catholic leaders created and administered a municipal unemployment insurance system, in which city funds subsidized the benefits received by members of Socialist, Catholic, and other unions. This "Ghent system" was studied and copied in Germany, Italy, Switzerland, and the United States. Despite their frustrations over the Catholic workers' movement, the religious and Flemish issues, and the necessity to compromise, the Socialists in Ghent represented, by pre–World War I standards, an impressive movement. Few working-class movements anywhere in the world so evenly brought together power in the spheres of politics, economic organization, and community life. At the same time, the persistence of dual working-class organizations, Socialist and Catholic, points to the multiple forms of social identity that workers held.

Brussels: Middle-Class and Artisanal Socialism

In Brussels, the Socialists spoke the language of class solidarity, but, in practice, the movement was even more clearly circumscribed by occupational, linguistic, and geographical divisions than in Ghent. Until the last few years before World War I, the Brussels Socialist movement was dominated by a coalition of middle-class individuals and craft unionists, who also led the Socialist party on the national level. Among the leaders were individuals such as Emile VanderVelde, chairman of the Second Socialist International that was headquartered in Brussels. The leaders were educated, French-speaking, and talented but oriented amost exclusively toward achieving power through the electoral process. They justified this, in part, by Marx's own emphasis on political power, but it also grew out of a bourgeois culture oriented to debate and the law and their fear of the craft unions. Belgium was so heavily industrialized, these leaders reasoned, that workers could eventually vote the Socialists into power. Patiently building up unions or other economic organizations of workers would be much more difficult given the depths to which heavy industrialization, low wages, and illiteracy had brought the workers.

At the same time, except for the strong Socialist unions that emerged in Ghent in the mid-1890s, what few unions existed in Belgium were craft unions that were often reluctant to organize workers outside their own trades and wary of the Socialists' talk of revolution and nationalization. In contrast to the Ghent Socialists, the middle-class leadership in Brussels tacitly agreed to leave the craft unions alone except for coaxing them to affiliate with the Socialist party. Hence, dozens of tiny "Socialist" unions jealously guarded their independence and did virtually nothing to organize or reach out to other workers. In 1908, for example, the 1,635 Socialist metal workers in Brussels belonged to twelve different unions. Ironically, these unions all belonged to the same national federation of metallurgists that the one unified metal workers' union in Ghent did. An exasperated Ghent metallurgist suggested that "someone should lock the Brussels metalworkers up in one room and not let them out until they form one union" (Landelijke Metaalbewerkersbond 1899, p. 32). Not without reason did many workers elsewhere in Belgium speak of the Brussels workers' *esprit de cloche* ("mentality of the local tower") or fierce local identity (*Journal des correspondances* 1908, p. 164).

The Socialist leaders also had difficulty coming to terms with the effects of urban geography and economic change in Brussels. As the largest and one of the fastest-growing cities in Belgium, Brussels did not have the dense network of workers' groups upon which the Socialists in Ghent had built. In fact, linguistic, economic, and geographical conditions combined to isolate the hard-core Socialist supporters, who were French-speaking or bilingual craft workers, in the center of the urban area. In the late nineteenth century, the majority of the skilled workers in the craft unions began to use the French of the middle and upper classes. The industrial workers in the more Dutch-speaking suburbs, who labored in small iron foundries, woodshops, and hat factories, were separated from the craft unionists in the bilingual center of Brussels almost as much as if they had lived in another city.

The division of the Brussels urban area into more than a dozen *gemeenten/communes* further prompted disunity. The emphasis that the Socialists placed on electoral politics encouraged workers to organize within each town to win control of the local government. Few new Socialist institutions, except the national party, stimulated any organizational solidarity, and there was no local Socialist union federation, as there was in Ghent. The unions in Brussels had organized only 6 percent of the industrial work force; the Ghent Socialists had organized over 20 percent. (See Table 10.1.) Though it was the largest in Belgium, the consumer cooperative in Brussels, the *Maison du peuple* ("House of the People"), had a much weaker presence in the city than *Vooruit*. By 1900, Brussels had almost three times as many inhabitants as Ghent, yet the *Maison du peuple* had only a few thousand more members.

The strength of the lower middle class in Brussels also contributed to the Socialists' failure to build up united working-class organizations. One reason they failed to create a mutual insurance society was because many craft unionists already belonged to societies that included small businessmen or were allied with middle-class societies through a non-Socialist federation. The *Maison du peuple,* too, faced a much greater amount of opposition from small shopkeepers and brokers than did *Vooruit:* A Catholic "worker" newspaper in the 1890s described the Socialists as "making war on small retailers" (*La Voix de l'ouvrier* 1893, p. 1).

The Socialists' failure to challenge the craft unions' conservatism or the power of the lower middle class meant that, in the long run, the Socialist movement in Brussels faced decline. The fastest growing group of workers in Brussels were less skilled, Flemish workers from outside the city whom the Francophone Socialist unions had failed to organize. To encourage workers from the countryside and small towns to find work in the large cities without moving there and increasing both urban crowding and the Socialist vote, the Catholic government created one of the world's most extensive systems of tramways and offered inexpensive workers' tickets on the national railroads. This investment in transportation was all the more striking because Belgian rents were low. Commuting soon affected Belgian urbanization as a whole: From about 1890 on, small towns and cities grew faster than the largest cities in Belgium, so that the country developed a rather decentralized pattern of urbanization (Strikwerda 1989). Already in 1896, employers broke one of the largest strikes in Brussels's history by bringing in workers "from other places in the country" (Gendarmerie 1896). At the same time, new factories sprang up in the Flemish towns around Brussels, beyond the reach of the Socialist craft unions in the city center. As late as 1911, the worst thing the Socialists could say about the Catholic unionists was that they were unskilled workers—*"ouvriers non-qualifiés"*—and Socialists usually referred to the Catholic workers, even in French, as *"dompers,"* Dutch for "stupes" or "duped ones" (*Journal des correspondances* 1906, p. 179; 1910, p. 14).

The Socialist movement in Brussels transformed itself only in the last few years before World War I when a group of unionists, allied with those in Ghent, finally broke down the old craft unions, created a mutual insurance society, and tried to recruit workers who had been neglected— the Flemish, commuters, women, and the unskilled. One goad to the Socialists was the fear that Catholics would organize these workers. After 1905, the Ghent Catholic unions sponsored a national Catholic union federation that sent organizers to Brussels. By 1913, even though the Socialist unions had almost tripled in size in about five years, Brussels had some 5,000 Catholic unionists to the Socialists' 18,000, nearly the same ratio as existed in Ghent. It is striking that Ghent, a much smaller, slower growing, poorer, and less literate city, had so much influence on Brussels. That it did points to the decisive but complex role of class relationships in the two cities. In Ghent, industrial workers could, with the help of a few leaders such as Anseele, deal with middle-class opponents from a position of self-confidence and relative strength. By contrast, in Brussels, the "labor aristocracy" of conservative though professedly Socialist craft unionists isolated themselves from other workers. They wished to defend their Francophone, urban culture against the Flemish, nonurban industrial workers as much as they wanted to defend their economic grievances against the employers or the lower middle class. The middle-class leaders typified by VanderVelde, furthermore, could be radical in their affirmations of Marxist or Socialist orthodoxy, but they were too cautious and too cutoff from the workers' world to see how a true Socialist working-class community could be created in the face of opposition from craft unionists and the lower middle class.

Not only did Socialist and Catholic labor organizers come from Ghent to Brussels, so, too, did the all-important unemployment insurance system that finally offered workers and union leaders an incentive to create strong unions. But, though the system helped create such unions, it deeply involved the Socialists in bargaining with other groups. In Brussels, it was much more complex to negotiate the subsidies that flowed from local governments to union members. In Ghent, the decision to grant unemployment subsidies through the unions could be worked out basically within the city itself and between the Catholic and Socialist camps. The heavily populated, Catholic-controlled countryside excluded the Liberals and Socialists from real power in the provincial government that had little to do with the city. In Brussels, the urban area made up a sizable portion of the province's population but was itself made up of a larger lower middle class, much of which voted Catholic and Liberal. The urban area also spilled over into more than a dozen communes and was fed by an army of commuting workers from outside the city. Only an intergovernmental unemployment system would work in Brussels and, even then, only with the approval of the provincial government in which Liberals, Catholics, Socialists, and middle-class groups all had a say.

The formation of this intergovernmental system revealed the logic inherent in the Ghent program. Government subsidies to union members, regardless of the ideology of their unions, gave working-class organizations a stake in preserving the status quo. The Catholic upper class could legitimize the transfer of funds through the unions by also granting subsidies to farmers' cooperatives and middle-class mutual insurance societies and by appealing to notions of distributive justice. Members of labor unions, even Socialists if their unions followed certain requirements, deserved help in maintaining their position in life (*stand* or *état*). It is striking that the unemployment system did not benefit, even in intent, all who needed aid. The Ghent system benefited those organized into an institutionalized group, not, as in the British or Scandinavian systems, either the neediest or the "deserving poor" or all the lower orders. The Ghent or Belgian system resembled, in some ways, that of Germany, a kind of de facto co-optation of certain potential challengers to the status quo, except that Belgium lacked the statist and authoritarian elements of imperial Germany.

What the case of Brussels shows, then, is the importance of middle-class influences and an artisanal economy in creating a peculiar Socialist movement and, secondly, the crucial force exerted by changes in the economy, urban geography, and interest-group politics that transformed an older working-class community.

Liège: Politics, Repression, and Socialist Syndicalism

It is tempting to argue that the Socialists' failure to create a unified working-class movement in Brussels was only due to the city's unique artisanal and middle-class economy. Similarly, the strength of Catholicism, Flemish linguistic nationalism, and the countryside all contributed, it seemed, to the Socialist movements in Brussels and Ghent being forced into the compromises that they made. Liège demonstrates that the choices that Socialist leaders made were as critical in shaping their movements as the economy and urban geography. Liège was overwhelmingly industrial, with an economy based on coal mining and metallurgy, yet Socialist leaders here, too, emphasized electoral politics at the expense of strong working-class organizations. The Catholic countryside around Liège made up such a small proportion of the electoral district that, from 1894 on, the Socialists won by far the largest vote in elections and often threatened to win absolute majorities against both Catholics and Liberals. (See Table 10.1.) Despite this political success, there was, even more so than in Brussels, no real Socialist working-class community in Liège until just before World War I. The Socialist cooperatives were small and divided, and many workers belonged to employer-controlled or non-Socialist mutual insurance societies. Because Socialists neglected unionization, most of the unions grew up among skilled workers, and members refused to affiliate with the Socialists. Socialist cooperatives and unions formed parts of the local Socialist party within each *commune* and supported the party's efforts to win political control of local government. Unfortunately, the *communes* had little relevance outside local politics: The industrial region sprawled through three river valleys and thousands of workers commuted between *communes* to work. Increasingly, as the low birth rate caused a labor shortage, thousands more commuted in from Flemish regions north of Liège via workers' tickets on the railroads or by tramways.

By emphasizing electoral politics and localism, Liégeois Socialists failed to challenge the enormous power of paternalism and repression exercised by employers. Socialist consumer cooperatives also failed to thrive because they had to compete with and live down the bad reputation of employer-controlled company stores that often called themselves "cooperatives." Liégeois industrialists organized themselves in a vastly different fashion than the textile factory owners in Ghent, where only the largest manufacturers employed as many as 1,000 workers. By contrast, the Cockerill and Ougrée-Marihaye coal and steel firms, based in the Liégeois suburb of Seraing, both employed over 7,000 workers across the Liège basin. The Ghent firms had never developed strong ties to investment banks and survived against English competition by offering lower wages and working the labor force longer hours. But Cockerill, Ougrée-Marihaye, and their fellow Liégeois firms borrowed from big banks in Brussels, Paris, and Frankfort, set prices with German and French cartels, and metamorphosed into some of the first multinationals. By 1914, they had investments and branches in Spain, Luxembourg, France, Russia, and China. They also had little to fear from localized Socialist unions.

Paternalism and repression by employers simplified class relationships to a clash between workers and employers. Employers squelched the rise of a progressive Catholic workers' movement. Catholic conservatives and Liberals combined to threaten Catholic activists and to get the Vatican to recall the leading progressive priest, Abbé Pottier (Gerin 1959). And upper-class employer power even drove many lower-middle-class shopkeepers into the Socialist camp for many of them resented the competition of the company stores and the upper-class hold on the Liberal party. Ironically, this influx further weakened the chances for Socialist consumer cooperatives. In the most proletarian of the three cities, the Socialist movement absorbed part of the petty bourgeoisie. Shopkeepers advertised in Socialist newspapers that they were "recommended to the comrades," were "suppliers to the cooperatives of the region," and were offering discounts to party members (Strikwerda 1983, p. 281–82).

The weaknesses of the Socialist movement in Liège were finally remedied by unionists who learned to combine elements of socialism and syndicalism. A number of Socialist union leaders, who supported the party's political slates but disliked its neglect of unionism, even allied for a time with the anarchists and syndicalists. The anarchosyndicalist movement eventually failed because both union leaders and most workers came to believe its emphasis on economic action was as one-sided as the Socialist party's emphasis on electoral politics. Syndicalism, shorn of its more ideological anarchistic elements, nonetheless influenced Liégeois militants to try to balance the emphases on economic action and politics. The unionists forced the Socialist party leaders to accept a more independent labor movement. They also built up cooperatives and insurance societies to challenge paternalism. Isi Delvigne, an ironfounder from Seraing who made the Liégeois metallurgists' federation into a powerful organization, helped to create regional federations of cooperatives and labor unions that were equal parts of the Socialist movement with the party.

Economic changes and influences from outside Liège allowed union leaders to transform the Socialist movement. Metallurgists such as Delvigne took the lead over miners, who had previously dominated the Socialist unions in Liège, because the region shifted from exporting coal to producing steel equipment. The increasing power of firms such as Ougrée-Marihaye and Cockerill and the growing number of commuting workers also forced the old-time Socialist leaders to abandon their support of local, political labor unions. The growing influence of the Ghent Socialists and the union leaders in Brussels brought funds to support labor organizations, speakers, and the distribution of literature. Just as Liégeois industrialists collaborated with the German coal and steel producers, so the Liégeois militants learned to time their strikes with those in Germany and even sent a delegation to study the structure of the German unions (Centrale des métallurgistes de la province de Liège 1914, p. 8).

By comparison with the Socialists in Ghent and Brussels, Liégeois Socialists had the strongest sense of class consciousness, as expressed in their language, attitudes, and voting patterns. "*Ouvrier,*" worker, defined the movement in opposition to the upper class, even on the lips of middle-class Socialist leaders. Liégeois Socialists had little awareness that other groups—Flemings, the lower middle class, farmers—had grievances against the upper class. They rarely discerned the ideological component in Catholic workers' opposition to socialism but saw only the hand of employers. Whereas Ghent and Brussels Socialists called the Catholic workers "dupes" or "blacks," meaning clericals, the Liégeois decribed them as "servants" (*domestiques*) or "yellows," meaning cowards. Yet, until well after 1900, Liège in many ways possessed the weakest Socialist movement among the three cities. The class consciousness of Liégeois workers was not enough to create strong organizations in the face of paternalism, repression, and deep divisions among workers and their leaders. The unified movement that arose by 1914 emerged out of the battles to reconcile syndicalism and socialism and the new tactics employed by working-class leaders.

Furthermore, the Liégeois Socialists, like those in Ghent and Brussels, began negotiating with other interest groups and accepting the role of the state. Despite the weakness of the Catholic and Liberal parties in Liège, Socialists had to win over progressive Catholics and left-wing Liberals in parliament to obtain passage in 1909 of a mandatory nine-hour day in coal mining. The major breakthrough in forcing coal mine owners to negotiate with the unions came in 1911 when the Catholic party's minister of industry intervened in a strike in Liège. Both Catholic and Socialist unions pressured the government, but it also acted out of its own interest to stabilize the crucial coal sector during a competitive international situation. Government-enforced negotiations had almost as big an impact on the unions as on employers, forcing the Liégeois unions, like those in Ghent and Brussels, to create a more bureaucratic staff and to educate their members on coal prices, profits, and the cost of living.

Conclusions: Power Relationships and Interest Groups

The three strikingly different Socialist movements in the three cities of Ghent, Brussels, and Liège demonstrate the multiple power relationships and cultural identities that shaped working-class movements. If, as E. P. Thompson (1966) has argued, class is not a thing so much as a relationship, than loyalties such as religion, ethnicity, and political ideology act as equally powerful relationships. In all three Belgian cities, socialism itself was a product of the diverse ideological and political involvements of the leaders and the rank and file. Socialists in all these cases were vehemently anticlerical: working-class consciousness often became synonymous, for them, with opposition to Catholicism, even in the face of workers' organizations that were both Catholic and attempting to defend workers' interests. Religion versus anticlericalism was not the only ideological tension shaping socialism; although Catholicism did not figure as a major issue in Liège, the battle over anarchosyndicalism affected the

Liégeois nearly as deeply. The Socialist movement in Brussels, especially, allowed the deep divisons that separated Flemings from French-speakers and rural commuting workers from urban natives to circumscribe their sense of solidarity.

Working-class solidarity, based on workers' shared economic experience, clearly acted as a powerful unifying force. Despite their ideological conflict, Catholic and Socialist unions in Ghent and Brussels frequently collaborated. Yet, a unified working-class movement, which writers such as Hobsbawm (1984) have argued is an essential component of working-class consciousness, seems to have been unimportant. Workers saw their own interests in complex ways. Many did not see collaboration on economic issues as reason to desert organizations that prevented cooperation on religious or political issues. But this need not be seen as a case of ideological issues deflecting workers from their true interests. Many rank-and-file Socialists accepted cooperation with upper-class Liberals in the name of anticlericalism but opposed them on economic issues. There is little evidence that strikes and economic antagonisms were less severe in Belgium because Socialist workers sometimes were divided from Catholic workers or sometimes allied with Liberal employers. The arguments of authors such as Michael Savage (1987) and Dennis Smith (1982) that workers act collectively on the basis of multiple power relationships seem to fit best with the conflict-ridden world of the Belgian working class.

The numerous allegiances that workers held can also help explain the emergence of interest-group politics. Creating the dense network of organizations that made up the Socialist and Catholic working-class communities was a natural result of the competition between rival movements and the desire to mark off workers from the Liberals or middle-class Catholics who were their sometimes allies. In turn, cooperatives, mutual insurance societies, labor unions, and the like gave Socialist leaders the resources—funds, meeting places, printing presses—with which to bargain with the state and other interest groups. Socialist leaders learned to make compromises with rival labor unions in strikes and with local governments and other political parties in setting up unemployment insurance systems. Eventually, this same bargaining process could be extended, albeit with difficulty, to negotiations between labor and employers, between farmers, the lower middle class, and big business, and, finally, between Flemings and Francophones.

The range of issues that the Belgian Socialists struggled with, furthermore, may have some relevance for other industrial societies. Scholars still need more understanding, for example, of the deep hold of religious and ethnic loyalties in shaping the working class in the United States (Laurie 1989; Mink 1986). Nineteenth-century prophets saw industrialization sweeping away all loyalties except class and all social groups except employers and workers. But the state and the market, in fact, allowed preindustrial loyalties to emerge on the national level and acquire bureaucratic status. By the mid–twentieth century, a new constellation of ideological and economic groups competed within a more powerful state. Only by seeing working-class militancy within the complex world in which it arose can we fully understand how the conflicts and compromises between workers and their opponents evolved into the interest-group politics of the twentieth century.

Acknowledgments

Research for this paper was supported by a Belgian American Educational Foundation Fellowship and a Newcombe Fellowship from the Woodrow Wilson Foundation. I thank Gail Bossenga, Scott McNall, and Steve Valocchi for their criticisms and suggestions.

References

Avanti [pseud.]. 1908. *Een Terugblik. Proeve eener geschiedenis der Gentsche Arbeidersbeweging gedurende de XIXe eeuw.* Ghent: Volksdrukkerij.

Berger, Suzanne, ed. 1981. *Organizing Interests in Western Europe.* Cambridge: Cambridge University Press.

Centrale des métallurgistes de la province de Liège. 1914. *Congrès du 23 aout 1914.* Liège: no publisher.

Cox, Andrew, and Noel O'Sullivan, eds. 1988. *The Corporate State.* Aldershot, UK: Edward Elgar.

Gendarmerie, Brabant. 1896. *Report of 13 octobre.* Carton 233, Procurer Général, Archives Générales du Royaume, Brussels.

Gerin, Paul. 1959. *Les débuts de la démocratie chrétiennes à Liège.* Brussels: Études sociales.

Hobsbawm, Eric J. 1984. *Workers: Worlds of Labor.* New York: Pantheon Press.

Huyse, Luc. 1980. *De Gewapende Vrede.* Leuven, Belgium: Kritak.

Journal des correspondances. 1906. May.

————. 1908. November.

————. 1910. February.

Kiehel, C. A. 1932. *Unemployment Insurance in Belgium: A National Development of the Ghent and Liège Systems.* New York: Industrial Relations Counselors.

Landelijke Metaalbewerkers van Belgie. 1899. *XIV Jaarlijksch Congres.* Ghent: no publisher.

Laurie, Bruce. 1989. *Artisans into Workers: Labor in Nineteenth Century America.* New York: Noonday.

McRae, Kenneth, ed. 1974. *Consociational Democracy.* Toronto: McClelland and Stewart.

Mink, Gwendolyn. 1986. *Old Labor and New Immigrants in American Political Development: Union, Party, and State, 1875–1920.* Ithaca, N.Y.: Cornell University Press.

Nolan, Mary. 1981. *Social Democracy and Society.* Cambridge: Cambridge University Press.

Perrot, Michelle. 1974. *Les ouvriers en grève.* The Hague: Mouton.

Quadragno, Jill. 1987. "Theories of the Welfare State." *Annual Review of Sociology* 13:109–28.

Savage, Michael. 1987. *The Dynamics of Working-Class Politics.* Cambridge: Cambridge University Press.

Scholl, S. H., ed. 1965. *150 Jaar Katholieke Arbeidersbeweging in Belgie 1789–1939.* Brussels: Arbeiderspers.

Smith, Dennis. 1982. *Conflict and Compromise: Class Formation in English Society 1830–1914.* London: Routledge and Kegan Paul.

Strikwerda, Carl. 1983. "Urban Structure, Religion, and Language: Belgian Workers, 1880–1914." Ph.D. dissertation, University of Michigan.

———. 1988. "The Divided Class: Catholics vs. Socialists in Belgium, 1880–1914." *Comparative Studies in Society and History,* 30:333–59.

———. 1989. "The Paradoxes of Urbanizations: Belgian Socialism and Society in the *Belle Epoque.*" *Urban History Yearbook* 16:82–96.

Thompson, E. P. 1966. *The Making of the English Working Class.* New York: Vintage.

Varlez, Louis. 1899. "La fédération ouvrière gantoise." *Le musée social* 1:1–41.

De Vier Getouwen. 1893. Ghent: no publisher.

De Vlasbewerker. 1898. Juni.

La Voix de l'ouvrier. 1893. 2 avril.

Zolberg, Aristide. 1986. "How Many Exceptionalisms?" In *Working-Class Formation: Nineteenth-Century Patterns in Western Europe and the United States,* eds. Ira Katznelson and Aristide Zolberg, pp. 397–455. Princeton, N.J.: Princeton University Press.

11 | The Politics of the Western Federation of Miners and the United Mine Workers of America: Uneven Development, Industry Structure, and Class Struggle

SHARON REITMAN

Metal and coal miners in the United States developed sharply contrasting union political traditions. Both groups formed militant unions in the early 1890s, but where the metal miners' Western Federation of Miners (WFM) advocated socialism, the coal miners' United Mine Workers of America (UMWA) embraced the liberal reform movement of the progressive era. And where the WFM founded the revolutionary Industrial Workers of the World, the UMWA became one of the strongest affiliates of the more conservative American Federation of Labor. Such political differences remained remarkably consistent throughout the twentieth century.

These opposing political trajectories are puzzling because Western metal miners and Eastern coal miners differed little on the variables traditionally thought to predict working-class political behavior. Most sociological explanations of such behavior focus on the industrial environment and explain variations in strike rates and political ideologies in terms of the organization of the labor process, the level of danger, or the geographic isolation associated with a given industry (Kerr and Siegel 1954; Lipset 1960; Blauner 1964; Gordon et al. 1982). Clark Kerr and Abraham Siegel's classic account of the sources of working-class militancy contends that the most strike-prone workers are those who engage in unpleasant, dangerous jobs in isolated environments where they have little contact with "neutral" parties capable of mediating labor disputes (Kerr and Siegel 1954, p. 191). Miners have become the archetypical proletarians precisely because they engage in arduous and dangerous labor, often live in single-industry communities, and have tended—regardless of national political contexts—to be militant. Why, then, did U.S. metal and coal miners gravitate toward opposing ends of the political spectrum of organized labor?

The theoretical anomaly posed by contrasting union traditions in the metal and coal mining industries suggests that the industrial environment alone is an insufficient explanation of working-class political behavior. Though high strike rates among miners in many countries support privileging the labor process as a source of industrial militancy, the diversity of political expression among miners indicates a need to disentangle the sources of industrial militancy from those of political behavior. Industry-centered explanations of working-class formation offer important insights into the structural parameters that guide class organization, but they neglect the concrete events that give political meaning to industrial struggles.

This chapter examines the political formation of working-class segments in terms of both the organization and practice of class relations. At the level of organization, it draws from the resource mobilization theory of social movements; at the level of class practice, it draws from historical and sociological works that emphasize the transformative potential of workers' participation in politically significant events (Thompson 1963; Zeitlin 1966; Katznelson 1986; Fantasia 1988; Kimeldorf 1988). Industry-related variables—especially product market competition—in conjunction with the degree of state autonomy from mining capital, contributed to the organizational and political resources of both employers and miners. Industry concentration facilitated organizational cohesion among metal mine employers by minimizing the number of competing firms that had to be organized into their associations. In the highly competitive bituminous coal mining industry, however, employer associations were repeatedly undermined by the presence of unorganized firms and a lack of organizational leadership. Moreover, the metal mining industry was situated in states whose economic development was dependent on the mining industry, but the coal industry was situated in more economically diverse states. As a result, metal mine employers enjoyed more stable support from state governments in repressing labor disputes. Miners in the metal mining industry also enjoyed greater organizational cohesion and political resources than their counterparts in the coal industry. They lived in communities that were autonomous from management control, but coal miners typically lived in company-dominated communities.

This analysis is consistent with the resource mobilization theory of social movements insofar as it examines how objective circumstances and institutional arrangements shape the organizational cohesion and political resources of contending groups (Morris and Herring 1987, pp. 144–45, 157–71). However, organizational capabilities do not in and of themselves produce political commitments. The political interpretation that members of the working class give to class relations is shaped by the degree of political repression they experience during industrial disputes. The political goals of the WFM and the UMWA were significantly influenced by the ways in which employers and miners brought their economic and political resources to bear on crucial strikes during the formative years of the two unions. As a result of contrasting organizational and political capabilities, industrial conflicts in the Western metal mining industry involved substantially more political struggle than industrial conflicts in the Eastern coal mining industry.

This chapter explores employers' and miners' resources and contrasts strikes in the metal and bituminous coal mining industries from 1870 to 1905, encompassing the period when miners formed the political agendas of their unions. I focus on metal mining in Colorado and coal mining in Pennsylvania—two states where union organizational efforts were substantial, and the volume of mineral output was high. The opposing political positions of the two unions were also starkly represented in Colorado and Pennsylvania.

The Origins of Organizational and Political Resources in the Metal and Bituminous Coal Mining Industries

From the discovery of gold in 1859 until well into the twentieth century, mining dominated the economic, social, and political life of Colorado. By 1890, the state produced close to one-third of the nation's silver and gold output (Neuschatz 1986, p. 42). The Silver State Investment and Mining Company assured investors that "the mining industry of Colorado is the source of its wealth; the mainstay of its prosperity; the foundation of all that it is now and all that it may become" (*Mine Report and Prospectus of the Silver State Investment and Mining*, n.d., p. 3). Colorado's mining industry developed in two phases, a labor-intensive prospecting phase and a capital-intensive corporate phase. And institutions that prospectors and independent merchants established during the prospecting phase became organizational resources for metal miners during the corporate phase.

The prospecting phase was dominated by independent miners and independent merchants. Self-employed miners were attracted to Colorado's placer deposits, pockets of gold located near the earth's surface. Placer mining techniques were simple, and capital requirements were minimal, making Colorado an ideal environment for minimally subsidized prospectors. The lack of a developed economic infrastructure also made Colorado an ideal environment for small, independent merchants. Mining towns required populations substantially larger than the number of men working in the mines. For example, one historian found that just one-third of the residents in a sample of mid-nineteenth-century Rocky Mountain mining towns were miners; the rest were "mining the miners," either as businessmen or land speculators (West 1979, p. 5).

Independent prospectors and merchants left a tremendous institutional legacy to the wage-working miners who later formed the WFM. Miners inherited a set of social institutions that augmented their organizational resources and enhanced their political power at the community level. Prospectors and merchants established rudimentary social and economic institutions when they arrived in the undeveloped West, including miners' courts to settle legal disputes, fire protection services, and boarding facilities (Wyman 1979, pp. 29–30). These critically shaped labor struggles in the West by providing miners with institutions that were autonomous from management and, therefore, capable of acting politically at the local level. The myriad of saloons common to the larger metal mining communities, for example, were multifaceted institutions that not only provided entertainment but became focal arenas for the practice of informal politics, as well (West 1979, pp. 73–96).

With the depletion of numerous placer deposits in the 1870s, prospecting in Colorado diminished and was gradually replaced by an era of large-scale capital investment and product market concentration. The state had vast reserves of silver and gold that were deeply buried beneath the earth's surface. The depth of the ores, the need for large and skilled work crews, and the primitive nature of milling and smelting processes made huge sums of capital essential to the development of these mines. Deep mining entailed investing in expensive machinery for hoisting men into the mines, pumping water out of the mines, ventilating the mines, and transporting the minerals from worksites to mine openings. Wages for the work crews tended to be high, especially during the first few years of deep mining when labor was scarce. Moreover, hardrock minerals occurred in complex formations with lower-grade ores attached to the more valuable ones; this meant that metal mine owners had to invest in expensive, complicated, and often experimental milling and refining procedures before their produce was marketable. Reflecting on these expenses, a leading engineer of the time concluded that there were really only three ingredients capable of producing success in the metal mining industry: "The first is money, the second is money, and the third is money" (quoted in King 1977, p. 56). Lacking these ingredients, many prospectors sold their claims to wealthy investors. In 1879 alone, Eastern investors spent an estimated $20 million in Western mines (King 1977, p. 83). Between 1893 and 1897, investors organized over three thousand new mining corporations in Colorado, each one capitalized at over $1 million (Dubofsky 1969, p. 22). By 1902, just 7 percent of Colorado's mining companies were responsible for 80 percent of the state's total hardrock mineral production (Neuschatz 1986, p. 50).

As Western mining capital became more concentrated, miners became more organized. They formed local unions whose primary goal was the maintenance of high wages (Wyman 1979, p. 156). In 1893, following a bitter strike in Idaho's Coeur d'Alene mining district, local miners' unions from several Western states amalgamated into the WFM. Like the independent miners who preceded them to the West, members of the WFM drew resources from their communities; unlike their counterparts in the Eastern coal fields who lived in company towns, many metal miners lived apart from company housing and had access to the independent saloons and social institutions common to the West. During the 1890s, miners enjoyed considerable autonomy and a degree of political power in the larger mining towns where they represented at least 30 percent of the population (Suggs 1968, pp. 323–24; Wright 1974, pp. 230–31; Neuschatz 1986, pp. 38–41).

Employers responded to metal miners' organizational cohesion by forming cohesive associations of their own in the 1890s (Wyman 1979, p. 228). They claimed that organization was necessary to keep the miners from "dictating" the affairs of the industry (*Idaho Springs News,* September 11, 1903, p. 3). Indeed, one historian claimed that metal mine employers organized as the *only* alternative to turning management entirely over to the miners (Wyman 1979, p. 53). In contrast to bituminous coal employers, metal mine employers faced few organizational constraints; the largest owners tended to dominate employer associations, setting precedents that smaller mine owners with less control over the market followed (Wyman 1979, pp. 227–29; Neuschatz 1986, pp. 81, 111–12).

Colorado's dependence on the metal mining industry, in general, and on several large companies, in particular, gave employer associations political leverage at the state level. In the words of one historian:

Colorado was keenly aware of its dependence upon outside capital. It was at the same time an intensely individualistic frontier community and a colony of alien capitalists. . . . The Colorado legislature was influenced by a strong desire to develop the natural resources of the State. Special privileges were given to water companies, mining companies and the railroads. Corporations enjoyed the benefits of vague laws, and were ready to take advantage of their friends in the legislature. Enforcement of the laws was weak, for the State officials were most concerned with the economic development of the State (Barnett 1966, p. 101; see also Wright 1974, pp. 90–91).

Moreover, mine owners in Colorado, arguing that their interests were synonymous with the economic development of the state, received military assistance in repressing several of the major strikes that occurred during the WFM's early years.

Bituminous coal employers, however, were unable to tie their interests to those of the state of Pennsylvania. Although mining was key, as it was in the West, Pennsylvania enjoyed economic diversity. It "was the keystone in the arch of the post–Civil War American economy" (Klein and Hoogenboom, 1973). Between 1860 and 1900, it was the second largest manufacturing state in the Union and the chief producer of coal, iron, steel, petroleum, and lumber (Klein and Hoogenboom 1973, p. 264). Pennsylvania's economy was also central in the manufacturing of glass, machinery, textiles, leather, and paper (Cochran 1978, p. 136).

Much like the prospecting phase in the metal mining industry, a period of rapid expansion and promising growth occurred in the bituminous coal mining industry's early years. The Civil War provided coal operators with immediate profits, and the burgeoning manufacturing sector of the economy promised more long-term returns. In addition, railroad companies tempted coal investors into unexploited regions with low ton-mile rates for long-distance hauls (Johnson 1979, p. 21). In the mid–nineteenth century, a "man owning coal lands considered himself in possession of a bonanza," one coal operator recalled (*Black Diamond,* March 1886, p. 5). These bonanzas were within the grasp of people of modest means because deposits of coal near the earth's surface kept capital requirements to a minimum (Gowaskie 1976, p. 670; Bowman 1989, p. 76).

The pervasiveness of shallow bituminous coal mines and the persistence of low capital requirements kept the coal industry accessible to small investors for a longer period of time than was the case in the West, but it also contributed to stiff intraindustry competition of a kind that was absent from the metal mining industry. With the decline of wartime prosperity, the coal industry entered into an era of overproduction and depressed prices. Continued railroad expansion contributed to this overproduction: By expanding their services, railroad companies exacerbated competition between coal operators by restructuring traditional market boundaries that, in turn, gave coal companies access to new markets. With more permeable market boundaries, employer competition shifted from a local to a regional level, increasing the competition for many established firms (Gowaskie 1976, p. 672). The discovery of other fuels that competed with bituminous coal, especially natural gas and lower-grade coal, in the face of a situation where productive capacity exceeded demand made competition in the coal industry all the more intense (Johnson 1979, p. 19).

Coal employers responded to unrelenting competition by drastically reducing their prices in a futile attempt to preserve their markets. Individual price reductions set into motion a chain reaction of reductions among competing firms, causing the price of coal to fall in virtually all regional markets (Bowman 1989, pp. 101–3). Operators complained that price wars sent profits lurching downward. Indeed, the average coal operator made only 3 or 4 percent profit from his coal (Nash 1982, p. 25).[1] "Lack of anything like organization and harmonious action," coupled with overproduction and sharp competition, "continually widens the breach and tends to destroy every vestige of profit that may yet be left," one employer lamented (*Black Diamond*, April 1887, p. 15). Three years later, the *Black Diamond* announced that "competition in the coal trade is simply suicide. That is the naked truth" (*Black Diamond*, February 1890, p. 495).

Many coal employers advocated organization as a means of regulating prices and overcoming low profits. Reflecting this sentiment, the employers' trade journal announced that the "watchword and motto of the *Black Diamond* for the coal trade, first and last, now and forever is organize, organize, organize" (*Black Diamond*, February 1, 1890, p. 495). Nevertheless, one employer association after another crumbled when less scrupulous members took advantage of price agreements to lower their own prices and gain a larger share of the market. This uncooperative behavior led one exasperated employer to the conclusion that the problem with the coal industry was that his colleagues were, quite simply, "a set of asses" (quoted in *Black Diamond*, May 1888, p. 16).

Yet, the problem was more complex. Coal employers lacked organizational leadership, and the smaller firms exerted an inordinate amount of market power. Furthermore, larger employers were vastly outnumbered by smaller establishments. For instance, of the coal mines operating in Pennsylvania in 1889, 525 were regular establishments, and 2,949 were small "country banks" (*Engineering and Mining Journal*, June 13, 1891, p. 696). Assuming that a stable price-fixing agreement requires the participation of the firms responsible for 70 percent of the industrial output, John Bowman demonstrates that this would have entailed organizing over 300 firms nationally in 1895 and 1905 (Bowman 1989, p. 71). Moreover, coal deposits that varied in geologic, climatic, and other conditions pertinent to mining were scattered across twenty-six states. Geologic diversity meant that size was not necessarily a market advantage because small producers with particularly favorable geologic conditions could easily capture the markets of their larger competitors (Everling 1976, pp. 9–10). Indeed, larger employers frequently accused the smaller ones, commonly referred to as "the disturbing element," of "ruining the coal business" because the lower operating costs of the "snowbird" mines enabled their operators to pay slightly higher wages and accept lower prices (Keir, n.d., pp. 18–22). In contrast to the market power of the larger metal mining companies, the bigger bituminous coal companies were constrained by small operations that stirred up wage controversies and depressed coal prices.

Rather than collectively addressing their disputes with labor, as their counterparts in the West did, disorganized employers in the labor-intensive bituminous coal industry resorted to frequent wage reductions and vertical integration in the form of company homes and stores. Miners' wages varied with the price of coal but were always at or near poverty levels, and an estimated two-thirds of all bituminous coal miners lived in company homes in the 1880s and 1890s (Nash 1982, p. 43, n. 40). Poverty-level wages and company paternalism led a legislative committee sent to investigate conditions in the western Pennsylvania coalfields in 1897 to the conclusion that the working and living conditions among mining families were "a rebuke to our civilization and a disgrace to our State" (Pennsylvania State Senate 1897, p. 2373).[2] These conditions also made organizing coal miners difficult. Lacking funds for strikes and benevolent services, several of the unions that preceded the UMWA were short-lived (Roy 1905). In addition, union representatives faced enormous obstacles to organizing on company property and in situations where miners depended on coal companies for their jobs, homes, and credit during lean times. One coal miner summarized the effects of paternalism in his description of the company store as "a standing octopus which withers, degrades and enslaves" (*United Mine Workers' Journal,* August 8, 1895, p. 4).

Employers' reliance on wage reductions and paternalism was a product of unstable political capacities as well as weak organization. Although state officials in Pennsylvania intervened on behalf of coal employers during an important strike in 1894, they refused similar assistance during the more crucial 1897 strike. Bituminous coal employers received inconsistent state support because state politics were relatively autonomous from mining capital. And not only was Pennsylvania's economy diverse but, between 1860 and 1920, its politics were controlled by a tightly knit Republican group. Only one Democrat served as governor of Pennsylvania during the entire period from 1861 to 1935 (Klein and Hoogenboom 1973, p. 321). The Republican machine, which also dominated the state legislature, was "notoriously corrupt" (Klein and Hoogenboom 1973, p. 318). Some historians claim that political corruption was responsible for the antagonism between state officials and business leaders. Legislators sold their votes to corporations and then blackmailed these same firms by threatening to pass liberal strike legislation (Klein and Hoogenboom 1973, p. 318). But the relative autonomy of the state of Pennsylvania did not mean that its officials were oblivious to the desires of capital. On the contrary, the state frequently assisted employers in their battles with workers (Holmes 1970, pp. 132, 135, 167–68, 173). Coal employers, however, lacked the organizational cohesion necessary to procure consistent state assistance.

A consequence of contrasting organizational and political resources in the two mining industries was that conflicts in the metal mining industry became more closely intertwined with political struggles than did those in the bituminous coal industry. Cohesive employer organization and Colorado's dependence on mining capital were, in no small measure, responsible for the substantial assistance from the state that employers received. At the same time, metal miners were well organized and enjoyed political autonomy at the local level. As a result, strikes in the metal mining industry during the WFM's first decade frequently involved conflict between state and community political institutions. By contrast, poorly organized bituminous coal employers enjoyed less consistent assistance from the more autonomous state government in Pennsylvania, and coal miners lacked community political organization comparable to that of their counterparts in the West. Strikes in the bituminous coal mining industry did not involve the same magnitude of political conflict as those in metal mining.

Class Struggle and the Development of Union Politics

Organizational and political resources limited the range of opportunities available to employers and miners, yet contrasting resources did not automatically produce political radicalism in the West and political moderation in the East. The effect of resources on political behavior was less direct: The organizational and political resources available to employers and miners helped to mold the character of the strikes during a critical phase of union political development. The political behavior of the WFM and UMWA is simultaneously the product of the objective circumstances that miners found themselves in and their own involvement in politically significant events. Metal and coal miners participated in several politically significant strikes just after they formed their unions. In this section, I briefly examine two such strikes in each industry,[3] which were significant because of their timing, their occurrence in a period of continuous conflict, and the involvement of state resources. Each of the strikes took place early in the unions' histories when miners were in the process of determining the political aspirations of their unions; each happened during a period marked by intense conflict and successive strikes; and state involvement influenced the outcome of each strike enormously.

The strikes that I have chosen illustrate the importance of organizational cohesion and access to state political resources. In 1894, well-organized metal miners in Cripple Creek, Colorado, achieved their goals with the assistance of a Populist governor, Davis A. Waite, who was sympathetic to labor. By 1903, metal mine employers utilized their enhanced resources to break a strike in Cripple Creek and expel the WFM from Colorado. Because competition between coal employers spanned regional boundaries, strikes in the coal mining industry were more likely to be successful if they, too, spanned regional boundaries, given that price increases in one locality were easily undermined by regional price wars among employers. The UMWA called two national strikes for increased wages, one in 1894 and another in 1897. In both instances, coal miners were poorly organized and poorly funded. Coupled with state repression, their lack of resources led to defeat in 1894. In 1897, by contrast, state governments refused assistance to coal employers and thus contributed to one of the UMWA's most important victories.

Shortly after the new year in 1894, several large mine owners in Colorado's Cripple Creek gold mining district increased the workday from eight to ten hours without a corresponding increase in wages, claiming that declining profits necessitated the change (Suggs 1968, p. 325). Cripple Creek's miners were skeptical of their employers' complaints and called a strike early in February (*Cripple Creek Weekly Journal,* February 18, 1894, p. 1, and June 3, 1894, p. 1). These men enjoyed ample resources during the 1894 strike. They struck only those mines that had instituted the ten-hour day, less than one-half of the district's total (Jameson 1987, p. 135). And although the struck mines employed a sizable fraction of the work force, striking workers were able to secure funds from the men who remained on the job. They also received credit and loans from local businesses and donations from miners in other localities. Significantly, members of the WFM occupied numerous political offices in the district, especially in the town of Altman where much of the strike action took place (Rastall 1905, pp. 10–12).

The level of conflict escalated in mid-March when employers made vigorous efforts to reopen their mines with strikebreakers. A district judge issued an injunction against the WFM, prohibiting interference with nonunion men (*Cripple Creek Weekly Journal,* March 18, 1894, p. 2). In protest, miners surrounded one of the struck mines in what to the superintendent appeared to be a threatening manner. The county sheriff sent a team of deputies into the town of Altman to protect the mine, and after a short battle between miners and deputies, city officials captured the deputies. A local judge, who was a member of the WFM, charged the deputies with carrying concealed weapons and sent them back to the town of Cripple Creek. The county sheriff retaliated by arresting Altman city officials and several prominent union men, but all were acquitted a short time later. The struck mines remained closed, and the situation remained at a standoff for the next six weeks. In May, mine owners made more determined plans to reopen their mines with strikebreakers, and the county sheriff deputized 1,200 men. Upon learning of these plans, miners established a military-like organization on top of Bull Hill, a steep bluff overlooking Altman and several important mines. Between 150 and 200 deputies marched to Bull Hill, and, in the battle with miners that ensued, one deputy and one miner were killed, each side took prisoners, and miners blew up a mine shaft. Governor Waite ordered the miners to lay down their weapons, and, believing that the deputies were illegally assembled, he ordered them to disband (*Cripple Creek Weekly Journal*, May 27, 1894, p. 1).

After arbitration meetings between the WFM and employers failed, Governor Waite, acting as a representative of the WFM, negotiated a settlement favorable to the union. The strike did not end immediately, however, because employer-supported deputies launched a second attack on Bull Hill. Governor Waite called out National Guard troops to force the deputies to disband, which they did only after being overwhelmed by militia forces. Despite much violence, the intervention of a Populist governor ensured the success of the metal miners.

Coal miners had fewer resources than their counterparts in the metal mining industry when the UMWA called a national suspension in April 1894, in order to increase coal miners' wages. A nationwide depression in 1893 had exacerbated destitution among coal miners, whose financial condition was already grim. One disillusioned miner, reflecting on the poverty-level wages he had received over the past fifteen years, remarked that "never during that time did I see such an ugly future before the miners of this country as I see today. Reductions and soup houses are about all we hear. God knows our wages are low enough already" (*United Mine Workers' Journal*, January 11, 1894, p. 8). Union membership, in addition, was disturbingly low, and the UMWA had only $2,600 in its treasury (Nash 1982, p. 33). Nevertheless, over 100,000 miners joined the picket lines. As one striker explained, "We might as well starve by taking it easy, as by starving working" (*United Mine Workers' Journal*, February 15, 1894, p. 2).

UMWA leaders pleaded with coal miners to engage only in peaceful picketing. But the miners in several towns were enraged by strikebreakers and injunctions. The threat of arrest carried little weight with them, and many shared the sentiments of Oscar Zamenski, who asserted that "I don't care what I do, if I get arrested and thrown into jail, then they can send my family to the poor house, where I know they will get enough to eat" (quoted in Nash 1982, p. 48). The UMWA leadership lost control of the strike, and coal miners across the country participated in violent protests. Meanwhile, governors in four states brought out the militia, and public opinion turned against the union (McConagha 1925, p. 68). By June, union officials recognized that they were fighting a losing battle and agreed to an unsatisfactory settlement to the strike (Nash 1982, p. 50).

When the UMWA called a second national wage strike in July 1897, destitution among bituminous coal miners had reached alarming proportions, union membership had declined to an all-time low of 3,973, and the UMWA had no strike funds. In spite of these constraints, 150,000 miners joined the picket lines (*United Mine Workers' Journal,* October 1, 1965, p. 11). The coal employer's failure to secure government assistance was a determining factor in preventing an outcome similar to that of the 1894 strike.

The UMWA's nonviolent stance had much to do with altering the role of state government officials in 1897. The union relied more heavily on local organization than it had in 1894, and, consequently, leaders were able to prevent serious violence during the 1897 strike. Their nonviolent position, coupled with massive press coverage revealing destitution in the coalfields, ultimately secured public support. Local communities, national relief associations, and individual citizens donated money, clothes, and food to the UMWA (*Black Diamond,* August 14, 1897, p. 183, and August 21, pp. 210–11). National and local presses portrayed coal employers as inhumane, dishonest, and incapable of managing the affairs of their industry. Strike coverage in a local newspaper in Buffalo, New York, exemplifies the prevailing opinion expressed in newspapers across the country:

> There can be no question but that the soft-coal miner is not receiving a fair proportion of the product of his labor in the shape of wages. Fierce competition among the coal-mine owners is the primary cause of the trouble—dishonest business methods is another. False weights and screens, with excessive prices charged for rent and goods from the companies' stores are common causes for complaint; besides the employment of more men than are needed in order that the [company] houses may be occupied, and trade at the companies' stores increased (quoted in *Black Diamond,* August 7, 1897, p. 153).

Government officials were equally harsh. A legislative commission in Pennsylvania sympathized with miners and sternly admonished employers for mismanaging their businesses (Pennsylvania State Senate 1897). Pennsylvania's governor refused military protection to strikebreakers imported by one of the leading coal companies, leaving 800 poorly organized local deputies to battle 800 angry miners. A month later, the company again tried to reopen, but 500 men and women drove the strikebreakers away (Nash 1982, pp. 58–59). A similar scenario took place in Illinois, where the governor refused troops to coal companies (*Black Diamond,* August 21, 1897, p. 211).

Even before government officials abandoned them, many employers had adopted an unusually sympathetic attitude toward the strike. Besides offering expressions of support, some even made financial contributions to the UMWA (*Black Diamond,* August 7, 1897, p. 154). Employers couched their support in notions of justice, though they had "cheerfully" welcomed the strike as a means of depleting the coal supply and increasing coal prices (*Black Diamond,* July 3, 1897, p. 11, and July 10, 1897, p. 40). Although they had originally maintained that the strike was a "godsend," these employers found themselves backed into a corner when nonunion states invaded their markets and their own state governments refused to intervene (*Black Diamond,* July 10, 1897, p. 40).

Coal miners won the 1897 strike, and it became one of the best-remembered events in UMWA history. Some sixty-eight years later, the *United Mine Workers' Journal* (October 1, 1965, p. 11) portrayed the strike as a "dramatic" and "spontaneous uprising of an enslaved people." Victorious coal miners convinced their employers to participate in an annual interstate joint conference where miners and employers collectively raised prices and wages. The interstate conference represented a means of solving industrial disputes without state intervention by providing a forum for miners and employers to discuss their disputes. After the 1897 strike, the UMWA turned its attention away from political change and concentrated instead on working with employers to stabilize competition and increase wages.

Political intervention in metal mining strikes, meanwhile, had become routine. Governors in Colorado ordered state troops to assist employers during mining strikes in 1896 and 1899. In 1901, prolabor Governor James Orman denied employers in Telluride, Colorado, troops and instead sent a team of investigators who sided with miners (Wright 1974, pp. 230–31). By 1902, metal mine employers were anxious for more decisive political action to end their continuing battle with the WFM, which had recently embarked on a campaign to organize mill and smelter workers in Colorado. This alarmed mine and mine-related employers: Not only did the WFM control many mining communities but it was threatening to control mill and smelter communities, as well. Cohesive organization and the support of employers in the highly concentrated smelter industry provided mine employers with an opportunity to elect a governor sympathetic to their interests. The Republican party supported George

Peabody in 1902 and ran a campaign that stressed the debilitating economic consequences of former Governor Waite's administration; mine employers asserted that the Populists had "disgraced" Colorado in the eyes of the world at large and, most critically, in the eyes of the Eastern business world. In the words of Peabody's supporters, "Capital is deterred from entering the state because of two years of misrule of a Populist governor, who has given the people of the East to understand that law and order have departed from Colorado" (Wright 1974, p. 188). In a state where labor was well organized, however, such arguments did not ensure a Republican victory. Competition between the previously allied Democratic and Populist parties was also a significant factor in the election of George Peabody (Wright 1974, p. 222).

Governor Peabody did not disappoint employers in what came to be their decisive battle with miners in Colorado. Mill employees in Colorado City struck for higher wages and union recognition shortly after the WFM sent a team of organizers there in 1903. The WFM then asked Cripple Creek mine owners to stop sending ore to the struck mills; their miners left work in sympathy with mill workers after several large employers continued ore shipments (Suggs 1972, pp. 47, 51–56). Governor Peabody sent employer-financed National Guard troops into the Cripple Creek district after a few sporadic acts of violence, despite the fact that there was no evidence that the WFM had been involved. Military officials imprisoned, without formal charges, union officials, city officials, and citizens who sympathized with the union on charges of "talking too much" (*Denver Post*, June 11, 1904, p. 3; Suggs 1972, pp. 95–96). The military was so thorough in its attempts to weed out union sympathizers that it was forced to set up a bull pen to hold the arrestees.

The actions of the National Guard in usurping local civil government incited public protest across the state. Citizens worried that Governor Peabody was depriving Colorado residents of their constitutional rights (*Denver Post*, June 11, 1904, p. 3). When the former state attorney general, Eugene Engley, went to court to defend four union men, armed soldiers surrounded the courthouse. Engley refused to proceed with the case on the grounds that

> the constitutional guarantee that courts shall be open and free and untrammeled for public business of a legal character has been invaded and overthrown. It is no longer under the constitution, a constitutional court; on the contrary, it is an armed camp. This court is surrounded by soldiery. The court and I and all other citizens present are now facing glimmering bayonets (quoted in Suggs 1972, pp. 97–98).

Public remonstrations were of little avail. Troops remained in Colorado throughout the fall of 1903 to assist in importing strikebreakers.

Governor Peabody granted the military almost unlimited power the following December for he believed that miners had attempted to derail passenger trains and had killed two mine managers in a shaft explosion. Although these acts were never traced to the union, Peabody empowered the military to arrest union leaders on whatever charges they could— usually vagrancy—in the hope of depriving the union of its leadership. According to Governor Peabody, unorthodox "heroic" steps were necessary "when dealing with a cancer, [because] nothing short of such measures will produce either relief or a permanent cure" (quoted in Suggs 1972, p. 106). In February 1904, after federal officials questioned the legality of Governor Peabody's tactics, he reduced military forces and allowed local officials to resume governance of the district (Suggs 1972, p. 108). However, the military reestablished control on June 6 after unknown parties blew up a depot station, killing thirteen nonunion men. Military troops and employer-led associations took over the county government and raided and destroyed union halls, cooperative stores, union libraries, and newspaper offices. Within days of the explosion, they began selecting unionists and "talkative" citizens for deportation. Governor Peabody established a military commission that deported 238 men to Kansas. "You better not return," military officials warned the men, "for something might happen to you" (*Denver Post,* June 15, 1904, p. 1). In addition, General Sherman Bell, in command of Colorado's military forces, closed the mine of an employer sympathetic to the union. He had these words for the mine's management:

> They can reopen at any time they want to, but let me tell you this: They can't have any of the men I have arrested. They will have to get other men, and those men won't be agitators. For so long as I am in control here, these agitators and dynamiters will not be per- mitted in the district. I deported seventy-nine this afternoon and I'll deport as many tomorrow. I'm going to clean up Colorado, so I'm sending them out of the state. And they won't come back (*Denver Post,* June 11, 1904, p. 3).

The extreme tactics that employers and state officials resorted to in 1903 undermined the WFM's organizational base in Colorado. They also contributed to the union's radical politics. According to one Colorado miner, strikes like the one in 1903 convinced him and his fellow miners that socialism was the only option left. "We miners of Colorado," he reported, "are today largely of the opinion that the old idea of freedom for the citizen seems to have become an impossibility" (*Miners' Magazine,*

May 19, 1904, p. 13). Former WFM president Edward Boyce maintained that "the action of the mine owners in Colorado—sanctioned and approved by the state and national government—in their treatment of the working people and those suspected of sympathizing with them, proves how bitterly the man who toils is hated by those who own the soil and control the government" (*Miners' Magazine,* September 1, 1904, p. 10). A short time later, metal miners approved by 80 percent a referendum to affiliate with the Industrial Workers of the World, a revolutionary organization that stressed direct action at the point of production in place of electoral politics.

Conclusions

The industrial environment occupies a privileged position in studies of working-class behavior. By acknowledging the industrial environment as a source of variation in working-class behavior, theorists assume that the work experience itself predisposes workers to a limited set of behaviors and political ideologies. Consistent reports of high strike rates among specific occupational groups—most notably miners—in different countries and time periods support the assumption of an association between work experience and industrial militancy. Yet, the sharply contrasting political trajectories of the WFM and the UMWA demonstrate that analogous work experiences do not necessarily beget analogous political commitments.

This does not mean that industry-related variables are insignificant with regard to working-class politics. Instead, it suggests that there is a missing link between work experience and union political commitments. This chapter has suggested that the missing link between industry and politics can be addressed by placing industry-related variables within the framework of the resource mobilization theory of social movements. Resource mobilization theorists assume that conflict is always present in situations where contending groups have competing interests (Morris and Herring 1987, p. 172). They therefore focus their attention on the objective conditions that facilitate movement mobilization and shape the character of movement organizations. Although both metal and coal miners had grievances associated with their labor and although both groups were militant, the organizational and political resources of miners and employers in the two industries differed markedly. Industry-related differences produced organizational cohesion among employers and miners in the West and organizational fragmentation in the East. These contrasting organizational resources existed in very different state economic and political environments, leading to a closer correspondence between in-dustrial and political conflict in the West.

This analysis of opposing union political traditions does not end at the level of class organization. Assuming, as E. P. Thompson does, that the "working class did not rise like the sun at an appointed time [but was] present at its own making" (Thompson 1963, p. 9), we must examine class at the level of practice as well as organization. We must look not only at how objective circumstances shape what is possible but at the events that transform possibilities into the first-hand experiences that workers carry with them to their union halls. I have argued that the timing of strikes early in the histories of the WFM and UMWA and their placement in a period of intense conflict influenced the significance of the strikes covered here. In the West, miners participated in more continuous conflict and experienced more explicit political repression than their colleagues in the East. Where the actions of Eastern state governments assisted coal miners in bringing their employers to the bargaining table, the actions of state officials in Colorado convinced members of the WFM that they have few rights under the existing political system. By examining class formation at the level of both organization and practice, this analysis suggests that the industrial environment is significant not because it mechanistically "breed[s] a distinctive social type" (Blauner 1964, p. 166) but rather because it helps to determine the extent to which industrial struggles become political ones.

Acknowledgments

I am grateful to Howard Kimeldorf, William H. Sewell, Jr., Terry Boswell, Rhonda Levine, Nicki Biesel, and Marc Steinberg for their valuable comments on earlier versions of this paper.

Notes

1. Reliable estimates of profits in the metal mining industry are difficult to obtain because figures usually include smaller prospecting ventures and new mines that do not show immediate profits. The *Engineering and Mining Journal* (July 26, 1884, pp. 57–58) estimated a 27 percent average gross profit in the mid-1880s. Though perhaps optimistic, this estimate indicates the greater profitability of metal mines relative to coal mines.

2. There was also a surplus of labor in the East that was associated with the immigration wave of the late nineteenth century. This surplus contributed to low wages.

3. These and other strikes are examined extensively in my dissertation (forthcoming, 1990), which the reader may refer to for richer descriptions and more complete documentation. In addition to newspaper accounts, I relied on the following sources to reconstruct the strikes in Colorado: Jameson 1987, pp. 133–47, 378–474; Suggs 1972; Rastall 1905.

References

Barnett, Paul S. 1966. "Colorado Domestic Business Corporations." Ph.D. dissertation, University of Illinois.

Black Diamond. 1886–1890, 1897.

Blauner, Robert. 1964. *Alienation and Freedom: The Factory Worker and His Industry.* Chicago: University of Chicago Press.

Bowman, John R. 1989. *Capitalist Collective Action: Competition, Cooperation, and Conflict in the Coal Industry.* Cambridge: Cambridge University Press.

Cochran, Thomas C. 1978. *Pennsylvania: A Bicentennial History.* New York: W. W. Norton and Co.

Cripple Creek Weekly Journal. 1894.

Denver Post. 1904.

Dubofsky, Melvyn. 1969. *We Shall Be All: A History of the Industrial Workers of the World.* Chicago: Quadrangle Books.

Engineering and Mining Journal. 1884, 1891.

Everling, Arthur Clark. 1976. "Tactics over Strategy in the United Mine Workers of America: Internal Politics and the Question of the Nationalization of the Mines." Ph.D. dissertation, Pennsylvania State University.

Fantasia, Rick. 1988. *Cultures of Solidarity: Consciousness, Action, and Contemporary American Workers.* Berkeley: University of California Press.

Gordon, David, Richard C. Edwards, and Michael Reich. 1982. *Segmented Work, Divided Workers.* Cambridge: Cambridge University Press.

Gowaskie, Joseph M. 1976. "From Conflict to Cooperation: John Mitchell and Bituminous Coal Operators, 1898–1908." *The Historian* 37:669–88.

Graebner, William. 1973. "Great Expectations: The Search for Order in Bituminous Coal, 1890–1970." *Business History Review* 48:49–72.

Holmes, Joseph John. 1970 "The National Guard of Pennsylvania: Policemen of Industry, 1865–1905." Ph.D. dissertation, University of Connecticut.

Idaho Springs News. 1903.

Jameson, Elizabeth Ann. 1987. "High-Grade and Fissures: A Working-Class History of Cripple Creek, Colorado, Gold Mining District, 1890–1905" Ph.D. dissertation, University of Michigan.

Johnson, James P. 1979. *The Politics of Soft Coal: The Bituminous Industry from World War I Through the New Deal.* Urbana: University of Illinois Press.

Katznelson, Ira. 1986. "Working-Class Formation: Constructing Cases and Comparisons." In *Working-Class Formation: Nineteenth-Century Patterns in Western Europe and the United States,* eds. Ira Katznelson and Aristide Zolberg, pp. 3–41. Princeton, N.J.: Princeton University Press.

Keir, John S. n.d. "The Pittsburgh District." Box 70, Record Group 68, National Archives.

Kerr, Clark, and Abraham Siegel. 1954. "The Inter-Industry Propensity to Strike— An International Comparison." In *Industrial Conflict,* eds. Arthur Kornhauser, Robert Dubin, and Arthur M. Ross, pp. 189–212. New York: McGraw-Hill.

Kimeldorf, Howard. 1988. *Reds or Rackets? The Making of Radical and Conservative Unions on the Waterfront.* Berkeley: University of California Press.

King, Joseph E. 1977. *A Mine to Make a Mine: Financing the Colorado Mining Industry, 1859–1902.* College Station and London: Texas A & M University Press.

Klein, Philip S., and Ari Hoogenboom. 1973. *A History of Pennsylvania.* New York: McGraw-Hill.

Lipset, Seymour Martin. 1960. *Political Man: The Social Basis of Politics.* Garden City, N.Y.: Anchor Books.

McConagha, William A. 1925. "The History and Progress of the United Mine Workers of America." Ph.D. dissertation, University of Illinois.

Mine Report and Prospectus of the Silver State Investment and Mining Company. n.d. Box 4. J. J. Blow Papers, Western History Collection, The University of Colorado, Boulder.

Miners' Magazine. 1904.

Morris, Aldon, and Cedric Herring. 1987. "Theory and Research in Social Movements: A Critical Review." In *Annual Review of Political Science* vol. 2, ed. Samuel Long. Norwood, N.J.: Ablex.

Nash, Michael. 1982. *Conflict and Accommodation: Coal Miners, Steel Workers, and Socialism, 1890–1920.* Westport, Conn.: Greenwood Press.

Neuschatz, Michael. 1986. *The Golden Sword: The Coming of Capitalism to the Colorado Mining Frontier.* New York: Greenwood Press.

Pennsylvania State Senate. 1897. *Legislative Record for the Session of 1897,* vol. 2. Harrisburg, Pennsylvania.

Portes, Alejandro. 1976. "The Sociology of National Development." *American Journal of Sociology* 82:55–85.

Rastall, Benjamin M. 1905. *An Inquiry into the Cripple Creek Strike of 1893.* In Colorado College Studies, vol. 2, pp. 1–48. General Series no. 17, Social Science Series no. 5, Colorado Springs, Colorado.

Roy, Andrew. 1905. *A History of the Coal Miners of the United States.* Westport, Conn.: Greenwood Press.

Sewell, William H., Jr. 1990. "How Classes Are Made: Critical Reflections on E. P. Thompson's Theory of Working-Class Formation." In *E. P. Thompson: Critical Debates,* eds. Harvey J. Kaye and Keith McClelland, pp. 50–77. Oxford, England: Polity Press.

Suggs, George G. 1968. "Catalyst for Industrial Change: The WFM, 1893–1903." *Colorado Magazine* 45:322–39.

———. 1972. *Colorado's War on Militant Unionism: James H. Peabody and the Western Federation of Miners.* Detroit: Wayne State University Press.

Thompson, E. P. 1963 [1966]. *The Making of the English Working Class.* New York: Vintage Books.

United Mine Workers' Journal. 1894–1895, 1965.

West, Elliott. 1979. *The Saloon on the Rocky Mountain Mining Frontier.* Lincoln and London: University of Nebraska Press.

Wright, James Edward. 1974. *The Politics of Populism: Dissent in Colorado.* New Haven, Conn., and London: Yale University Press.

Wyman, Mark. 1979. *Hard Rock Epic: Western Miners and the Industrial Revolution, 1860–1910.* Berkeley: University of California Press.

Zeitlin, Maurice. 1966. "Political Generations in the Cuban Working Class." *American Journal of Sociology* 71:493–508.

12 | The Irish Land War: Peasants, Politics, and Parliament

Kathleen Stanley
Dean Braa

Between the years 1879 and 1881, Irish peasants engaged their landlords in a bitter war over proprietary rights, also known as the "land question." Specifically at issue were the "three Fs": fixity of tenure, fairness of rents, and freedom to sublet all or part of a tenant holding. The Land War included agrarian violence, the widespread use of social ostracism or "boycott," and party politics in the British House of Commons. This multifaceted struggle led ultimately to the dissolution of the landed estates in Ireland.

The central argument of this chapter is that this struggle was a *class* war. Class is, first and foremost, a relational category; classes are determined by their relationship to one another within a system of social production. Social relations of production form the material basis of class and define, very broadly, class interests.[1] And class struggles, as opposed to other forms of human conflict, are over these relationships. In the case of the Land War, the struggle concerned the relations of tenancy that determined access to land—the most important force of production in an agrarian society—and through which landlords appropriated the surplus labor of peasant producers.

The Land War is also the story of how the Irish peasantry became a class for themselves and how they affected the course of Irish history.[2] In discussing this process, we have tried to transcend a simplistic "structure versus agency" formulation. On one side of this issue is Louis Althusser (1970, 1971, 1977), who explains the historical process in terms of transformations necessitated by structural contradictions within which individual human beings and social classes act as the "conveyances" (*trager*) of economic, political, and ideological structures (*practices*). On the other side is E. P. Thompson (1963, 1978), who regards historical transformation as essentially the result of human agency, i.e., of the goal-oriented pursuits of human actors who can and do transcend structural determinations. Both positions are theoretically and empirically untenable and have been criticized elsewhere at greater length (Calhoun 1982; McNall 1987; Porpora 1985). Class processes are neither automatic and mechanical, as in Althusser's model, nor unstructured and voluntaristic, as Thompson would have us believe.

Perhaps the most serious weakness of an "either/or" formulation is that it fails to address the more interesting issue—the relationship between structure and agency (or, as we prefer, "praxis").[3] Class struggle necessarily includes material, political, and ideological elements that are combined and used to motivate and shape action. Although material conditions may determine class interests, they are not in and of themselves sufficient to explain class formation and struggle. Class struggle also includes the intentional and creative use of politics and ideology. It is only through historical analysis of particular class formations that the interrelationship between these elements can be understood. Consequently, our analysis of class struggle during the Irish Land War will focus on these three components of class. We begin with an analysis of the material conditions of the various class participants. This includes the identification of the various relations of production among and between peasants and the specific forms of surplus appropriation imposed on tenants by the landlords. It was the contradiction between tenant production and landlord appropriation, within a context of agricultural depression, that formed the material basis of class struggle during the Land War. Second, the forms of political struggle will be examined with emphasis on the structure and logic of collective action at both the grass-roots and the regional/national levels. This section will focus on the combined organizations of the Land League and the Home Rule Party and their linkage of the land question and nationalism—the "New Departure." Third, the ideological components of the political struggle will be examined. The emphasis here is on the ideology of the New Departure that included a form of agrarian socialism, Celtic revival, and nationalism. The creative synthesis of these elements was instrumental in establishing a united national struggle against British domination and landlordism.

The Agrarian Sector in Postfamine Ireland

The Great Famine of 1845–1849 marks a structural turning point in Irish history. The period that followed the famine was distinct politically, economically, and socially from that which had preceded it. Especially important were changes in the agricultural system and in the agrarian class structure. These changes had two important consequences for the process of class formation and class struggle by (1) making possible a broad-based peasant alliance, and (2) precipitating the agricultural downturn that was the most immediate cause of the Land War.

The late eighteenth and early nineteenth centuries in prefamine Ireland had been marked by rapid population increases, drastic subdivision of land into smaller and smaller holdings, and increasing dependence on the potato crop. About half of the agrarian population depended almost entirely on the potato for subsistence, and when the entire crop failed for several years in succession (beginning in 1845) the results were devastating. Due to death and emigration, the population was cut from over 8 million in 1841 to about 6.5 million in 1851.

The famine had a profound impact on the structure of Irish agriculture. As population size decreased, the average size of peasant landholdings increased. In 1844, the median size of holdings of over one acre was 10.8 acres; by 1876, it was 18.5 (Clark 1979, p. 108). Associated with this were changes in land-use patterns as Irish agriculture shifted from tillage to livestock. The change in land usage resulted from a shift in agricultural prices: Prior to the famine, agricultural prices had favored tillage crops, but after about 1850, they strongly favored livestock and dairy products (Solow 1971). This shift in prices was, in part, a consequence of improved methods of transportation and greater competition from North American farmers in the grain markets. Higher living standards in England made possible a greater volume of meat consumption at the same time that the development of railroads in Ireland and steam transport between Ireland and England made it possible to ship Irish livestock to English cattle markets (Clark 1979, p. 108; Solow 1971, pp. 96–97).

Land in Ireland, both before and after the famine, was held by a very small group of landowners, many of whom were also members of the British Parliament. In 1870, there were fewer than 20,000 proprietors in the entire country, and 3,761 of these controlled 80 percent of the land (Hooker 1938, p. 23). An important class of estate agents managed the properties of absentee landowners.

Peasant producers held land through a rather complex system of tenancy. The more privileged tenants (usually Protestants in Ulster) held leases in perpetuity (or something very close to it) and typically operated large grazing farms. In 1870, approximately 20 percent of the Irish peasantry were leaseholders. The vast majority of tenants—77 percent in 1870— held land from year to year on the basis of oral agreements (Hooker 1938, p. 27). These "tenants-at-will" were forced to bid for holdings at auction, which kept rents high. Rarely were their holdings compact; most held a number of scattered plots of land. In addition to excessive rents, tenants-at-will had to make extra payments to estate agents and pay two different taxes, yet, unlike leaseholders, they enjoyed no security of tenure and had no right to compensation for any improvements.

There was also an extensive system of subtenancy. "This happened when—either because the landlord was generous, or because the tenant had made improvements since the rent was fixed, or because agricultural prices had risen or for any other reason—the tenant could obtain rent at a higher rate than he was paying to the landlord. Sometimes the tenant let the entire holding; more frequently he subdivided the holding, letting part and cultivating the rest himself" (Hooker 1938, p. 29). Leaseholders very frequently sublet part of their holding, and tenants-at-will also did so, though less commonly. There were two principal types of subtenancy. "Cottiers" were allowed merely a cabin and a potato garden in exchange for rent and sometimes labor. Most cottiers also sought wage work wherever they could find it. The second type of subtenancy was "conacre," a form of sharecropping in which arable land was taken on a seasonal basis. Because the lender had the responsibility of preparing the ground and providing tools and seed, conacre, in essence, provided land-poor peasants with a portion of the crop in return for their labor. The system of subletting, particularly in the prefamine period, led to deep divisions within the peasantry. By reputation, the relations between direct tenants and their subtenants were worse then those between landowners and tenants. There were several reasons for this. Subtenants enjoyed even less security of tenure than did tenants-at-will, those from whom land was sublet charged double (or more) the rent they themselves paid, and subtenants usually worked for more prosperous peasants. "During the pre-Famine period the demand for agricultural labour was declining while the supply was rising, so that employment was inevitably insecure and poorly paid. Relations between farmers and labourers were frequently bitter" (Clark 1978, p. 25). Tensions and conflicts were further exacerbated by the preference of leaseholders for grazing despite the fact that tenants-at-will and cottiers depended on the preservation of tillage land to obtain potato plots and agricultural employment.

A major effect of the famine was the decline (though by no means disappearance) of subletting. As population size decreased, as landholdings increased in size, and as production shifted from tillage to pasture, leaseholders and tenants-at-will were under less pressure to sublet. Cottiers, not surprisingly, had been hardest hit by the famine, and there was a significant drop in their numbers. Those who did survive found it increasingly difficult to sublet land through either cottier or conacre forms of subtenancy, and they became more dependent on wages (including seasonal migration to England) for their livelihood (Clark 1979, pp. 229–30).

As subletting decreased, the exploitative relations of production between tenants and landowners (and their agents) were brought into sharp relief. Before the famine, the system of subtenancy had created deep antagonisms among peasants and effectively prevented any alliance against the land-owners. But after the famine, although divisions remained, there was a greater potential for tenants to coalesce around issues of rent and the general conditions of tenure.

The agricultural depression of the 1870s gave these issues added impetus and brought them to the fore. Until about 1876, Irish agriculture prospered. The next three years, however, witnessed disastrous harvests due to poor weather. In the past, bad harvests had resulted in higher agricultural prices as supply constricted. By the late 1870s, however, Irish agriculture was facing increasing competition from North American grain farmers. For the first time, low yields were accompanied by low prices (Solow 1971, p. 123). And yields for the primary subsistence crop, the potato, declined even more precipitously than those for cash crops. The livestock economy also suffered losses as the price of butter fell and the wet weather reduced the yields and quality of fodder crops and spread disease. The situation was made even worse by a decline in the demand for seasonal agricultural labor in England, where the effects of the agricultural depression were also being felt. Poor peasants (the vast majority) had always depended on this labor as their primary source of cash for paying rents, and its loss added to the general hardship.

Irish tenants already faced a difficult process of economic reproduction in the decades after the Great Famine. In the late 1870s, "with what is commonly called the luck of the Irish, everything failed them at once" (Solow 1971, p. 127). The plight of the peasantry was made even more precarious by the inelasticity of rents and the absence of fixity of tenure. By 1879, famine had become, once again, a distinct possibility in Ireland. This agricultural crisis was the spur to social upheaval in the form of the Land War. Coming under specific attack was the system of land tenure that kept Irish farmers continually teetering on the brink of disaster. Peasant opposition to the land tenure system "included resentment against the historical fact of confiscation; tenants' lack of security of tenure; the insufficient rewards for tenants whose efforts had enhanced—indeed, largely created—the land's value; opposition to absentee landlords; and frustration at the lack of any prospect of alternative employment for the Irish peasant in Ireland" (Bew 1979, p. 2).

The Land War began primarily as an attempt to persuade landlords to reduce rents. Many tenants believed they were entitled to rent reductions as a matter of right and that it was the obligation of the landlord to help them during economic adversity. Beginning in 1878, tenants began to submit appeals for rent reductions, and the number of such appeals increased as the crisis deepened. For their part, however, the landlords did not believe that the level of distress, particularly when measured against the Great Famine, was sufficient to justify abatements (Clark

1979, p. 235). Moreover, in an era of consolidation and conversion to pasture, there was little economic rationale in preserving small tenants. Some did grant abatements, but they were generally small and were insufficient to provide any real relief. Inevitably, many tenants began to fall into arrears, and landlords began evicting those who would not or could not pay. "By the third decade of the nineteenth century a fierce struggle had developed between the two groups. Landlords fought to collect rents and to evict tenants who were not paying, while tenants resisted payments and, above all, resisted evictions" (Clark 1975, p. 486).

The Political Struggle

The combination of agricultural crisis and exploitative relations of production forced the Irish peasantry to fight for its material survival, but it did not determine the form that struggle would take. Yet, the development of political organization and strategy was not completely open-ended either. Rather, the political struggle during the Land War was shaped by several elements, including previous struggles and the possibilities created by a shifting class structure. These elements were combined in new and creative ways through the process of struggle. The Land War marked an important point in Irish history when new strategies and alliances were used to political and economic advantage. Of crucial importance was the linkage of the land question and the national question through the combined organization of the Land League and the Home Rule party.

The formation of the Irish National Land League in October, 1879, was a direct response to growing peasant distress and unrest and the culmination of several decades of agrarian agitation. "The more active political life of the 1870s derived much of its character from the ideas and events of the preceding twenty years; for it was during these years that the land question acquired a central importance in the public mind, and that the connection between land and politics, implicit in the Irish situation for centuries, came to be generally recognized" (Becket 1973, p. 351). The Land League had two important antecedents, the Tenant League of the 1850s and the Fenians.

The Irish Tenant League was itself the outgrowth of the "tenant protection societies" formed in the postfamine years. These tenant societies had as their common goals reducing rents and resisting evictions; their support came primarily from leaseholders in more prosperous regions of the country (Clark 1979, pp. 212–13). The Tenant League had some measure of success in electing representatives to Westminster but soon foundered when two of its leading members accepted positions in a coalition government in what was regarded as an act of co-optation. As an organized movement, the Tenant League disintegrated rapidly, without realizing any of its concrete goals. A small number of farmers' clubs, whose support came mainly from large farmers, survived, but very few remained continuously active (Clark 1979, p. 215).

Although the tenant right movement faltered, a great mass of discontent remained. In 1858, the Fenian Brotherhood (also known as the Irish Republican Brotherhood) was formed as an oath-bound secret society. The Fenians believed that revolution was the only way to free Ireland from English domination. Fenian support came primarily from the poorest farmers and laborers, and agrarian secret societies flourished in the 1860s as a series of bad harvests caused widespread distress. The Fenians staged a "rising" in 1867 that was quickly and easily defeated by forces of the Royal Irish Constabulary and the British Army. Fenianism remained, however, "a powerful political force, a rival and spur to constitutional nationalism, and even, on occasion, its ally" (Becket 1973, p. 361).

The Home Rule party, the other principal political organization of the Land War, also had its historical antecedent. During the 1850s and 1860s, a small group of nationalist politicians had kept alive the constitutional demand for Irish self-government. The early home rule movement drew its supporters largely from the southern and eastern parts of the country and from the Catholic middle classes in towns and cities. A small measure of support for home rule and a number of its most important leaders came from the Anglo-Irish ascendancy, whose ruling class aspirations were blocked by English rule. Home rule did have considerable rural appeal, although most tenants were most interested in land issues. The activities of the Fenians played an important part in pushing the parliamentarians toward greater militancy. The constitutional nationalists, for fear of appearing to ally themselves with the British government against true Irish patriots, were forced into a cautious support of Fenian goals, particularly land reform. The early home rulers were also concerned that centuries of English mismanagement and neglect were leading to revolution and believed that the only real guarantee against open revolt "would be the government of Ireland by her natural rulers—the nobility, the gentry, and the substantial middle classes" (Becket 1973, p. 377). Though the Home Rule party was successful in electing representatives to the British House of Commons, it made little headway in gaining an Irish parliament.

This situation began to change in 1875 when the policy of obstructionism, which became a major tactic of the Land War, was initiated. Obstructionism involved the deliberate abuse of the rules of procedure for the express purpose of holding up business. Specific tactics included the introduction of numerous bills by the Irish party (thereby filling up the docket) and lengthy speeches and attempts at amendment for purposes of delay (filibustering) (Thornley 1960). Obstructionism was certainly not new, but, in the past, its use had been restricted by "gentlemen's agreement." The Irish Home Rule party's novelty lay in its aggressive use of these tactics to further the Irish political cause by obstructing all manner of debate and legislation, not simply those bills dealing with Irish issues. This tactic often made it impossible to pass any legislation, particularly bills of finance, and it was very effective in disrupting the administration of the British Empire.

Obstructionism was taken up by a handful of Irish MPs, most notably Charles Stewart Parnell, and had been developed into an effective political weapon by 1877. To increase his popular support and gain control of the Home Rule party, Parnell, a landowner, actively sought a closer alliance with those espousing land reform. The man responsible for forging this alliance was Michael Davitt, an Irish Fenian whose family had been evicted from their holding during the famine. In 1877, Davitt had emerged from a long spell in prison determined to bring the land question to the center of Irish politics. In the summer of 1879, Davitt and other Fenians engaged in informal negotiations with Parnell. Although the details are obscure, some sort of working agreement was reached in which the more radical section of the Home Rule party pledged itself to land reform in order to win the allegiance of rural Ireland. In October of that year, Davitt organized the Land League and persuaded Parnell to be its president.

An open connection was thus established between the land movement and the most active section of the Home Rule party (Becket 1973, p. 386). This alliance between the land movement and the Home Rule movement became known as the "New Departure," and each side received something important through these ties. The Home Rule party found that the land movement could provide the popular base of political support that it had been lacking. In return, the land movement received the political support of a group of politicians who were now committed to land reform and were in a position to take their demands to Parliament.

The Land League was effective in harnessing and directing the unrest that grew as the agricultural crisis deepened. League goals reflected the interest of tenants, including specific demands for implementation of the "three Fs," reduction of rents, and an end to evictions. A new demand that arose during the Land War was the call for peasant proprietorship (ownership) of the land and, by extension, an end to landlordism. These demands reflect the primary class contradiction of Irish society in the late nineteenth century—that between tenants and landowners. The level of agitation continued to increase in 1880. Very large public meetings, with thousands of participants, were held, and hundreds of local Land League branches were formed. The public demonstrations served both as a platform to express League demands and as a means of intimidating its opponents. The League sought to disrupt the land system by encouraging tenants to withhold their rents and by organizing tenants to resist evictions. Landowners and their agents, baliffs, process servers, and "landgrabbers" (peasants who took land from which the previous tenant had been evicted) were assaulted and, with increasing regularity, ostracized.

Organized ostracism was actively promoted by the leaders of the agitation. The most celebrated instance was directed against land agent Captain Charles Boycott. The "boycott" against him denied him the use of laborers to harvest his crops, servants to do the household chores, workers to care for the horses and other livestock, as well as the privilege of receiving his mail, shopping in the local stores, or getting his horses shod at the blacksmith (Palmer 1940, p. 200). Boycotting quickly became one of the most effective strategies of the Land War. According to Clark (1979, p. 312), its success provides clear evidence of the authority of the Land League and the extent to which it was grounded in the stable structure of agrarian community relations.

Violence and the threat of violence were important features of the Land War. "Violence helped to enforce the laws of the Land League. Most often the objective was to prevent or punish landgrabbing, the payment of normal rents, or the eviction of tenants; in addition, violence or the threat of it was often employed during boycotts. . . . The single most common motive for outrage was the prevention or punishment of landgrabbing, and the victims in such cases were almost always tenants" (Clark 1979, pp. 320–21). The League did not, however, officially condone violence, although its members did participate in it and League speakers frequently incited it, whether intentionally or not. Those directly responsible for agrarian violence typically had some personal stake in the case at hand (Clark 1979, p. 325). Ultimately, however, agrarian agitation would have had a far more limited effect were it not for the linkage of the land question and the national question. The real basis of landlord power lay in the British system of property, law, and colonial domination and could thus be challenged only through a direct attack on the British state. The efforts of Parnell and other nationalist politicians were therefore a crucial element of the Land War.

In the election of 1880, the balance of power within the Home Rule party shifted in favor of the Parnellites. Sixty-one home rule candidates were returned, approximately two dozen of whom were loyal to Parnell and one dozen of whom were connected with the agrarian agitation. The election of 1880 also brought down the Conservatives, led by Benjamin Disraeli; the Liberals, led by William Gladstone, came to power. Gladstone's return to office was dependent on the support of the Irish

Home Rule party, and in return, the Irish expected land reform and concrete steps toward Irish self-government.

The levels of agrarian agitation in Ireland and obstructionist agitation in Parliament led Gladstone to propose emergency measures to protect tenants who were in arrears because of the agricultural depression. When the bill was defeated in the House of Lords, there was an almost immediate increase in agrarian disturbance, including the beginnings of the large-scale organized boycotts. As the agitation and violence increased, certain members of Gladstone's cabinet pressed for more coercive measures to reassert government authority. "When the new session opened in January 1881 the cabinet's Irish policy presented the familiar combination of coercion and concession: a bill for the suspension of *habeas corpus* and a bill for the reform of the land system" (Becket 1973, p. 390). Attempts by Parnell and his allies to obstruct the coercion bill (Protection of Person and Property Bill) led to the implementation of a "closure" resolution that would put an end to obstructionist tactics.

The Land Act of 1881 was a victory for the land movement for it essentially conceded the basic demands of the Land League, in particular the "three Fs." Under the terms of the act, land courts were set up to adjudicate rents that would remain fixed for a period of fifteen years. Yearly tenants were to have fixity of tenure as long as they paid their rents, did not sublet, and did not erect buildings without the landlords' consent. Tenants were also given the right to sell their interest in the holding. The newly established Land Commission would also lend up to three-quarters of the purchase price to tenants wishing to buy their holdings. "By these provisions, and by recognizing the permanent interest of the tenant in his holding, the act of 1881 established a system of dual ownership, and reduced the landlord to little more than a receiver of rent" (Becket 1973, p. 391). The more radical elements of the Land League attempted to subvert the Land Act, which they believed did not go far enough in establishing peasant proprietorship. Parnell did not denounce the act completely but complained that it did little or nothing for tenants already in arrears and that it excluded leaseholders from any immediate benefit. He warned tenants not to make application for rent arbitration to the new land courts until the League had satisfied itself about their character with a number of test cases (Becket 1973, p. 392). Opposition to the Land Act led to Parnell's arrest under the Protection of Person and Property Act.

Parnell's arrest only heightened his prestige in Ireland and led to further agrarian agitation. The Land League called for a total rent strike and assumed a position of open rebellion. The government used the "No Rent Manifesto" as an occasion for suppressing the League and declaring it illegal. The result was a wave of agrarian violence and demands for Parnell's release. This proved, however, to be the last gasp of the Land League.

By autumn of 1881, the movement was in disarray, and much of the central leadership was imprisoned. The majority of tenant farmers turned their attention away from political agitation and toward the land courts, which were immediately swamped with applications for rent arbitration. Parnell was eventually released from prison under terms of what came to be known as the "Kilmainham Treaty" between himself and Gladstone. Gladstone agreed to relax coercion and amend the Land Act, and Parnell agreed to use his influence to calm the country and assure the acceptance of the Land Act in its amended form. For all intents and purposes, the Land War was over.

The Land League did not achieve its goal of peasant proprietorship but did set in motion a chain of events that led to its realization by the turn of the century. "The Land War had generated a new political force in Irish politics that did not disappear even after the movement as such had collapsed. . . . The Land War had not resolved a conflict, but rather had intensified it" (Clark 1979, pp. 342, 344).

Although the Land League was officially defunct, tenant farmers remained organized. After his release from prison, Parnell formed the Irish National League on the basis of reconstituted Land League branches. The National League was still an agrarian-based organization, although nationalism, rather than land reform, was now the principal goal. Because the peasantry remained organized, they were in a position to respond quickly when, in the mid-1880s, economic conditions again deteriorated. This time, tenant farmers were experienced and organized, and they rapidly increased their antilandlord agitation with many of the same tactics they had used only a few years earlier during the Land War. The major demand was that rents fixed by the Land Act of 1881 should be reduced. The new agitation was very much grass-roots in its origins for the Home Rule party was busy with its political battles at Westminster.

Throughout the 1880s and 1890s, agrarian unrest flared whenever the harvests were poor or agricultural prices depressed. Even the Conservative government (which came to power largely because of Gladstone's inability to solve the "Irish problem") was becoming convinced that the only real solution to the Irish problem would be the transfer of land ownership to the tenants.

Although landlords were not yet being driven from their estates, their fortitude was showing signs of wear. The administration of their estates was becoming difficult and costly, sources of credit were drying up as the value of their properties declined, and competition from North American farmers was undermining the profitability of their estates.

Tenant struggles and the shifting world market made landowners willing, even eager, to sell their estates.

The Wyndham Act of 1903 finally estalished terms for the transfer of land that were acceptable to both tenants and landowners. The new act "proved so satisfactory to both sides that without making the sale of estates compulsory it went far toward making it universal. . . . At the time of its passage there were still more than half-a-million tenant-farmers. By 1909 some 270,000 purchases had been negotiated, and a further 46,000 were pending. Little more than a decade later, landlordism in rural Ireland had become a thing of the past" (Becket 1973, p. 407). More than twenty years after the end of the Land War, the final goal of the Land League, peasant proprietorship, was achieved.

Agrarianism and Nationalism

The ideology of agrarian nationalism was not a simple reflection of structural transformation. Rather, it represented a creative synthesis of three distinct ideological frameworks: the bourgeois nationalism of the Home Rule party, the radical republicanism of the Fenians, and the agrarianism of the Land League. It was the combination of these ideologies in thought and their adherents in political action that made the Land War successful. Ideological transformation and the creation of a "counterhegemony" were thus crucial aspects of the class struggle (Gramsci 1971). Changes in the Irish economy obviously played a role in the development of this counterhegemony. The famine and continuing emigration, in particular, left an important legacy of nationalism and hatred toward the British (Hutchinson 1987, pp. 114–15).

Both the home rule movement and Fenianism were part of this nationalist legacy, although they employed rather different strategies. Under Parnell, the Home Rule party took up a very pragmatic nationalism (Brasted 1983). It was the growing realization that home rule had little chance of success without a popular base of support that led Parnell into an alliance with the land movement. Fenianism, on the other hand, had its roots in the Catholic peasantry (the poorest tenants and cottiers) and was consequently more committed to land reform. The Fenians' advocacy of armed rebellion came from the belief that national independence was the necessary first step toward any program of social reform. Unlike the home rulers, the Fenians took their inspiration from Ireland's Gaelic past. The name "Fenian" was derived from "Fianna"—the army led by Fionn MacCuchail (Finn MacCool), the legendary Celtic warrior.

A more explicit ideological connection between nationalism and the land question was provided by Davitt's agrarianism, derived from the writings of James Fintan Lalor, a participant in the Young Ireland movement of 1848. Lalor, and Davitt after him, argued that the basis of Irish nationality was not a desire for self-government but a love of the land that the Irish depended upon for their livelihood. What both men advocated was a form of agrarian socialism.

> I acknowledge no right of property . . . which takes away all right of property, security and independence, and existence itself, from a population of eight millions. . . . I hold and maintain that the entire soil of a country belongs of right to the entire population of that country, and it is the rightful property, not of any one class, but of the nation at large . . . the enjoyment of the people of this right of first ownership in the soil is essential to the vigor and vitality of all other rights (Lalor, quoted in Davitt 1970, pp. 60, 63).

This view was apparently widely shared because hundreds of thousands of Irish peasants were mobilized during the Land War to fight for what they believed were their natural rights to the land. The roots of this belief are to be found in the system of land tenure that existed before the English confiscations of the sixteenth and seventeenth centuries. Before the English arrived, the Irish were organized into clans that held land in common. Every member of the clan had a right to an allotment of the clan's land, and no system of private ownership existed. Upon this communal order of landholding, the English superimposed their own system of private ownership, seizing land from the native occupiers through conquest and confiscation. Through the centuries, Irish peasants remained "determined to revive their communal rights and to destroy the system which had been forced upon them. The circumstances of the conquests and confiscations became a part of their tradition and heritage. Often it was the only history they knew" (Palmer 1940, p. 5). The Land League was thus an outgrowth of a long-standing cultural tradition.

The success of the Land War lay in its linkage of the land question and the national question (the New Departure). Either one, taken separately, had little chance of succeeding. The earlier nationalists, both bourgeois and revolutionary, had failed to attract sufficient peasant support, and, as a consequence, their efforts were ineffective. Earlier peasant struggles had basically taken the form of agrarian crime. Because they lacked a political organization and agenda, they were unable to challenge the real foundation of the land system that was based in English property rights and the system of colonial domination.

The ideology of the New Departure proved to be counterhegemonic, a powerful motivating force capable of uniting, even if only temporarily, divergent classes in a national struggle against the land system. Ideology, in the case of the Land War, was not a secondary issue derived in some simple way from material conditions. The New Departure as a form of political and ideological praxis was the beginning of an ultimately successful challenge to the power of the British Empire.

Conclusion

Our analysis of the Irish Land War highlights several important issues in the historical study of class formation and class struggle. Perhaps most important is the demonstration of the interconnections between material, political, and ideological dimensions of class. Class cannot be reduced to any one of these elements or to a "structure versus agency" issue. Such formulations miss the complexity of class processes.

Structural transformations in the Irish economy brought certain contradictions, namely the exploitative relations between landlords and tenants, into sharp relief and made a broad alliance of tenants possible. Agricultural depression threatened the material survival of the peasantry and made some kind of response necessary. Although structural contradictions were thus the motivating force of class struggle, they did not determine the form or outcome of that struggle. The political and ideological practices of the Land War were created by the participants from an array of possibilities derived from the collective experiences (history) of the social actors. These experiences were recomposed in ways that gave meaning and legitimation to the struggle for land.

Historical change is neither automatic nor mechanical; class struggle does, indeed, matter. The abolition of landlordism was in no way predetermined. The outcome of the Land War was affected by conjunctural factors, such as changing world agricultural markets (which, along with agrarian agitation, helped render the large estates unprofitable) and elections in England (which allowed the Home Rule party to exert considerable power). Crucial to the outcome was the success of the Land League in mobilizing and organizing the peasantry and forming interclass alliances. In the absence of coordinated agrarian and parliamentary struggles, the trajectory of Irish development would have been very different.

Notes

1. Social relations of production refer to (1) the relation to the means or forces of production, and (2) the form of surplus product (value) appropriation. In this chapter, peasants are seen as subject to various forms of surplus appropriation (rents) and various forms of tenancy as relations to the land. Land is a force of production or, as Marx suggested, a subject of labor.

2. We are using "peasantry" as a descriptive term that refers to all tenant producers in the agrarian sector. As we indicate later, the peasantry is divided into various relations of production with common and contrary interests.

3. Praxis is used here as an epistemological proposition. Human beings must act upon the material world in order to apprehend and comprehend their existence. But, as John McMurtry suggests, following Marx, acting in a material world includes the process of "projective consciousness." In other words, humans build a structure in imagination as a precondition for acting upon a material world, i.e., constructing something in reality (McMurtry 1978, pp. 22–24). The construct in imagination is not the "reflection" of material reality, and, yet, it is necessary in order to transform the material world. For example, we argue that the linkage of the land and national questions was a strategy that resulted in the dissolution of the landlord class. This strategy was formulated "in imagination" by various social actors and used to transform relations of production in the agrarian sector. We prefer to call this an exercise in "creative praxis."

References

Althusser, Louis. 1970. "The Errors of Classical Economics: An Outline for a Concept of Historical Time." In *Reading Capital,* eds. Louis Althusser and Etienne Balibar, pp. 91–118. London: New Left Books.

———. 1971. *Lenin and Philosophy.* New York: Monthly Review Press.

———. 1977. "Marxism and Humanism." In *For Marx,* ed. Louis Althusser. London: Verso.

Becket, J. C. 1973. *The Making of Modern Ireland, 1603–1923.* New York: Alfred A. Knopf.

Bew, Paul. 1979. *Land and the National Question in Ireland, 1858–1882.* Atlantic Highlands, N.J.: Humanities Press.

Brasted, H. V. 1983. "Irish Nationalism and the British Empire in the Late Nineteenth Century." In *Irish Culture and Nationalism, 1750–1950,* eds. Oliver MacDonagh et al. London: Macmillan.

Calhoun, Craig. 1982. *The Question of Class Struggle: Social Foundations of Popular Radicalism During the Industrial Revolution.* Chicago: University of Chicago Press.

Clark, Samuel. 1975. "The Political Mobilization of Irish Farmers." *Canadian Review of Sociology and Anthropology* 12:483–99.

———. 1978. "The Importance of Agrarian Classes: Agrarian Class Structure and Collective Action in Nineteenth-Century Ireland." *British Journal of Sociology* 29:22–40.

———. 1979. *Social Origins of the Irish Land War.* Princeton, N.J.: Princeton University Press.

Davitt, Michael. 1970. *The Fall of Feudalism in Ireland, or The Story of the Land League Revolution.* Shannon, Ireland: Irish University Press.

Gramsci, Antonio. 1971. *Selections from the Prison Notebooks.* London: Lawrence and Wishart.

Hooker, Elizabeth R., 1938. *Readjustments of Agricultural Tenure in Ireland.* Chapel Hill: University of North Carolina Press.

Hutchinson, John. 1987. *The Dynamics of Cultural Nationalism: The Gaelic Revival and the Creation of the Irish Nation State.* London: George Allen and Unwin.

McMurtry, John. 1978. *The Structure of Marx's World-View.* Princeton, N.J.: Princeton University Press.

McNall, Scott. 1987. "Thinking About Class: Structure, Organization, and Consciousness." In *Recapturing Marxism,* eds. Rhonda F. Levine and Jerry Lembcke, pp. 228-46. New York: Praeger.

Palmer, Norman D. 1940. *The Irish Land League Crisis.* New Haven, Conn.: Yale University Press.

Pomfret, John E. 1930. *The Struggle for Land in Ireland, 1800-1923.* Princeton, N.J.: Princeton University Press.

Porpora, Douglas V. 1985. "The Role of Agency in History: The Althusser-Thompson-Anderson Debate." *Current Perspectives in Social Theory* 6:219-41.

Solow, Barbara Lewis. 1971. *The Land Question and the Irish Economy, 1870-1903.* Cambridge: Harvard University Press.

Thompson, E. P. 1963. *The Making of the English Working Class.* New York: Vintage.

———. 1978. *The Poverty of Theory.* New York: Monthly Review Press.

Thornley, David. 1960. "The Irish Home Rule Party and Parliamentary Obstruction, 1874-87." *Irish Historical Studies* 12:38-57.

Culture, Ideology, and Consciousness

The selections in the final section of this volume explore the complex and sometimes contradictory ways in which human actors express their experience of class structure and class action. Class consciousness is mediated, as the following chapters show, by the specific cultural context in which dominant and subordinate classes interact.

As David Halle demonstrated in an earlier work, the workplace is but one of several sources of class identity and experience. For Halle, the house itself is an important material basis of cultural identity and, in his contribution to this volume, he examines the art displayed in working- and middle-class houses as indicators of class distinction and taste. His findings point to the importance of a materialist approach to culture, but also suggest that the relationship between taste and class may not always be a clear and obvious one.

From Michael Yarrow's study of Appalachian coal miners, we learn how male occupational culture is combined with an intense class consciousness to produce a contradictory set of meanings in which the gender consciousness created by male social relations simultaneously strengthens the solidarity of miners and significantly limits its scope. Where the division of labor is sharply gendered, class consciousness is intersected and constituted by a consciousness of gender.

Marc Steinberg's critique of poststructuralist theory argues against the increasingly prevalent view that language itself shapes the contours of class conflict. Drawing from his study of nineteenth-century English cotton spinners, he offers an analysis of class conflict that suggests that discourse is not a simple referential guide but is inscribed by meanings generated in the context of material relationships as well. Steinberg shows how the cotton spinners of Ashton-Stalybridge drew from an available historical language of subordination to construct a discourse of class conflict that "spoke" to their specific experiences of exploitation.

Based upon his previous theoretical contributions and his experience as a steelworker in Hungary, Michael Burawoy suggests that the working classes of Hungary and Poland, continually called on to act out a vision of socialism that was contradicted by their own experiences, developed a critique of socialism based upon its failure to live up to its own promises. Burawoy describes the ritual process of "painting socialism" within the factory regime of bureaucratic despotism and the ways in which this regime hindered collective mobilization. He then compares this to the "painting of democracy" in advanced capitalist societies and notes that the rise of the market in the East carries the potential for a serious working-class struggle for democratic socialism.

13 | Bringing Materialism Back In: Art in the Houses of the Working and Middle Classes

David Halle

Materialist Approaches to Art and Culture

Materialist approaches to the study of art and culture have fallen out of favor in some circles these days. This is especially true of the historical materialism associated with Marxism. As one commentator put it:

> Perhaps the sole characteristic common to virtually all contemporary varieties of Western Marxism is their concern to defend themselves against the accusation of materialism. Gramscian or Togliattian Marxists, Hegelian-Existentialist Marxists, Neo-Positivizing Marxists, Freudian or Structuralist Marxists, despite the profound dissensions which otherwise divide them, are at one in rejecting all suspicion of collusion with "vulgar" or "mechanical" materialism (Timpanaro, 1975, p. 29).

Yet, if "vulgar" Marxist theories of the influence of the mode of production on culture are out, the new "sophisticated" Marxism has difficulties, too. For example, in a number of his later writings, Raymond Williams (1977, 1978) rejects the "naive reductionism" of many Marxist accounts of the link between culture and material base. But he runs into problems, which he acknowledges he cannot solve, when thinking about a more sophisticated model of the relation between base and superstructure, between ideas and material production. As he says, many of these models are either unclear, are posed at such a level of generality as to be unhelpful, or are without meaning. The metaphor, beloved of vulgar materialists, that art "reflects" the material world may be too simple, but it is a dubious advance to substitute the more complex and less clear metaphor that art "mediates" the world. To stress the "complexity and autonomy" of the superstructure in relation to the base may be to replace a simple theory with an empty one.[1]

Rather than refine and fine-tune the model of the relation between ideas and mode of production, some of the recent Marxist theoreticians of art and culture have rejected materialism altogether. The results are not always encouraging. For example, Herbert Marcuse (1978, p. x), in *The Aesthetic Dimension: Toward a Critique of Marxist Aesthetics,* denies many of the "materialist" propositions of Marxist aesthetics, including the idea that there is a "definite connection between art and the material base, between art and the totality of the relations of production." Marcuse argues that "authentic art" or "great art," which is his focus, is "largely autonomous vis-à-vis the given social relations" for the defining characteristic of great art is that it is critical of existing social relations, "breaking through the mystified (and petrified) social reality and opening the horizon of change." Thus, art is not a reflection of society but "goes beyond it." This theory has several problems. One consequence of Marcuse's view would appear to be that it excludes from the realm of "authentic art" a wide range of works, including most Christian art, most impressionist art, and most abstract art of the twentieth century; little of this art is particularly critical of society, still less does it suggest an alternate one.[2] Moreover, Marcuse ends by grounding his theory of the critical nature of art in archaic biology, specifically in Freudian drive theory. Thus, he argues that great art (critical art) pertains to the domain of Eros the Beautiful, representing Freud's pleasure drive, for great art strains toward the liberation from oppression. Uncritical works, by contrast, represent Freud's destructive drive for they collaborate in domination. Yet, given the highly controversial status of Freudian drive theory in modern psychoanaltyic thought and given the various psychoanalytic schools that reject drive theory altogether (of which interpersonal theory and object relations theory are the two foremost), it is untenable to simply assert the truth of drive theory, as Marcuse does.[3]

My argument in this chapter is that Marxists and other analysts of culture may have rejected a materialist approach to art and culture too soon. By a "materialist approach" here, I mean the view that art and culture should be studied and understood in the material context in which it is located and that this material context has an important causal impact on the existence and persistence of that culture. The problem with many attempts to apply materialism to art and culture in the twentieth century lies not with the materialist perspective in general but with the choice of the *particular* material context used to provide the explanation.

In the twentieth century, the salient material context for art is, in many respects, the house and its material surroundings. This is just as important as the mode of production in analyzing, for example, painting. Certainly, in the last 150 years, the majority of paintings have been originally purchased by individuals who wish to hang them in their homes. Thus, French impressionist art now occupies a prominent place in many leading Western art museums because, for many years, people bought the paintings to hang in their homes. Indeed, the French state museums refused to buy works by living artists for a long time.)

Some observers have, in fact, commented on the importance of the house in understanding art in the nineteenth and twentieth centuries. Analyzing the emergence of impressionism, Harrison and Cynthia White (1965) pointed to the fact that most paintings in France in the 1830s and 1840s were purchased for the homes of the bourgeoisie, rather than the aristocracy. This affected both the form of the art (for huge ceiling paintings were too large for most bourgeois homes) and its content (for panoramic battle scenes were inappropriate for bourgeois homes); genre paintings and landscapes were more suitable. Yet, there are few systematic studies of painting in the context of the house and almost none for the twentieth century.

Similar arguments can be made for many other items of modern culture. For example, the meaning of primitive artworks for the societies that produce them has been amply studied, yet, in the twentieth century, primitive artifacts have been increasingly displayed as art in contexts far removed from that of their creators—in people's homes in the West. Religious artifacts and representations have likewise been overlooked. These have long pervaded the homes of Catholics, and their images can be striking. Wassily Kandinsky (1913), for instance, was deeply influenced by the vivid religious images he saw in Russian peasants' houses. But there are almost no studies of religious artifacts in Western homes. All this suggests that, in seeking to understand the meaning of art for a modern audience, works should be examined in the context of the social life, architecture, and material surroundings of the house.[4]

The study I am presently conducting is designed to remedy the absence of accounts of art and culture in the material context of the modern house. My research is based on samples of houses and people drawn from three neighborhoods in the New York City area, representing a cross section of social classes—upper class, middle class, and working class. These neighborhoods include the fashionable and expensive town-houses of Manhattan's East Side; the modest wood frame houses in working- and lower-middle-class Greenpoint, an urban enclave in Brooklyn; and the large houses in a group of adjoining affluent suburbs on Long Island's North Shore—Manhasset, Plandome, and Flower Hill. (For convenience, I will refer to these three suburbs as "Manhasset.")

From each of these areas, I chose a random sample of houses based on a list of all homes in the area, prepared by touring each neighborhood. I then interviewed residents in their homes, recording and asking about the art and cultural items on display and locating these in the context of the house and neighborhood. In addition, I took a full set of photographs of the interior of most dwellings and drew a floor plan. The vast majority of persons interviewed were homeowners, rather than renters. In total, the analysis encompassed 115 houses, 35 from each area.

In this chapter I will focus on landscape art, for reasons that I explain later.[5] Ultimately, I will suggest that, for a full understanding of twentieth-century art and culture, this materialist approach, based on the study of art in the context of the house and neighborhood, should be combined with a materialist approach based on an analysis of the impact of the mode of production. Clearly, we need both versions of materialism.

Landscape Pictures: The Historical and Material Contexts

I classified by subject matter the paintings, reproductions, and photographs in the houses studied. I then selected a subsample consisting of those pictures that were prominently displayed—those that occupied a wall alone or were displayed alone except for other paintings of the same subject matter. Table 13.1 shows the results. (To focus on the subject matter of the pictures I do not distinguish between original paintings and reproductions here or between paintings by recognized artists and those by obscure or anonymous artists. I will deal with these distinctions later.)

Landscapes are the most popular pictures in all the neighborhoods studied. They constitute 35 percent of the paintings in Manhattan, 25 percent of those in Manhasset, and 31 percent of those in Greenpoint. They are either the first or second most common subject of the prominently displayed pictures in 79 percent of the houses in Manhattan, 74 percent of those in Manhasset, and 60 percent of those in Greenpoint. (A "landscape" is defined here as a picture in which land, water, or sky occupies more than half the surface area.) Thus, the landscape motif is popular among residents of all social classes—i.e., working-class people in Greenpoint and upper- and upper-middle-class people in Manhattan and Manhasset.

Certain other types of subject matter do show clear differences between the working class, on one hand, and the upper and upper middle class, on the other. Pictures of religious figures, for instance, are common in Greenpoint (representing 15 percent of the pictures there) but not elsewhere. Conversely, abstract art is present in Manhattan (in 12 percent

TABLE 13.1 The Subject Matter of the Paintings and Photographs Prominently Displayed on Walls in Houses, by Type of Neighborhood in Which the House Is Located[a-f]

	Neighborhood		
Subject Matter	Working- and lower-middle-class urban (Greenpoint) $(n=178)^a$ %	Upper-class urban (Manhattan's East Side) $(n=275)$ %	Upper-middle class suburban (Manhasset) $(n=253)$ %
Landscape	31.7	35.3	25.0
Cityscape	5.0	4.4	2.0
People			
Religious persons	15.4	1.1	5.9
Family members (photos and portraits)	22.7	13.8	14.6
Friends and acquaintances	—	1.1	—
Others	4.5	16.4	16.8
Abstracts	—	12.2	4.7
Flowers	12.3	4.0	24.9
Animals, birds, or fish	4.5	5.8	2.4
Still life (fruit, vegetables, or drinks)	3.9	2.2	2.4
Buildings (noncity)	—	—	0.7
House interior	—	1.6	—
Other	—	2.2	0.4
TOTAL	100.0	100.1	99.8

Notes:

a. The data refer to pictures, not to households.

b. The data include reproductions and photographs as well as original pictures. They also include items by little known or anonymous artists, as well as items by recognized artists.

c. The data include only topics that are prominently displayed. A topic is defined as "prominently displayed" if pictures depicting that topic constitute all (scored as one point) or at least three-quarters (scored as half a point) of the topics of the pictures on a wall. For example, a picture of a landscape that occupies a wall alone or only with pictures of other landscapes, counts for one point; a landscape picture or a group of landscape pictures, that constitute at least three-quarters of the pictures on a wall count half a point.

d. The data in Table 13.1 include pictures in the following rooms and areas of the house: the hallway, foyer, living room, dining room, kitchen, library, den, sitting room, family room, master bedroom and guest room. It excludes pictures in the bathroom(s), children's bedrooms and basement.

e. Some topics are displayed not just on walls, but for instance on the flat surfaces of tables, dressers, and shelves. Examples are family photos and religious figures. The data in Table 13.1 will therefore underestimate their presence in the home.

f. For the purposes of the data in Table 13.1, a "landscape" is defined as a picture in which land, water or sky occupies more than half of the surface area.

of the pictures) and Manhasset (in 4 percent of the pictures) but not in Greenpoint.

Because landscape pictures pervade the houses of all social classes, I want to focus on them here. First of all, I will look at the historical and material context for the popularity of landscape pictures. There is a close historical connection between landscape art and the house and its surroundings, which is of great significance for materialist theories. The very emergence of landscape painting in the West as a distinct genre has been linked to the development of a villa or country-house culture in the Renaissance. Such painting was unknown in the medieval world; landscape appeared simply as background for the figures depicted in the works of that age (Friedlander 1949; Gombrich 1966). In the Italian Renaissance, urban dwellers began to buy villas in the country to serve as second homes (Coffin 1979); at the same time, the taste for landscape art developed (Turner 1966, ch. 10).

Similarly, the movement of urban dwellers to rural or quasi-rural (suburban) areas in the United States seems to have stimulated the demand for landscape art. In the early days of U.S. cities, when residents lived close together in an urban core (the "walking city"), portraits dominated the art scene (Richardson 1956). But by the mid-nineteenth century, when suburbs began to develop and large numbers of middle-income people moved from the city to semirural suburbs and commuted (by ferry, omnibus, and railroad) to jobs in the city, landscapes emerged as a flourishing art in the United States. The popularity of this art grew throughout the rest of the century (Novak 1980). In the twentieth century, the automobile accelerated the pace and scale of suburbanization, and since World War II, blue-collar as well as white-collar citizens have moved in large numbers to newly created suburbs. Today, most urban residents with moderate incomes or more consider a move to the suburbs, even if they ultimately reject the idea as undesirable or beyond their economic means. Thus, it is understandable that landscape paintings are now of central importance in the houses of working-class people in Greenpoint and upper- and upper-middle-class people in Manhattan and Manhasset as suburbanization pervades modern U.S. culture. The broadly popular landscape is embedded in people's material lives, above all in their houses.

Landscape Pictures: The Content

There are two striking features common to almost all landscapes in the houses sampled, regardless of the social class of their owners. And like the taste for landscapes itself, these features are embedded in people's ordinary, material lives—not in the mode of production but in the context of their houses, residential neighborhoods, and leisure lives.

Tranquil Nature

First of all, these landscapes reflect an overwhelming preference for a nature that is sedate and tranquil. Turbulent landscapes are rare in the houses studied; almost all of them depict a calm natural setting, where rivers flow peacefully, oceans are placid, trees are unruffled by wind, and snow lies evenly—fallen but never falling. In the 263 landscapes prominently displayed in the houses I studied, only one depicted a turbulent nature. This was an eighteenth-century religious picture (in reproduction) by Alesandro Magnasco (1677–1749), entitled *The Baptism of Christ*, and it hung in a Catholic rectory on Manhattan's East Side. Jesus stands in this painting amid a stormy ocean and dark skies. But when I questioned a priest who lives in the rectory about the painting, he told me he intended to remove it. The painting bothered him, but he was unable to say why. A year later, I returned to the rectory and found the picture gone, banished to the choir room in the church next door. The priest was still unable to articulate what it was in the picture that disturbed him, but a reason suggests itself from the vantage point of this study. Surely, it was not the religious content of the painting; the rectory was full of religious pictures. And the landscpe genre itself could not have been the problem, either, for displayed in the rectory guest room were other landscapes that gave the priest no pause. But these other pictures all depicted calm scenes. Thus, it appears that the turbulence of Magnasco's canvas was responsible for its demise.

The reasons people give for liking landscapes paralled this finding about calm versus turbulent settings. When I asked homeowners what attracted them to the landscapes on their walls, they mentioned most frequently the tranquility of the subject matter: The pictures on their walls were "calm" and "restful"; they offered "solitude" and "quiet"; they soothed. As one Manhattan man commented, referring to a Chinese garden scene with mountains in the background: "It's so calm. That's what I like about it." This comment is echoed in those of other respondents. For example, a Manhattan woman said of her photographs of the coasts of Greece and Mexico: "They have a feeling of solitude, beauty, quiet, and peace," and a Greenpoint woman, speaking of a landscape of trees and a river, said, "It's very restful." Another Greenpoint woman commented on a rural street scene lined with autumn trees: "It's peaceful and restful." And a Manhasset man said of his two beach scenes: "They're peaceful."

The second reason given by respondents for liking a landscape was that it recalled a place or person of which the respondent was especially fond. But this reason is a distant second in terms of the frequency with which it was expressed.

There are a number of causes for this overwhelming preference for calm landscapes, and most of them derive from the material context of the house and its surroundings. First, there is the perception of the home as a refuge from the perceived hustle and hubbub of the world of work and its trappings. A Greenpoint man who teaches high school science in the New York public schools touched on this cause when he cited his reasons for liking the serene landscape in his living room (interviewer's questions are in parentheses): "I like it because it's calm. (Why do you like a calm landscape?) For fifteen years, I ran the lunchroom at school. Have you ever heard the sound of six hundred teenagers having lunch? It was murder."

Second, the preference for calm landscapes seems to stem from the widespread aversion of homeowners in urban and suburban areas of the United States to poorly maintained yards and gardens, to an unkempt landscape on their doorsteps. A few residents in the areas I studied permit their yards and gardens to grow wild, but such practices are almost universally condemned by other residents.

A third cause derives from the common modern orientation to the countryside and the shore as scenery to drive past, whether as commuter or tourist, or as the arena for vacation trips and leisure time. A Manhasset woman explained that what came to mind when she looked at the landscape of autumn leaves in the den was her yearly visit to the country. Another Manhasset resident associated the landscape of Maine in her living room with the scenery she and her husband drive past on their way to visit their daughter in Quebec. Thus, the vision and experience that many of these residents have of the landscape is partly shaped by the culture of the automobile itself. (See Venturi et al. [1980] for a similar phenomenon relating to roadside commercial architecture.) Many residents also associate the landscapes they display in their houses with favorite vacation spots, an orientation to the landscape that has been growing in popularity since the mid-nineteenth century and that builds on an earlier tourist orientation to the landscape (Jackson 1980). When landscapes are perceived as places to drive past or to drive to for short visits or long vacations, it comes as no surprise to find them represented as calm and serene locales in people's homes.

Modern America is, of course, not alone as a society favoring calm landscapes. Renaissance Italy, for example, shared the same preference (Turner 1966, ch. 10). Yet, there is something different about the modern vision of landscapes, which is underlined by the second main feature of the landscapes I studied. And, like the first, it tends to characterize the landscapes in the houses of all the social classes sampled.

The Empty Terrain

The idea conveyed by the landscapes in the houses I studied suggests that people are considered appropriate in landscapes depicting non-industrial societies or industrial societies in the past but that the human figure is deemed inappropriate and unwelcome in landscapes that represent the modern world, especially the contemporary United States. The vast majority of the landscapes I saw in the residences of Greenpoint, Manhattan, and Manhasset are unpeopled when they depict modern U.S. scenes. Land, sea, and sky are there, but rarely people; 85 percent of the landscapes of contemporary settings in the study have no figures in them at all. Yet, when landscapes depict this nation's past or the past of another industrial society or when they depict simple societies (in the past or present), they often are, indeed, populated; 67 percent of such landscapes contain figures. In fact, the presence of figures—in period dress or native clothing—provides the key to identifying landscapes as depicting a nonindustrial society or an earlier period in the history of an industrial one. This is true in all three areas studied, as Table 13.2 makes clear. In Greenpoint, not one of the landscapes that depict a contemporary U.S. scene is peopled; in the Manhattan and Manhasset houses, only 22 percent are.

In one Manhasset house, for example, there are a number of historical landscapes, all peopled. These include a lake scene set in early nineteenth-century France, which contains two women. By contrast, in the kitchen, there is a depopulated land/seascape, which reminds the residents of their house in the Hamptons, and in the living room there is a painting, again without figures, of their Manhasset house, set in the context of the lavish grounds. In another Manhasset house, neither of the only two landscapes contain people. Both represent contemporary California; one is the desert not far from the place where the wife grew up, and the other is of Laguna Beach, which the couple likes to visit. A Greenpoint living room has a landscape, painted by the residents' adult daughter, that depicts the scenery around the family's vacation cabin in upstate New York; there are no people in this landscape. On the other hand, in the couple's bedroom is a populated landscape of a nineteenth-century U.S. scene.

When asked to comment on these landscapes, the residents corroborated these findings. They said they did not *want* figures in their landscape pictures of modern U.S. life. In about half the cases, they could not really say why; they just felt figures would be "wrong," "inappropriate,"

Table 13.2 Whether landscape is peopled, by society depicted and neighborhood of house where displayed[a]

	Neighborhood					
	Working-class urban (Greenpoint)		Upper-class urban (Manhattan)		Upper-middle-class suburban (Manhasset)	
	Society depicted		Society depicted		Society depicted	
Whether Landscape Is Peopled	Contemporary U.S. (n=40)	Non-industrial or industrial in the past (n=33)	Contemporary U.S. (n=23)	Non-industrial or industrial in the past (n=64)	Contemporary U.S. (n=36)	Non-industrial or industrial in the past (n=53)
	%		%		%	
Peopled	0	64	22	67	22	66
Not peopled	100	36	78	33	78	34

p<.001

[a]The data refer to the subsample of pictures defined in Table 13.1—pictures prominently displayed.

or "would not fit in." However, other residents gave clearer reasons, almost all of which had to do with the idea that, when they actually experienced the modern U.S. landscape, they did not want other people to be there, which is why they liked to see the landscape depicted without people. One view often expressed was that people ruin landscapes, in various ways. As one Greenpoint woman said, "People spoil a lot of beautiful places. They're noisy, they come in with their radios."

Another view expressed by residents is that one goes somewhere scenic to enjoy nature and get away from people, so the latter do not belong in landscapes. A Manhasset woman put it this way: "My view of nature is that it is separate from people. I like to enjoy nature by itself, without other people around." A third view accurately reflects the mechanization of modern agriculture and of the methods of taking care of scenic landscapes: Most natural landscapes have no people, so it is inappropriate to portray them in pictures. A Greenpoint man said this about his picture featuring an inlet lake, trees in the water, and birds: "I wouldn't want to see a person in this picture. Where would a person be, standing on the water [laughs]!"

That there is a strong preference for an empty terrain in landscapes of the modern world is significant for it distinguishes this culture from almost all previous cultures. A culture whose attitude to the landscape was the exact reverse provides an interesting counterpoint. From about 1830–1850 in France, lithographs of the countryside were enormously popular. However, the public demanded that this countryside be filled with people—at least one or two peasants or other ordinary men or women were required. The public would not buy a depopulated landscape. So important were the figures in the pictures that a division of labor emerged among the artists: certain artists, often the lesser known ones, first painted the physical countryside and so on; other artists, who often became famous for their talents in depicting figures, then specialized in adding the people (Adhemar 1938).

The Landscapes of Cézanne, Monet, and Gauguin

Looking at landscapes in this material context—that of the house and neighborhoods in which they are displayed—throws new light on the direction taken in the twentieth-century taste for landscape art in the West. The clear and widespread preference for empty terrains when landscapes depict modern society and the desire for landscapes of non-industrial societies or industrial societies in the past to contain figures is prefigured by Cézanne and Monet, on one hand, and by Gauguin, on the other—perhaps the three most important influences on twentieth-century landscape art. The work of Cézanne and Monet, whose major landscapes are set in France—the apex of society at that time—is an interesting place to begin. The absence of figures from Cézanne's landscapes is striking and has often been commented upon (for example, in Schapiro 1962, p. 14). It is, in fact, rare to find human figures in his landscapes. In contrast with much of the landscape painting of the time, in Cézanne's pictures there are almost no promenaders, vacationers, or picnickers. Roads are empty, or, more often, there are no roads at all.

Monet did paint landscapes with people. Yet, it is his haystacks and water lilies—both depopulated scenes—that so influenced twentieth-century art. Kandinsky (1913), for example, wrote of how enormously he was affected by Monet's paintings of haystacks.

Gauguin's later landscapes are almost all set in Tahiti—a society clearly seen as primitive by comparison with metropolitan France—and these paintings are full of figures. Indeed, it seems that, in Gauguin's mind, the scenery and the inhabitants were almost inseparable for he rarely painted the former without including the latter (Rewald 1954).

The division between modern artists who paint landscapes—without figures—of their own societies and artists who paint landscapes—with figures—of a primitive society, an earlier historical period of their own society, or a fantasy society informs twentieth-century art. Cézanne, Monet, Kandinsky, and Mondrian, on one side, and Gauguin and the later surrealists, on another, mark a clear pattern in the world of art. This study demonstrates the same pattern.

Although this is not the place to argue what motives might have led these artists to paint as they did, it is appropriate to suggest some reasons for their popularity among modern audiences. These artists' landscapes fit a constellation of tastes that I have touched on in this chapter. These, too, are anchored in the material lives, above all in the residential and leisure lives, of those who purchase their works, whether in original or in reproduction.

Landscape Pictures and the Mode of Production

I have so far said nothing about materialist theories that might relate the subject matter discussed above to the mode of production. Such theories are certainly important, but I argue they must be tempered by looking at the art in the material context of the house and neighborhood, as well. Consider the theory of Pierre Bourdieu (1984), which is one of the most interesting of recent attempts to relate art and culture to the mode of production (actually, to the occupational structure of advanced industrial society). Bourdieu's data are from France, but he argues that his theory of art and culture is applicable to societies like that of the United States.

Bourdieu stresses the role of culture in maintaining class inequalities, in preserving and reproducing the class structure of advanced capitalist societies. He points to survey data, including his own, that show that "consumption" of high culture (for instance, the taste for modern art or classical music or attendance at museums or symphony concerts) varies by social class. The upper and middle classes are more likely than the working class to go to a classical music concert or the opera or to read a "quality newspaper." The reason for this, Bourdieu argues, is that the taste for high culture is unequally distributed among social classes. This is, in turn, because the capacity to comprehend high culture is taught, above all, in the higher education system; it is also taught in the families of the upper-middle and upper classes. Thus, the working class and the poor have little chance of acquiring the capacity—which Bourdieu refers to as "culture capital"—to appreciate high culture. Instead, they develop a taste for popular culture, which is associated with the dominated classes.

Finally, Bourdieu argues, high culture preserves and reproduces the class structure in two main ways. First, knowledge of the arts is used to control access to the dominant class: Only those with a competence in the high arts are admitted, on a permanent basis, to elite circles. Second, high culture operates to build solidarity among the dominant classes. For example, attending common cultural occasions or discussing cultural phenomena creates class solidarity.

In this interesting and complex way, Bourdieu relates art and culture to the mode of production for, in the end, it is the occupational structure of advanced industrial society that explains and generates artistic and cultural tastes, practices, and beliefs.

A number of features of the landscapes in the houses I studied are certainly consistent with this theory. These features do distinguish the pictures of the working class in Greenpoint from those of the upper-middle and upper classes. Far more clearly than the shared features discussed earlier, they relate to artworks as items of prestige and indicators of social superiority, as part of a system of class domination rooted in the stratified occupational structure. These features concern the identity and standing of the artist; how often foreign societies, in general, are depicted; how often particular foreign societies, such as Japan, Britain, and France, are depicted; and the frequency of landscapes that depict the historical past.

There are clear differences here between houses in working-class Greenpoint and those in upper-class Manhattan (see Table 13.3). Manhattan residents can often name a professional artist who painted at least some of their pictures. Thus, they identify a professional artist for 56 percent of the landscape pictures. Further, these residents usually know if the

TABLE 13.3 Selected Status-raising Characteristics of Landscape Pictures, by Neighborhood[a]

	Neighborhood		
	Working- and lower-middle-class urban (Greenpoint)	Upper-class urban (Manhattan's East Side)	Upper-middle-class suburban (Manhasset)
Characteristic	(n=73.5)[a] %	(n=95) %	(n=96.5) %
Percentage of landscapes painted by a professional artist whose identity the owner knows	12	56	60
Percentage of landscapes that refer to the past	31	55.8	52.8
Percentage of landscapes that refer to foreign societies (in past or present)	19	83	36
Percentage of landscapes that refer to Japan, Britain, or France	4	44	16.6

[a]The data refer to the subsample of pictures defined in Table 13.1—pictures prominently displayed.

artists have reputations in the art world and therefore a high resale value attached to their work. By contrast, residents of working-class Greenpoint can seldom identify a professional artist who painted their pictures. They know who painted only 12 percent of the landscapes displayed, and that is always because the artist was a relative or friend. Not a single original landscape displayed in Greenpoint is by an artist of stature, and, therefore, none of the pictures has much, if any, market value. Further, Greenpoint residents have little or no interest in the identity of the artist, and most know little about art history. For example, although several Greenpoint residents have small reproductions of Leonardo da Vinci's *Last Supper* in their kitchens or dining rooms, not one could supply the artist's name.

Another difference between social classes is the extent to which landscapes portray foreign societies. Such depictions are much more common in East Side Manhattan houses than in those of Greenpoint. Eighty-three percent of the landscapes in Manhattan homes depict foreign societies, but only 19 percent of those in Greenpoint do. A third difference lies in the kind of foreign societies depicted. Japan, England, and France (in that order) are the most likely subjects in the landscapes in Manhattan houses—together, they account for 47 percent of all the landscapes. Nor are these usually the countries of origin of the residents. By contrast, in Greenpoint, only two landscapes featured Britain, France, or Japan, and half of the foreign landscapes in Greenpoint are of the residents' country of origin (notably Poland or Italy). Finally, historical landscapes are far more common on Manhattan's East Side than in Greenpoint. Thus, 55 percent of the Manhattan landscapes referred to the past, only 31 percent of those in Greenpoint did.

These distinctions, if taken alone, do provide material for a theory such as Bourdieu's. Yet, based on the earlier discussion of the features common to the landscapes in the houses of the working, middle, and upper classes, a number of objections occur to Bourdieu's full theory. For one thing, the extent to which there are two distinct taste structures—that of the dominant and that of the dominated classes—is unclear. Both the working class and the middle class share a fervent interest in landscape art, and both share an interest in seeing calm landscapes that, when they depict contemporary U.S. scenes, are depopulated. Further, these interests and tastes derive much more obviously from the material context of the modern house and its surroundings than from occupational distinctions associated with the mode of production. In addition, it is uncertain how far "high culture" serves certain vital class functions. Bourdieu has argued that it acts both to limit access to the dominant class—one needs familiarity with high culture to gain admission to the dominant class—and to foster class solidarity by providing a common set of topics and interests around which that class can unite. Yet, the survey data we have on "high culture," including Bourdieu's own, suggest that high culture has, in fact, penetrated only a *minority* of the dominant class. For example, Bourdieu (1984, p. 527) asked his working-class, middle-class, and upper-class respondents to select, from a list of well-known artists, their favorite. Kandinsky, Braque, and Dali were the modern artists on the list. But no more than 13 percent of any social class named one of these artists as their favorite. By contrast, impressionists—either Renoir or Van Gogh—were the favorite artist of every social class; no less than 47 percent of any social class named one of these as their favorite. U.S. survey data likewise show that less than half the middle and upper-middle classes (and usually far less than half) are interested in such high-culture items as quality newspapers, the opera, ballet, and classical music (see Wilensky 1964; Ford Foundation 1974; and Robinson 1979). It is, then, difficult to see that high culture can, in general, be pivotal either for controlling access to the dominant class or for fostering solidarity within it. If high culture does function in that way, it probably is among those sectors of the dominant class that are involved in the production and control of high culture. For example, knowledge of high culture may help gain access to museum and university circles but be of far less value in the corporate and political worlds.

Two Types of Materialism

Materialism—the view that the material context in which ideas and culture are located is important both for understanding their meaning and for explaining their existence and persistence—has an impressive lineage of adherents, of whom Marxists and Durkheimian sociologists are among the foremost. I have argued that the proper applications of this perspective to twentieth-century art demands that we view that art in two materialist contexts. We need to see it in the context of the political and economic structure of modern society—the mode of production—and we need to view it in the context for which much of it is purchased and displayed— the modern house. Without the latter perspective, the former is often thin and incomplete. Although my argument here has concentrated on landscape art, I believe it is applicable to many of the other major art genres of the twentieth century.

Notes

1. Compare Engel's famous formulation that the base influences the super-structure only "in the last analysis."
2. Marcuse acknowledges the major objection to his theory of art:

> The objection that I operate with a self-validating hypothesis seems justi-fied. I term those works "authentic" or "great" which fulfill aesthetic crite-ria previously defined as constitutive of "authentic" or "great" art. In de-fense, I would say that throughout the long history of art, and in spite of changes in taste, there is a standard which remains constant. This standard not only allows us to distinguish between "high" and "trivial" literature, opera and operetta . . . but also between good and bad art within these genres. There is a demonstrable qualitative difference between Shakespeare's comedies and the Restoration Comedy, between Goethe's and Schiller's poems, between Balzac's "Comedie humaine" and Zola's "Rougon-Macquart."

This claim that, in the history of art, certain works have always been recognized as "great" or "authentic" is false as an empirical statement about the reception of the works by either general audiences or "experts"; the fluctuating reputation of Leonardo's *Mona Lisa* is one of many counter examples. See Wolff (1983) for similar objections to Marcuse's theory.

In his theory of what constitutes "great art," Althusser (1966) puts forward a notion similar to Marcuse's, minus the psychoanalytic underpinnings. (But in his more general approach to ideology, he definitely does not reject materialism.) Both Althusser's and Marcuse's theories of art constitute, in many ways, what has aptly been referred to as "veiled idealism" (Alexander 1988, p. 93).

3. For a critical discussion of Freudian drive theory and of competing schools and perspectives in psychoanalytic theory, see Greenberg and Mitchell (1983).

4. Some people will say that it is the museum, rather than the house, that is the main context for modern art and culture. Indeed, in recent years, a number of writers have critically examined the role of the museum in modern art. See, for example, Foucault (1977); Lebensztejn (1981); Krauss (1982); DiMaggio (1982); Stocking (1985); Clifford (1988); and Jonaitis (1989). The museum cannot, of course, be overlooked. Yet, most of the art and culture items produced in the last 150 years that are now displayed in museums reached this status because they, or similar items, were once displayed in private homes.

5. Some of the data that follows have been treated from a different theoretical point of view in my article "Class and Culture in Modern America." See Halle (1989).

References

Adhemar, M. Jean. 1938. "Les Lithographes de Paysage en France à L'Epoque Romantique." *Archives de l'Art Français: Nouvelle Période* 19:230–32.

Alexander, Jeffrey. 1988. "The New Theoretical Movement." In *Handbook of Sociology,* ed. Neil Smelsner, pp. 77–101. Beverly Hills, Calif.: Sage Press.

Althusser, Louis. 1971 [1966]. "A Letter on Art in Reply to André Daspre." In *Lenin and Philosophy and Other Essays,* pp. 221–28. London: New Left Books.

Bourdieu, Pierre. 1984. *Distinction: A Social Critique of the Judgement of Taste.* Cambridge: Harvard University Press.

Coffin, David. 1979. *The Villa in the Life of Renaissance Italy.* Princeton, N.J.: Princeton University Press.

Clifford, James. 1988. *The Predicament of Culture.* Cambridge: Harvard University Press.

DiMaggio, Paul. 1982. "Cultural Entrepreneurship in Nineteenth-century Boston: The Classification and Framing of American Art." *Media, Culture and Society* 4:303–22.

Ford Foundation. 1974. *The Finances of the Performing Arts: A Survey of the Characteristics and Attitudes of Audiences for Theater, Opera, Symphony, and Ballet in 12 U.S. Cities,* 2 vols. New York: Ford Foundation.

Foucault, Michel. 1977. "Fantasia of the Library." In ed. Michel Foucault, *Language, Counter-Memory, Practice,* trans. D. F. Bouchard and S. Simon, pp. 87–109. Ithaca, N.Y.: Cornell University Press.

Friedlander, M. J. 1949. *Landscape, Portrait, Still-Life: Their Origin and Development,* trans. R. C. Hull. New York: Philosophical Library.

Gombrich, E. H. 1966. "The Renaissance Theory of Art and the Rise of Landscape." In *Norm and Form in the Art of the Renaissance,* ed. E. H. Gombrich. London: Phaidon Press.

Greenberg, Jay, and Stephen Mitchell. 1983. *Object Relations in Psychoanalytic Theory.* Cambridge: Harvard University Press.

Guilbaut, Serge. 1983. *How New York Stole the Idea of Modern Art.* Chicago: University of Chicago Press.

Halle, David. 1989. "Class and Culture in Modern America." *Prospects* 14:373–406.

Jackson, J. B. 1980. "Learning About Landscape." In *The Necessity for Ruins,* ed. J. B. Jackson, pp. 1–18. Amherst: University of Massachusetts Press.

Jonaitis, Aldona. 1989. "Franz Boas, John Swanton, and the New Haida Sculpture at the American Museum of Natural History." Paper series, Institute for Social Analysis at SUNY Stony Brook.

Kandinsky, Wassily. 1964 [1913]. "Reminiscences." In *Modern Artists on Art,* by Robert Herbert, pp. A–44. Englewood Cliffs, N.J.: Prentice-Hall.

Krauss, Rosalind. 1982. "Photography's Discursive Spaces: Landscape/View." *Art Journal* 42:311–19.

Lebensztejn, Jean-Claude. 1981. *Zigzag.* Paris: Flammarion.

Marcuse, Herbert. 1978. *The Aesthetic Dimension: Toward a Critique of Marxist Aesthetics.* Boston: Beacon Press.

Novak, Barbara. 1980. *Nature and Culture: American Landscape and Painting.* New York: Oxford University Press.

Rewald, John. 1954. *Paul Gauguin.* New York: Harry Abrams.

Richardson, E. P. 1956. *Painting in America: From 1502 to the Present.* New York: Thomas Cromwell.

Robinson, John. 1979. *How Americans Use Time.* New York: Praeger.

Rosand, David. 1984. Review of Serge Guilbaut's *How New York Stole the Idea of Modern Art. The New York Times Literary Supplement,* October 12.

Schapiro, Meyer. 1962. *Paul Cézanne.* 2nd ed. New York: Harry Abrams.

Stocking, George, ed. 1985. *Objects and Others.* Madison: University of Wisconsin Press.

Timpanaro, Sebastiano. 1975. *On Materialism.* London: New Left Books.

Turner, Richard. 1966. *The Vision of the Landscape in Renaissance Italy.* Princeton, N.J.: Princeton University Press.

Venturi, Robert, Denise Scott Brown, and Steven Izenour. 1980. *Learning from Las Vegas: The Forgotten Symbolism of Architectural Form.* Cambridge, Massachusetts: MIT Press.

White, Harrison, and Cynthia White. 1965. *Canvases and Careers: Institutional Change in the French Painting World.* New York: John Wiley and Sons.

Wilensky, Harold. 1964. "Mass Society and Mass Culture." *American Sociological Review* 29:173–97.

Williams, Raymond. 1977. *Marxism and Literature.* Oxford: Oxford University Press.

———. 1978. "Problems of Materialism." *New Left Review* 109:3–17.

Wolff, Janet. 1983. *Aesthetics and the Sociology of Art.* London: George Allen and Unwin.

14 | Talkin' Class: Discourse, Ideology, and Their Roles in Class Conflict

MARC W. STEINBERG

In *Gender and the Politics of History,* Joan Wallach Scott observes that "we cannot write about class without interrogating its meanings—not only its terminology and the content of its political programs but the history of its symbolic organization and linguistic representations" (Scott 1988, p. 90). Her comments are broadly representative of the semiotic turn in the analysis of class, ideology, and conflict that has gained increasing currency. This theoretical movement, which I term poststructuralism, views the investigation of social structure, thought, and action as the analysis of discourse. In this perspective, class, ideology, and conflict are seen as semiotic systems to be dissected as any other *text* would be (Callinicos 1985).

Poststructuralists span a spectrum of positions on Marxist class analysis. Some have sought an eclectic (though often uneasy) alliance between semiotics and materialism (Coward and Ellis 1977; Ryan 1982; Spivak 1987). Others have found in the theoretical corpus a foil for a radical critique of Marxism (Laclau and Mouffe 1982, 1985, 1987; Mouffe 1983, 1988; Scott 1988). Regardless of their stance on this issue, however, poststructuralists approach the analysis of ideological conflict and collective action as discursive contention.

In this chapter, I critique both theoretical and historical representatives of poststructuralism. For the historical case, I focus on Gareth Stedman Jones's (1982, 1983) recent reexamination of chartism work for three reasons. First, his rereading of chartist politics is illustrative of the way in which poststructuralists view discourse as the fount of ideological production and conflict. Second, there is a growing trend in the social and political history to draw from poststructuralist theory, of which Scott's work is but one of the more prominent examples.[1] Third, Stedman Jones's work has been cited as a foundation piece for understanding the role of discourse in the production and transformation of ideology in other historical contexts.[2]

The chapter is divided into five parts. In the first section, I briefly note some of the important precepts in the poststructuralist analysis of discourse and ideology. In the second section, I outline Stedman Jones's examination of chartist politics. In the third section, I offer brief critiques of both. In the fourth section, I extend this critique through an examination of the discourse of conflict used in a major industrial action by the cotton spinners of the Ashton-Stalybridge region of England during 1830. Finally, in the conclusion I summarize my criticism of poststructuralism and the lessons of the case study.

Poststructuralist Tenets

Whether attempting to find a happy marriage with Marxism or to surpass it entirely, poststructuralist social theories share several axioms.[3] Foremost amongst these is the proposition that social life is constructed in and through discourse (Coward 1977, p. 103; Coward and Ellis 1977, p. 23; Laclau and Mouffe 1985, pp. 96, 108, 114).[4] Within the terms of the poststructuralists, discourse can be defined as all social practices of signification, giving it an encompassing scope. From this perspective, discourse overlays an intelligibility on people and their situations, actions, and beliefs.

Classes and ideologies are therefore structured and realized in discourse. In a quasi-Marxist approach, discourse takes the form of an autonomous social formation that infuses the activities in other formations with illusory meaning (Coward and Ellis 1977, pp. 94–95). In more extreme (non-materialist) formulations, class position and ideology are taken to be the contextual products of the discourse that constitutes the situation (Laclau and Mouffe 1985, p. 142; 1987, p. 96). In this sense, the ideologies and rationalities that guide social action, like the actors themselves, are products of discursive moments.[5] A fundamental idea in both perspectives is that meaning is relative and relational, born of the positioning of the elements of discourse. The boundaries of ideology are thus the limits that discourse imposes.

By extension, domination is also a discursive act. It is realized through the construction of an illusory coherence and freedom or the suppression of alternative meanings within a partially fixed field of signification. In the former case, actors are imbued through discourse with an ideology that poses the world in nonconflictual terms (Coward and Ellis 1977, pp. 68, 75; Coward 1977, p. 95). In the latter, a partial hegemony is achieved when dominant meanings reinforce one another, creating a closure in which other articulations are forced to remain latent (Laclau and Mouffe 1985, p. 136; Mouffe 1988, p. 90).

Finally, class conflict is a process of semiotic disruption and change. Both dominant classes and ideologies are undermined when the contradictions of their ascendancy are exposed by the articulation of antagonistic meanings (Laclau and Mouffe 1985, p. 131). Struggle is a "war of position" over how collectivities are constituted through discourse. And success is achieved when the ruse of the illusory is fully exposed or when a group defines itself in its own discursive field. Importantly, subordination may be defeated, but the threat is never wholly eradicated. In a discursive world, there is no finitude for the possibility of alternative meaning is in the very nature of discourse itself.

In sum, poststructuralists view class ideology, conflict, and transformation as discursive constructions. In each variant of the perspective, it is discourse that defines peoples' interests and consciousness. Through it, class struggle can be effected. Indeed, for the poststructuralists, discourse is the only avenue for social change.

Gareth Stedman Jones and Chartism

Gareth Stedman Jones's recent writings on chartism have a clear affinity with poststructuralist theory. In them, he provides us with a detailed historical analysis of the role of discourse in ideological (class) conflict. In his most extensive piece, "Rethinking Chartism" (Stedman Jones 1983), he argues that a coherent political discourse is critical for the sustained mobilization of actors around collective grievances. Discourse is an integral part of class conflict because it mediates between consciousness and experience, thus bringing intelligibility to the latter. A successful political discourse palpably diagnoses the problems of those it seeks to reach, providing a clear and encompassing analysis of their grievances and a ready vocabulary for collective alternatives (Stedman Jones 1983, pp. 95–96).

Stedman Jones's criticism of the historiography of chartism emanates from this understanding.[6] He observes that the locus of analysis of the movement has been the social or economic experiences of the working class, its discourse being seen as an epiphenomenal vehicle of reaction. All interpretations (including Marxist) have viewed the movement as a collective class response to the disruptions of industrial capitalism. This referential analysis of its political discourse and program cannot explain why such a discourse was drawn upon to express grievances, the particular form that the mass movement took, nor its national character (Stedman Jones 1983, pp. 92–94, 99).

Stedman Jones argues against extant historiography, which he claims views chartist discourse as a secondary product of (economic) class struggle. Instead, he finds this discourse reveals chartism to be, first and foremost, a political movement, rooted in grievances against political corruption, not class oppression. Political action, a mass movement for political inclusion and equal rights, was the solution (Stedman Jones 1983, pp. 100, 105). Chartism's working-class character and life course were due to the political exclusion and repression of the working class in the early 1830s and the easing of repression and growth of reform in the latter 1830s and into the 1840s (Stedman Jones 1983, pp. 107, 158–59, 175–77).

The core of this chartist discourse was a political radicalism rooted in the 1770s, which emphasized constitutionalism and natural rights. Drawing from a heritage that included Painite republicanism, it recognized the legitimacy of gains through honest labor and condemned those garnered through political corruption. Democratic governance safeguarded the community from monopolist tendencies that threatened such rights. Though the discourse increasingly was reformulated to reflect working-class concerns, these central ideological tenets were never compromised (Stedman Jones 1983, pp. 104, 111, 122, 126, 134, 153, 156, 159).

The resiliency of these conceptions allowed political radicalism to surmount challenges from trade unionism and Owenism in the mid-1820s through the mid-1830s. Though they respectively championed class solidarity and an apolitical community devoid of competition, neither ideology was ultimately dyssynchronous with the discourse's premium on natural rights and political equity (Stedman Jones 1983, pp. 113–15, 117, 145).

For Stedman Jones, then, the history of chartism is one of how an ideology, conveyed through a discourse, structured working-class mass action. As he observes, "Radicalism . . . determined the form taken by the movement" (Stedman Jones 1983, p. 126). Its prognoses of social ills were nested in a critique of the monopolization of power; its prescriptions for change illuminated the state as the principal target for redress. Challenges to radicalism required accommodating mutations in this discourse, but they never ruptured the core ideological tenets. In the end, however, they were the movement's undoing, as the political realities of governance passed it by.

Refutations and Reformulations

Poststructuralist theories and Stedman Jones's historical analysis suffer from parallel problems regarding social agency, change strategies, and ideology. The paramount problem in poststructuralist accounts is that discourse acts upon people, rather than people acting through discourse. By subsuming the social within the discursive, these theories cast into serious doubt people's agency and autonomy for collective action. The dynamics of class conflict are rooted in the impulses of semiotic change, and the actors themselves are animated by a system of meanings over which they exercise little control. Class conflict often is reduced to battles of signification. And consciousness is confounded by the transitory nature of signification for collective identity and purpose are subservient to an increasingly complex montage of contexts and traces of the past. In effect, it becomes little more than a discursive cage of collective understanding.[7]

In such a world, the flux of meaning should inevitably overwhelm the ability of collectives to establish and sustain collective goals. Instead, contentious groups become interlopers for change when and where contradictions of meaning allow. Yet, the organized pursuit of change seems chimerical because collective goals may be confounded by a latent infinitude of meaning. In the end, discourse is the imperious impresario of events.

Finally, discourse as apprehended by poststructuralists would seem to be an impediment to the construction of ideology—if ideology can be recognized within its theoretical scheme at all. In neo-Marxist versions, it becomes consumed by the discourse that conveys it; in nonmaterialist theories, the seamless semiotic world reduces all understanding to signification in context.[8] In neither case is it clear where (if at all) an ideology serves as a sociomoral guide, charting the relations between class actors, as well as the possibilities for change.

In Stedman Jones's analysis we find similar issues of agency and change at the historical level. Critics have taken him to task for presenting a reified history of ideas, largely devoid of context. They argue that he portrays radical discourse with a false coherency, failing to see its dynamism, the extent of its polysemy, and its class transformation over time.[9]

These criticisms direct attention to the larger question of the role of discourse in chartism. Stedman Jones depicts political radicalism as the engine of chartism, defining issues and directing collective action. It hangs ethereally above class conflict, infusing meaning and autogentically changing to accommodate new grievances. When its cogency evaporates, so, too, does the contention. Chartism's working-class legions have little agency in determining the course of the movement. They receive their ideology from on high and troop its colors in their ensuing struggles.

From his account, we fail to apprehend that this radical discourse was produced through struggle and was itself a locus of contention. Part of this conflict was ideological; radicalism (composed of many strands) was drawn upon in reaction to political economy and other combatants. Together, they circumscribed a field of discourses that was the site of hegemonic conflict.[10] Thus, the use of radical discourses was fundamentally relational and grounded in class conflict. Its sources were multiple, and the meanings produced through them were attuned to both the structure of class relations and the context in which they were used. By placing discourse before people, Stedman Jones obscures these dynamics and conflates ideology and discourse.

In sum, poststructuralism, though it is intent on elucidating the ways in which discourse underlies class conflict, leads us to a paradoxical conclusion. Discourse can be seen as restricting agency and inhibiting sustained collective action.

In contrast, I outline here an alternative framework by which we can understand the role of discourse in class conflict. I define discourse as the historically and contextually bounded social processes of language use that dialogically frame actors and contexts (Macdonnell 1986; Ricouer 1976; Rossi-Landi 1975, 1983). Through this process, people create propositional and evaluative accounts about themselves, their relations with others, and other social and material processes (Volosinov 1986). Their production is governed by a system of logonomic rules, which prescribe how actors use signifiers, govern the production of meaning, and define the actors' roles in the process (Hodge and Kress 1988). These rules can complement the extant power structure by defining the legitimate participants and boundaries of meaning production and by precluding possibly subversive meanings and actors. In short, discourse is a partly hegemonic process that takes sides (Blakar 1979; Gramsci 1971, 1984; Hodge and Kress 1988; Salamini 1981; Volosinov 1986; R. Williams 1976).

These processes are partially routinized by the recurrent aspects of social life (and because of our need for experientially grounded accounts of these) into discourse streams. Streams are dialogically tied to social action, and they carry a common stock of signifiers that are drawn upon in the process of meaning production. Streams are loosely structured and contain finite possibilities for meaning. Their use is, nonetheless, an active social process involving collective choice. Collective actors bring their experience to discourse, and its use is a choice of how best to frame these with the available streams. For any given context, there are a set of streams that define its discursive field. How actors construct meaning within this field is a joint product of the social structuring of relations, constraints imposed by the power structure, previous experience, and the polysemy of the streams (Callinicos 1985; Doyal and Harris 1983; Ricouer 1976).

Discourse streams are essential to conflict because they present the interpretive boundaries within which it can unfold. Part of conflict itself is the attempt to dominate the definitions of the acceptable and possible. Moreover, their intersection in use produces larger dynamic frames of meaning that form the core of ideologies. These provide inductive maps of the relations between actors, activities, and contexts, a moral framing of these relations, and alternative possibilities to them (Therborn 1980). Discourse and ideology are thus recursively tied, making ideology a collective and historically circumscribed process that operates in a loosely ordered fashion (Summer 1979; Therborn 1980; J. B. Thompson 1987).

Discourse is thus an important intermediate process in class conflict. To reformulate ideology, denude the givenness of ruling-class hegemony, and define commitment and purpose (as well as alternatives to the current order) involves discursive struggle. This is a hegemonic, piecemeal conflict in which class actors seek to appropriate the use of streams and reformulate their meanings. The process and its results are neither formulary nor guaranteed. It is contingent on the collectivity's capacity to restructure the logonomic rules, the availability of alternative discourse streams and their potential polysemy, and the effectiveness of counterdiscursive strategies on the part of the ruling class. In a Gramscian sense, it is clearly a "war of position" (Mouffe 1979). The verbal bloodletting of this trench warfare nonetheless can play a determinant part in the course of mobilization and contention. In protracted conflict, the role of discourse is no small matter.

The Discourse of Labor Conflict Among the Ashton-Stalybridge Cotton Spinners, Ca. 1830

To illustrate the above theoretical outline, I return to Stedman Jones's England, briefly examining a few texts of discourse used by factory hands in their conflicts with the factory owners in the Ashton-Stalybridge area of Lancashire. Southeast Lancashire is inscribed in history books as the birthplace of the Industrial Revolution, and the Ashton-Stalybridge area, a few miles south of Manchester, was the heartland of the cotton industry juggernaut.

The Ashton-Stalybridge Region: A Thumbnail Sketch[11]

In 1800 Ashton and its diminutive neighbor Stalybridge were bucolic market towns for their relatively poor agricultural hinterlands. By 1830, the parish containing them had more than tripled in size, and one enthusiastic contemporary had already designated the region as "the most important commercial area in the world" (*Manchester Guardian,* April 3, 1827). Such was the impact of the cotton industry.

By the end of the 1820s, the Ashton-Stalybridge region was a manufacturing center of enormous magnitude. Within the immediate area of Ashton town alone there were perhaps seventy cotton mills, and the whole region roughly equaled the industrial capacity of Manchester. These mills produced one-eighth of the entire output of the English cotton industry and were tied to a burgeoning world market. The growth of the regional industry had begun modestly in the 1790s with the investments of the indigenous bourgeois, many of whom had deep roots in the local woolen trade. Their substantial early profits were reinvested, and, from the early 1820s, the area experienced an unparalleled expansion. By 1830, the largest establishments were employing over 1,000 operatives.

This industrial boom gave shape to a regional class structure that was starkly divided between a powerful but small industrial bourgeoisie and a large proletarian population. By the 1830s, Ashton was over 80 percent working-class, and the other towns in the region contained even higher proportions. The vast majority of these workers were dependent on the cotton industry. In between was a small and relatively supine petty bourgeoisie, a "shopocracy" whose fortunes ebbed and flowed with the industry.

Members of the Ashton-Stalybridge bourgeoisie, typical of nouveau industrial capital, were ardent supporters of liberal politics, political economy, and religious nonconformity. With their wealth and power, they constructed a world of their own design. Stately houses (pretentiously named) were erected on the hillcrests that ringed the towns. In Ashton, they financed the construction of a gasworks and a city hall to meet their growing commercial needs. They also built a comfortable Independent chapel in which they found an equally comfortable faith of their own terms. Socially, they were well integrated, and many of the leading families were tied through marriage.

By 1830, these "cotton lords" had also gained political ascendancy. They had created and controlled borough governments for Ashton and Stalybridge and, prior to the passage of the Reform Bill, had secured a parliamentary seat for Ashton itself (despite its modest size). Through diplomacy and mutual economic interest, they effected a cordial relationship with the Earl of Stamford, the preeminent landholder of the parish. The factory owners also established a well-heeled network with many of the area's lesser gentry. With their factory workers, though, they maintained considerable distance. Beyond the confines of the mill walls, their primary contact was in the running of Sunday schools for working-class children. Little else bridged the transparent gap between the classes.

In the closely packed housing of the factory hands, a vibrant, independent working-class culture took hold. Factory workers founded their own scientific and literary societies and constructed a fairly extensive network of fraternal clubs and burial societies. The public house was the hub of much (male) social activity, Ashton having one pub for every 113 people (Manchester Statistical Society 1838, pp. 7–8). Wakes and fairs, insalubrious nuisances for the local elite, were the social high points. Gaming, cockfighting, pugilism, and bullbaiting were fixtures of local recreation.

In matters of religion and politics, the working-class members were far removed from their employers. Spiritually, they expressed little of the fervor of their superiors, with as many as 40 percent of workers openly professing no religious affiliation in some of the region's towns (Manchester Statistical Society 1838, Appendix, p. XIX). Of those who did note ties to a church, most were nominal members. Politically, the region's working class fostered an entrenched radicalism. The eminent radical Richard Carlile (a Painite disciple and rational deist) found such fervor for his creed that he was moved to note, "Nothing can be better than the hopes of Infidelity here at Ashton" (*Lion,* July 24, 1829, p. 104). Many radical causes found a welcome home here, both in established organizations such as a branch of Carlile's Zetetic Society, to the many informal radical groups of long duration.[12]

Within political and fraternal societies, the spinners in particular often took an active role. They were skilled adult male factory workers who manned the spinning machines that produced the finished cotton yarn. Spinners constituted about 13 percent of the factory work force in the district and were the largest adult male group in the mill. They were a highly paid factory elite and clearly the most contentious faction.

The spinners of Ashton-Stalybridge had a long history of organization and had been affiliated with attempted regional trade unionism from the early 1800s. They were among the key actors in the first regionwide spinning strike in 1818, and various locales also engaged in lesser strikes in 1824–1826. Ashton and Stalybridge spinners were among the most well-organized and militant of all town groups.

By the end of the 1820s, industrial relations were at the breaking point. In 1828, many of the local mill owners had forced the spinners to formally renounce the union, in the wake of a bitter nearby strike. The cotton industry's market, still suffering the effects of a depression in 1826, was weak and unstable. Recent reductions of piece rates elsewhere were a signal for the local cotton lords to reduce wages. The spinners were steadfast in their opposition to such cuts. Coupled with complaints of "grinding" at work, exorbitant rents for some of the firm-owned cottages, and the rise among some employers of truck (payments in kind rather than cash), the threat of reduced rates solidified an intense enmity toward the factory owners.

The strike of 1830–1831 was the largest of its kind in decades. Two thousand spinners from fifty-two district firms turned out on December 12, idling a total of no less than 20,000 factory hands. The strike had been preceded by several firm-specific turnouts in the spring and summer, as well as almost continuous mobilization efforts by the union during the period. Sporadic summer negotiations had forestalled it, but, by the end of November, the issues were clearly insoluble.

The strike was a rancorous affair, lasting over ten weeks during the dead of winter. Violence, though used strategically and sparingly by the spinners, was dramatic and greatly heightened tensions. From the first strikes in the summer through the end in early February, there was one attempted bombing of a mill owner's house, one assassination of a mill manager (and son of a mill owner), and two other attempted assassinations. Eventually, a large contingency of the military (replete with mounted infantry and artillery) was billeted in the area to preserve the peace. The spinners conducted a well-orchestrated campaign throughout. They employed a wide array of tactics, including a carefully conceived picketing strategy, mass demonstrations, parades, and attacks upon mills. In the end, however, they found themselves organizationally well-to-do but materially poor. By the second week in February, defeated spinners were trickling back to work. Several hundred, permanently blacklisted by the mill owners, were forced to seek livelihoods elsewhere.

The discourse samples I discuss below are drawn from this heady period and focus on the relations of exploitation between mill owners and spinners. There was no relatively stable, internally coherent discourse stream concerning the labor exploitation during this period. The spinners therefore had to construct a discourse of exploitation from extant streams, one that clearly denoted the antagonisms between themselves and the mill owners. In the samples that follow, we have a brief glance at how they accomplished this.

A Discourse of Exploitation

By May of 1830, vituperative sniping between the spinners and mill owners was already surfacing in the local press. Each group sought to establish a context for an impending conflict. For the spinners, the local union leader, John Joseph Betts, was at the forefront. Betts was not only active within trade affairs but outspoken as a political radical and community organizer. For him, the issue was patently clear. At a meeting in early May, he contrasted the state of the factory workers to that of the slaves of the colonies. The slaves, he noted, had a decided edge.

> The only real difference is, that the negroes are slaves in *name,* while hundreds of thousands of our poor countrymen, here, are slaves in *reality.* There the slaves are comfortably housed, wholesomely fed, worked to the best economy of their health and strength, and I dare say sometimes overworked. Here the slaves are miserably lodged, starved, beggarded, abused, neglected, and over-

worked, always, and at all times without pity, without mercy, without hope. . . . The metallic machinery is far more valued here than that which we are told is moved by immortal souls. . . . But poor humanity has overstocked the market. Muscles, bones, and nerves are cheaper than stale mackerel. . . . A broken bone would not be thought of half a consequence as a broken spindle. The most humane manufacturers would never think of estimating humanity as equal to machinery. Their reasoning is, that machinery is expensive, but humanity—is—(oh it is!)—dust and ashes: and stock of living cogs and spindles, is more valuable in their esteem, for the poor spark of mucilage of life that holds it together in animated parcels.—To keep their machinery in order stands them a cost: to suffer to get out of order would be ruinous—but their whole cheap beyond the effect of prodigality, excessive above superfluity itself, not to be missed, not to be wanted, not to be reckoned on more than clouds of smoke that issues from the mouths of their thousand terrestrial hells (*United Trades' Co-operative Journal,* May 8, 1830, p. 78).[13]

Betts's depiction of the mill owners' rapaciousness was elaborated upon by an Ashton factory hand shortly after in the same periodical. The piece, entitled "The Cotton Spinners and Power-Loom Weavers' Lesser Catechism," portrayed the cotton lords as imbued with fanatical greed.[14] "Question—What is thy duty towards thyself? Answer—My duty towards myself is to take all advantages, whether by falsehood or truth, by which I shall be enabled the more readily to make a fortune; to worship nothing but money; to give thanks to no one; and to serve (except myself), no one all the days of my life" (*United Trades' Co-operative Journal,* June 6, 1830, p. 115). The mill owners lacked all semblance of scruples, and their singular drive was for accumulation and class privilege. "Q. Rehearse the articles of thy belief? A. I believe in the omnipotent power of the steam engine, the prime mover of all machinery . . . I believe in the holy combination of Masters, the holy rules by which they are held together—the communion that exists among them—the forgiveness of none who transgress their laws—heedless of the resurrection of life to come" (*United Trades' Co-operative Journal,* May 22, 1830, p. 92). The commandments of the cotton lords were a litany of debaucherous cupidity and stylish barbarity.

1....Thou shalt have no other god but Mammon. 2. Thou shalt not make unto thyself any image in the likeness of machinery that is not turned by power.—Thou shalt not employ any hands except to assist machinery to do their work, for the master with which thou are united are jealous masters, visiting the sins of the fathers upon the children and the sins of the children upon the fathers unto the third and fourth generation. 3. Thou shalt not use the names of the masters irreverently, for they will not hold him guiltless that so useth their names. 4. Remember that whilst others keep holy the Sabbath day, after six days of labour, and in it do no manner of work—thou and thy son and thy daughter, thy man servant and thy maid servant, they cattle and the stranger that is within thy gates shall all be fully employed,—some cleaning thy boilers and retort-flutes, some inspecting thy steam-engine, thy horizontal shafts, joints, and boxes, and some posting thy accounts or preparing a balance sheet of thy week's gainings. Thou, in the mean while, must see thy friends at dinner, or go out to dine with them...6. Thou shalt not do open murder. 7. Thou shalt not commit adultry, except if thy pleasure and thy profit is increased in doing so. 8. Thou shalt suffer no one to steal from thee. 9. Thou shalt not allow witnesses to testify against thee. 10. Thou shalt covet thy neighbor's house, thy neighbor's wife, and his servant, and his maid, and his ox, and his ass, and everything that is his, if by doing so thy profit and thy advantage is further secured (*United Trades' Co-operative Journal,* May 22, 1830, pp. 92–93; June 12, 1830, p. 114).

Such invective continued to be produced during the summer and fall months. By November, the spinners believed in the inevitability of a major contest. Betts went about the hinterlands speaking to large assemblages to mobilize and coordinate the spinners. Early that month, a minor excise officer passing through the town of Audenshaw heard Betts's thunder before a crowd of 10,000 workers. Shocked and thoroughly frightened, he summarized the speech and forwarded it immediately to the Home Office. As he described events,

Betts observed that Trade Unions and Political Ones were now so intimately blended together that they must be looked upon as one. He proceeded to state that we lived under the Worst, the most Rascally, Despotic, Tyrannical Government that ever existed. He told the meeting of the Glorious Victory that had been achieved in France by only 8000 Men over Tyranny and said there were more than 80,000 men ready for a similar proceeding in England.[15] He then sat down apparently exhausted by the Efforts he had made and was followed by a person of the name of Buckley who resides in North Street near this place. He informed the Meeting that he was the chief cause of the Repeal of the Combination and Conspiracy Acts. He stated that every Master was a Tyrant, and they had a right to participate in whatever property any Man had, that they must down with the Cotton Lords who had no right to any such profits, that they were Omnipotent in power, that if they would be United no Force could stand against them and that they must repel Force by force; they must rouse from their Apathy and let their Despotic Tyrannical Masters know theirs was the power and that they would use it. Betts again addressed them assuring him that he fully concurred in the Sentiments of the last Speaker, he told them that this and other Meetings in the Villages were only preparatory to the great Meeting which would be held shortly in Staley Bridge or Ashton. He told them to recollect their Power was Omnipotent that they must shortly use it, that Petitions were of no use, they might write to the Ministers but they must write in such a way that the Writer should never be known. He knew that their writing would be of no use. He hoped that they would be united, that they would be determined to be Free. Let Liberty or Death be their Cry and Spreading out a small Flag with various Devices on it, told them that this was the Tricoloured Flag under which they must Act, that they must be Firm or this Opportunity would be Lost, and concluded with hoping that they would be united and all attend the meeting at Staley Bridge or Ashton as the placards were to inform them, that all of the Factories would Stop on that Day, and on that Day he intimated a Decisive Step would be taken (Great Britain Public Record Office, Home Office Papers 40/27, pp. 338–39, Nightingale to Home Office, November 11, 1830).

As Betts announced, the mass meeting did take place on December 4 near the factory town of Dukinfield. The pageant prefatory to the meeting is, itself, worth noting because it resembled in form the mass platform meeting that had become an integral part of radical demonstrations (see Belchem 1978, 1981; Pickering 1986). At noon on that day, a procession formed in Stalybridge with hundreds of boys taking the lead; a band displaying a tricolored flag and a sardonic banner with the phrase "Free Trade" followed closely behind. Factory hands, including women, came next in military formation, many wearing tricolored ribbons and armed with guns and bludgeons. At its peak, the procession stretched more than a mile. Twenty thousand finally assembled in a meadow to hear a contingency of speakers. Among the orators was Jonathan Hodgins, a leading member of the National Association for the Protection of Labour, as well as of the Manchester spinners' union. Hodgins put the issues before them in stark terms.

He rose for the purpose of declaring his opinion, that if the masters persevered in their list, the consequences would fall on their heads. He did not mean to say that it was their duty to riot, but he did mean to say, that in all cases, and in all countries, there was an evident boundary, beyond which oppression could not be borne: and when it had reached that point, those who were the cause of that oppression were the first to suffer. He did not believe that the masters of Ashton and Stalybridge intended to bring about a revolution; if they did not, they must be mad indeed. It was not for the purpose of effecting a reduction that they put forth the list, but for the fear the operatives should have the strength to take possession of the mills. They would prefer their list, even when they knew it would bring distress to the neighborhood. Had the operatives ever attempted to take their mills by storm?—(No, no.) Had they not laboured in them as many hours as were allowed by act of parliament?—(We have.) The masters said they would take possession of the mills. Had the operatives ever been guilty of insubordination?—(No.) Insubordination among the slaves in the West Indies meant, kicking when the master put too heavy a burden on their backs, and he did hope that they would kick most manfully if the burden became too great. He hoped that it would be such kicking as would kick the burden away (*Manchester Guardian*, December 11, 1830).

In the subsequent ten weeks, the spinners took these words to heart.

Dissecting the Discourse

This was the discourse used by the spinners to depict their exploitation. Noteworthy beyond its often eloquent style are the elements that composed it. Having no internally coherent discourse stream of labor exploitation, the spinners drew from other streams, constructing a poignant heterogloss. Specifically, they appropriated other streams in finding homologies in the discourses on slavery and revolution and in that of middle-class Christianity.

The use of the slavery metaphor was more than a neat trope. The contemporary abolition campaigns included in their numbers some of the most vaunted liberal bourgeois politicians of the age (Howse 1953; E. Williams 1944). Although they attacked the institution of slavery on moral grounds, they also championed the principles of political economy. By appropriating the discourse of abolition, the factory workers were thus also trying to usurp the moral authority of the users of this discourse stream, exposing their duplicitous immorality to the public. It was all fine to thunder against the exploitation across the ocean, but it was the silence on it at home that was truly deafening.

In the vituperative "Lesser Catechism," we find a transformation similar to that employed in the discourse of abolition. In this context, there are two intertwined facets in the appropriation. First was the relation between the employers and workers in the district. As I noted, the only concerted action taken by the factory owners to bridge the class gap was the organization of a Sunday school union. From their inception in the early twenties, these schools were the only organized venue for working-class education in the rudiments of reading and writing. By the early 1830s, over half of all children in Ashton and Stalybridge were being subjected to regular doses of Bible study and catechisms. Thus, by appropriating the form of the catechism, the worker was not only vilifying the factory owners but turning their means of inculcating deference on its head.

The second point to be observed is the wide use of Christian morality to buttress the popular political exonomy that was purveyed to the working class of this era. Writers such as Jane Marcet, Hannah More, and Harriet Martineau liberally intertwined such morality in their explications of political economy, providing it with a moral facade that the technical structure lacked (Goldstrom 1985; Richardson 1975; N. W. Thompson 1984).[16] The factory workers of Ashton seemed to have little truck for such "knowledge," as witnessed by the history of the local Mechanics' Institution.[17] Founded in the town in 1825 and initially drawing a group of over 400, it was languishing close to demise by 1827. By 1831, it had closed its doors.

In the discourse of revolution, we see a different turn. In these cases, the discourse stream of political radicalism (in which the Ashton workers were skilled hands) was extended to labor exploitation. Depiction of the moral limits of *political* oppression was transformed into an analysis of those of *economic* oppression. The extension was not an example of political radicalism's hegemony, as Stedman Jones would have us believe. Rather, the use of revolutionary discourse (and its attendant symbols, such as the tricolor) was a transference of the legitimacy of revolt into the context of labor struggle. Government corruption was *not* the issue. What was depicted was an industrial problem that begged an industrial solution.

The discourse of revolution provided a system of meaning that was clearly interpretable for the workers. In each sphere of power, tyrants could be exposed, and the immorality of their actions made evident. Politicians robbed through taxes, employers through profits. Each took Mammon as their guide, and, in each case, the situation demanded redress, though in distinctly different manners.

Through these discursive transformations, the spinners constructed a discourse of labor exploitation. They were engaged in a war of position to determine the moral limits of emergent capitalist labor relations. That they did not have an extant discourse stream did not prevent them from comprehending their situation. How, in the longer term, such appropriations may have become problematic is the subject for further investigation. Nonetheless, I believe it is clear that, within the boundaries of extant discourse, the spinners did produce a system of meanings that was an important facilitator in their struggle with the factory owners.

Conclusion

In the case of the Ashton-Stalybridge cotton spinners, we have seen the role of discourse in class conflict. Through extant discourse streams the spinners ideologically framed the nature of their exploitation and their struggle against it. This was a loosely structured process, tied to the dynamics of the contention and bounded by the context of the class conflict and the discursive field.

Poststructuralists, in examining such a case, argue that it is discourse that fashions the dynamics of class conflict. Neo-Marxist versions posit this as a materialist "dialectic between history, language and ideology" (Coward and Ellis 1977, p. 92). For them, material processes are given shape in the semiotic. In nonmaterialist formuations, discourse is viewed as the progenitor of all, the process in which class itself is constituted. Stedman Jones, in his analysis of chartism, broadly applies this perspective to the working-class agitations of the late 1830s and 1840s. His is a history in which an ideology of constitutionalism and natural rights, conveyed through the discourse of political radicalism, orchestrated the working-class pursuit of social change.

The case of the Ashton-Stalybridge spinners, however, reminds us that class actors struggle through discourse, rather than being impelled by its imperious meanings. People start with their collective understanding and memory of the material relationships that define their situation. Through discourse, actors inscribe meaning in these relationships and the contexts in which they transpire, though not just as they please. Meaning is not transparently referential. And the polysemy of this process is limited by the experience actors bring to discourse and the practices that give rise to its necessity.

Within these limits, class actors engage in important wars of position to parse out the world in their own terms. In so doing, working-class groups have the opportunity to disrupt the domination imposed through social structure, a structure that is dialogically tied to discourse. They cannot, though, eviscerate domination. Such collective actors can define the nature and limits of their struggle and, through this, solidify their internal organization and enhance resource flaws. Conversely, they can impair similar processes among capitalists. If working-class groups are successful in these endeavors, they can define the meaning of the conflict for the wider community. The spinners, as we have seen, were able to convey the virtuousness of their cause, the necessity of commitment, and perhaps even the importance of violence and sacrifice to their peers and kindred factory hands.

In short, the cardinal lesson of the spinners' case is that class actors do have agency through discourse, albeit bounded. Contrary to the ideas of the poststructuralists, it is people that actuate meaning—not the other way around.

Acknowledgments

My thanks to Nicki Beisel, Geoff Eley, Michael Kennedy, Chalmers Knight, Sharon Reitman, William Sewell, Margaret Somers, and Charles Tilly for their helpful comments. I would also like to extend special appreciation to Rick Fantasia, Rhonda Levine, and Scott McNall for making this chapter possible. Any problems of meaning in this work are due to the operation of the signifiers in the text and not to those above.

Notes

1. For a valuable overview of the varieties of discourse analysis in historical literature, see Schöttler (1989).

2. An example of his influence in the U.S. case is found in Kazin's (1988) article on the political language of the U.S. labor movement.

3. Exemplary of the former is the work of Rosalind Coward and John Ellis (Coward 1977; Coward and Ellis 1977). For critique and debate, see Chambers et al. (1977–1978), Coward (1977–1978), and Adlam and Salfield (1978). Representative of the "post-Marxist" strain is the recent work of Chantal Mouffe and Ernesto Laclau (Laclau and Mouffe 1985; Mouffe 1983, 1988). They have used poststructuralist theory (particularly deconstructionism) to censure what they define as an essentialist economism in Marxism (Laclau and Mouffe 1985; Mouffe 1983). Their critique has sparked several strident debates with Marxists (Geras 1987, 1988; Laclau and Mouffe 1987; Meiksins and Meiksins Wood 1985; Meiksins Wood 1986; Mouzelis 1988). For additional criticism, see Rosenthal (1988) and Rustin (1988).

4. As Laclau and Mouffe observe, "Every object is constituted as an object of discourse" (Laclau and Mouffe 1985, p. 107).

5. As Chantal Mouffe, for example, argues, "Interests never exist prior to the discourses in which they are articulated and constituted" (Mouffe 1988, p. 90).

6. The rubric "chartism" was derived from the slate of six demands that were established in the early phases of the agitation in 1838 and served as the bedrock

of this reform agitation. The six "points" of the charter were universal male suffrage, annual parliaments, equal electoral districts, vote by secret ballot, salaried representatives (MPs), and the eradication of property qualifications for office-holding. As a movement covering a decade of agitation, there were, of course, a variety of other political and economic platforms that ebbed and flowed during its course. For recent histories of the movement, see Epstein (1982), Epstein and Thompson (1982), Goodway (1984), Saville (1987), and D. Thompson (1984).

7. For critiques of both the Lacanian and Derridean epistemologies employed by poststructuralists, see Chang (1988), Ryan (1981), K. Silverman (1983), D. Silverman and Terode (1980), and Turkle (1978).

8. Indeed, Laclau has stated that "if we assert the discursive nature of all social relations, the basis for the distinction between base and superstructure collapses and with it disappears the only terrain on which the concept of ideology made sense" (Laclau and Mouffe 1982, pp. 97–98).

9. Among the various critiques are Belchem (1988), Claeys (1985a), Cronin (1986), Epstein (1986), Foster (1985), Gray (1986), Kirk (1987), McCord (1985), Palmer (1987), Saville (1987), Schöttler (1989), Scott (1987), Stansell (1987), and D. Thompson (1987). Epstein, Foster, Kirk, Saville, and Thompson in particular rebuke Stedman Jones for slighting the working-class bases of chartism.

10. For some recent works that relate to the transformation of discourse and the contention surrounding it for this period, see Belchem (1988), Claeys (1985b, 1986), Cunningham (1981), Goldstrom (1985), Gray (1988), Meuret (1988), Smail (1987), N. W. Thompson (1984), and Tribe (1978).

11. The following background material is drawn from an extensive case study of the Ashton-Stalybridge region from my dissertation (Steinberg 1989). The study draws from a wide array of both primary and secondary sources that are too numerous for citation in this short space. For complete source documentation, I refer the reader to the dissertation.

12. For a history of this informal radical tradition, see Epstein (1988). This lively political tradition, coupled with other social organizations, produced what was perceived to be a vibrant intellectual life among the working class. John Bowring, a leading utilitarian, government functionary, and future editor of the *Westminster Review,* was highly impressed by this culture, observing in a letter to the Home Office during a tour of the region that "in every town I have visited are men incomparably superior in intellectual capacity to most of their masters" (Bowring to Lamb, December 30, 1830, Lancashire County Record Office, DDX/880/2).

13. There were a number of such meetings to mobilize the factory workers in the spring and summer. One from a branch of the National Association for the Protection of Labour (NAPL) in Ashton is particularly of note in light of Stedman Jones's thesis. At this meeting, the prominent NAPL member, Thomas Oates, emphasized the need to focus on unionization and not parliamentary reform:

After talking some time about the Reform Bill, he said there was a class of men, which he was disposed to rank even lower in degree of crime, than the detested boroughmongers; men who raised a loud cry of "stop thief" against the boroughmongers, had their own hands in the poor man's pocket, and were recklessly plundering him. Unless by their own exertions or otherwise, the working classes obtained an advance in wages, *they would find radical reform itself ineffectual to relieve them* (*Manchester Times,* May 29, 1830, emphasis added).

The "class of men" was, of course, the factory owners.

14. In the somewhat confused terminology of the period, mill owners were also called cotton spinners and power-loom weavers (depending on their mill operations). This is a vestige of the old master-servant discourse in which hands were distinguished by the epithet "journeymen," and owners by "master."

15. The "Glorious Victory" in France refers to the July revolution. The "80,000 men in England" refers to the NAPL, a confederation of unions led by the spinners that had as its purpose the universal unionization of the working classes. By some estimates, the union had some 80,000 adherents by the time of the strike, though the true number cannot be known (Kirby and Musson 1975).

16. For an excellent example of this, see Martineau's *A Manchester Strike: A Tale* (1833), number 7 in her series *Illustrations in Political Economy.* The story tells of factory hands led into an ill-conceived strike by unionists, which eventually brings ruin to all.

17. Mechanics' institutions were established by the bourgeoisie to create an avenue for working-class education and self-enlightenment. They emphasized political economy, mechanics, and other sciences in the hopes of inculcating proper motivation among workers. They met with mixed success, and their staple populations were sometimes members of the lower middle class (such as clerks) rather than the workers for whom they were targeted. The institution in Ashton was spearheaded by Charles Hindley, a leading mill owner and future MP for Ashton (Hindley 1825; Tylecote 1957, pp. 248–49, 254).

References

A. *Archives*

Great Britain Public Record Office. Home Office papers, series 40.
Lancashire County Record Office. Miscellaneous papers, DDX/880, letters to the Right Honorable Robert Peel and from Bowring to Lamb.

B. *Contemporary Periodicals*

Lion, 1829.
Manchester Guardian, 1827.
Manchester Times, 1839.

United Trades' Co-operative Journal, 1830.

C. Secondary Sources

Adlam, Diane, and Angie Salfield. 1978. "A Matter of Language." *Ideology and Consciousness* 3:95–111.

Belchem, John. 1978. "Henry Hunt and the Evolution of the Mass Platform." *English Historical Review* 93:739–73.

––––––. 1981. "Republicanism, Popular Constitutionalism, and the Radical Platform in Nineteenth-Century England." *Social History* 6:1–32.

––––––. 1988. "Radical Language and Ideology in Early Nineteenth-Century England: The Challenge of the Mass Platform." *Albion* 20:247–59.

Blakar, Rolv M. 1979. "Language as a Means of Social Power: Theoretical-Empirical Explorations of Language Use as Embedded in a Social Matrix." In *Pragmalinguistics: Theory and Practice,* ed. Jacob L. Mey, pp. 131–69. The Hague: Mouton.

Callinicos, Alex. 1985. "Postmodernism, Post-Structuralism, Post-Marxism?" *Theory, Culture, and Society* 2:85–101.

Chambers, Iain et al. 1977–1978. "Marxism and Culture." *Screen* 18:109–14.

Chang, Briankle G. 1988. "Deconstructing Communication: Derrida and the (Im)possibility of Communication." *History of European Ideas* 9:553–68.

Claeys, Gregory. 1985a. "Language, Class and Historical Consciousness in Nineteenth-Century Britain." *Economy and Society* 14:239–63.

––––––. 1985b. "The Reaction to Political Radicalism and the Popularisation of Political Economy in Early Nineteenth-Century Britain." In *Expository Science: Forms and Functions of Popularisation,* eds. Terry Shinn and Richard Whitley, pp. 119–36. Dordrecht, the Netherlands: D. Reidel.

––––––. 1986. "Individualism, Socialism, and Social Science: Further Notes on a Process of Conceptual Formation, 1800–1850." *Journal of the History of Ideas* 47:81–93.

Coward, Rosiland. 1977. "Class, 'Culture' and the Social Formation." *Screen* 18:75–105.

––––––. 1977–1978. "Response." *Screen* 18:120–22.

Coward, Rosiland, and John Ellis. 1977. *Language and Materialism.* London: Routledge and Kegan Paul.

Cronin, James E. 1986. "Review Essay: Language, Politics and the Critique of Social History." *Journal of Social History* 20:177–83.

Cunningham, Hugh. 1981. "The Language of Patriotism, 1750–1814." *History Workshop* 12:8–33.

Doyal, Len, and Roger Harris. 1983. "The Practical Foundations of Human Understanding." *New Left Review* 139:59–78.

Epstein, James. 1982. *The Lion of Freedom: Feargus O'Connor and the Chartist Movement, 1832–1842.* London: Croom Helm.

––––––. 1986. "Rethinking the Categories of Working-Class History." *Labour/Le Travail* 18:195–208.

––––––. 1988. "Radical Dining, Toasting and Symbolic Expression in Early Nineteenth Century Lancashire: Rituals of Solidarity." *Albion* 20:271–91.

Epstein, James, and Dorothy Thompson, eds., 1982. *The Chartist Experience: Studies in Working-Class Radicalism and Culture, 1830–1860.* London: Macmillan.

Foster, John. 1985. "The Declassing of Language." *New Left Review* 150:29–45.

Geras, Norman. 1987. "Post Marxism?" *New Left Review* 163:40–82.

———. 1988. "Ex-Marxism Without Substance: Being a Reply to Laclau and Mouffe." *New Left Review* 169:34–61.

Goldstrom, Max. 1985. "Popular Political Economy for the British Working Class in the Nineteenth Century." In *Expository Science: Forms and Functions of Popularisation,* eds. Terry Shinn and Richard Whitley, pp. 259–73. Dordrecht, the Netherlands: D. Reidel.

Goodway, David. 1984. *London Chartism, 1838–1848.* Cambridge: Cambridge University Press.

Gramsci, Antonio. 1971. *Selections from the Prison Notebooks,* eds. and trans. Quintin Hoare and Geoffrey N. Smith. New York: International Publishers.

———. 1984. "Notes on Language." *Telos* 59:127–50.

Gray, Robert. 1986. "The Deconstructing of the English Working Class." *Social History* 11:363–73.

———. 1988. "The Language of Factory Reform in Britain, c. 1830–1860." In *The Historical Meanings of Work,* ed. Patrick Joyce, pp. 143–79. Cambridge: Cambridge University Press.

Hindley, Charles. 1825. "An Address Delivered at the Establishment of the Mechanics' Institution, Ashton-under-Lyne, June 22, 1825." Ashton-under-Lyne: Thomas Cunningham.

Hodge, Robert, and Guenther Kress. 1988. *Social Semiotics.* Ithaca, N.Y.: Cornell University Press.

Howse, Ernest M. 1953. *Saints in Politics: The "Clapham Sect" and the Growth of Freedom.* London: George Allen and Unwin.

Kazin, Michael. 1988. "A People Not a Class: Rethinking the Political Language of the Modern U.S. Labor Movement." In *Reshaping the U.S. Left: Popular Struggles in the 1980s,* eds. Mike Davis and Michael Sprinkler, pp. 259–86. London: Verso.

Kirby, R. G., and A. E. Musson. 1975. *The Voice of the People: John Doherty, 1789–1854, Trade Unionist, Radical and Factory Reformer.* Manchester, England: Manchester University Press.

Kirk, Neville. 1987. "In Defence of Class: A Critique of Revisionist Writing upon the Nineteenth-Century English Working Class." *International Review of Social History* 32:2–47.

Laclau, Ernesto, and Chantal Mouffe. 1982. "Recasting Marxism: Hegemony and New Political Movements," interview by David Plotke. *Socialist Review* 16:91–113.

———. 1985. *Hegemony and Socialist Strategy: Toward a Radical Democratic Politics.* London: Verso.

———. 1987. "Post-Marxism Without Apologies." *New Left Review* 166:79–106.

Macdonnell, Diane. 1986. *Theories of Discourse: An Introduction*. Oxford: Basil Blackwell.

Manchester Statistical Society. 1838. *Report of a Committee of the Manchester Statistical Society, on the Condition of the Working Classes, in an Extensive Manfacturing District, in 1834, 1835, and 1836*. London: James Ridgway and Son.

Martineau, Harriet. 1833. *A Manchester Strike: A Tale*. 3rd ed. London: Charles Fox.

McCord, Norman. 1985. "Adding a Touch of Class." *History* 70:410–19.

Meiksins, Peter, and Ellen Meiksins Wood. 1985. "Beyond Class?: A Reply to Chantal Mouffe." *Studies in Political Economy* 17:141–65.

Meiksins Wood, Ellen. 1986. *The Retreat from Class: A New "True" Socialism*. London: Verso.

Meuret, Denis. 1988. "A Political Genealogy of Political Economy." *Economy and Society* 17:225–50.

Mouffe, Chantal. 1979. "Hegemony and Ideology in Gramsci." In *Gramsci and Marxist Theory*, ed. Chantal Mouffe, pp. 168–204. London: Routledge and Kegan Paul.

––––––. 1983. "Working-Class Hegemony and the Struggle for Socialism." *Studies in Political Economy* 12:7–36.

––––––. 1988. "Hegemony and New Political Subjects: Towards a New Concept of Democracy." In *Marxism and the Interpretation of Culture*, eds. Cary Nelson and Lawrence Grossberg, pp. 89–104. Urbana: University of Illinois Press.

Mouzelis, Nicos. 1988. "Marxism or Post-Marxism?" *New Left Review* 167:107–23.

Palmer, Bryan D. 1987. "Response to Scott." *International Labor and Working-Class History* 31:14–23.

Pickering, Paul. 1986. "Class Without Words: Symbolic Communications in the Chartist Movement." *Past and Present* 112:114–62.

Richardson, William. 1975. "Sentimental Journey of Hannah More: Propagandist and Shaper of Victorian Moral Attitudes." *Revolutionary World* 11:228–39.

Ricouer, Paul. 1976. *Interpretation Theory: Discourse and the Surplus of Meaning*. Fort Worth: Texas Christian University Press.

Rosenthal, John. 1988. "Who Practices Hegemony?: Class Division and the Subject of Politics." *Cultural Critique* 9:25–52.

Rossi-Landi, Ferruccio. 1975. *Linguistics and Economics*. The Hague: Mouton.

––––––. 1983. *Language as Work and Trade: A Semiotic Homology for Linguistics and Economics*. South Hadley, Mass.: Bergin and Garvey.

Rustin, Michael. 1988. "Absolute Voluntarism: Critique of a Post-Marxist Concept of Hegemony." *New German Critique* 43:146–73.

Ryan, Michael. 1981. "New French Theory in New German Critique." *New German Critique* 22:145–61.

––––––. 1982. *Marxism and Deconstruction*. Baltimore, Md.: Johns Hopkins University Press.

Salamini, Leonardo. 1981. "Gramsci and Marxist Sociology of Language." *International Journal of the Sociology of Language* 32:27–44.

Saville, John. 1987. *1848: The British State and the Chartist Movement.* Cambridge: Cambridge University Press.

Schöttler, Peter. 1989. "Historians and Discourse Analysis." *History Workshop* 27:37–65.

Scott, Joan W. 1987. "On Language, Gender, and Working-Class History." *International Labor and Working-Class History* 31:1–13.

———. 1988. *Gender and the Politics of History.* New York: Columbia University Press.

Silverman, David, and Brian Torode. 1980. *The Material Word: Some Theories of Language and Its Limits.* London: Routledge and Kegan Paul.

Silverman, Kaja. 1983. *The Subject of Semiotics.* New York: Oxford University Press.

Smail, John. 1987. "New Languages for Labour and Capital: The Transformation of Discourse in the Early Years of the Industrial Revolution." *Social History* 12:49–72.

Spivak, Gayatri S. 1987. "Speculation on Reading Marx: After Reading Derrida." In *Post-Structuralism and the Question of History,* eds. Derek Attridge, Geoff Bennington, and Robert Young, pp. 30–62. Cambridge: Cambridge University Press.

Stansell, Christine. 1987. "A Response to Joan Scott." *International Labor and Working-Class History* 31:24–29.

Stedman Jones, Gareth. 1982. "The Language of Chartism." In *The Chartist Experience: Studies in Working-Class Radicalism: 1830–1860,* eds. James Epstein and Dorothy Thompson, pp. 3–59. London: Macmillan.

———. 1983. *Languages of Class: Studies in English Working Class History, 1832–1982.* Cambridge: Cambridge University Press.

Steinberg, Marc W. 1989. "Worthy of Hire: Discourse, Ideology, and Collective Action Among English Working-Class Trade Groups, 1800–1830," vol. 2. Ph.D. dissertation in sociology, University of Michigan.

Sumner, Colin. 1979. *Reading Ideologies: An Investigation into the Marxist Theory of Law and Ideology.* New York: Academic Press.

Therborn, Goran. 1980. *The Power of Ideology and the Ideology of Power.* London: Verso.

Thompson, Dorothy. 1984. *The Chartists.* New York: Pantheon.

———. 1987. "The Languages of Class." *Bulletin of the Society for the Study of Labour History* 52:54–57.

Thompson, John B. 1987. "Language and Ideology: A Framework for Analysis." *Sociological Review* 35:516–36.

Thompson, Noel W. 1984. *The People's Science: The Popular Political Economy of Exploitation and Crisis 1816–34.* Cambridge: Cambridge University Press.

Tribe, Keith. 1978. *Land, Labour and Economic Discourse.* London: Routledge and Kegan Paul.

Turkle, Sherry. 1978. *Psychoanalytic Politics: Freud's French Revolution.* New York: Basic Books.

Tylecote, Mabel. 1957. *The Mechanics' Institutes of Lancashire and Yorkshire Before 1851.* Manchester, England: Manchester University Press.

Volosinov, V. N. 1986. *Marxism and the Philosophy of Language.* Cambridge: Harvard University Press.

Williams, Eric E. 1944. *Capitalism and Slavery.* Chapel Hill: University of North Carolina Press.

Williams, Raymond. 1976. *Marxism and Literature.* Oxford: Oxford University Press.

15 | The Gender-Specific Class Consciousness of Appalachian Coal Miners: Structure and Change

MICHAEL YARROW

The point of departure for this chapter is a study of working-class consciousness. The term "class consciousness" has often been used in Marxist theory to mean the full realization by a class of its position in the class system and of the actions it must take to revolutionize the system to reflect its interests. The problem with this use of the term is that it often carries with it the assumption of an unconscious or falsely conscious working class up to the revolutionary moment when material conditions arouse the class like a slap in the face (Jacoby 1978). This Lukacsian essentialist conceptualization either ignores the role of subjectivity in the historical process, except in extraordinary times, or views subordinate classes as hopelessly bewildered. It treats the development of class consciousness and class struggle as essentially inexplicable (Gintis 1980). I am interested in just this development and believe with Herbert Gintis that it must be scrutinized from the perspective of the lived experience of the class as well as how it is affected by macrostructural and ideological developments. I will use the term "actual class consciousness" to connote what workers believe and feel about the class system they experience.

In viewing working-class subjectivity from the perspective of lived experience, we experience class and gender relationships together. As Cockburn observes, "The sex/gender system is to be found in all the same practices and processes in which the mode of production and its class relations are to be found. We don't live two lives, one as a member of a class, the other as a man or woman. Everything we do takes its meaning from our membership of both systems" (Cockburn 1983, p. 195). Attempts to understand class consciousness in isolation from gender ignore an important element of consciousness that powerfully shapes action, for work and other aspects of life under patriarchal capitalism are structured by gender as well as by class.[1] Class consciousness is expected to be gendered. The fruitfulness of the new approach can be seen in the work of Paul Willis (1977, 1979), Roberta Goldberg (1981), Cynthia Cockburn (1983), David Knights and David Collinson (1985), and Sallie Westwood (1985). They demonstrate that, for men and women in a variety of jobs, class consciousness is refracted through a gender prism.

This chapter is an attempt to apply this analysis to workers in an occupation that has been socially constructed as the epitome of "men's work," underground coal mining. It departs from previous work in this area in two ways:

1. Whereas Willis (1979), Bertell Ollman (1986), and Knights and Collinson (1985) analyze male workers' gender consciousness chiefly as a "limitation" to class consciousness, I suggest that miners have adapted the received definition of manliness to meet their class needs and that, depending on the structural conditions, their gender consciousness may act either to stimulate or inhibit class consciousness.[2] My difference with those who see male workers' gender consciousness as a limitation to their class consciousness may also be due to a different way of conceptualizing class consciousness. Most theorizing on this topic starts from an epistemological problematic—the problem of knowing what the society is really like (Eyerman 1982).[3] With this problematic, the question of class consciousness becomes: Under what conditions does the working class perceive and understand society the way academic Marxists or sociologists do?

    The notion of class consciousness, at least in its Marxist version, grew out of a different problematic, one of working-class revolution. When viewed from this problematic of collective struggle, it seems clear that the rationalist bias of most theorizing and research in the area is misplaced. To act collectively against the powerful requires not only good analysis but appropriate emotions. I contend that the gender consciousness of male miners reinforces their class consciousness in important ways, both emotional and cognitive. I also explore the ways in which gender consciousness contradicts class consciousness.

2. Earlier work, except for Cockburn's (1983) to some degree, looks at the gender-specific class consciousness of male workers at one point in time and tends to assume that its chief features are enduring. I have interviewed miners over a ten-year period of dramatic changes in material conditions and ideological climate.[4] With this data, I can begin to assess the dynamics of their gender-specific class

consciousness. And during this decade, I detected interesting changes in emphasis within the general gestalt of miners' consciousness.

In approaching the analysis of the actual consciousness of coal miners, I will first sketch how the logic of capitalist and patriarchal domination has shaped the class/gender experience of Appalachian coal miners. Then I will describe important features of their gender-specific class consciousness and its adjustments to the current coal employment crisis.

The Class/Gender Experience of Appalachian Coal Miners

Macrofactors Determining Class/Gender Location

As an extractive energy industry delivering a resource that is plentiful in the United States, the coal industry has been plagued by periodic overproduction crises that have brought destruction of capital and hardship to miner families. Because coal is an important fuel for the economy, when a high proportion of production is unionized, miners possess the power to shut down the economy. This has led to a sense of power among miners and an extraordinary amount of state involvement in managing the industry's labor relations. The market for coal in the United States is presently split between domestic electric utilities and both domestic and foreign steel industries. Utility demand for coal is relatively stable, varying slightly with the business cycle, the price of oil, and the political climate regarding nuclear power, acid rain, and global warming. The demand for the higher-priced metallurgical coal has been in secular decline in the United States and subject to increasing competition in the export market. The metallurgical coal market fluctuates wildly with the business cycle. In the 1980s, the employment experience of miners has differed, depending on whether they worked in the steam or metallurgical coalfields.[5]

The organization of property in an industry powerfully affects the class experience of its workers. The coal industry has become increasingly concentrated in the last few decades, with oil, mineral, and large conglomerate corporations buying the major coal companies. Yet, it is still less concentrated than many other industries, with the largest twenty producers accounting for only 45 percent of production in 1980 (Chapman 1983). Since 1980, the U.S. coal industry has experienced increased competition in domestic markets from Colombia and South Africa, in European markets from those countries themselves and Australia, and in Japan from Australia and China. Increased competition and the declining domestic steel industry have resulted in a substantial drop in the demand for U.S. metallurgical coal and in its price, which has fallen by half.

Coal companies have used a combination of strategies to protect profits. They have rushed the introduction of efficient longwall technology, shut marginally productive mines, externalized inefficiencies by subcontracting production, increased control of the labor process to achieve a substantial speed up, lobbied for lower taxes and relaxation of governmental regulation, and sought to lower wages and benefits through weakening the union. Coal companies are coercing miners and mining communities to subsidize higher profits in the name of making the industry competitive.

The organization of coal mine labor has been fiercely fought by the companies, from the mine wars between 1910 and 1930 to the violent resistance to organizing efforts in nonunion mines in the 1980s. There has been a secular decline in the proportion of coal produced by the United Mine Workers from 80 percent in 1960 to half that in 1983. The decline results from the recent antiunion offensive of the Eastern operatives and several decades of development of strip-mining in the West, where the United Mine Workers are weak. During periods of strong demand for mine labor (most recently in the 1970s), the UMWA has been able to achieve a relatively high wage and benefits package and a strong position, vis-à-vis management at the minesite. Now, with excess capacity (especially in metallurgical coal) and technological redundancies, the union is gradually being forced to make concessions (Simon 1983).

As is typical of extractive industries, coal mining involves placing industrial plants in rural areas. And, as with other extractive industries in the past, this typically involved the construction of company towns and the recruitment of a labor force dependent on the one industry. This has fostered the development of occupational communities, culture, and personality traits.

The gender relations of Appalachian miners are distinctive. Because mining has been socially constructed as "men's work" in a one-industry region, women have had difficulty finding paid employment other than minimum-wage service jobs. This employment picture enforces the economic dependency of miners' wives on their husbands and of miners' families on the coal operator. Responding to the lack of family wage jobs outside the mining sector in coal regions, women in the 1970s took legal action to gain jobs in the mines. By the late 1970s, several thousand had gained entry into this bastion of "men's work," although the mass layoffs of the 1980s have since expelled most of these women miners, who tended to be the last hired. Appalachian mining communities are, of course, isolated from urban feminist organizations, but they are increasingly exposed to feminist ideas by the media, primarily television. And though economic dependency undergirds a patriarchal ideology of miners' wives as helpmates, mining culture also celebrates strong women who must provide for their families when their husbands are killed or injured (Yarrow 1982). And miners' wives often belittle traditional middle-class notions of the woman's role (Stewart 1989).

This is the structural context in which miners' lives are lived and their understandings developed. Along with the physical aspects of work, production technology, and miners' culture, these conditions shape the miners' work and nonwork experience.

Work Experience

Since the 1920s, mechanization has resulted in higher productivity, but, because the miner still controls the speed and direction of the machines, it has not resulted in significant loss of power or skill (Dix 1977; Seltzer 1977; Yarrow 1979). Specialization occurred as each miner's job was defined by the machine he operated. But with frequent job changing, the miner's skills have not been fragmented. Also, management is still hindered by poor visibility in its efforts at surveillance of the work force because the majority work away from management's view most of the time. Mechanization and the increasingly cooperative nature of the labor process make attribution of production to individual miners impossible, so payment by the ton has been converted to hourly pay. With this change in the terms of labor exchange, management has lost a powerful work incentive but has gained flexibility in introducing new technologies and speed-ups.

Although the production work force has been concentrated in a smaller area and the level of supervision has increased twelve-fold from 1890 to 1969 (Seltzer 1977, p. 57), miners have been able to retain considerable control of the labor process by applying power resources marshalled through group unity. Several aspects of the work seem to foster unity. First, the relatively small work force in a mine allows miners to know their workmates. The time miners spend in the bathhouse dressing for work and showering after the shift, their often long rides to work locations in the mine, and rest breaks and machine breakdown breathers throughout the day provide ample time to communicate with their mates without being overheard by management.

Second, the work necessitates cooperation among miners. Members of the crew must anticipate each other's actions to avoid bottlenecks in production, and they must help out when a mate runs into trouble. High production is a collective achievement. So is safety. Operating huge machines in tight, dark, explosive surroundings requires watching out for your "buddies." And shoddy work is not shipped out, as on an assembly line, but creates the environment in which miners have to work for the next few weeks. Typically, miners collectively socialize a new recruit to work safely and to think about his buddies (Yarrow 1979).

They attempt to keep masculine traits of competitiveness and bravado in check to avoid divisiveness and danger by applying strong sanctions to those who go beyond acceptable limits. Common struggles against the foreman, protected by the union contract, and the miners' willingness to strike locally to prevent disciplinary action against a mate also reinforce solidarity.

When the union was strong in the 1970s, workers were successful in countering most of the operator's attempts to mobilize paternalistic principles of control. In the crisis conditions of the 1980s, operators reasserted paternalistic control and created the conditions under which it would be effective. With hundreds of coal company bankruptcies, the operators' claim to a paternalistic harmony of interests with their employee "sons" has increased plausibility. Precarious operators ask for help from their employees in the form of giving up some contract rights and benefits or not insisting on union representation. And in the nonunion mines, production bonuses underscore operator benevolence.

Foremen appeal to the male values of competition, physical strength, and courage. They promote competition between sections and shifts in terms of tons of coal mined. Cautious miners may be ridiculed as unmanly. One told me of being assigned with two other men to lift heavy steel rails. The miner remarked that it looked like a four-man job. The foreman asked, "What's the matter? Aren't you man enough?" (Miner #143, July 1978, southern West Virginia).

Miners and mine management have tended to react hostilely as a male group to the intrusion of women into the mines. Their definition of mining as "men's work" and of men as stronger, tougher, more skilled with machinery, and both dirtier and braver than women convinces them that women cannot do the work. Both seem to fear the degradation of the status of their occupation if women can also do it. Male miners are apprehensive about the possible disruption of their brotherhood but have typically made accommodations in order to maintain the unity of the crew.

In the work experience of underground miners in Appalachia, class conflict is often refracted through the prism of gender. Miners have sought to create worker unity as a brotherhood of male workers. Bosses have tried to weaken the brotherhood by labors of division, including bureaucratization and emphasis on the divisive tendencies in the dominant definition of masculinity or gaining acceptance as part of the brotherhood.

Experience Beyond the Mines

During the early decades of this century, miners in central Appalachia lived in company-owned coal camps where an overweaning paternalism was practiced by mine management. Miners were beholden to the operator not only for their jobs but for most services, from police and groceries to teachers and preachers (Brophy 1964; Goodrich 1925; Simon 1978; Yarrow and Dorris 1985; Yarrow 1986).

The present pattern in the Appalachian coalfields can be thought of as a giant step toward the pattern typical of the rest of the working class. But, in some important ways, it seems as though the "occupational community" has ballooned but not yet burst. Miners have dispersed geographically but still maintain neighborhood, peer, and kin ties with other miners. Although the union has brought miners protection from many abuses of power, land and employment monopolization still result in a concentration of power in the coal and land companies. The cultural isolation of the Appalachian coalfields has been pierced by mainstream culture purveying the dominant ideology, but the mining subculture has remained strong, as reflected in shared institutions, norms, and language. This subculture remains useful as a culture of struggle and resistance, providing miners with a framework and counter values with which to debunk at least some aspects of the invading culture (Johnson 1976; Branscome 1978; Lewis et al. 1978). Miners inhabit a bicultural milieu in which many elements of the two cultures are contradictory (Yarrow 1982).

Some observers have argued that the social cohesion of the mining communities has changed from a family-centered structure, in which kin networks were the foundation of all social relations, to a peer group society, in which same-age, same-sex groups are dominant (Lewis 1970). Although the evidence on this point is far from conclusive, and the family continues to be an important institution, there may be a trend toward a greater importance of peer groups, especially among young male miners. On the other hand, the mass layoffs of the 1980s seem to have reversed this trend to some extent for the unemployed miners are expelled from daily participation in the underground peer group, and a lack of spending money inhibits participation in many aboveground peer activities.

During the coal camp hand-loading éra, miners had considerable autonomy and independence at work, but their nonwork hours were closely controlled in the company-owned camps. Perhaps miners whose working conditions encouraged a sense of independence, power, and confidence felt particularly galled by their infantilization in the camps after work. The present pattern is a reversal of the coal camp structure; now, work is more closely controlled, and leisure is approaching the norm of bourgeois consumer freedom. But if the experience of work and leisure in the coal camp structure promoted a militant conflict class consciousness, how can the reverse have a similar outcome? It would appear that the touchstone of continued militance under altered conditions is the working-class brotherhood, forged in the mine work groups' response to the increasingly cooperative labor process and its defense against intensifying managerial control attempts. It is this unity that spills over into peer relations outside work. Peer leisure relations, in turn, strengthen the workplace solidarity by recognizing its reality aboveground (Yarrow and Dorris 1985). This class gender experience can be expected to encourage a distinctive, gender-specific class consciousness.

The Gender-Specific Class Consciousness of Miners

The class and gender elements in the consciousness of central Appalachian coal miners coalesced during the boom of the 1970s. And, in response to the crisis of the 1980s, that consciousness was changed, yielding new harmonies and antimonies between its class and gender elements.

Class/Gender Consciousness of Miners During
Rank-and-File Mobilization

The following portrait of miners' consciousness is based on interviews conducted at the apex of one of the most militant rank-and-file mobilizations in the postwar U.S. labor movement. Since the late 1960s, rank-and-file miners, pensioners, and widows had organized to get black lung compensation and new, tougher mining health and safety laws, to depose an autocratic union president, and to democratize the miners' union. At their union conventions in 1973 and 1976, they adopted radical negotiating demands that included the right to strike during the life of a contract and the improvement of community services in the coal towns. In the four years prior to the interviews, rank-and-file miners, in opposition to their union leadership, participated in a wave of wildcat strikes, a number extending across the entire Eastern coalfields. In the first eight months of 1977, the man-days lost to strikes as a percentage of available workdays was 10.33 percent as compared with 0.17 percent for all industries— 6,076 percent of the average rate! (Bituminous Coal Operators' Association 1977). When interviewed in March 1978, miners were in the third month of a contract strike. They had turned down two proposed contracts negotiated by the union leadership and ignored a back-to-work injunction imposed by President Jimmy Carter under the Taft-Hartley Law. They were receiving support from other unions, farmers' associations, and citizens' groups from as far away as New England, Georgia, and California.

Miners frequently refer to the views and actions of the older generation as sources of ideas, justifications, and points of comparison: "Our grandaddies fit for this union" (Miner #130, January 1978); "The coal operators killed my dad" (Miner #145 II, July 1978); "Well the union is, originally more so than now, what's made America really! I mean it's done away with slavery, just about" (Miner #133, March 15, 1978); "We don't know how to work the way the oldtimers did" (Miner #130, March 13, 1978).

The emotional proximity of the past is undoubtedly due to the fact that most Appalachian miners are the sons and grandsons of miners. Although conditions in the mines and beyond have changed substantially, frequent references to the views of miners of a previous era reflect a judgment that they are still deemed relevant. Miners during the 1970s appreciated their fathers' bequest of a union won with sacrifice and struggle. They accepted the older generation's perception of the operator/miner conflict.

One indication that miners' consciousness in the 1970s involved a melding of class and gender understandings is the term they used to identify a respected coworker—"good strong union man." It involves a combination of gender and class terms, but each term has both class and gender meanings: A man is only "strong" if he can take a militant stance, and the union is conceived of as a brotherhood. A good strong union man is contrasted with a "scab" or "company suck," who is neither manly nor true to his class.

Listen to three southern West Virginia miners in their forties talk about the difference:[6]

Dennis: We have a percentage of good strong union men, but even with the scabs you can take good strong leaders and break their backs. See, a scab won't rebuke you, if you got a good leader. A scab ain't nothin but a yellowbelly anyhow. He's the next thing to Judas. . . . They put it out if you are a good union man, you are out to destroy production, you're out to destroy the country. That's the biggest lie that a man ever told. Because a real down-to-earth union *man,* he *wants* production.

Don: If you go in or around the mines the good strong union men is the ones that is doing all the work.

Bud: We have to mine the coal that pays our wages.

Don: He [the good strong union man] wants a safe place to work and he wants enough to live on. All poor people are now realizing that that's all there's going to be out of life. If he can stay healthy, if he has got a healthy, safe place to work and he comes home, he's got warm and plenty to eat, that's about all he asks for. That's all I have ever wanted, you know, and plenty of friends" (Miners #127, 145, and 146, July 22, 1978).

These miners see life as a series of harsh tests of manhood that the good strong union man passes and the scab fails. Not only is the work dangerous, strenuous, skilled, and dirty but the daily work experience involves constant managerial attacks. Manhood is won in daily personal combat with both the boss and the work.

Since the hand-loading era (1880–1930), there seem to be subtle changes in emphasis in the notion of toughness. Hard work waned slightly in significance and technical competence became an important requirement for gaining the respect of peers. News of somebody's mistakes spread quickly through the mine. Also, toughness in "standing up" to the boss was stressed during the period of mobilization. It seems that miners have adopted the norm of autonomy from their fathers, but to try to practice it under a labor process with much closer supervision requires constantly fighting off managerial encroachments. Toughness involves the courage and skills of this self-defense. And the strong labor demand of the 1970s reduced the chances of being fired for this aggressive stance.

For militant miners, manhood also required softness—a supportive, nurturing stance—toward one's brothers. The union man is "bighearted." Typical male competitive individualism that scorns dependency is directed at the relationship with management, but a collective ethic of interdependency is promoted for relations with workmates. Because competitive individualism is a pervasive manly value in the dominant culture (Wilkerson 1984), miners must struggle to overcome it. Consequently, they use tough manly sanctions and harsh initiation rites to attack it in members of their work groups (Vaught and Smith 1980). The discipline of collective production and safety under the current mechanized production process and the ample time for communication reinforce miners' efforts to form a solidary brotherhood. The "company suck" violates the brotherhood in two ways: He is solidary with the boss (and thus not with his union brothers), and he is unmanly because he does not have the courage to stand up to the boss and therefore cannot be depended upon to stick up for a wronged brother. He is also selfish in his relationships with workmates. During the 1970s, miners became especially sensitive to the necessity for unity in their rank-and-file strikes. They evaluated each proposed contract in 1978 in terms of its effects on various categories of "brothers," including the young, the older working miners, and the pensioners. Because their strength came from unity, any potentially divisive element was seen as weakening.

Although few miners think about it in this way, they seek to redefine the meaning of masculinity to meet their perceived class needs. Male combativeness is not condoned in relations with mates but is honored in relations with class enemies. Commendable behavior toward mates should include support, caring, mutual respect, and love as a form of collective resistance against management.

Union miners see two contending worldviews extant among miners, which they tend to regard as stable character traits. The consciousness of "good strong union men" involves a calculus of collective betterment, manly "backbone" to "stand up" to the boss, and "bigheartedness" to buddies. The "scab" consciousness of the "company sucks" entails a calculus of individual advantage, unmanly cowardice, and selfishness. The good strong union men dream of collective transcendence, of a strong and vibrant working-class community that is able to defend its rights in the workplace. The scabs dream of individual transcendence by getting rich.

There has been a debate in the British literature about the sources of workers' views of class structure. David Lockwood, in a 1966 article, argued that "for the most part men visualise the class structure of their society from the vantage points of their own particular milieux, and their perceptions of the larger society will vary according to their experiences of social inequality in the smaller societies in which they live out their daily lives (Lockwood 1975, p. 16).

J. H. Westergaard (1975) countered that macrostructural conditions such as crises, concentration of capital, dequalification of labor, and nationwide strikes have promoted a more cosmopolitan working-class consciousness in Britain with a vision of societal transcendence. Michael Mann (1970, 1973) has argued that both immediate experience and the dominant ideology influence workers, leading characteristically to contradictory class consciousness. In trying to understand Appalachian miners' consciousness of the national class system, I find substantial evidence to support Lockwood's model, but there are some indications that macrostructural developments have caused revisions in their "proletarian traditionalism."

Miners' consciousness of class beyond the coalfields is typically derived from a few sources of information. Their union provides one source, and a conglomerate owning their mine may provide another. But on many issues, they rely on local newspapers and television. Because their experience is powerfully affected by macropolitical and economic developments such as governmental reactions to national strikes and the secular trend toward the export of manufacturing jobs, they pay close attention to these developments. They tend to evaluate national events according to assumptions about class relations as they have experienced them and have been taught about them by their fathers. Though their images of a national class structure tend to be vague, their impressions about class relations are sharp.

Miners have a strong sense of class conflict in relations with management in the mines. One miner reported his response to a foreman who tried to establish a brotherly relationship as: "Let's get one damn thing straight right now! You ain't our damn buddy. You're our enemy!" Even rather conservative union miners see a conflict of interest with their employers over the goals of production and safety. Although some miners view coal operators as especially "dirty" in their dealings with their employees, many generalize their view of coal companies as their "enemies" to big businesses in general and would endorse the following statement made by a moderate miner: "Actually the big companies in the United States is what run it. They can choke you, they can drown you, they can do what they want to do, if the people let them. And they'd be more of it if they would be let more" (Miner #135, March 15, 1978). As this quote suggests, many miners see the class relationship as a desperate struggle with high stakes. They have to fight for their lives, their families, their rights, and their dignity.

Involvement in struggles with the coal companies over black lung, safety, and labor legislation, as well as strikes, has given miners an opportunity to evaluate the roles of government, the media, and various types of professionals in class conflict. Asked what lessons he learned from the 111-day strike, one miner responded: "Number one is you know who all your enemies are and never underestimate your enemies. Another good lesson is that the federal government and big business are one and the same. They are like Siamese twins. If you hit one, the other one hollers" (Miner #128, July 3, 1978).

Few miners see the relationship between big business (usually called "money") and government in the structural terms of Marxist state theorists. Rather, most see it as responding to pressure, as in the pluralist theory, but with big business having the most effective means of influence. Many miners assess the state's role in class conflict by analyzing the influences on the personnel in governmental positions. Either they see personnel as having business interests, such as their speculation during the 1978 strike that President Carter must have had investments in the coalfields, or as being easily influenced by the elite. Gender comes into this analysis in the common belief that it takes "a real man" to withstand seductive and intimidating elite influences, just as it does to "stand up" to bosses in the mines.

In their desperate struggle against the powerful money interests, miners see the unions as their only source of support: "The union is the only thing in this whole country that stands up for the working man. If you don't have a union you don't have no rights at all" (Miner #139, March

16, 1978). Because the union is so important in the class struggle, miners must sacrifice to save it from being destroyed: "These men might as well face it. They are going to have to fight. They are going to fight or they are going to die!" (Miner #141, March 13, 1978).

To fight, miners feel they need courage, toughness, and weapons. They see the strike as their primary weapon. When laws and slack demand for coal labor make it ineffective, they become discouraged: "I don't care how good a man is, if he ain't got no weapon, he can't fight" (Miner #139, March 16, 1978). Miners see the contract, governmental safety regulations, guns, and other forms of physical intimidation as other important weapons in their arsenal. They differ in the degree to which they disapprove of illegal or violent actions, but most approve of them in extreme circumstances because they perceive the stakes to be so high and feel that legal actions have been blunted by the companies.

Although most of my respondents see the system as enduring and are suspicious of revolutionary ideologies, the experience of rank-and-file mobilization during the 111-day strike and of the symbolic aid from other unions and farmers encouraged some to think that rank-and-file power could force major societal changes. They saw working people as historical actors who, through their unions, had brought the wider distribution of the fruits of their labor and human rights. In that situation, they tended to view their role defensively as fighting off a business and governmental attempt to crush the unions: "If you keep all the unions together, then you can beat the companies. But if you don't we're going to end up on the short end" (Miner #147, March 18, 1978). But some thought more expansively of beating the enemy once and for all: "I mean if you ain't a big man you're liable to get stomped in the mud in this country. And it is getting worse. But what they don't know is rank and file still runs the government same as the union. And I want to see the day when the United States marches on that D.C. up there and cleans it out. And the Bible says it will happen. We're going to throw them all in the Potomac. All them rich dudes is going down in the Potomac with their money in their pockets 'cause they'll be afraid to leave it" (Miner #141, March 13, 1978).

This brief description of the main contours of the gender-specific class consciousness of Appalachian miners during a period of mobilization suggests that they had developed an analytic and emotional frame for understanding the world from the earlier generation of miners and from their work and community experiences. Their consciousness involved a fusing of class and gender perspectives into a particularly aggressive and solidary conflict class consciousness and a notion of manliness. In the enthusiasm of mobilized rank-and-file power, some even had visions of achieving a society in which workers exercised more power.

Change in the Consciousness of Miners
with the Coal Employment Crisis

In attempting to understand the coal employment crisis that has had such devastating effects on their life chances, miners are presented with two competing interpretations: the corporate and the union. The corporate explanation was available from President Ronald Reagan, coalfield newspapers, coal associations, and many coalfield politicians. It contends that U.S. unions, especially the miners' union, have become too strong and bargained up wages, benefits, and working conditions to the point where they are not competitive on the world market. Unions have protected lazy, unproductive workers and wasteful work practices that lead to massive inefficiencies. The solution offered includes cutting labor costs by lowering wages and benefits, increasing managerial control, and destroying unions. The United Mine Workers of America tries to counter this explanation with one of its own. It argues that miners did not price themselves out of the market but that the market was fundamentally altered by forces beyond their control. They point to the fact that, as U.S. coal has been losing out to foreign coal, the labor costs of U.S. coal have decreased by almost 50 percent due to a doubling of productivity. They see a corporate plot to destroy domestic unions and reduce labor costs by producing in low-wage, low-tax, lax-regulation countries. Their answer is protectionism: saving U.S. jobs by reducing imports.

Although varying in their analyses, miners tend to combine elements from both these explanations because they each resonate with their experiences. They look back on the 1970s from the perspective of the present crisis as a time in which they did live "high off the hog" compared with their parents and grandparents and as a time when they did exert considerable power over the labor process. They remember protecting unproductive workers and defending unproductive practices and now view the tighter discipline under which their parents worked as necessary. On the other hand, they see a corporate plot to destroy their union by opening nonunion mines and importing coal. They experience this directly in the closing of large union mines and the subleasing of the coal rights to small nonunion operators or the investment in large, new, government-protected "scab" mines that pay above union scale. In the strategic debate about contract concessions, the strongest voices in favor come from the unemployed, and the strongest voices against from union organizers who are already having difficulty advocating their cause to nonunion miners with above-union wages. But most miners are reluctant to give up hard-won gains that are a measure of their collective achievements.

The miners' assessment of the present crisis is accompanied by shifts in their gender-specific class consciousness. Perhaps the most dramatic change in consciousness is in an emphasis on the two criteria of manliness. In 1978, the stress was on a miner's ability to face down the boss; now, it is on how hard a man works. Thus, gender identity has become less class combative. This change has been accompanied by an altered use of history. In 1978, the elders were cited for their struggle against operator oppression; today, they are revered as hard workers. The new generation of miners hired in the 1970s, then lauded for their militance, are now seen by many as a cause of the downfall of the industry and the union because they "were not interested in working for their buddies' welfare." In times of crisis, harmony of interests with precarious operators becomes more plausible, and hard work is stressed as a way to keep the company in business and protect jobs.

Miners also seem to have reevaluated the exercise of rank-and-file power. At the peak of rank-and-file mobilization during the 1978 strike, they considered themselves to be powerful, able to win the strike and possibly to force more far-reaching structural changes. The perceived loss of that strike caused them to reevaluate their power position with respect to their corporate opponents. Ten years of gathering crisis convinced most that the companies were practically invincible. They saw change as possibly due to an upswing in the business cycle or the election of a Democratic president but viewed either development as beyond their power to influence. Without change, many saw their union being destroyed in the near future.

As miners perceive the diminishing power of the rank and file, they reassess militance. The wildcat strikes of the 1970s, which were seen in 1978 primarily as a noble attempt to fend off operator aggression, are now typically seen as foolish and often ignoble—the view the operators have had all along. Rank-and-file power is also questioned by way of increasing criticism of union democracy. Although not optimistic, miners hope that their union leaders will be able to find a way out of the present crisis, since they perceive themselves as powerless to accomplish the feat. Thus, they want to give their leaders as much power as possible. They want a smart, tough, manly leader to win the battle they can no longer win themselves.

The brotherhood has begun to unravel as a result of the layoffs and the inability of the union to protect jobs. Unemployment means the bonds are not reinforced by the daily work experience. It also means that miners do not have the disposable income to participate in many leisure activities with peers. They are thrown back on kin support networks for survival. Miners who are still working appreciate the precariousness of their positions. They resist the demand of the brotherhood that they refuse overtime while others are laid off. Instead, they try to get all they can to provide a nest egg for their families when they are sacked. They have reluctantly and with a bad conscience adopted the calculus of individual advantage in place of the collective betterment they believe in. In the crisis, when collective struggle seems implausible, family loyalty takes precedence over loyalty to the brotherhood.[7]

Miners resist working in nonunion mines or leaving for the low-wage nonunion jobs in the South because, according to their gender-specific class consciousness, these jobs would deprive them of the working conditions they have fought for, the brotherhood they cherish, and their sense of self-respect. But their work-related, gender-specific consciousness is not very helpful in developing alternative strategies. Miners see their power as deriving from their positions as wage laborers. When there is no demand for their labor, they see themselves as powerless. Collective strategies that involve finding new sources of power and new allies, such as women and other male workers, are unimaginable for most. They also reject visions of the future that detach them permanently from the underground brotherhood, the basis for their proud class/gender identity. In the crisis, the miners' union does not seem to be formulating strategies for a collective struggle to make an economic transition from coal. But unemployed miners are fish out of water gasping for breath, and they are hard to convince that there might be plausible collective strategies in the absence of capital's need for their underground brotherhood.

Harmonies and Antimonies in the Class and Gender Elements of Miners' Consciousness

1. *Miner Toughness.* Rupert Wilkinson lists the traits constituting toughness in U.S. culture as mastery, dynamism, competence, self-defense, competitiveness, endurance in dangerous and stressful situations, willpower, and autonomy (Wilkinson 1984, p. 7). These traits are all part of the meaning of the term as used by miners. The core meaning for miners seems to be a mental and physical stance toward the world; it is a cognitive and performance style focused on combat. Whereas survival strategies of subordinate people may involve invisibility and subtle passive resistance or ingratiating oneself to the powerful, toughness for miners involves a declaration of independence from and challenge to the authority of the bosses. It includes class and gender elements that reinforce and contradict each other. Although women may be tough, it is necessary to the achievement of manhood in the mines. Toughness in U.S. culture stresses competition with other men (Wilkinson 1984; Howell 1973), but miners direct their combat toward their class enemies, the representatives of mine management. Socialization to masculine toughness, especially in the coal miners' subculture, teaches men many of the conflict skills of verbal and physical combat, bluffing, and strategic thinking useful in taking a militant stance toward management. For a vulnerable working-

class man confronted by a powerful enemy, learning to be tough allows him to act in defense of rights rather than out of fear. The tough miner can thus achieve a relationship with the boss that is consistent with a conflict class consciousness. On the other hand, fighting with the boss has been a test of masculine identity.

Tough-mindedness is the attendant cognitive style, disciplined for conflict. It involves distilling the implications of information for the conflict. Tough-mindedness is impatient with complex analyses that impede action. It involves "facing the facts" even if they are intimidating for unrealistic assessments lead to ineffective action. It values practical experiential knowledge rather than abstract knowledge, which tends to be ridiculed as impractical and mistrusted as manipulation by class enemies. The experience of having a union leader, Arnold Miller, who came from the ranks but was perceived as not sophisticated enough to hold his own in the elite world has led many miners to value "book learning" as well as practical experience. However, it was Miller's perceived weak will that garnered the most criticism. As one miner put it, "Well, we proved that our union can run without much brains in these past two elections [when Miller was elected president]. But we also proved that it can't operate very efficiently without backbone" (Miner #130, July 5, 1978). Tough-mindedness demands that one's analysis be harnessed to an iron will—"backbone."

Willis (1979) has observed that the masculine toughness of British factory workers is easily co-optable and is thus a block to class consciousness. Because tough men are preoccupied with defense of their dignity, they can be mollified with a managerial apology rather than structural change. I have found a similar concern for the style of command among coal miners. They tend to go along with a boss who asks and fight one who orders. On the other hand, miners conceive of their dignity as involving the preservation of an expansive set of rights. These include free speech, freedom to do the job the way they want without supervision, freedom to make judgments about their own safety, freedom to work as fast as they want and to strike when they want, and the right to high wages, family health care, and pensions. Aggressive assertion of these rights is, to put it mildly, an impediment to management's control project. Miners make little distinction between rights to personal dignity on the job and citizens' rights beyond the job: All must be protected by struggle against the powerful. Herbert Gintis (1980) has argued that, in the West, the class struggle has been waged in terms of human rights versus property rights. Although sometimes co-optable with gestures, coal miners' tough defense of expansive human rights catapults them into this struggle.

The tough conflict class consciousness of male miners was relatively well adapted to the boom conditions they faced in the 1970s. But as conditions changed, miners experienced a disjuncture between consciousness and action. The militant, collective, contestation survival strategy, in a period of layoffs, mine closings, and a demobilized rank and file, becomes increasingly vulnerable to capitalist reprisals. Survival strategies and their attendant consciousnesses are also labeled by bosses and dealt with accordingly: The "good strong union man" is a "troublemaker"; the "company suck" is a "good man." Miners know that their consciousness is not a private affair but can have powerful ramifications. In the present crisis, miners who wish to avoid the "troublemaker" label but retain the concomitant combative class consciousness feel very uncomfortable with concessions they must make at work. As one miner put it, "Sometime you have to eat crow to survive" (Miner #229, January 22, 1987). I found a greater tolerance for "scab" behavior among even the most militant miners in 1987 than was evident in 1978. To relieve the painful sense of hypocrisy, some miners began to adjust their consciousness toward a more harmonious view of employer-employee relations. In this context, the overwhelming support for the Pittston strikers can be viewed as a reaffirmation of the militant perspective.

Possibly because standing up to the boss is no longer as practical a test of toughness, being able to do hard work, to endure discomfort, and to brave danger is regaining the importance it had during the hand-loading era. This test gives the work significance in the achievement of manliness. In this way, the miners' celebration of toughness is an impediment to seeing their class interests as opposed to those of capital. It is only the most conflict-conscious who are fully aware of this and resist it consistently. One reported that, when asked at the end of a shift by other miners how many buggies his section had mined, he would reply, "Too . . . too damn many!" (Miner #128, March 17, 1978).

Toughness undermines class solidarity in three ways. First, because it is regarded as a manly virtue, women are not generally viewed as tough and so cannot be worthy members of the brotherhood and are therefore ignored as class allies. Second, to the extent that toughness is a posture of independence from influence, this may make it difficult for miners to compromise and cooperate as a group. Third, the miners' desire for tough leaders can be a block to class consciousness. They tolerate the undemocratic practices of a leader as part of the toughness they want and as the way to intimidate hopelessly weak miners into taking the proper militant actions. In the process, they tend to ignore building the structures of class unity and accountability of leadership and set themselves up for betrayal by their leaders. In the national political arena, their quest for a tough leader led some of the younger militant miners to vote for antiunion Ronald Reagan in 1980 because of his tough stance toward other countries.

Male toughness as construed by Appalachian coal miners has contradictory effects on their class consciousness. Toughness supports, prepares, and endorses class combative actions (which enhance conflict class consciousness with its emotional dimensions of courage) and indignation at attempts at subordination. It is packaged with a tough-mindedness disciplined to struggle. On the other hand, it excludes women, tends to be competitive, and ignores some important aspects of class analysis.

2. *Male Bonding and Class Solidarity.* Male bonding can pose an impediment to class solidarity by encouraging miners to see a bond with male managers. This happens to some degree in the shared hostility of foremen and male miners to the introduction of women into the mines. It also occurs in the masculine meaning given to hard, dangerous work, obscuring its reality as class exploitation. But miners guard against these claims to solidarity with class antagonists by defining brotherhood as excluding bosses and by making an ability to fight the bosses a membership criterion.

Class solidarity is also obstructed by male competitiveness and sense of superiority (Gray 1984). Miners struggle to overcome this by stressing the importance of their brotherhood. Although they participate in competitive games, they strive to set limits and curb behavior that threatens unity. They have been so successful over the decades that they have been able to unite beyond the workplace and conduct wildcat strikes across multistate regions in spite of opposition by union leadership. In a culture where the capitalist ideology of competitive individualism is dominant, miners have been successful in maintaining a collectivist code and practice in their working-class brotherhood. During the periods of rank-and-file mobilization, their solidarity has inspired visions of social transcendence of the class system but not of the gender system.

The biggest block that the miners' brotherhood erects to class solidarity is its exclusion of women. Women are considered to have essentially different and, to some degree, opposite traits from men, and they are seen as outsiders and viewed with suspicion. Although there are many examples of male miners who welcomed women coworkers into the brotherhood rather than see the brotherhood weakened, it seems to be a provisional membership. Wives have joined strikes and other union struggles on an episodic basis but are typically not welcomed to union meetings and are not thought of as part of the group. Their abilities are not used well, and strategic thinking typically excludes them. In fact, militants often see wives as blocks to militant actions because their presumed preoccupation with "paying the bills" leads them to pressure their husbands to go back to work. In an important way, miners have less in common with their wives now than their parents did in the coal camps of the past. They do not jointly face the operator as the landlord, storekeeper, and controller of services in the community, as the coal camp family did. To protect family members from the worry and guilt that might be produced if they knew details of the dangers and indignities of the job, miner couples construct a barrier between work and family spheres that widens the gulf between husband and wife. Some militants imagine overcoming this problem by bringing wives into the union but are discouraged from pushing this project by membership resistance.

3. *The User and the Used.* Stan Gray (1984) has pointed out that male workers under capitalism share with women under patriarchy the experience of having their bodies used as objects of others' purposes. My interviews are filled with references to how coal operators use and abuse miners for the sake of profit. This might be grounds for empathy with the women's plight and cross sex class solidarity. Under coal camp paternalism, there were structural reasons why miners may have made the connection between their exploitation and that of women. Their wives were often subject to sexual harassment by their bosses, and they viewed it as a form of class, as well as sex, oppression (Long 1985). Now, sexual harassment seems to be mostly a problem for women miners. And instead of seeing it as class or sex oppression, male miners often see it as class collaboration by the women intruders—as evidence that they are not part of the brotherhood. According to their male identity, miners are users of women. In many of the mines I have visited, there is much banter about women as sexual objects. This reflects an oppressor's consciousness that blocks class solidarity across the gender line and may inhibit a clear appreciation of class oppression. Although, in patriarchal ideology, miners can be bosses of their families, I have found this tendency pronounced among only a minority of miners.

4. *Subordination at Work Versus Superordination in the Family.* There is a contradiction for the male worker under patriarchal capitalism between his subordinate position at work and his superordinate position in the family. As noted above, the patriarchal family position may compensate for the subordination to the boss. Cockburn (1983) and Willis (1979) argue that, because men feel they owe their breadwinner role to their employer, they feel grateful to that employer, especially when jobs are scarce. The breadwinner role also discourages militant actions that might jeopardize the job or interrupt the cash flow due to strikes. But miners have often struggled for a family wage, job security, better safety and benefits in order to fulfill the breadwinner role more adequately. These demands have cut into the rate of exploitation and have been resisted

by companies. Such resistance leads miners to regard capital as opposed to their attempts to provide for their families, heightening their sense of class conflict. They also often express indignation at the unmanly subordination they experience at work. Thus, their gender consciousness reinforces their consciousness of class conflict.

5. *Images of Leadership: Paternalism Versus Collective Leadership.* The experience of most of my respondents with rank-and-file mobilization and class conflict led to profound disillusionment with the whole gamut of authority figures. The union president Miller, President Carter, and governors of coal states were seen to be on the side of the operators. Judges who issued injunctions for the operators and police who "baby-sat" scabs who were harassing strikers were also found to be partisan. The supposed neutral role of the state, according to dominant ideology, was critically reassessed. This led to a blanket condemnation. In terms of their gender-specific class consciousness, none of them stood the test.

Few thought of the solution in terms of building structures of collective leadership or accountability to the working class. The neglect of such an option may have been partly due to their recent disillusionment with a rank-and-file group that had been secretly led by a Maoist sect. The most important factor seems to be their reading of their experience with union presidents. From their class/gender perspective, John L. Lewis and Tony Boyle were tough men who could stand up for the membership, and Miller was weak and sold them out. In making this judgment, they ignored the accommodationist actions of Lewis and Boyle and the benefits they had won under Miller. Although few had experienced Lewis's rule, they viewed him as the leader nobody could control, who remained true to his followers and thus commanded their respect and obedience. The way miners read the historical evidence was influenced by their own experience with class conflict. They know it takes "backbone" to stand up for their buddies at the mine and increasing sophistication to fight effectively against lawyers, company executives, and government bureau-crats. They wanted a leader to "stand behind us," backing the rank-and-file demands and, at the same time, standing in front as the "big man" enforcing discipline and taking charge. Only a few were concerned about the problem of creating a new autocrat. Because standing up to corporate executives and presidents takes combat skills they lacked, they wanted a paternalistic champion to do right by them. Their class/gender con-sciousness directed them toward the search for a tough, educated man. As the conditions became more intimidating in the 1980s, they elected tough-talking Rich Trumka as union president, hoping that his mining experience and law degree prepared him to fight the companies effectively.

Conclusion

This chapter began with two theoretical questions: What is the impact of gender on the class consciousness of male blue-collar workers? And how do we understand the shifts in consciousness that accompany shifts in the material and ideological context? I will summarize briefly what I believe can be concluded.

The evidence I have collected from Appalachian miners indicates that their gender consciousness is an adaptation of the prevailing U.S. male gender consciousness, resonating better with their militant conflict class consciousness. Miners' gender consciousness reinforces their class consciousness by stiffening their class militance with masculine toughness and cementing their solidarity with male bonding. The impulse of laborers to struggle with bosses is reinforced by the fact that they view subordination to capital as beneath their manly dignity. Because of its aggressive defense of this dignity, the militant stance is more consistent with cosmopolitan and local definitions of manliness than an accommodationist stance would be.

This consciousness contains contradictions. Miners' gender consciousness impedes working-class consciousness by the exclusiveness of the "we" group that is conceived as the brotherhood of male miners rather than all working people, by the dependence on a paternalistic union leader, by manly pride in alienated labor, and by a sense of superiority over women. The contradictions in this consciousness make it more dynamic. They create tensions that disrupt its solidification. Emphasis within the set of themes may change without completely disrupting accepted truths—viz., the recent change of emphasis in the definition of manliness from "standing up to the boss" to "hard work," which has accompanied the demobilization of the rank-and-file movement and the crisis in coal employment.

Consciousness does not simply reflect changing conditions. With the radical changes in the class and gender relations of coal mining in this century, there has been an amazing continuity in consciousness despite shifts in emphasis. Some analyze this as a result of cultural inertia, but other working-class subcultures have altered quite radically with changing conditions. However, the changes often do not come until the next generation, which views its parents' perspectives as quaint and inappropriate to the new conditions. One reason for the intergenerational continuity in miners' consciousness is undoubtedly that, with all the change, some basic relations remain similar in form. Miners have a continuing sense of class conflict largely because they have continued evidence that coal operators often do not act in their best interests. Therefore, they see a continuing need for the union in spite of its present weakness and past mistakes. It enables them to assume a manly stance at work. And because gender is such a powerful source of identity, the gender element in miners' consciousness is a source of resistance to change: Although the elements of gender consciousness may be adapted slightly to new conditions, major change would cause an identity crisis for many.

Acknowledgments

Research for this paper was supported by a sabbatical leave from Ithaca College, an Appalachian Studies Fellowship, and a James Still Fellowship. I am grateful for the help of Ruth Yarrow, who conducted some of the interviews and made numerous suggestions about the analysis.

Notes

1. I adopt the term "patriarchal capitalism" from Eisenstein (1979) who uses it to mean a mode of production in which a male-dominated sex/gender system is fused with a capitalist political economy. Hartmann (1981) argues that patriarchy and capitalism are sometimes integrated and sometimes contradictory. I believe, with Hartmann and Cockburn (1983), that it is often fruitful to separate analytically the logics of class and sex/gender relationships.

2. There seems to be an assumption among many theorists of class consciousness that consciousness of any other structure of inequality distracts from consciousness of class. This belief is based on an assumption that these other factors obscure perception of class. In practice, this assumption has led to denying the importance of racial and gender oppression. I think this assumption must be explored empirically, as begun by Willis, Cockburn, and Westwood, for it is conceivable that elements of gender or race consciousness may reinforce class consciousness (for race consciousness promoting class consciousness, see Leggett 1968; Leiter 1986; Zingraff and Schulman 1984).

David Knights, in marginal notes on an earlier draft of this chapter, raised the question of intentionality. He asked if I am arguing that miners or a few leaders intentionally design the most advantageous class/gender consciousness for their strategic position. I do not mean that, but I have found that many thoughtful and involved miners both in and out of leadership positions discuss not only the strategic implications of the current conjuncture but also the qualities of character they respect in their mates. And it goes beyond talk. They teach and discipline new recruits about certain acceptable perspectives and behaviors. So, I believe it is accurate to describe them as active participants in the shaping of their class/gender consciousness.

3. Willis's categories of "penetration" and "limitation" clearly arise out of this problematic.

4. The analysis of Appalachian miners' consciousness in this chapter is based chiefly on almost 200 lengthy (1½ to 4½ hours), semistructured interviews with 100 underground miners and 30 miners' wives, conducted between 1978 and

1987. Twenty-five of the miners have been interviewed at least two times, and several were seen eight times.

5. The long and bitter A. T. Massey and Pittston strikes of the 1980s both took place in the metallurgical coalfields and were provoked by aggressive cost-cutting strategies by management aimed at maintaining their global competitiveness. Most of the interviews in this study were conducted in the central Appalachian metallurgical coalfields.

6. The names have been changed.

7. The pain of this violation of the principle of brotherhood is underscored by the attempts to reaffirm it during the 1989–1990 Pittston strike. Over 40,000 miners struck in solidarity with the Pittston strikers, and material aid poured in to the strikers from other mines.

References

Bituminous Coal Operators' Association (BCOA). 1977. Statement presented at the first session of the National Bituminous Coal Wage Agreement Negotiations, Washington, D.C., October 6.

Branscome, Jim. 1978. "Annihilating the Hillbilly." In *Colonialism in Modern America: The Appalachian Case,* eds. Helen Lewis et al., pp. 211–27. Boone, N.C.: Appalachian Consortium Press.

Brophy, John. 1964. *A Miner's Life,* edited and supplemented by John D.P. Hall. Madison: University of Wisconsin Press.

Chapman, Duane. 1983. *Energy Resources and Energy Corporations.* Ithaca, N.Y.: Cornell University Press.

Cockburn, Cynthia. 1983. *Brothers: Male Dominance and Technological Change.* London: Pluto Press.

Dix, Keith. 1977. *Work Relations in the Coal Industry: The Hand-Loading Era, 1880–1930.* Morgantown: Institute for Labor Studies, West Virginia University.

Eisenstein, Zillah R. 1979. "Developing a Theory of Capitalist Patriarchy and Socialist Feminism." In *Capitalist Patriarchy and the Case for Socialist Feminism,* ed. Zillah Eisenstein, pp. 5–40. New York: Monthly Review Press.

Eyerman, Ron. 1982. "Some Recent Studies in Class Consciousness." *Theory and Society* 11:541–53.

Gintis, Herbert. 1980. "Communication and Politics: Marxism and the 'Problem' of Liberal Democracy." *Socialist Review* 10:189–232.

Goldberg, Roberta. 1981. "Dissatisfaction and Consciousness Among Office Workers: A Case Study of a Working Women's Organization." Ph.D. dissertation, American University.

Goodrich, Carter. 1925. *The Miners' Freedom: A Study of the Working Life in a Changing Industry.* Boston: Marshall Jones.

Gray, Stan. 1984. "Sharing the Shop Floor: Women and Men on the Assembly Line." *Radical America* 18:69–88.

Hartmann, Heidi. 1981. "The Unhappy Marriage of Marxism and Feminism: A More Progressive Union." In *Women and Revolution,* ed. L. Sargent, pp. 1–41. Boston: South End Press.

Howell, Joseph T. 1973. *Hard Living on Clay Street*. Garden City, N.Y.: Anchor Press.

Jacoby, Russell. 1978. "Political Economy and Class Unconsciousness." *Theory and Society* 5:11–18.

Johnson, Linda. 1976. "Reflections on Women and Appalachian Culture." *Win Magazine* 12:9–10.

Knights, David, and David Collinson. 1985. "Accounting for Discipline in Disciplinary Accounting: A Case Study of Shopfloor Resistance to Management Accounts and Its Disciplinary Outcomes." Presented at the "Inter-Disciplinary Perspectives on Accounting Conference," Manchester, England.

Leggett, John C. 1968. *Class, Race and Labor: Working Class Consciousness in Detroit*. New York: Oxford University Press.

Letter, Jeffrey. 1986. "Reactions to Subordination: Attitudes of Southern Textile Workers." *Social Forces* 64:948–74.

Lewis, Helen. 1970. "Coal Miner's Peer Groups and Family Roles." Paper read at American Anthropological Association meeting, San Diego, California, November.

Lewis, Helen et al. 1978. "Family, Religion and Colonialism in Central Appalachia." In *Colonialism in Modern America: The Appalachian Case*, eds. Helen Lewis et al., pp. 113–39. Boone, N.C.: Appalachian Consortium Press.

Lockwood, David. 1975. "Sources of Variation in Working-Class Images of Society." In *Working Class Images of Society*, ed. M. Bulmer, pp. 16–31. London: Routledge and Kegan Paul.

Long, Priscilla. 1985. "The Women of the Colorado Fuel and Iron Strike, 1913–14." In *Women, Work, and Protest: A Century of U.S. Women's Labor History*, ed. Ruth Milkman, pp. 62–85. Boston: Routledge and Kegan Paul.

Mann, Michael. 1970. "The Social Cohesion of Liberal Democracy." *American Sociological Review* 34:423–39.

———. 1973. *Consciousness and Action Among the Western Working Class*. London: Macmillan.

Ollman, Bertell. 1972. "Toward Class Consciousness Next Time: Marx and the Working Class." *Politics and Society* 3:1–24.

———. 1986. "How to Study Class Consciousness . . . And Why We Should." Paper read at American Sociological Association meeting, New York, September.

Seltzer, Curtis I. 1977. "The United Mine Workers of America and the Coal Operators: The Political Economy of Coal in Appalachia, 1950–1973." Ph.D. dissertation, Columbia University.

Simon, Richard M. 1978. "The Development of Underdevelopment: The Coal Industry and Its Effects on the West Virginia Economy, 1880–1930." Ph.D. dissertation, University of Pittsburgh.

———. 1983. "Hard Times for Organized Labor in Appalachia." *Review of Radical Political Economics* 15:21–34.

Stewart, Katie. 1981. "The Marriage of Capitalist and Patriarchal Ideologies: Meanings of Male Bonding and Male Ranking in U.S. Culture." In *Women and Revolution*, ed. Lydia Sargent, pp. 269–311. Boston: South End Press.

――――. 1989. "Speak for Yourself: Gender as Dialogic in Appalachia." In *Negotiation of Gender in American Culture,* eds. Faye Ginsburg and Anna Tsing. Boston: Beacon Press.

Suffern, Arthur E. 1926. *Coal Miners' Struggle for Industrial Status.* New York: Macmillan.

Vaught, Charles, and David Smith. 1980. "Incorporation and Mechanical Solidarity in an Underground Coal Mine." *Sociology of Work and Occupation* 7:159–87.

Westergaard, J. H. 1975. "Radical Class Consciousness: A Comment." In *Working Class Images of Society,* ed. M. Bulmer, pp. 251–56. London: Routledge and Kegan Paul.

Westwood, Sallie. 1985. *All Day, Every Day: Factory and Family in the Making of Women's Lives.* Chicago: University of Illinois Press.

Wilkinson, Rupert. 1984. *American Tough: The Tough-Guy Tradition and American Character.* New York: Harper and Row.

Willis, Paul. 1977. *Learning to Labor.* New York: Columbia University Press.

――――. 1979. "Shop Floor Culture, Masculinity and the Wage Form." In *Working Class Culture,* eds. John Clarke et al., pp. 185–98. London: Hutchinson.

Yarrow, Michael. 1979. "The Labor Process in Coal Mining: Struggle for Control." In *Case Studies on the Labor Process,* ed. Andrew Zimbalist, pp. 170–92. New York: Monthly Review Press.

――――. 1982. "How Good Strong Union Men Line It Out: Explorations of the Structure and Dynamics of Coal Miners' Class Consciousness." Ph.D. dissertation, Rutgers University.

――――. 1986. "Capitalism, Patriarchy and 'Men's Work': The System of Control of Production of Coal Mining." In *The Impact of Institutions in Appalachia,* proceedings of the Appalachian Studies Conference, eds. Jim Lloyd and Anne G. Campbell, pp. 29–47. Boone, N.C.: Appalachian Consortium Press.

Yarrow, Michael, and James Dorris. 1985. "Work, Leisure, and Social Cohesion: The Changing Basis of Coal Miner Solidarity." In *Transitions to Leisure,* eds. B. G. Gunter et al., pp. 71–88. New York: University Press of America.

Zingraff, Rhonda, and Michael D. Schulman. 1984. "Social Bases of Class Consciousness: A Study of Southern Textile Workers with a Comparison by Race." *Social Forces* 63:98–116.

16 | Painting Socialism: Working-Class Formation in Hungary and Poland

Michael Burawoy

The Soviet locomotive cannot go any further because there are no more rails. The socialist train comes to a stop. Brezhnev instructs the steel industry to make more rails. It is done, and the socialist train continues until once more it comes to the end of the track. Andropov is now general secretary of the party and discovers there is no more steel to be had. So he orders that the track behind the train be put in front of it. The socialist locomotive continues until once more it comes to a standstill. Now there is no track either in front or behind the train. Chernyenko has assumed leadership, but there are neither steel nor rails. So he instructs all the Communists to get out of the train and rock it backwards and forwards so that the passengers inside should think that the socialist locomotive is once more on its way.

—Pre-Gorbachev Joke

A specter is haunting the Soviet Union and Eastern Europe. It is the specter of Solidarity, a working-class revolt staged in the name of the unfulfilled promises of state socialism. In 1980–1981, the Polish working class attempted, for the first time in history, a societywide Marxian revolution. The working class gave the revolt its energy and determined its direction. Its leaders came from the working class, hardened by experiences in the earlier revolts of 1956, 1970, and 1976. Intellectuals played a subsidiary, although often critical, role. Initially, Solidarity resisted taking over the means of production, but later in the spring of 1981, when its fate was already sealed, economic crisis compelled it to initiate such a struggle. Now, nearly a decade later, it has formed the first non-Communist government in forty years of Soviet domination in Eastern Europe.

If it was Marxian in its class basis and its goals, its context and idiom violated all conventional Marxian norms. It did not take place in an advanced capitalist society but in a society that claims to be socialist.

It was not bound by a commitment to Marxism or even socialism but was profoundly anti-Marxist, nationalist, and permeated by religious symbolism and commitment. Yet, despite itself, Solidarity, inasmuch as it can be regarded as a homogeneous movement, aspired to socialist goals, a proletarian democracy in which workers would direct society in the collective interest.

Was this convulsion of state socialism a freak case, peculiar to Poland, or did it have broader significance? Historians stress the heritage of an old culture that has enabled an underground society to develop and persist for almost two centuries of occupation, with brief and partial respites in the last century, and for twenty-five years of disenchanting independence between the two world wars. They give special attention to the legacy of Roman Catholic faith, noble democracy, and a rich spiritual and literary heritage that fed and consoled the political frustrations of an oppressed nation. Solidarity is but the most recent of a series of uprisings—in 1733, 1768, 1791, 1794, 1830, 1863, 1905, 1920, 1944—against foreign and, in particular, Russian occupation. These are the pegs upon which the Polish collective consciousness is hung. Social scientists, on the other hand, have tried to subsume the rise of Solidarity under some universal rule: the colonized rising up against the colonizer, the working-class struggle for trade union recognition, or the rebellion of civil society against the state.[1]

In the first interpretation, working-class revolt is the enactment of a unique history; in the second, it is the working out of a general principle. But in both, we lose sight of the world historical significance of Solidarity because Poland's state socialist character becomes an incidental or contextual factor. Within a Marxist framework, the question has to be reformulated: Do the working-class struggles in Poland signify something distinctive about social movements under state socialism? Are the working classes created by state socialism more likely than those created by advanced capitalism to form a "class-for-itself" striving toward a democratic socialism? Or are they inclined to seek the restoration of capitalism? In answering such a fundamental question, it is necessary to return to basics.

Theories of Class Formation

The compelling logic of Marx's original theory of the collapse of capitalism and transition to socialism lies in the confluence of objective laws that spell the demise of capitalism and subjective struggles that guarantee the transition to socialism. On the objective side, the argument is as follows. Capitalists compete with one another in the pursuit of profit and, in so doing, introduce new machinery, deskill workers, and increase the reserve army of unemployed. Individual capitalists have no alternative but to keep up with the latest mode of expropriating surplus if they are to survive as capitalists. The survival of each capitalist depends on the degradation of workers. But the effect for collective capital, for the system of capitalism, is the generation of crises of overproduction and of profitability. These crises lead to the destruction of capitalists, who become fewer and fewer even as they become larger and larger. Increasingly, they are concentrated into trusts, cartels, and joint stock companies until the state eventually assumes ownership of an increasing share of the means of production. Capitalists reveal themselves to be incompetent to deal with the deepening crises and superfluous to the organization of production, so exploitation becomes transparent. Capitalism brought to a head must topple over.

Marx and Engels, therefore, assume that the end of competitive capitalism is the end of all capitalism. They do not conceive of a new form of capitalism—an organized capitalism. Why not? The answer lies in the development of class struggle that coincides with the worsening crises. As individual capitalists pursue profit and drive capitalism to its doom, they also generate a class structure that is increasingly polarized between working class and capital. Intermediary classes (in particular small capitalists and peasantry) disappear into a working class that itself is becoming homogenized, dependent, and degraded. But this "class-in-itself" is still made up of individuals competing for the crumbs preferred by capitalism. Class struggle, then, counteracts the atomizing effects of competition. At first in scattered and isolated confrontations with individual capitalists but then through combinations into trade unions, the working class pursues its interests within capitalism. Only with the formation of a working-class political party, which sees the proletariat's fate as a question of controlling state power, is capitalism itself challenged. In the political, as well as in the economic, arena, the bourgeoisie proves to be its own gravedigger. It continually draws the working class into the political arena to fight battles against other classes (particularly the landed aristocracy) or against other national bourgeoisie. Moreover, Marx was convinced that universal suffrage would demystify class relations and pierce any illusions that workers would be able to substantially improve their circumstances within the framework of capitalism. Universal suffrage would unchain class struggle by clarifying the opposition of interests between capital and labor and by fostering the organization of the working class into a political party. Not only does capitalism necessarily sow the seeds of its own destruction but the working class recognizes that necessity and develops the means of seizing power and going beyond capitalism.

The leap from class-in-itself to class-for-itself has not occurred, and contemporary Marxism has sought to revise the theory in two essentially different ways. The first is to reexamine Marx's conception of class-in-itself and to argue against the polarization and homogenization theses. Far from disappearing, the middle class—variously understood as a "contradictory class location" or "the professional managerial class"—is continually reconstituted under capitalism. And even within the working class, reskilling is as important as deskilling. Others point to divisions within the working class created by the balkanization of labor markets, reflecting segregation by race and gender, and the separation of core and peripheral sectors of the capitalist economy. Yet others speak of the re-creation of an aristocracy of labor. However, these theories, which point to divisions within the working class, do not explain why these divisions override class solidarity. They do not explain why, even in the absence of such divisions, workers do not challenge capitalism. Or, in other words, they do not explain the vertical coordination of interests of workers and capital. They presuppose what has to be demonstrated, namely, the inherent opposition of the interests of workers and capitalists.[2]

The second approach examines precisely how class interests are organized. Here, the point is to examine class-for-itself or, to use another term for the same phenomenon, class formation. As in Marx, the focus moves from the economic to the political arena, to the formation of working-class parties and their struggle for and insertion into capitalist democracy.[3] However, the working class and its allies, rather than being the gravediggers of capitalism, become its saviors. The extraction of concessions, facilitated by electoral democracy, reequilibrates capitalism through the intervention of the state, tempering competition among capitalists and reducing crises of overproduction. In this argument, interests are shaped by actors in the political arena, but there is no connection back to the arena of production itself. The economy provides the conditions of class compromise, but there is no attempt to understand the shaping of interests as it goes on in the lived experience of production— the experiential foundations for compromise at the level of the state. This argument criticizes Marx for not recognizing capitalism's capacity to extend concessions to the working class and fails, therefore, to comprehend why workers do not develop a more radical class consciousness when concessions are not forthcoming.

In short, the revision of Marx's theory of polarization and homogenization, on one side, and of his theory of class struggle, on the other, both ignore the microfoundations of class formation—the political and ideological apparatuses of production and the consciousness that corresponds to them. In other words, they ignore what I call the *regime of production,* which mediates between class-in-itself and class-for-itself. Its form determines how and whether a class-in-itself gives rise to a class-for-itself.[4]

Antonio Gramsci's understanding of hegemony has to be transplanted from the realm of superstructures to the realm of the base, from the state back to civil society. Here, private appropriation of the product and wage labor establish the basis of consent to capitalism. In a fully developed *hegemonic regime*, we find the coordination of the economic interests of workers and capitalists through the dependence of the former on the latter. That is, workers cooperate with capital in order to keep their jobs when profits are threatened and to extract concessions when profits are increasing. At the same time, in the workplace, workers are constituted as individuals with rights and obligations defined by the production regime. Consent presupposes force that, at the level of production, ultimately rests with the employers' right to hire and fire. In a hegemonic regime, the application of force is, itself, the object of consent, bound by certain rules. Individual workers are disciplined or fired for violations of the regime's code, but they can appeal against the employer. Here, the rule of law applies, but in layoffs, the rule of profit applies. Capitalists engineer consent to closure on the grounds of their right to make a profit.[5]

Marxism has too easily removed questions of politics and ideology to the "superstructure" while confining the base to its economic moment. Marx showed how the production of useful things was simultaneously the production of the capitalist, who depends on profit or surplus value, and of the worker, who depends on the wage or paid labor. To maintain themselves (that is, to survive economically), workers must keep on coming to work each day, just as the survival of the capitalist depends on making profit. Under capitalism, relations of production reproduce themselves of themselves. But this presupposes what is, in fact, problematic—the turning of labor, the capacity to work, into sufficient labor for the capitalist to make a profit. The generation of surplus is not automatic but requires institutions or "apparatuses" for eliciting the cooperation of workers in the pursuit of profit—apparatuses that have consequences for class formation. These production regimes are various and demand examination in their own right. Thus, although the manufacture of things is simultaneously the manufacture of relations, it is also the manufacture of an experience of those relations. And here I argue (contra Marx) that, under advanced capitalism at least, hegemonic regimes *manufacture consent*.

Under state socialism, a different regime of production emerges—what I call *bureaucratic despotism*. Central appropriation and redistribution of surplus involves a parallel central direction of production. The state appears at the point of production as the troika of management, party, and trade union. These are branches of the state, very different from the privatized hegemonic regimes of capitalism. Here, workers are guaranteed security of employment, which means that coercion is applied *within* the framework of production and not at its perimeter. Employers apply punitive sanctions in arbitrary ways, whether through fines, denial of bonuses, piece rate systems, or access to scarce goods, in order to elicit cooperation from workers. The coordination of the interests of workers and managers is not made on the basis of profitability but on their common interest vis-à-vis central planners.

Capitalism based itself on private appropriation as something given and natural. Exploitation and, indeed, capitalism as an economic system lies concealed. All that is required is the organization of consent. In state socialism, on the other hand, the state is the appropriator of surplus. Exploitation is palpable and, therefore, has to be legitimated. Those who direct society, whom George Konrad and Ivan Szelenyi call the teleological redistributors,[6] do so in the name of their claimed knowledge of the collective interest and their capacity to satisfy that interest in a just and efficient manner. Direct producers are continually called on to act out a vision of socialism that is at odds with the reality around them. It is not a matter of manufacturing consent but of *painting socialism.* In so doing, they become all the more critical of socialism for failing to live up to its promises. Painting socialism potentially turns into struggles for its realization.

The struggle for socialism is most clearly expressed in the Polish Solidarity movement of 1980–1981. But my argument should apply to all state socialist societies, not just those that have experienced working-class revolt. Contemporary Hungary is the worst-case scenario for my theory because we find very few traces of working-class mobilization even though its history is quite similar to that of Poland. It, too, experienced national humiliation at the hands of surrounding powers; it, too, experienced working-class revolt in 1956; and it, too, has had a relatively open civil society. But there the parallels stop. For Hungary today possesses none of those characteristics that made the rise of Solidarity so distinctive. Instead of a collective memory inspired by nationalism and Catholicism, binding society into a force hostile to the state, Hungary is a fragmented society, ambivalent about its past and driven by individualism and entrepreneurship. Hungarian workers have learned to maneuver within the socialist order rather than revolt against it. They are contemptuous of the Solidarity movement that plunged Poland into economic chaos. "They got what they deserved. Unlike we Hungarians who work for our living the Poles expect to have meat on their table by striking." From being a land of brothers and sisters, Poland overnight became a nation of loafers and hustlers. Their collective mobilization sent shivers down the Hungarian spine.

Surely, Hungary points to the uniqueness of the Polish Solidarity movement, doesn't it? As I shall argue, this is only partially correct. Despite their differences, Polish and Hungarian workers share a common class consciousness—one that is critical of socialism for failing to realize its own proclaimed goals of efficiency and equality. But class consciousness leads to class mobilization only under certain conditions—namely, the development of collective interests and collective capacities to pursue those interests. So, the possibilities of collective mobilization are undermined by channels for individual mobility and the absence of autonomous institutions operating in a relatively open civil society.

This argument is based on my experiences in Hungarian factories, particularly in Miskolc, Hungary's second biggest city. There, I worked as a furnaceman in the huge Lenin Steel Works for three periods: for six months in 1985, for two months in 1986, and for a further two months in 1987. The chapter begins with the ritual painting of socialism and the distinctive negative class consciousness to which it gives rise. It traces this to the imperatives of the broader political economy and how these are transmitted by a regime of bureaucratic despotism. I then turn to the way class mobilization is undermined by the creation of individual channels of mobility and the absence of collective actors. Finally, I bring the discussion up to the present, examining the implications of democratization for transitions beyond state socialism.

The Prime Minister Is Coming

It was a freezing February morning in 1985 when I began my first shift at the huge basic oxygen converter.[7] There was a lull in production, and I was casually talking to Feri, whose job was to clean the oxygen lance, when Stegermajer, the plant superintendent, came up yelling at us to get on with sweeping the place clean. The look of disgust on Feri's face made clear what he thought of the idea. Who had ever heard of keeping a steel mill clean? And, anyway, it was not his job. But there was no arguing with the menacing look on Stegermajer's face, so we lazily took up our brooms and began brushing away at the railings, creating clouds of dust and graphite that would descend elsewhere to be swept again by someone else's broom. Aggressiveness and shouting seemed a way of life here at the Lenin Steel Works. The bosses were always on edge. What were they so nervous about? How different it was from Bánki, where I had worked before.[8] There, we were left to our own devices to handle our machines or not, to take a walk or visit a mate as we pleased. There was no make-work at Bánki.

No sooner had we brushed the railings to reveal a dull green and yellow layer than painters appeared, brightening up the surroundings at least for a few minutes until the dust and graphite descended once more. "Was this normal?" I wondered. The next day, the painting continued, and I heard that some delegation would be visiting, but no one cared who, why, or when. As became clear in succeeding days, this was to be no ordinary visit: No less a person than the prime minister himself would be visiting. The automatic chute that used to send alloys from the bunkers overhead down into the ladle below, broken now for many weeks, was being repaired. We would no longer have to shovel the alloys into a wheelbarrow and tip them down the chute ourselves, choked by clouds of silicosis-producing dust as we did so. Thank God for the prime minister.

On the Friday before his Tuesday visit, production had come to a standstill. Welders were out in force with their tanks of acetylene, resting uncomfortably near the converter. New silver doors, threaded by water pipes to prevent warping, were being erected to fence off the converter. Hoards of young lads from neighboring cooperatives were swarming around to give the converter its final touch. Preparations were as elaborate as those for a satellite going into orbit. Soldiers were shoveling the snow away from the entrances below and cleaning up the debris that they uncovered. It seemed that the entire land had been mobilized for the visit of the prime minister.

I found Józsi swearing in our eating room: "This is a steel mill, not a pharmacy." He had just been told to change into new overalls, with a new hat and gloves. I looked at him in disbelief, assuming I had not understood him properly. "You won't even be working when the prime minister comes," I said. He looked at me as though I had come from the moon. "What's that to do with anything? Everybody has to conform. This is window-dressing politics." So, we all trooped off to get our new outfits and came back mockingly giving our hard hats a final polish. Five minutes later, let alone next Tuesday, we would be filthy again.

Today was our turn for a Communist shift. In aid of charity, such as support for a children's hospital or the National Theatre, we work an extra shift. It's a socialist form of taxation. We were assigned to paint the slag drawer, a huge machine that skims off slag from the pig iron as it passes on the way to the converter. There were not enough paint brushes to go around; I could only find a black one. What could I paint black? What better than the most treasured of the furnaceman's tools— his shovel? I had hardly begun this critical task when Stegermajer came storming over, with his hand behind his back and his hard hat bobbing, his head bowed for combat. "What the hell are you doing?" "Painting the shovels black," I replied as innocently as I could. But he was not amused, so I added, "Haven't you got any more brushes so I can help the others?" No, there were no others. "So I can't help build socialism?"

I continued, somewhat riskily. My mates cracked up, amused at the thought of their "yogurt furnaceman" building socialism.[9] Even Stegermajer caved in when Józsi interceded, "Misi, Misi you don't understand anything. You are not *building* socialism, you are *painting* socialism. And *black* at that."

The "painting" continued on Monday when we hauled out the always ascending graphs demonstrating the superiority of the converter over the old Siemen's Martin furnaces. Party slogans and directives for the forthcoming party congress, as well as photographs of earlier visits by dignitaries, were displayed at resting points for Tuesday's scenic tour. At noon on Monday, Stegermajer came over to me with an embarrassed look and said, "You know the prime minister is coming tomorrow." I nodded and smiled. "Well, why don't you take a holiday?" he said. They surely did not want their yogurt furnaceman upsetting the visit.

I assume the prime minister came; I saw his picture in the newspaper peering into the wondrous converter. When I returned on Wednesday, the flags were down and the graphs were returned to their storeroom, together with the party directives and photos. The filming was over. Once more we were a steel mill, at least until the next painting.

Workers looked upon this cabaret as just another instance of socialist waste and deception. "This is the Communist sector," begins the furnaceman's joke, "If there's pig iron, then there's no scrap. If there's scrap, then there's no pig iron. If there happens to be both, then someone must have stolen something." On seeing workers melting ice with a gas flame, Gyuri shakes his head in dismay, "Money doesn't count, the prime minister is coming." Socialism, it seems, can only conjure up an image of efficiency by calling on its workers to collaborate in a desperate and farcical cover-up. But are all irrationalities of a piece, as they appear to the workers? Is there a rationality behind the irrationality—a deeper meaning in the painting? What interests parade behind the facade?

Ideology Versus Reality

The growth of a capitalist enterprise depends on its profitability; growth of a state socialist enterprise depends on state-dispensed investment funds. There are three steel mills in Hungary. Their common interest in expanding the resources available to the steel industry is broken by an intense rivalry over the distribution of what is available. The rivalry is made all the more intense by the unequal efficiency of the mills. Dunaújváros, built after the war with modern Soviet technology, is the most profitable of the three. LKM and the smaller Ozd, both much older and, in places, operating with the last century's technology, barely break even. Just as critical is the production profile of the different enterprises. In an economy driven by shortage, the enterprise that produces a relatively homogeneous product is able to plan ahead for its material requirements and is in a much better position than a company that produces a wide variety of products and whose material supplies fluctuate correspondingly. This makes Dunaújváros, with its sheet steel production, a more efficient enterprise than LKM, which produces diverse high-quality steels for the machine industry. Furthermore, with quality being less important at Dunaújváros, it is less vulnerable to supply constraints, heightening its image of greater efficiency. The companys' distinctive products lead to a corresponding distribution of influence—Dunaújváros with the ministry of finance, Ozd and LKM with the ministry of industry. Thus, competition between enterprises becomes competition between government bodies.

In theory, the entire production of steel in Hungary could be located at Dunaújváros. Certainly, the capacity and space is available, and, indeed, such was the proposal of a secret Soviet report. (At LKM, they are skeptical that Dunaújváros has the expertise to produce the high-quality steel LKM specializes in.) In any event, the plan came to nothing simply because it is impossible to close down steel plants in a state socialist society.[10] (Miskolc society would, for example, be decimated if LKM closed down, and, in fact, a management proposal to reduce employment by just 800 workers met with instant rejection by party authorities.) The balance of political forces leads, therefore, to a roughly equal distribution of resources among the three enterprises: LKM gets its Combined Steel Works, Ozd receives new rolling mills, and Dunaújváros receives a coking plant and two 120-ton Soviet basic oxygen converters. Rather than concentrating investment in one enterprise, it is distributed among all three, and its effectiveness is drowned in the surrounding obsolete technology. Thus, the new Combined Steel Works is marooned among antiquated rolling mills and blast furnaces. The distribution of resources through political bargaining in a hierarchical order leads not only to a characteristic uneven development of technology but to widespread short-ages in raw materials and machinery. Because there are no hard budget constraints, enterprises have an insatiable hunger for resources—insatiable because the success of enterprises and, thus, of their managers' careers depends on garnering resources for expansion. And that explains the seemingly absurd preparations for the visit of the prime minister. As a very influential person, he had to be convinced that LKM was at the forefront of the building of socialism.

Consequently, by its own logic, *building* socialism turns into *painting* socialism, reminding all of the gap between what is and what should be, deepening the critical consciousness of workers and managers alike. This ritual juxtaposition of the real and the imaginary is not confined to the exceptional: It is part and parcel of factory life—the union elections, the production conferences, competition among Socialist brigades and the Communist shifts. Because it is embedded in real practices, the pretense unwittingly assumes a life of its own, a spontaneous critique of existing society and a potential force for an alternative one.

Nor is critique confined to economic rationality. It extends to the principles of social justice that socialism proclaims. "Money doesn't count, the prime minister is coming" expresses the powerful resentment toward the red barons who direct society, those we must entertain with these charades. Furnacemen are fond of the joke about the contribution made to socialism by three men. "The first receives 5,000 forints a month. He builds socialism. The second receives 15,000 forints a month. He directs the building of socialism. The third receives 50,000 forints a month. For him, socialism is built."

Csaba, neither a member of the party nor of the trade union, says all the best jobs go to the party people. Thus, I am told how "connections" dictate membership in the famous inside contracting systems—self-selected, self-organized worker collectives (VGMKs) that receive specific lump-sum payments for the completion of specific tasks outside normal working hours. Pay can be three or four times the normal wage, which could easily double the pay a worker received each month. Karsci related the story of the VGMK assigned to clean up the roof of the Combined Steel Works—it included the party secretary, the trade union secretary, and the Communist youth secretary. How often we berated Hegedus, the day foreman, for being more concerned about his VGMK work than his formal duties. When we were on afternoon shift, we would see him wandering around, sometimes supervising, sometimes opening bags of cement as his token contribution to the VGMK that rebuilt the walls of the ladles.

Resentment is not leveled at inequality per se for everyone wants to be rich but against undeserved wealth accumulated through the exploitation of contacts or scarce skills without corresponding effort. Moreover, there are those who, in the eyes of the steelworkers, deserve to be poor, such as the half-million Gypsies who, I am forever being told, continue to malinger and steal, live in a cesspool of poverty because they know no better, and thereby heap disrepute onto a nation of honest, decent, and hardworking people, despite the fact that they receive government assistance.

Many workers hold up East Germany as their model. Many have worked there and come back impressed by its egalitarianism, as well as its efficiency. Bela, the steelmaker and a party member, often entered into heated arguments about the merits of the East German society, where the cleaning lady and the enterprise director received the same pension, where inflation was insignificant and one could survive on a single wage. "If there's socialism anywhere, it's in East Germany," Bela concluded. For Kálmán, a young and ambitious furnaceman, on the other hand, NDK (East Germany) is "too political"—one can't travel abroad so easily, and, to move up, one must be a party member. Even though he is married to an East German woman, he wouldn't consider living there permanently. He's interested in getting ahead: "To hell with socialism."

But socialism is all around, even in Hungary, compelling compliance to its rituals of affirmation. Painting *over* the sordid realities of socialism is simultaneously the painting *of* an appearance of brightness, efficiency, and justice. Socialism becomes an elaborate game of mutual pretense that everyone sees through but that everyone is obliged to play. It is an intermingling of a desultory reality and a fabricated appearance in which the appearance takes on a reality of its own. The pretense becomes a basis against which to assess reality. If we have to paint a world of efficiency and equality—as we do in our production meetings, our brigade competitions, our elections—we become more sensitive to and outraged by inefficiency and inequality. Very different is the capitalist game through which workers spontaneously consent to its directing classes by *obscuring from themselves* its *system* of domination and inefficiency. Under socialism, we are called on to *cover up* injustice and irrationality and to paint a vision of equality and efficiency. The very conditions that are hidden through participation in capitalist production, the veritable relations of production, become the focal concern of the players in socialist production.

The compulsion to participate in the socialist game is potentially explosive—the pretense becomes an alternative turned against reality. But what turns the potentiality into a reality, class consciousness into class mobilization? Here, we must look not at the consciousness workers in state socialist society share and what distinguishes it from the consciousness of capitalist workers but at the different modes of structuring interests within and among state socialist societies. Poland and Hungary represent extremes: In one, the tendency is toward the mobilization of collective resources; in the other, the tendency is toward the mobilization of individual resources. The divergence presents a puzzle for, in both countries, civil society has been relatively open. For an answer, we must look to everyday life, both at work and beyond.

The Decline of Bureaucratic Despotism

Our model of competitive capitalism is one in which workers can be hired and fired at the will of the employer. Anarchy of the market, competition among capitalists for profit and among workers for jobs, gives rise to production regimes that can be subsumed under the category of market despotism. Under advanced capitalism, however, protections for workers emerge in the form of compensation for loss of job and machinery to defend workers against arbitrary firings. There is still force, but it is applied according to rules and is subject to appeal. Under these circumstances, employers must elicit the workers' consent to managerial goals and managerial domination. We have, in short, hegemonic regimes of production.

In state socialism, on the other hand, employment guarantees preclude the threat of losing one's job as a means of extracting cooperation. Alternative modes of organizing force must be found. Instead of employment insecurity, we find wage insecurity, introduced through piece rates, bonuses, and premiums. Moreover, these remunerations for cooperation are themselves subject to continual change and wielded in an arbitrary manner by management, party, and trade union. This troika rules over the workplace in the form of bureaucratic despotism—bureaucratic insofar as it is tied to the state and the distribution of scarce resources that are monopolized by this state.[11]

Management dictates not only when and where we shall paint socialism but when and where we shall work and the rewards and punishments for what we do. The party and trade union buttress its arbitrary domination. As our chief steward said, "The trade union is good for one thing. Keeping your mouth shut." It collects our dues, 1 percent of our earnings, sending half upstairs to headquarters and redistributing the rest as assistance in times of need—when members are ill for an extended period, have a child, or face funeral expenses. The union officers distribute places in the holiday homes. It is a bureaucratized friendly—or should I say unfriendly—society with little or no power to fight for workers' rights. Quite the contrary, it withholds assistance to members with bad disciplinary records. An X or two (absence without permission) means no benefits. Józsi, always a victim of Xs, shows me his pile of old trade union books at home and expresses his disgust by wiping them on his bottom. Long ago, he gave up his membership. Recognizing where its interests lie, management threatens to withdraw premiums from workers who are not union members or who have not paid up all their dues.

The party and Communist youth organization (KISZ) form the second arm of managerial domination. KISZ and then party membership is the way up, Gabi assures me, still struggling to find the two party references necessary for entry. He points to Bandi, who, he says, will have nothing to do with the party and will be stuck in his present job as "operator"— the steelmaker's assistant. Long before the formal elimination of party organization in the workplace in 1989, its importance had been eroding. It had lost its grip on the channels of internal mobility as credentialing, seniority, experience, and, to a lesser extent, patronage (*protekció*) became more important than party membership. Peter proudly tells me how he managed to get into a VGMK, although one of his friends—a party member—had been excluded. Karsci, ambitious though he is, does not see the point in joining the party and sacrificing some two hundred forints a month. Nevertheless, he is promoted.

Although the bureaucratic shell of the regime of production has remained, its despotic content has been crumbling for many years under pressure from expanding market forces. Management used to be able to control the movement of workers from one enterprise to another by virtue of its control over their work book. Now, a labor market directs the flow of labor, and workers seek out credentials that will place them in the most lucrative jobs. Thus, fewer and fewer men attend the technical high school for steelworkers. Among the entering cohort, the majority are now women, not because they want to become steelworkers but because it is now the easiest secondary school credential to obtain. Men are no longer interested in becoming steelworkers. Once the aristocrats and heroes of labor, the steelworkers now lag behind electricians and mechanics, who can ply their skills in the private sector (*maszek*) as well as the state sector. Who wants to work on continuous shifts the rest of his life at a salary little better than the average?

The possibility of moving from workplace to workplace weakens management's control in production for workers care less about punitive sanctions. And the sanctions themselves are weaker than ever. The resources available for enterprises to distribute—access to schooling, housing, kindergartens, and, in the past, sometimes even food—all these have diminished so that workers have less to lose when they incur the displeasure of management. The reproduction of labor power has become increasingly unhinged from performance at work. Housing, for example, is now distributed independently of one's place of work or work references. There is a long waiting list for council flats, but the relevant criteria are family size, income, and present accommodation. There is also cooperative housing distributed through the National Savings Bank. Here, protekció may count, but more critical is the ability to pay.

At the same time that the enterprise's control over access to public goods (education and housing) is weaker, it has also become less important as a source of income. First, families with two wage earners are taken for granted in the working class. The state facilitates this by relatively generous maternity and childcare benefits, allowing women to stay home for three years at 75 percent of their normal wage and guaranteeing them their jobs at the end of the period. In such dual-earner families, the individual worker is less dependent on his or her employer. Second, the last two decades have seen an expansion of opportunities to obtain extra earnings in the informal or private sector, known in Hungary as the second economy or *maszek.* Even though steelworkers are doubly handicapped in this respect—shiftwork makes a regular second job impossible, and the skills they learn are not generalizable—nevertheless, they have found ways to make extra money in the second economy. Gyuri, who lives in a village about an hour away, cultivates a big garden for home consumption and breeds nutria to sell their fur. Karsci's rabbit business brought him enough money to take a honeymoon in Italy. His defective pig business brought in some 20,000 forints, which took him to Germany where he bought a music center and electronic game that he later sold at home for a great profit.

Moreover, it is worth making money. Unlike the situation in other East European countries, you can buy almost anything—from specialty foods to computers and videos—all for local currency, provided you have enough of it. Budapest is the consumer paradise of Eastern Europe, a bustling city attracting more and more tourists. There are no special shops for the apparatchiks, but the market rules, at least in consumer goods. Hungary has used some of its foreign currency to make imported luxury goods available to all, holding out rewards for those prepared to work hard or find other routes to riches. For the working class, day-to-day life is ruled by the almighty forint, not the queue or the party.

Rather than making the second economy illegal, the state has consistently sought to exploit it. The state compensates for wages falling behind inflation by creating more openings for private initiatives, by opening up the second economy. Workers can only maintain their standard of living by laboring longer and longer hours, and the state assumes that the work capacity of the Hungarian family is inexhaustible. Life is ordered according to a giant piece rate system. As workers struggle to make ends meet, they must exceed the norm, which, in turn, justifies norm revision. Socialism has a long history of organizing production in this way, but now it is extended to the sphere of consumption. Workers are helpless as they clamber up the down escalator, whose downward speed increases every year. Many collapse exhausted with heart attacks, some commit suicide, and others take to drink. Most are trapped in huge housing projects such as the Avas, where I used to live. There, 80,000 struggle to make ends meet. In this maze of identical concrete blocks, families, pressed into one- or two-room panel apartments, crack at their seams. Divorce rates increase, along with violence.

An increasing few, usually with the helping hand of others, manage to perch themselves on top of the escalator, building fancy houses in the Buda Hills or Tapolca, trying to remove themselves from the scramble below. At the same time that opportunities for entrepreneurship are being monopolized by fewer and fewer people, the state has introduced taxes on earnings from extra work. This hits the working class most hard.

Inequalities intensify and become more visible, but, for the time being, workers are more intent on keeping up with, rather than combining to stop or slow, the down escalator.

The market offers opportunities to all, though increasingly to some more than to others. Here, individualism pays, providing there are goods to be purchased. Mutatis mutandis, where shortages prevail as in Poland, market forces do not engender the same entrepreneurial energies from the working class. The market continually fails, and administrative allocation—that is, rationing—steps in to substitute. Well-being depends on networks based on ties of family, friendship, religion, profession, or work. Whom one knows and what one has to offer decides one's fate. If such patronage is further limited to a party elite and its hangers-on, then individual striving can prove fruitless and collective rebellion become more attractive. Always a potentiality, such a solution becomes a reality when the state is not just illegitimate but shows itself to be weak, when there is an alternative institution such as the Roman Catholic church commanding the allegiance of the population, when powerful national sentiments galvanize into a vibrant collective memory, and when there are rudimentary channels for conveying information and engaging in public discussion.

But this is only half the solution to the Polish puzzle. The other half is to be found in three decades of painting socialism that inadvertently created a working class that was not only organizationally strong but hostile to the socialism that actually existed for its systematic violation of all it was supposed to be. This spontaneous socialist consciousness became the switch track that guided Solidarity along its ascendant path from independent trade union to worker-directed society in 1980 and 1981 and that, eight years later, voted its leaders into power.

Classes and Social Movements: East and West

History has played a cruel trick on Marx. The society that was supposed to give way to emancipation under seige from a revolutionary working class has managed to contain challenges to its order, and the society that was to realize emancipation is threatened by the very class it was supposed to liberate. I have tried to resolve this puzzle by focusing on the regime of production—itself a reflection of the relations of production. In advanced capitalism, the movement from class-in-itself to class-for-itself is stymied by the hegemonic regime that organizes consent to capitalism. But this movement in state socialism is given impetus by a bureaucratic despotism that organizes a critique of state socialism for failing to live up to its promises.

But are there not "paintings" in capitalism, too? There are, but they are paintings *within* capitalism, not *of* capitalism. When the chief executive officer of General Motors visits one of his divisions, there is, to be sure, a painting, a celebration of the virtues of General Motors and a demonstration of the division's efficiency. But there is no celebration of capitalism per se. There is no ritual performance that clearly marks the separation of the ideology of capitalism from its reality. We may say that capitalism is *painted out* of our daily lives. Capitalism works not with a single but with a multiplicity of ideologies that meld with our lived experience without raising that experience to the level of critique. The effect of ideology is as ubiquitous as it is invisible. It acts behind our backs, so to speak.

If we paint our society at all in this global sense, it is a painting of democracy. We do partake in rituals that speak to the rights and freedoms of individuals—the language of political liberalism. If advanced capitalism does not generate a radical working-class movement, it is certainly true that it does generate social movements of a multiclass character that are rooted in the discrepancy between the ideals and reality of democracy. Civil rights movements, the women's movement, ecology movements, peace movements—all work on the terrain of the failed promises of democratic rights. But, as Marx long ago demonstrated, the pursuit of political emancipation is quite compatible with the expansion of capitalism and its denial of human emancipation. Important as they undoubtedly are, modern social movements do not challenge the fabric of capitalism. Indeed, by making capitalism a better "place" to inhabit, they actually protect it against its tendencies toward self-destruction.

If it is true that we do not paint capitalism, is it not also true that workers in Hungary and Poland have, in the last two years, ceased to paint socialism and begun to dismantle the apparatus of bureaucratic despotism? In both countries and, indeed, in the Soviet Union, old paintings have been unveiled, and a new painting has begun—the painting of parliamentary democracy. What happens when parliamentary democracy is grafted onto a centrally controlled economy? For many in both the West and the East, parliamentary democracy is so closely identified with capitalism that the transformation now occurring in Hungary and Poland can only be a transition to capitalism. They assume that the end of "communism" must spell the beginning of capitalism. Certainly, the rhetoric of Hungarian and Polish leaderships and their determination to obtain loans from the West encourage such an assumption.

But these commentators may be making the same mistake that Marx did. Just as he assumed that the end of competitive capitalism spelled the end of all capitalism and overlooked the possible emergence of a second stage of capitalism, so we now all too easily regard the end of state socialism as the end of all socialism and overlook the possibility of the rise of a democratic socialism. In another play on Marx's theory of history, we now have to consider the transition from "communism" to "socialism." Although debates in the Hungarian parliament celebrate the expansion of democracy and the pluralization of property forms, workers in the Lenin Steel Works are very nervous about the prospects of an expanding market, the loss of jobs, rising inflation, and increasing taxation. The more they are told about the virtues of the market, the more suspicious they become as they see the few becoming richer at the expense of the many. We have still to hear from the working classes of the Soviet Union, Hungary, and Poland, who have been painting socialism all their lives and now want to realize *it,* not capitalism.

To continue our opening joke: Gorbachev may jump onto the socialist locomotive and tell everyone to get out and push the train. He says he will pay them later. But they—the members of the working class—may demand payment before he is ready and not necessarily in the currency he has to offer.

Acknowledgments

My thanks to those about whom this story is told are no less than my total reliance on their convivial cooperation. Their names, however, have been disguised. One actor absent from the story but who made it all possible is my collaborator Janos Lukacs. He not only organized the necessary permissions for me to do this research from countless authorities but on many occasions relayed crucial information from his own interviews with management. The discussions over our joint research have inevitably shaped some of my ideas, but I alone take complete responsibility for what is expressed here.

Notes

1. The literature on Solidarity is considerable and still growing, and there is no space to do justice to it here. For an understanding that traces Solidarity's evolution through Polish history, see Norman Davies, *Heart of Europe* (Oxford: Oxford University Press, 1980), for an example of the more generalizing approach, see Andrew Arato, "Civil Society vs. the State," *Telos* 47:23–47, and Alain Touraine et al., *Solidarity: Poland 1980–81* (Cambridge: Cambridge University Press, 1983).

2. Apart from Lenin's *Imperialism: The Highest Stage of Capitalism* (Peking: Foreign Language Press, 1970), examples of such analysis include Erik Wright, *Classes* (London: Verso, 1985), and David Gordon, Richard Edwards, and Michael Reich, *Segmented Work, Divided Workers* (New York: Cambridge University Press, 1982).

3. Foremost among recent contributions to the theory of class compromise is the work of Adam Przeworski, *Capitalism and Social Democracy* (Cambridge: Cambridge University Press, 1985). His writings expand on a specific reading of Gramsci's prison writings. Przeworski underlines the importance of material concessions granted to the working class, but the Frankfurt School has stressed the importance of the way ideology mystifies class relations under advanced capitalism and, in some versions, the way the psyche is shaped by and adapted to advanced capitalism.

4. I have developed this concept further in *The Politics of Production* (London: Verso Books, 1985). There is now a wide range of attempts to link the experience of production to class formation. See, for example, Edward Thompson, *The Making of the English Working Class* (New York: Vintage, 1963); Ira Katznelson and Aristide Zolberg, *Working-Class Formation* (Princeton: Princeton University Press, 1986); William Sewell, *Work and Revolution in France* (Cambridge: Cambridge University Press, 1980); Rick Fantasia, *Cultures of Solidarity* (Berkeley: University of California Press, 1988); and Jeffrey Haydu, *Between Craft and Class* (Berkeley: University of California Press, 1988).

5. For further details, see Michael Burawoy, *Manufacturing Consent* (Chicago: University of Chicago Press, 1979).

6. George Konrad and Ivan Szelenyi, *Intellectuals on the Road to Class Power* (New York: Harcourt, Brace, Jovanovich, 1979).

7. For a detailed account of the labor process at the Combined Steel Works where I worked, see Michael Burawoy and Janos Lukacs, "What Is Socialist About Socialist Production: Autonomy and Control in a Hungarian Steel Mill," in *The Transformation of Work,* ed. Stephen Wood, pp. 295–316 (London: Unwin Hyman, 1989).

8. See Burawoy, "Piece Rates, Hungarian Style," *Socialist Review* 79:43–69, and Burawoy and Lukacs, "Mythologies of Work: A Comparison of Firms in State Socialism and Advanced Capitalism," *American Sociological Review* 50:723–37.

9. They referred to me as their "yogurt furnaceman" (*'kefir olvasztar'*) because I refused to indulge in their meals of pork fat and preferred instead to drink cartons of *kefir*—cat food, as they called it. Of course, they were also jokingly referring to my physical weakness and ineptitude. They called me a "50 percent" furnaceman.

10. For several years now, pressure to close down large sections of the Ozd steelworks has been resisted for fear of "social unrest." The numbers of employees have fallen through attrition and what is called soft unemployment, but major layoffs have yet to take place. Ozd has become a test case for the imposition of hard budget constraints in the era of new economic reforms.

11. In his fascinating study of Chinese industry, Andrew Walder argues that there is a typically "communist" form of authority, what he calls "communist neo-traditionalism," that stems from the dependence of workers on the enterprise not just for income but for the provision of a wide variety of scarce goods. This model may still be approximated by some enterprises in the Soviet Union, but it has not been true for Hungarian and Polish enterprises for at least three

decades. As we shall see, many scarce and important goods and services are distributed directly by the Hungarian state; others can only be obtained in the marketplace. Hence, we find very different patterns of authority and control within the workplace. See Andrew Walder, *Communist Neo-Traditionalism* (Berkeley: University of California Press, 1986).

About the Book and Editors

In recent years, a flurry of "poststructuralist," "post-Marxist," and "state-centered" approaches have emerged in historical and sociological scholarship. Far from ignoring these developments, the study of class has shaped and been shaped by them. As the selections in this volume indicate, class analysis changes and develops, while sustaining itself as a powerful, refined working tool in helping scholars understand the complexities of social and historical processes.

This volume provides a cross-section of the rich body of social theory and empirical research being produced by scholars employing class analysis. It demonstrates the variety, vibrancy, and continuing value of class analysis in historical and sociological scholarship. The work of promising young scholars is combined with contributions from well-established figures to produce a volume that addresses continuing debates over the relationship between structure and agency, the centrality of class relations, and the dynamics of class formation, class culture, and class consciousness.

Scott G. McNall is dean of the College of Arts and Sciences at the University of Toledo. **Rhonda F. Levine** is associate professor of sociology at Colgate University. **Rick Fantasia** is associate professor of sociology at Smith College.

About the Contributors

Dean Braa completed his doctoral degree in sociology at the University of Kansas in the spring of 1990 and has begun his career as a professor at Western Oregon College. He conducted research in County Donegal, Republic of Ireland, for his master's thesis on the Irish peasantry. His Ph.D. dissertation dealt with urban redevelopment and tenant struggles in Kansas City, Missouri.

Michael Burawoy teaches sociology at the University of California, Berkeley, and is completing a book on the transition from socialism to capitalism. His earlier publications include *Manufacturing Consent* (1979) and *The Politics of Production* (1985).

Rick Fantasia is an associate professor of sociology at Smith College. He is the author of *Cultures of Solidarity* (1988), a work that deals with many of the issues raised in this collection.

Shelley Feldman is an assistant professor in the Department of Rural Sociology, Cornell University. Her research interests include gender stratification, the political economy of development, peasant studies, state and society, and contemporary theory. She has special interests in the South Asian region, where she has carried out extensive field research. Among her publications are "Rural Women Discovered . . . ," in *Development and Change* (1983), with Florence E. McCarthy, and "Human Rights and the New Industrial Working Class in Bangladesh," in Claude E. Welch, Jr., ed., *Human Rights in Developing Countries* (1989).

David Halle is a visiting scholar at the Russell Sage Foundation, associate director of the Institute for Social Analysis, and associate professor of sociology at the State University of New York at Stony Brook. He is completing a book on class and culture in the modern home and is the author of *America's Working Man* (1984).

Jerry Lembcke is an adjunct professor of sociology at Holy Cross College. He is the author of *Capitalist Developments and Class Capacities* (1988), *Race and Urban Change* (1988), and coeditor (with Rhonda Levine) of *Recapturing Marxism* (1987). He is currently working on uneven industrial development in the United States and its relationship to working-class formation.

Rhonda F. Levine is an associate professor of sociology at Colgate University. She is the author of *Class Struggle and the New Deal: Industrial Labor, Industrial Capital and the New Deal* (1988), coeditor (with Jerry

Lembcke) of *Recapturing Marxism* (1987), and coeditor (with Martin Oppenheimer and Martin J. Murray) of *Radical Sociologists and the Movement: Experiences, Lessons, and Legacies* (1990). She has been chair of the Marxist Sociology section of the American Sociological Association, on the board of directors of *Critical Sociology,* and active in the Labor Studies Division of the Society for the Study of Social Problems.

Scott G. McNall is dean of the College of Arts and Sciences at the University of Toledo. He continues his work on class formation and is writing a book on theories of class. He is the author of, among other works, *The Road to Rebellion* (1988).

Beth Mintz is professor of sociology at the University of Vermont. Her recent publications include *The Power Structure of American Business,* with Michael Schwartz (1985), "Class vs. Organizational Components of Director Networks," in Perrucci and Potter, eds., *Networks of Power* (1989), and "The United States Capitalist Class," in Bottomore and Brym, eds., *The Capitalist Class: An International Study* (1989). Her current research focuses on the changing structure of the medical industry.

James R. Orr is a doctoral candidate in the Department of Sociology at the University of Kansas. He is engaged in dissertation research that examines the influence of fraternal orders on the process of class formation in the United States.

Sharon Reitman is a doctoral candidate in the Department of Sociology at the University of Michigan, Ann Arbor. Her research interests include labor history, class formation, social movements, and social change. She is completing a comparative historical analysis of the origins of contrasting union politics in the U.S. coal and metal mining industries during the late nineteenth and early twentieth centuries.

William G. Roy is an associate professor of sociology at the University of California, Los Angeles. His major research interests are long-term economic and political transformations in the United States, particularly the rise of corporate capitalism and the bureaucratic state. His current research concerns the rise of U.S. industrial corporations from 1880 to 1913. Among his recent publications are: "Interlocking Directorates and Communities of Interest Among American Railroad Companies, 1905" (with Philip Bonacich), *The American Sociological Review* (1988), and "Time, Place, and People in History and Sociology: Boundary Definitions and the Logic of Inquiry," *Social Science History* (1987).

Kathleen Stanley is a doctoral student in sociology at the State University of New York at Binghamton. Her dissertation is a case study of immigrant refugee labor in the restructuring of the midwestern meat-packing industry.

Marc W. Steinberg is a research associate at the Center for Research on Social Organization, University of Michigan. His current research is on the ideological bases of collective action among trade groups in early nineteenth-century England.

Carl Strikwerda is an assistant professor of history at the University of Kansas. He has published articles on European social history in *Journal of Urban History* (1987), *International Labor and Working Class History* (1988), and *Urban History Yearbook* (1989). He is editing, with Camille Guerin-Gonzales, a book on *The Politics of Immigrant Workers.*

Stephen Valocchi is an assistant professor of sociology at Trinity College in Hartford, Connecticut. His research interests include political sociology, social stratification, and social movements. He has published articles on comparative welfare policy, state theory, and social movements during the New Deal. His present research evaluates the notion of protest cycles as it pertains to the New Deal. Recent publications include "The Unemployed Workers Movement of the 1930s," *Social Problems* (1990), and "The Relative Autonomy of the State and the Origins of British Welfare Policy," *Sociological Forum* (1989).

Löic J.D. Wacquant is an amateur boxer who has completed doctoral degrees in sociology at the University of Chicago and at the École des Hautes Études en Sciences Sociales in Paris. His current research combines a historical study of the formation of Chicago's black subproletariat since World War II and an ethnography of boxing in the city's ghetto. He will pursue this project as a junior fellow of the Society of Fellows at Harvard University. His other interests include social theory, the history and epistemology of the social sciences, and economic and cultural sociology. Among his recent publications are "The Ghetto, the State, and the New Capitalist Economy," *Dissent* (1989), and "Sociology as Socio-Analysis," *Sociological Forum* (1990). He is also the author of two monographs on the colonial society of New Caledonia and editor of *Practice, Class, and Culture: Selected Essays by Pierre Bourdieu* (forthcoming).

Erik Olin Wright teaches sociology at the University of Wisconsin, Madison. His works, e.g., *Classes* (1985), have served as a catalyst for many of the recent debates about how to define and conceptualize class.

Michael Yarrow is an associate professor of sociology at Ithaca College. The major focus of his research has been the labor process in underground mining, the development of the control system for mine labor, and the class and gender consciousness of miners. His work is grounded in field observations and interviews with over 100 miners and their families in Virginia, West Virginia, and Kentucky. Among his publications are "Voice from the Coalfields," in John Gabenta, Barbara Smith, and Alex Willingham, eds., *Communities in Economic Crisis* (1990), and "Miners' Wisdom," *Appalachian Journal* (1988).

Index